ENGLISH LITERATURE AND THE CRUSADES

The period from the Mamlūk reconquest of Acre (1291) to the Ottoman siege of Constantinople (1453) witnessed the production of a substantial corpus of Middle English crusade romances. Marcel Elias places these romances in dialogue with multifarious European writings to offer a novel account of late medieval crusade culture: as ambivalent and self-critical, animated by tensions and debates, and fraught with anxiety. These romances uphold ideals of holy war while expressing anxieties about issues as diverse as God's endorsement of the crusading enterprise, the conversion of Christians to Islam, the sinfulness of crusaders, and the morality of violence. Reinvigorating debates in medieval postcolonialism, drawing on emotion studies, and excavating a rich multilingual archive, this book is a major contribution to the cultural history of the crusades. This title is part of the Flip it Open programme and may also be available open access. Check our website Cambridge Core for details.

MARCEL ELIAS is Assistant Professor of English at Yale University. His essays on crusade literature, European representations of Muslims and Islam, and the history of emotions have appeared or are forthcoming in *Speculum*, *Review of English Studies*, *New Medieval Literatures*, *Studies in Philology*, and elsewhere.

CAMBRIDGE STUDIES IN MEDIEVAL LITERATURE

Founding Editor
Alastair Minnis, *Yale University*

General Editors
Marisa Galvez, *Stanford University*
Daniel Wakelin, *University of Oxford*

Editorial Board
Anthony Bale, *Birkbeck, University of London*
Zygmunt G. Barański, *University of Cambridge*
Christopher C. Baswell, *Barnard College and Columbia University*
Mary Carruthers, *New York University*
Rita Copeland, *University of Pennsylvania*
Roberta Frank, *Yale University*
Alastair Minnis, *Yale University*
Jocelyn Wogan-Browne, *Fordham University*

This series of critical books seeks to cover the whole area of literature written in the major medieval languages – the main European vernaculars, and medieval Latin and Greek – during the period c.1100–1500. Its chief aim is to publish and stimulate fresh scholarship and criticism on medieval literature, special emphasis being placed on understanding major works of poetry, prose, and drama in relation to the contemporary culture and learning which fostered them.

Recent titles in the series

Emma O. Bérat *Women's Genealogies in the Medieval Literary Imagination: Matrilineal Legacies in the High Middle Ages*
Anne Schuurman *The Theology of Debt in Late Medieval English Literature*
Jennifer A. Lorden *Forms of Devotion in Early English Poetry: The Poetics of Feeling*
Harriet Soper *The Life Course in Old English Poetry*
Taylor Cowdery *Matter and Making in Early English Poetry: Literary Production from Chaucer to Sidney*
Olivia Holmes *Boccaccio and Exemplary Literature: Ethics and Mischief in the "Decameron"*
Joseph Taylor *Writing the North of England in the Middle Ages: Regionalism and Nationalism in Medieval English Literature*
Mark Faulkner *A New Literary History of the Long Twelfth Century: Language and Literature between Old and Middle English*
Mark Chinca and Christopher Young (eds.) *Literary Beginnings in the European Middle Ages*
Andrew M. Richmond *Landscape in Middle English Romance: The Medieval Imagination and the Natural World*
David G. Lummus *The City of Poetry: Imagining the Civic Role of the Poet in Fourteenth-Century Italy*
Richard Matthew Pollard *Imagining the Medieval Afterlife*

A complete list of titles in the series can be found at the end of the volume.

ENGLISH LITERATURE AND THE CRUSADES

Anxieties of Holy War, 1291–1453

MARCEL ELIAS

Yale University

Shaftesbury Road, Cambridge CB2 8EA, United Kingdom

One Liberty Plaza, 20th Floor, New York, NY 10006, USA

477 Williamstown Road, Port Melbourne, VIC 3207, Australia

314–321, 3rd Floor, Plot 3, Splendor Forum, Jasola District Centre, New Delhi – 110025, India

103 Penang Road, #05-06/07, Visioncrest Commercial, Singapore 238467

Cambridge University Press is part of Cambridge University Press & Assessment, a department of the University of Cambridge.

We share the University's mission to contribute to society through the pursuit of education, learning and research at the highest international levels of excellence.

www.cambridge.org
Information on this title: www.cambridge.org/9781108832212

DOI: 10.1017/9781108935463

© Marcel Elias 2024

This publication is in copyright. Subject to statutory exception and to the provisions of relevant collective licensing agreements, no reproduction of any part may take place without the written permission of Cambridge University Press & Assessment.

When citing this work, please include a reference to the DOI 10.1017/9781108935463

First published 2024

A catalogue record for this publication is available from the British Library.

Library of Congress Cataloging-in-Publication Data
NAMES: Elias, Marcel, 1985- author.
TITLE: English literature and the crusades : anxieties of holy war, 1291-1453 / Marcel Elias, Yale University, Connecticut.
DESCRIPTION: Cambridge ; New York, NY : Cambridge University Press, 2024. | Series: Cambridge studies in medieval literature | Includes bibliographical references and index.
IDENTIFIERS: LCCN 2024004239 (print) | LCCN 2024004240 (ebook) | ISBN 9781108832212 (hardback) | ISBN 9781108940702 (paperback) | ISBN 9781108940702 (epub)
SUBJECTS: LCSH: Romances, English–History and criticism. | English literature–Middle English, 1100-1500–History and criticism. | Crusades in literature. | Emotions in literature. | Islam–Relations–Christianity. | Christianity and other religions–Islam. |
LCGFT: Literary criticism.
CLASSIFICATION: LCC PR321 .E45 2024 (print) | LCC PR321 (ebook) | DDC 820.9/358207–DC23/eng/20240314
LC record available at https://lccn.loc.gov/2024004239
LC ebook record available at https://lccn.loc.gov/2024004240

ISBN 978-1-108-83221-2 Hardback

Cambridge University Press & Assessment has no responsibility for the persistence or accuracy of URLs for external or third-party internet websites referred to in this publication and does not guarantee that any content on such websites is, or will remain, accurate or appropriate.

For Esme

Contents

Acknowledgments		*page* viii
	Introduction	1
1	Royal Emotions, Blasphemy, and (Dis)unity in *The Siege of Milan* and *The Sultan of Babylon*	18
2	Hopes and Anxieties of Conversion in the *Otuel* Romances	50
3	Women, God, and Other Crusading Motives in *Guy of Warwick*	70
4	Therapeutic Crusading and Excessive Violence in *The Siege of Jerusalem* and *Richard Coeur de Lion*	99
	Conclusion	131
Notes		135
Bibliography		199
Index		231

Acknowledgments

This study began as a doctoral dissertation funded by the Gates Cambridge Trust and was reworked during a Research Fellowship at St Catharine's College, Cambridge. I accumulated many debts of gratitude during my years in Cambridge. Above all, I would like to thank Helen Cooper for being the most supportive, inspiring, and intellectually generous doctoral supervisor I could have hoped for. Special thanks are also due to Laura Ashe and Siobhain Calkin for reading and commenting on chapter drafts, and to Corinne Saunders and Nicolette Zeeman, my doctoral examiners, for providing feedback that helped me sharpen my ideas and better understand what this book is about. For their friendship and encouragement, I am grateful to Aliya Bagewadi, Vaibhav Bhardwaj, Hanna Baumann, Andrew Chen, Kate Crowcroft, Matthias Goetz, Christoph Grossbaier, Natasha Magnani, and Milan Pajic.

The Department of English at Yale University, my academic home for the past three and a half years, has offered a supportive and stimulating environment in which to finish this book. I am especially grateful to Ardis Butterfield, Jessica Brantley, and Emily Thornbury for welcoming me into the community of medievalists, for consistently offering (or agreeing) to read my work, and for their wise counsel. I have benefited immensely from their mentorship. Feisal Mohamed provided valuable feedback on an entire draft of this book, and Cajetan Iheka on a version of the introduction. My sincere gratitude goes to both. For conversations about or around this book, I thank Joe Cleary, Hussein Fancy, Marta Figlerowicz, Ben Glaser, Naomi Levine, Ernest Mitchell, Priyasha Mukhopadhyay, Stephanie Newell, Cathy Nicholson, and Joe North. The Faculty of Arts and Sciences generously funded a manuscript workshop that brought together Suzanne Akbari, Chris Chism, and Cecilia Gaposchkin, to whom I am deeply indebted for reading an earlier version of this study and supplying incisive, constructive criticism. Yale also provided valuable

Acknowledgments

support in the form of a Morse Fellowship and a Publication Grant from the Whitney Humanities Center.

Two anonymous reviewers appointed by Cambridge University Press offered feedback that considerably enriched the manuscript. I cannot thank them enough for their time and attention. I also wish to extend profound gratitude to Emily Hockley, Alastair Minnis, Dan Wakelin, and Marisa Galvez for their commitment to this book and editorial support. In the later stages of the book, Claire Adler, Claire Crow, and Celine Vezina helped format the footnotes and check the quotations and references; I thank them too. I am also grateful to *New Medieval Literatures* and *Studies in Philology* for permission to reuse previously published material: roughly half of Chapter 2 appeared in an earlier form in "Mixed Feelings in the Middle English Charlemagne Romances: Emotional Reconfiguration and the Failures of Crusading Practices in the *Otuel* Texts," *New Medieval Literatures* 16 (2016), 172–212; and Chapter 4 substantially reworks a few paragraphs that appeared in "Violence, Excess, and the Composite Emotional Rhetoric of *Richard Coeur de Lion*," *Studies in Philology* 114:1 (2017), 1–38. My final academic acknowledgment is to two remarkable scholars and teachers, Marco Nievergelt and Denis Renevey, who sparked my interest in medieval literature and encouraged me to apply for graduate programs.

My academic trajectory, this book, and pretty much everything else would not have been possible without the inspiration and unwavering support of my parents, Peter and Jane. My sisters – Tamara, Lisa, and Lana – have sustained and encouraged me over the years. Their partners – Antoine, Raphael, and Mike – have offered their interest and encouragement along the way. Gunda, Bernhard, and Emil, my in-laws, welcomed me into their family and provided vital assistance during our transition from England to the United States via Germany. My singular gratitude, finally, to my wife, Gesa, for her love, companionship, fierce intelligence, and boundless energy; and to my sons, Aaron and Jonah, for the happiness they bring to me every day.

With Gesa, Aaron, and Jonah, I have shared the greatest joys and deepest sorrows. This book is for Esme, beloved daughter and sister, who was born and died as I completed it.

Introduction

A Christian cleric, upon hearing of the rout of a crusader army, accuses the Virgin Mary of failing to protect her followers. A Muslim knight, struck by an epiphany, converts to Christianity, bringing with him qualities – strength, obedience to superiors, and a sense of communal responsibility – previously lacking in Christians. Envoys of a powerful sultan lament the cruel execution of their friends and relatives by an English king. These are some of the characters populating the literary texts that I examine in this book: Middle English crusade romances produced from around the time of the Mamlūk reconquest of Acre (1291), the last major crusader stronghold in the Levant, to around that of the Ottoman siege of Constantinople (1453). In the following chapters, I argue that these characters and others performed complex cultural work, speaking to some of greatest crusade-related concerns of the post-1291 era: God's will and support of wars waged in his name, the selfish ambitions these wars could satisfy, Latin Christendom's ability to compete on the global scene, sinfulness and divisions within the Christian community, questions of poor leadership, notions of shared humanity across religious and racial divides, and the morality of violence, even when sanctioned by the Church.

Middle English crusade romance, as I conceive it, is a subgenre that imaginatively engages with the history of the Levantine crusades, geopolitical circumstances in the Holy Land after 1291, and late medieval realities of religious warfare in other locations, including North Africa, Iberia, the Baltic, the Balkans, and Anatolia.[1] My reasons for concentrating primarily on this subgenre are twofold. First, it is the most comprehensive testimony to the crusade imaginary of late medieval England. Second, I see it as especially well suited to bringing out the heterogeneity of, and conflicts within, contemporary crusade culture.[2] As I hope to show in this study, crusade romances take up, dramatically enact, distill to their essentials, combine, and place in tension ideas featuring in an eclectic range of more "historical" sources on the crusades, from those whose agendas are

2   Introduction

unambiguously celebratory and propagandist to the more critical. These include letters of invective against heaven, penitential treatises by ex-crusaders, poems denouncing the hypocrisy of combatants, chronicles registering discomfort at the human costs of holy war, and various works staging what I call "reverse Orientalism" – a mode in which the achievements and opinions of Muslim figures (real or imaginary) are made to reflect critically on Christians. In assembling these materials, the overall picture I seek to paint is of a deeply conflicted post-1291 English crusade culture: one committed to the ideals of crusading, yet harboring profound anxieties about these ideals – about their providential underpinnings, potential success, enactment, debasement, and even justification. Here and elsewhere in this study, I use the term "anxiety" in its general sense, to mean "worry" or "uneasy concern," a sense that goes back to the Middle English *anxiete*, the Old French *anxieté*, and the Latin *anxietas*.[3] This term, and its near-synonym "concern," are especially apt for my purposes because of their connotations of durability. Indeed, the moral, political, and providential issues that I discuss in the chapters that follow persisted, unresolved, for long periods of time.[4]

My approach in this book is informed by a tradition of postcolonial scholarship that developed in part out of studies of the modern colonial novel, which may (I think productively) be viewed as the literary successor to the crusade romance.[5] To situate my work in relation to previous scholarship on crusade literature and within the broader field of postcolonial studies, I will briefly discuss some general tendencies in the reception, by modernists and medievalists, of Edward Said's epochal *Orientalism* (1978). Postcolonial scholarship on the nineteenth to mid twentieth centuries has often echoed Said in arguing for the complicity of Western literature in the ideology of imperialism. However, much of this scholarship has considered Said's conception of Orientalism as a discourse whose essence is "the ineradicable distinction between Western superiority and Oriental inferiority" too homogenizing and restrictive, stressing the need to attend to the "heterogeneities and ambivalences" of colonial culture, and the "anxieties and tensions" it carries, to quote Lisa Lowe and Yumna Siddiqi.[6] Said himself in his later *Culture and Imperialism* (1993), a study that focuses on the modern novel, affirmed the capacity of European literature not only to uphold but also to unsettle dominant ideologies and civilizational polarities.[7] In *Culture and Imperialism*, Western culture is described as "heterogeneous," "unmonolithic," and traversed by "critical and often contradictory energies," a view supported by readings of novels such as Joseph Conrad's *Nostromo*, which Said sees both "criticizing and

Introduction 3

reproducing the imperial ideology" of its time.[8] In the wake of *Culture and Imperialism*, most scholarship exploring colonial themes in novels has aligned more closely with this study than with *Orientalism*,[9] often emphasizing the role of imperial setbacks and indigenous resistance in rendering the terrain of colonial writing more diverse and conflicted.[10] Elleke Boehmer argues that, in the aftermath of the Second Boer War (1899–1902), which "laid bare the vulnerability of the Empire," British novels came increasingly to express uneasiness and critiques, if rarely about colonialism per se, about the practices, effects, and abuses of colonial rule.[11] Boehmer notes that in many of these works of latter-day empire, rather than serving as foils for Western rationality, colonized cultures serve as "agents for metropolitan self-questioning."[12] In a similar vein, Priyamvada Gopal argues that, under the pressure of armed insurrection in the colonies, British novelists began "to ask troubling questions about the imperial project."[13] And Jennifer Yee, drawing attention to French colonial losses, traces a "littérature coloniale" that responded to these events with "anxiety and doubt." Yee writes that alongside depictions of Eastern cultures as radically Other, what she calls "first-degree Saidian Orientalism," the novels in her corpus feature "Critical Orientalism: a discourse on the Orient that foregrounds a critique of its own modes of understanding."[14]

If scholars of modern colonial literature have often highlighted its tensions and self-critical elements, much of the pioneering work to which we owe the field of medieval postcolonialism has tended to read crusade epics and romances in ways that align quite closely with Said's approach in *Orientalism*.[15] John V. Tolan, for example, sees the imaginative crusade literature produced in Europe from the First Crusade (1095–99) to the fall of Acre and beyond operating as part of a specifically medieval Orientalism, used to justify military action, celebrate crusaders, and establish boundaries between Christianity and Islam.[16] In a study that also aims at unearthing the roots of modern Orientalism, Suzanne Conklin Akbari considers the depiction of Muslims in *chansons de geste* and romances composed circa 1100–1450 in terms of two negative stereotypes, serving "to differentiate the Western self from its Eastern other" along religious and racial lines: the polytheistic, idolatrous "Saracen" who rebukes his "gods" and the intemperate Arab whose irascible character is a product of both "the Oriental climate" and "the deviant 'law of Muhammad.'"[17] In *Empire of Magic*, Geraldine Heng argues that the First Crusade gave rise to the genre of romance, which she sees functioning throughout the centuries (much like modern Orientalism, in Said's conception) as an

4   Introduction

"ideological instrument" of colonization, authorizing Christian conquest and settlement in the Levant, and following the Mamlūk reconquest of Acre, exercising a form of "cultural domination."[18] Romance "projects," according to Heng, include constructing a "discourse of essential differences among peoples," voicing "triumphant celebration" of crusaders, and "exercising a will-to-power in geographically conceiving the world as the hinterland of Europe and the playground of the Christian faith."[19] In her more recent *Invention of Race*, Heng draws on imaginative and historical crusade writings spanning the First Crusade to the rise of the Ottomans to argue for an understanding of holy war as "a matrix conducive to the politics of race," which she defines flexibly, in language coterminous with that deployed by Said in his 1978 study: "a tendency to demarcate human beings through differences" that are "selectively essentialized as absolute and fundamental."[20] In the field of Middle English studies, scholars have often read crusade romances as projecting a world where Christians are heroic and divinely supported, while Muslims are monstrous, religiously frustrated, and "wholly Other."[21]

While in many ways indebted to this scholarship, the present book seeks to expand the study of crusade literature in directions that are broadly consistent with those taken by much postcolonial criticism on modern colonial literature since *Orientalism*. In the rest of this Introduction, I discuss issues of periodization, methodology, and genre that are key to my thinking about Middle English crusade romances, while unpacking my arguments and offering some hints of the analyses to come. I then present the rationale behind my selection of romances and offer a more detailed summary of the chapters. Let us start with periodization. In his important *Des Chrétiens contre les croisades*, which has yet to receive the attention it deserves in the Anglo-American academy, historian Martin Aurell shows that critiques related to the crusades, while expressed following the First Crusade, increased and diversified as the Muslim countercrusading movement gained traction and Christian defeats multiplied: Imād al-Dīn Zangī's reconquest of Edessa (1144), Ṣalāḥ al-Dīn's recovery of Jerusalem (1187), Louis IX of France's two failed expeditions (1248–50 and 1270), and the Mamlūk campaigns culminating in the siege of Acre, to name only some central events.[22] The attitudes that Aurell examines, focusing on the twelfth and thirteenth centuries and drawing mainly on nonliterary sources, range from disapproval of particular practices to interrogation of the very concept of crusade. My book extends this line of inquiry to the period after 1291 and into the realm of literature, placing English crusade romances in dialogue with a large body of evidence to

Introduction 5

illuminate the hopes and ambitions, as well as the anxieties and critiques, that animate them.[23] Chapter 1 argues that, in a post-1291 context, literary depictions of both Christians and "Saracens" or Muslims voicing divinely addressed frustration should be understood as expressive of collective anxieties about God's lack of support to the crusading enterprise.[24] Chapter 2 discusses how late medieval England's "fantasy of conversion," whereby a strong and virtuous Muslim warrior embraces Christianity, exposing and then rectifying the moral shortcomings of his new coreligionists, engages concerns about Christian vulnerability and sinfulness caused by the Mongol conquests, the Mamlūk recovery of Acre, and Ottoman victories at Nicopolis (1396) and Constantinople.[25] Chapters 3 and 4 explore how crusade romances articulate tensions – between devotion to God and worldly ambition, and between legitimate and illegitimate violence – which, while going back to the beginnings of the enterprise, were subject to late medieval developments in the context of crusading in the Baltic, North Africa, and Iberia. Although clearly invested in perpetuating ideals and realities of holy war, Middle English crusade romances are far more self-critical and troubled by anxiety and tension than a clear-cut Orientalist approach would allow.

If European responses to crusading diversified under the pressure of Christian defeats in the Levant, so too did views of Muslims and Islam.[26] As Tolan, Akbari, Heng, and others have demonstrated, derisive representations of Islamic doctrine, lurid biographies of Muhammad, and stereotypes of Muslims as irrational, driven by bodily pleasures, and overall lacking moral discipline are constitutive elements of Orientalist and racializing discourses – discourses that retained currency throughout the high and later Middle Ages.[27] Yet, while some European authors writing after 1291 portrayed Islam as manifestly different and Muslims as inferior Others, those pondering the implications of crusading defeats often reversed these representational tendencies. They presented Islam as akin to Christianity in the values and practices it enjoins, and extoled the merits of Muslims to highlight the failures of Christians. This representational mode is well illustrated by the English Dominican friar John Bromyard's *Summa praedicantium* (c. 1330–48), a widely disseminated manual for preachers composed a few decades after the fall of Acre.[28] Like many fellow churchmen, Bromyard explained crusading defeats via the linkage between morality and fortune: they had occurred because the crusaders, and Christians in general, were sinful. Yet Bromyard brought this moral and providential rationale to bear not only on Christians, but also on Muslims. He asks his audience to ponder the following question: "Sed diceret quis

6   Introduction

infideles Terram illam inhabitantes, bona opera non faciunt, quare ergo tradidit illis Deus terram, vel quare illos malos permittit, terram inhabitare, qui nihil boni faciunt?" ("But if someone says that the infidels who inhabit that land [the Holy Land] do no good works, then why did God give them that land to inhabit?"). His answer is to suggest that, while Christians were able to conquer the Holy Land at a time in which they served God well, Muslims now occupy it because they are less evil (*minus malis*).[29] Accordingly, throughout the *Summa*, Bromyard focuses on perceived similarities between practices in Christianity and Islam (including almsgiving, kindness to strangers, marital fidelity, and avoidance of profanity), highlighting the good works (*bona opera*) of Muslims, and ascribing to them pointed critiques of Christians, to shame and educate his fellow coreligionists.[30] The coexistence of Orientalism and what may be called "reverse Orientalism," a mode that I further discuss in Chapter 2, goes a long way in explaining the varied and often contradictory representations of Muslims in Middle English romance. In post-1291 romances, representations that uphold and unsettle Orientalist and racializing ideologies collide. Constructions of difference compete with an emphasis on sameness. And the voices and behaviors of Muslim characters (or previously Muslim characters, in the case of those who convert to Christianity) are frequently used to edifying, self-critical ends.

My primary methodology in this book is engaged historicism, which I practice to meet a critical need: due to disciplinary boundaries and emphases, Middle English romances of religious warfare are only rarely studied in light of wider traditions of crusade writing, especially works produced after 1291.[31] Despite the "cultural turn" in crusade studies, historians have largely ignored these romances.[32] In literary scholarship, a major tendency since the 1990s has been to focus on the ways in which they articulate national and regional identities, often (though not always) without reference to the broader English and European archive of extant crusade documents.[33] To date, the study of insular crusade romances to most fully engage with the historical discourses, ideologies, and practices of crusading is Lee Manion's 2014 monograph, *Narrating the Crusades*, which analyzes these romances as evidence of crusading's narrative-generating power, situating them within a paradigm of "loss and recovery" and exploring their afterlives in early modern works.[34] My study aligns with Manion's in its interdisciplinary, historicist approach, but draws on a largely distinct, more linguistically diverse and international body of contextualizing sources, some insular (in English, French, and Latin) and others continental (in French, Occitan, German, and Latin), including

Introduction

writings produced by crusaders and travelers in North Africa and West Asia. I draw on this vast, multilingual corpus – a substantial portion of which has been overlooked or sparsely explored by literary scholars and historians alike – to offer new readings of Middle English crusade romances and a new interpretation of the post-1291 political culture to which they belonged. But I also do so to reveal their internationalism: their engagement with concerns, ideas, and traditions that overran European national boundaries. This book thus joins a chorus of recent work that, building on foundational studies by scholars including Ardis Butterfield and David Wallace, seeks to "de-insularize" insular literature and expose the limitations of traditional nation-bound approaches to literary history.[35]

As well as practice a particularly engaged historicism, I pay special attention to processes of translation/adaptation, since Middle English crusade romances are anonymous and most of them rework earlier materials: Anglo-Norman romances and *chansons de geste*, as well as Latin chronicles and histories.[36] Many of the Middle English romances themselves survive in substantially different versions. Influential to my reading practice is the New Philology, which posits that interpretations of medieval literary texts should be underpinned by a detailed investigation of what Bernard Cerquiglini calls "variantes": textual variations in successive manuscript renderings of a given narrative (whether or not translation from one language to another is involved).[37] As the following chapters demonstrate, the anonymous writers of insular crusade romances took a highly dynamic approach to translation or adaptation, exploiting the instability of manuscript culture to alter, expand on, and reconfigure the stories they inherited from previous generations. For example, these authors added altogether new scenes in which Christian and Muslim characters voice religious frustration and doubt.[38] They rendered crusaders more intemperate and sinful while endowing non-Christians with qualifiers of valor and praise.[39] They heightened inter-Christian rivalry and dissent.[40] They established continuities in their characterizations of Christians and Muslims, serving to probe the boundaries of crusader violence.[41] At the hands of writers who conceived of translation or adaptation as an act of creative innovation and topical engagement, romance became a crucial literary site for addressing the fraught questions faced by post-1291 Europe: Was heaven to blame for crusading defeats? Did God support the enterprise? Were God's agents – the crusaders – inadequate? Could Christendom achieve victory without an infusion of Muslim strength and virtue? Could Christians put an end to their internal conflicts and cooperate militarily? Had crusading devolved into a self-serving activity, driven by expectations of worldly fame and social advancement? Did the extreme violence in holy war even conform to God's teachings?

Additionally, my critical approach attends closely to emotional language and characterizations, especially as they intersect with discourses on the vices and virtues. The texts themselves guided me in this methodological choice: while researching this book, I noticed that emotion words and descriptions of emotional displays are often at stake in moments when the romances of my corpus depart from their sources, revealing their own distinctive perspectives.[42] This study thus contributes to the history of emotions movement, which has demonstrated continuities and differences in expressions of, and attitudes toward, emotions across a dizzying array of cultures and contexts.[43] Yet, though scholars of medieval literature such as Anthony Bale, Rita Copeland, Sarah McNamer, Sif Ríkharðsdóttir, and Megan Moore have produced important work on emotions in noncrusading texts and contexts,[44] and while Stephen J. Spencer, Susanna A. Throop, and others have drawn on historical sources of the crusades circa 1095–1291 to contribute fruitfully to the history of emotions,[45] my book is the first to bring this approach to bear on imaginative crusade literature, and on post-1291 writings of any kind.[46] In the following paragraphs, I explain why emotions were an essential resource for authors or translators of crusade romances, outlining their place in crusade propaganda, in crusade culture more broadly, and in the pastoral education of the laity in late medieval England.

My thinking in this area is indebted to scholarship on modern colonial and neocolonial cultures by Sara Ahmed, Leela Gandhi, and Jane Lydon, who have studied emotional language and rhetoric to understand the workings of dominant ideologies, as well as the contradictions within, and practical limitations of, these ideologies.[47] Love of God, charitable assistance to Christian "brothers" in the East, sorrow for injuries inflicted on Christ's patrimony, righteous vengeance against wrongdoers, and zealous anger (*ira per zelum*) against the sinful – such emotional "scripts" were common in ecclesiastical propaganda, especially in crusade sermons, which played a key role in shaping and perpetuating the ideology of the movement throughout the centuries.[48] Ahmed's notion of "affective economy," invoked to explain how emotions circulate across both psychic and social fields, is useful for thinking about the emotional and ideological work of crusade propaganda.[49] For the individual, a potential recruit, emotional rhetoric served to appeal to a sense of spiritual obligation to take the cross. For the collective, it worked to create and reinforce Christian identity, defined in opposition to a threatening, sinful religious and racial Other.

Introduction 9

As the following chapters show, key components of this emotional rhetoric feature prominently in Middle English crusade romances.

Yet, from a very early stage in the history of the crusades, and increasingly over time as contemporaries were forced to face up to disparities between ideals and reality, the emotional repertoire of crusade writing broadened to incorporate elements of self-questioning and self-critique.[50] The First Crusade, while militarily successful, raised troubling questions about the human implications of holy war – questions that were asked by chroniclers using the evaluative and empathic possibilities of emotional language. Albert of Aachen's account is a case in point: narrating the horrific massacres perpetrated by the crusaders at the siege of Jerusalem in 1099, he presents his coreligionists not as virtuous conquerors but as pitiless murderers (*percussores*), raving and venting their rage (*bachantes ac seuientes*) at their victims, whose perspective he adopts and whose sorrow he laments (see Chapter 4).[51] Beginning with the reconquest of Edessa by Imād al-Dīn Zangī and the debacle of the Second Crusade (1145–49), the starkly delineated moral hierarchies of crusade propaganda were further complicated by military defeats that, drawing on Old Testament models, contemporaries widely ascribed to Christian pride and envy (see Chapter 2). The long period from the Ayyūbid recovery of Jerusalem in 1187 to the Ottoman victory at Nicopolis in 1396 saw the development of a highly influential tradition in which Muslims, rather than Christians, are portrayed as righteous avengers, endowed with the authority to punish crusaders for their emotional intemperance and moral transgressions (see Chapter 1). Yet, at the time of Louis IX of France's Egyptian and Tunisian campaigns and of the Mamlūk campaigns leading to the reconquest of Acre, crusaders and laypeople, no longer satisfied with receiving the blame for military failure, turned to heaven for accountability. They wrathfully rebuked God, Christ, and the Virgin Mary, and often threatened to abandon their faith (see Chapter 1). During the fourteenth century, the emotion of love came to occupy a central position in debates on the motives of crusaders, rendered pressing by the Christian loss of the Holy Land and the rise of "chivalric crusading" in the Baltic and North Africa (see Chapter 3). In reworking their sources, writers of crusade romances drew extensively on and contributed creatively to this complex emotional culture.

In this study, I tend to avoid the term "affect," as in recent critical practice it has often carried with it the sense of a preconscious and prediscursive experience, favoring instead the term "emotion," frequently employed by scholars to emphasize the conscious, verbal, interactive, and performative dimensions of feeling – dimensions that crusade romances strongly emphasize.[52] Broadly speaking, my approach to the study of emotions is social constructionist, in that I believe, like Barbara H. Rosenwein and many others whose research is historically oriented, that societies "bend, shape, encourage, and discourage the expression of various emotions."[53] To elucidate the emotional depictions of crusade romances, I delve not only into crusade documents but also into treatises on the passions and the vices and virtues, homiletic literature, medical books on the humors, and manuals for the instruction of knights and kings. I follow Damien Boquet, Piroska Nagy, Carla Casagrande, and Silvana Vecchio in regarding the later Middle Ages as a period when "the Church became particularly concerned with the emotional education of the faithful."[54] Treatises on the vices and virtues reached unprecedently wide audiences during the thirteenth to fifteenth centuries, when they were translated into vernacular languages, incorporated into other literary traditions, and used by priests in their daily practices. This development may be traced back to the Fourth Lateran Council of 1215, which devised a broad-ranging agenda of reform that included the laity's compulsory annual confession.[55] In England, Archbishop John Peckham's Lambeth Constitutions of 1281 refined this emphasis on pastoral education by imposing quarterly seminars, first in the province of Canterbury and later in York, for the doctrinal instruction of lay congregations.[56] Crucially, as Vecchio has noted, this vernacular approach to pastoral education placed considerable emphasis on the emotional underpinnings of virtuous and sinful behavior.[57] In this tradition, emotions, while not inherently ethical, were considered the raw material for moral acts, whether good or evil.[58] Their moral outcome was thought to rest on the will: in the words of Reginald Pecock, one is to "refreyne hem whanne þei moven aȝens doom of resoun or of feiþ" and to "cherische hem whanne þei moven answeryngli to þe doom of resoun or of feiþ."[59] Anger, when controlled by reason, could be harnessed in the service of virtue. Stirrings or feelings of pride and envy were to be contained lest they give rise to homonymous sins (i.e., prideful or envious acts).[60] When properly regulated and directed, love put God before the self. As noted by Boquet and Nagy, this late medieval "pastoral of emotions" knew no social boundaries, targeting "Western society from top to bottom."[61]

At the same time, growing clerical attention to the education of knights and princes led to the production of a remarkable number of chivalric manuals and *specula principum* in which the emotions feature prominently.[62] A notable example is Giles of Rome's *De regimine principum*

Introduction 11

(c. 1270–85), which circulated extensively among the English nobility and gentry. Giles's treatment of the emotions in the context of royal ethics, strongly influenced by Thomas Aquinas, offers nothing less than a code of emotional conduct.[63] Each emotion could be positive or negative, according to object and direction, and certain emotional dispositions were to be followed while others avoided. Properly expressing one's emotions was viewed as important not only to the moral and political lives of contemporaries but also to their physical well-being. Medieval humoral theory, inherited from classical medical philosophy, established the connection between imbalanced bodily humors and the excessive display of emotion.[64] The link between emotional expression and somatic effects meant that emotions could be both the cause and cure for physical ailments. Moreover, the purported interdependence between body and soul endowed discourses of sickness and healing with an ethical quality. Homiletic literature typically viewed illness and other more minor indispositions as physical manifestations of problematic and often sinful actions, choices, and lifestyles.[65] Thus, within all of these types of literature, which were at times conflated within single works, discourses on the emotions were inherently tied up with notions of favorable and unfavorable conduct.[66]

Due to this collective effort to theorize their place in moral and political life, and to their important role in crusade culture, emotions proved highly attractive tools for authors of Middle English crusade romance. Within and between these romances, emotional depictions have myriad intra- and extradiegetic functions and effects, which I cursorily sketch out here and discuss in detail in the following chapters. Sorrow is an emotion that binds Christian characters together, and that invites the audience to identify with their cause. But it is also used to elicit judgment of Christians and sympathy for non-Christians, who are at times cast as sorrowful victims of wrongful actions. Righteous anger frequently underpins legitimate vengeance (or the threat thereof), and is ascribed to both Christians and Muslims. Unbridled wrath serves to pose probing questions about communal politics, crusader violence, and the relations between the human and divine. Fear and shame, often combined, heighten the sense of religious antagonism, as well as that of Christian vulnerability. Envy and pride are the disruptive crusader emotions par excellence. Love – romantic and spiritual – enables explorations of rivaling motives for, even "philosophies" of, crusading. If, in reworking earlier sources drawing on the repertoire of emotions, romance writers were often more interested in unsettling than upholding conventional oppositions (such as virtuous

Christian and sinful non-Christian, righteous crusader and harmful oppressor, divinely protected and religiously frustrated, and just war and illegitimate violence), it is because they sought to inscribe in their narratives the greatest crusading preoccupations of the world around them.

But they also did so because of the generic contract they had with audiences, what Hans Robert Jauss calls the "horizon of expectations."[67] There is a scholarly tradition, going back to influential work by Northrop Frye, that associates the romance genre with schematic dichotomies (good/evil, heroes/villains) and best examples.[68] Critics subscribing to this view have sometimes set the medieval romance against the modern novel, contrasting the former's discursive directness and ideological straightforwardness with the latter's discursive complexity and multiple ideological valences.[69] A different picture has, however, emerged from a number of genre-based discussions of romance as it developed in late medieval England. In attempting to map broad defining parameters for Middle English romance in diachronic and synchronic perspective (i.e., in relation to contiguous contemporaneous genres, such as the *chanson de geste* and the saint's life), scholars such as Jane Gilbert, Christine Chism, and Neil Cartlidge have focused not just on its subject matters and thematic interests but also on various more general tendencies: its ability to encode "a multiplicity of inscribed reader-positions and ideological identifications," the ambivalence and admiration it sustains toward protagonists and antagonists alike, the tensions it explores between ideology and experience, and the critical perspectives it offers on dominant social practices.[70] It is to this view of Middle English romance that the present book contributes. Writers saw romance as a propitious space for articulating ambivalent, self-interrogative meditations on the crusades in late medieval England in part because this is the kind of cultural work that audiences had come to expect of the genre.

These expectations were shaped by the mode in which Middle English romances were delivered and the environment in which they were consumed. Scholars now commonly agree that the target audience of these romances consisted of wealthy nonaristocrats and the gentry. Yet this audience was not the only one to consume them: there is evidence of works filtering up and down the social levels, to kings and to household servants. These romances were commonly read aloud in communal settings and, given that contemporary English households did not tend to segregate according to class, they reached a diversity of listeners in this context, bridging literate and nonliterate segments of the population.[71] Due to its wide, heterogeneous audience, Middle English romance may be

Introduction   13

productively thought of as popular fiction, as long as one avoids deeming it "unsophisticated" and allowing only for passive, uncritical absorption.[72] Helen Cooper offers a compelling account of how romances would have been received. The centrality of debate to late medieval English culture, the oral delivery and communal reception of romance, the emphasis that writers placed on meaning alongside story, the questions they sometimes explicitly and often implicitly asked their audiences to reflect upon – all of these factors, Cooper argues, suggest an engaged, socially interactive literary consumption. "Romances could provide a secular forum analogous to academic debate," writes Cooper. "Their audiences expected to respond actively to them, and the writers encouraged such a response."[73] In the case of the Middle English crusade romances, the issues that audiences were invited to discuss and debate were topical and pressing: God's endorsement of the crusading enterprise, the apathy and misdirected priorities of European kings, the selfish motives and competitiveness of knights, Christendom's beleaguered state and military vulnerability, and the morality of violence.

The large number of Middle English romances featuring encounters and battles between Christians and non-Christians has resulted in different scholarly understandings of what qualifies as a "crusade romance." But basing our conception of this subgenre on historical evidence of contemporary identification with the crusading movement puts us on solid ground.[74] The oft-neglected Matter of France or Charlemagne romances – five of which I discuss here (*The Siege of Milan, The Sultan of Babylon, Otuel, Otuel and Roland,* and *Duke Roland and Sir Otuel of Spain*) – occupy a central position in this corpus since references to the Carolingian king and his peers as protocrusaders permeate European writings of the high and later Middle Ages. *Guy of Warwick* contributed to the familial crusading tradition of the Beauchamps, earls of Warwick. The siege of Jerusalem of 70 CE by the Roman generals Titus and Vespasian, imaginatively rendered in the alliterative *Siege of Jerusalem,* was conflated with the crusader conquest of the city during the First Crusade in various chronicles and treatises. And *Richard Coeur de Lion* is loosely based on the events of the Third Crusade (1189–92).[75] As well as offer thickly historicized readings of these narratives, I weave other relevant romances into my discussion to highlight intertextual relations and broader thematic patterns.

The book's structure is text-based and emotion-based. Each of its four wide-ranging chapters discusses one to three romances and two or more emotions. Chapter 1 focuses on articulations of sorrow, anger, and vengeance in *The Siege of Milan* and *The Sultan of Babylon* to illuminate underlying anxieties about poor leadership, internal disunity, and perceived lack of divine support. *The Siege of Milan* engages two of the most significant crusading disappointments of the post-1291 era. The first concerns the inability or unwillingness of European kings to unite and launch a large-scale campaign to "recover" the Holy Land. The second emerges as a troubling question: why would a God who possessed the power to intervene in human affairs allow for wars fought on his behalf to persistently end in failure? The romance features a striking scene of Christian rebuke of the Virgin Mary, the rationale of which I elucidate in light of an important body of evidence that surfaced in the lead-up to and aftermath of the fall of Acre: a series of letters to the celestial *curia* composed by an Italian Dominican missionary in Baghdad; the poem of a Provençal troubadour Templar in the Levant; and numerous other literary works and chronicles in Latin, Occitan, and German. Creatively reworking the Anglo-Norman *La Destruction de Rome* and *Fierabras*, the writer of *The Sultan of Babylon* addresses a contiguous set of preoccupations by heightening historically charged problematic behaviors. King Charlemagne repeatedly succumbs to wrath, resulting in collectively detrimental fratricidal quarrels. Sultan Laban, while presented as politically virtuous and justified in his military actions against Christians, is constantly disappointed by his "gods," whom he physically abuses and threatens to forsake. As I argue, the motif of the "afflicted Muslim," which proliferated within the genre of Middle English romance, encapsulates a prominent aspect of post-1291 cultural development, whereby Christian frustrations at God's perceived inaction and anxieties about religious apostasy were projected onto the Muslims of fantasy.

Chapter 2 continues to investigate the Charlemagne romances' fraught reflections on divine will and the politics of communal crusading, but with a focus on anxieties related to the conversion of non-Christians, Latin Christendom's beleaguered state, and rash crusader conduct. These concerns underlie the three Middle English *Otuel* romances, which recount the story of a Muslim knight (Otuel) who, after nearly defeating Christendom's chivalric champion (Roland), miraculously converts to Christianity. The adaptors of these romances, I argue, reconfigured their Old French and Anglo-Norman sources according to the emotional rhetoric mobilized in contemporary political discourse in response to the westward conquests first of the Mongol Empire and then of the Ottoman Empire, drawing in particular on the vocabulary of fear, fearlessness, and shame. In these romances, religious conversion does not change

Introduction 15

Otuel: he was already fierce, noble, courteous, and pious as a Muslim, attributes that he carries into his "new" Christian life. Following his conversion, the three *Otuel* romances depart from the French tradition in having him reprove Charlemagne's closest peers (Roland, Oliver, and Ogier) for their pride and envy, thus situating him in relation to, if not directly within, a tradition that suffused European chronicles, treatises, travel literature, sermons, and poems. The motif of the righteous, admonitory Muslim, as I demonstrate, was grounded in contemporary beliefs in the providential relationship between morality and military outcomes; and it came to be most pervasively used to comment on the Christian loss of the Holy Land and the Ottoman victory at Nicopolis, which was itself interpreted by Jean Froissart and Philippe de Mézières through the cultural prism of Charlemagne's legendary wars against Muslims.

Chapter 3 turns to anxieties about the motivations of crusaders, focusing on the romance of *Guy of Warwick* as it features in the Auchinleck manuscript. In fourteenth-century Europe, an ideology of "chivalric crusading" that sought to harmoniously combine knight-errantry, courtly love, the pursuit of fame, and service to God gained wide popularity, disseminated by works such as Guillaume de Machaut's *La prise d'Alixandre*, the anonymous *Livre des fais* of Marshal Boucicaut, Geoffroi de Charny's *Livre de chevalerie*, and Nicolaus of Jeroschin's *Krônike von Prûzinlant*. But this ideology was not without its critics: writers including John Gower, Philippe de Mézières, and Henry of Grosmont seized on the notion of crusading as love-service to articulate complex critiques of the worldly ambitions of crusaders. *Guy of Warwick* intervenes in this debate by exploring the practical implications of fighting for worldly love and, following the protagonist's confession, love of God. Garnering accolades from peers and social superiors is a stipulation of Guy's love-service to Felice, the Earl of Warwick's daughter. Yet this quest for praise and fame becomes so all-consuming that it leads him to nearly forget about Felice and abandon the Christian faith. Reconfiguring the Anglo-Norman *Gui de Warewic*, the Auchinleck *Guy of Warwick* enhances tensions between the protagonist's pre- and postconfessional lives by rendering his rejection of earthly concerns more emphatic and having him translate religious devotion into martial acts of selfless friendship. Drawing on biographical evidence, I suggest that the ascetic ethos purveyed by the romance, harking back to the inception of the crusading movement, held considerable purchase in fourteenth-century English chivalric spheres, and was particularly rife among participants in the Barbary crusade of 1390 to Tunis. I conclude by arguing that Geoffrey Chaucer modeled his Knight and

16   Introduction

Squire in the General Prologue to the *Canterbury Tales* on the rivaling "philosophies" of crusading documented in the chapter.

Chapter 4 examines tensions between beliefs in the "healthy," salvific character of crusading and anxieties about the morality of violence. It argues that, finding their origins in events that took place during the First Crusade, these tensions became especially pronounced in post-1291 crusade culture, crystallizing in works by John Gower, John Wyclif, John Clanvowe, and Michel Pintoin, among others, and complexly articulated in *The Siege of Jerusalem* and *Richard Coeur de Lion*. The chapter returns to the emotions of anger, sorrow, and fear, but to explore non-Christian emotional and physical reactions to acts of Christian violence, framed as troublingly excessive. In my subchapter on *The Siege of Jerusalem*, I analyze the romance's juxtapositions of unrestrained Christian anger and violence with compassion-arousing Jewish agony in light of comparably ambivalent historical reports of the crusading pogroms against Europe's Jewish communities and the massacre of Muslims in Jerusalem at the conclusion of the First Crusade. Similar concerns, I suggest, shaped the creative adaptation of *Richard Coeur de Lion*, which, in some versions, casts the eponymous king as a cannibal. To elucidate the king's actions, I reassess the long historiographical and literary tradition of crusader cannibalism that originated in events at the siege of Ma'arra (1098), arguing that by the time *Richard Coeur de Lion* was written and rewritten, cannibalism had come to symbolically stand for the necessities *and* the worst excesses of the enterprise. The romance's two episodes of anthropophagy invoke this cultural legacy. The first restores the king to good health while the second exposes the baser instincts to which crusading could appeal.

To read crusade romances with an eye to the anxieties, tensions, and critiques they carry, as I propose to do here, is to pursue critical aims that align with those animating a substantial body of postcolonial scholarship on modern colonial literature in the wake of Said's *Orientalism*. My hope is that the following chapters will stimulate further work in this vein, and further contributions by medievalists to debates in the expansive field of postcolonial studies. At the same time, this study seeks quite simply to provide scholars and students of Middle English crusade romances with a stronger sense of the historical consciousness of these texts, their engagement with broader European traditions of crusade writing, and the pressures exerted on them by contemporary geopolitics. It unearths a variety of new contexts for understanding tropes of romance that have long been recognized yet remain underanalyzed (the "afflicted Muslim," the

Introduction 17

"blasphemous bishop," the "worthy sultan," the "heroic convert," the "love-spurred crusader," and so on). Finally, what I hope to illustrate are the benefits of a hybrid methodology combining historicist inquiry, attention to practices of translation or adaptation, and analysis of emotions. This methodological blend is especially useful for my study, on the grounds discussed above, but might be fruitfully applied to other medieval literary texts and corpora.

CHAPTER I

Royal Emotions, Blasphemy, and (Dis)unity in The Siege of Milan *and* The Sultan of Babylon

The Carolingian king Charlemagne, whose invasion of al-Andalus (Islamic Spain) in 778 forms the historical basis of the foundational *Chanson de Roland*, was an icon of the crusading movement.[1] Preaching the First Crusade at Clermont in 1095, Pope Urban II is said to have invoked the deeds of Charlemagne to enjoin his audience to take the cross, expand the frontiers of Christendom, and liberate the Holy Sepulchre in Jerusalem.[2] Four centuries later, in his *Epistre au roi Richart* (1395), Philippe de Mézières called upon the Carolingian king's example to urge Richard II of England to join forces with Charles VI of France to reconquer the Holy Land.[3] A wealth of evidence attests to how closely contemporaries identified the crusading preoccupations of their time with the cultural and literary tradition of Charlemagne as it developed in high and late medieval Europe.[4]

Yet scholars seldom study the Middle English Charlemagne romances for their engagement with late medieval crusading concerns.[5] Those who mention the crusades tend to do so in passing while focusing on other issues: the place of these texts, which derive from *chansons de geste*, within the genre of romance, for example, or the paradox of casting the Frankish king as a literary hero in England during a period of Anglo-French war.[6] Phillipa Hardman and Marianne Ailes observe that the heroes of the French epic were subject to a process of "supranationalization" in the insular versions, whereby national affiliations are replaced with Christian identities. The narrative effect, according to Hardman and Ailes, is an enhanced sense of "us" – the transnational Christian community – and "them" – its Muslim enemy.[7] In a similar vein, Robert Warm argues that the insular romances "are deliberately ignoring the deadly rivalry" between England and France and "constructing an idealized vision of the past, within which true Christian knights fought the infidel rather than one another."[8] For these critics and others, crusading is not so much a narrative focus as a means to an end: the promotion of a Christian collective identity in the context of the Hundred Years War.

18

Royal Emotions, Blasphemy, and (Dis)unity 19

One aim of this chapter is to show that the Middle English Charlemagne romances are in fact deeply invested in late medieval debates about the crusades, including the question of whether western European kings should prioritize domestic issues, such as the Hundred Years War, or crusading activity. Another aim is to complicate the frequently aired notion that these romances imagine the Christian community as cohesive and stable, and to center the many episodes of disunity and infighting in this corpus, probing their historical, political, and religious significance. Indeed, while these romances invariably culminate in Christian unity, in the course of the narration they stage dramatic conflicts – between Christians but also between the human and divine – that would have carried strong topical resonances for contemporary audiences bearing the legacy of Christendom's crusading failures in the Levant. It is, I argue, in these ubiquitous moments of friction, negotiation, and dissent that the Middle English Charlemagne romances express anxieties related to the crusades.

For authors of crusade romances, and for those who wrote the cultural and historical narratives of the crusades more generally, the language and rhetoric of emotions proved instrumental to expressing concerns about Christian cohesion and the lack thereof. In this chapter, I discuss the narrative function of emotions in the articulation and disruption of communal solidarity, focusing on anger and sorrow, and their connection to vengeance. In my subchapter on *The Siege of Milan* (c. 1400), I show that these emotions serve to promote collective crusading efforts and criticize those who obstruct them.[9] *The Siege of Milan* enacts complaints against the misdirected priorities of Charlemagne that find close analogues in the historical record. Yet the romance's most powerful critique is of heaven – the Virgin Mary in particular – for failing to protect her followers in combat. In the post-1291 era, as in earlier years, the explanation diffused by ecclesiastical authorities to solve the dilemma of crusading defeats was that God's perceived inaction was a manifestation of wrath against Christian sinfulness. The more straightforward reaction, however, staged in *The Siege of Milan* and a substantial body of little-studied writings, was to accuse heaven of dereliction of duty.

In my subchapter on *The Sultan of Babylon* (c. 1400), I harness this body of evidence to offer a new interpretation of the pervasive motif of the "afflicted Muslim" who rebukes his "gods," arguing that such depictions were in fact projections of European anxieties about divine will and support, and the conversion of Christians to Islam.[10] If in some scenes Laban, the eponymous sultan, expresses divinely addressed anger and sorrow, in others he is portrayed as morally and politically virtuous: a worthy ruler who is provoked to righteous vengeance by an unsanctioned attack on his men by Christian Romans, a polity defined by its sinfulness, before engaging in battle with the internally divided forces of Charlemagne. As scholars have argued, *The Sultan of Babylon* constructs a discourse of racial alterity in its depiction of Laban's army. What remains to be noted, however, is the way in which the romance also troubles this discourse, setting up representational continuities between Christians and Muslims and orchestrating shifts in perspective that invite the audience to relate to, and even sympathize with, the predicaments of both parties. In *The Sultan of Babylon*, cultural discourses are notably unstable.

NEGOTIATING CHRISTIAN EMOTIONAL SOLIDARITY IN *THE SIEGE OF MILAN*

The Siege of Milan (hereafter *Milan*) is often ascribed a distinctive place within the corpus of Middle English Charlemagne romances, in part because it is one of only two of these texts for which there is no extant source material.[11] Critics have pondered the poem's generic makeup as incorporating elements from hagiography and homily, and exploiting devotional and eucharistic themes.[12] Yet in its emotional assertions and transgressions of communal solidarity, and in its engagement with late medieval crusading concerns, *Milan* conforms to broader narrative patterns common to the romances of this corpus. In what follows, I first examine theoretical codifications of anger that would have informed contemporary interpretations of the romance's key scenes of conflict between Church and Crown, Bishop Turpin and King Charlemagne. I then elucidate the narrative's rhetoric of sorrow in light of cognate uses and elicitations of this emotion in crusade propaganda, chronicles, and complaint literature produced by Latin Christian authors in Europe and the Near East.

Coercive Wrath and the Misdirected Priorities of Christian Kings

Depictions of meritorious and reprehensible anger in *Milan* are indebted to two related traditions: biblical, based on the model of *ira dei*; and political, stemming from the codes and conventions regulating royal and aristocratic anger. Traditionally, Christian doctrine categorized anger as a deadly sin. Yet a form of praiseworthy human anger emerged in late antiquity and the early Middle Ages, due in part to the presence of *ira dei* in the Bible. In the Old Testament, God's anger is inherent to his role as judge. Concurrent with his love for humankind, anger is a response to sin yet contains an edifying, "constructive" dimension: it aims to coerce into virtuous action, and therefore leads humans to salvation.[13] Writing in the early fourth century, Lactantius warns of the dangers of immoderate human anger but asserts that God endowed humankind with the emotion for the sake of correcting faults.[14] In *De civitate dei* (completed 426 CE), Augustine of Hippo stresses the importance of considering emotions in causal terms, in counterpoint to Stoic thought, and upholds the righteous performance of anger: "Irasci enim peccanti ut corrigatur . . . ne pereat nescio utrum quisquam sana consideratione reprehendat" (For I do not think that any right-minded person would condemn anger at a sinner in order to correct him).[15] In Alcuin of York's view, expounded in an early ninth-century treatise on the vices and virtues, anger is disruptive of sound judgment and causes countless social ills but is good when directed against one's own sins.[16] A few years later, Hincmar of Reims enumerates the social evils ensuing from the emotion while acknowledging the benefits of anger driven by zeal and virtue.[17] The same two criteria for positive anger are retained in Thomas of Chobham's *Summa confessorum* (c. 1216). Although generally strict in his assessment of the emotion's harmful effects, Thomas identifies the founding component of zealous anger – the vicious nature of the target – and goes as far as labeling this type of anger a virtue: "Ira autem per zelum est quando irascimur contra vitia et contra vitiosos, et possumus optare quod talis ira crescat, quia virtus est" (Anger through zeal is when we are angry against vice and against the vicious, and we can hope that this anger increases, because it is a virtue).[18] Highlighting the perils of anger, these authors also recognize its merits, when deployed to reprove and correct wrongdoers (including oneself).

But this legitimate form of anger was only to be expressed in certain circumstances and had to respect specific modalities, which later authors rigorously defined. For Thomas Aquinas, the key criterion demarcating righteous from censured anger is whether it is bound to reason. He asserts that anger is required at times, and that expressing it and desiring vengeance to punish vice and maintain goodness and justice is commendable; on the other hand, anger against an undue object, or manifested in an undue or immoderate manner, is sinful.[19] Similarly, Giles of Rome's *De regimine principum* warns against the dangers of impulsive royal wrath but highlights the value of the emotion when harnessed as an instrument of reason in the service of virtue.[20] Finding its source in William Peraldus's *Summa de vitiis*, Chaucer's *Parson's Tale* likewise denounces "sodeyn Ire or hastif Ire" vented "withouten avisement and consentynge of resoun," while commending "nat wrooth agayns the man, but wrooth with the mysdede of the man."[21] Here, as is the case with other Middle English words signifying anger (including *tene* and *gref*), *wrooth* and *ire* are not morally weighted, but are used interchangeably. In sum, anger was approved of when morally justifiable and controlled by reason and was condemned if excessive, impulsive, and/or unreasoned.

Such theoretical treatments of anger informed uses of the emotion in narrative sources. The way a writer framed the wrathful actions of a given character could serve to assert his or her endorsement or denunciation of the person or actions in question, and invite readers or listeners to do the same. Imputing unrighteous or unchecked wrath was one way of conveying and eliciting reproof. An equally effective formula was to present a person's unwarranted behavior as provoking the legitimate anger of others. Moreover, when authors ascribed anger to kings and lords, they often invested it with a communicative function, as Stephen D. White illustrates in analyzing twelfth-century French chronicles and other historical narratives. White writes, "More than an emotional response to a past political act, a display of anger also involves a quasi-juridical appraisal of the act and of the person or persons deemed responsible for it."[22] The expression of anger signaled that an offense was committed, and that if reparations were not made, vengeance would ensue. But more often than not, in the narratives analyzed by White, the threat of retribution suffices to initiate a settlement between parties, leading to restructured social relationships.[23] Anger therefore contained a conciliatory dimension that, as we will see, is invoked in *Milan* to mediate royal and ecclesiastical power.

In crusade sermons, a form of zealous anger (*ira per zelum*) against the perceived injuries inflicted by Muslims was sometimes encouraged, as Susanna A. Throop has shown.[24] Yet far more often, preachers ascribed the emotion to God, whom they portrayed as angered by human sin, whether that of the Muslim enemy or reluctant Christian recruit. Indeed, the threat of divine wrath, and the fear it entailed, were frequently invoked to pressure potential recruits into taking the cross. As Jacques de Vitry warned: "Qui autem noluerunt audire levem sibilum predicationis saltem audiant magnum clamorem Crucifixi, alioquin audituri sunt tonitruum terribilis vocis: Ite, *maledicti!*" (Those who do not want to listen to the soft murmur of the sermons, should at least listen to the loud call of the Crucified, else [sic] they will hear the thunder of a dreadful voice: Go, *you who are cursed!*).[25] Or, in the words of Gilbert de Tournai, speaking of the sign of the cross that separates crusaders from others: "Virga enim

Coercive Wrath and Misdirected Priorities 23

crucis et sanguine Christi sanctificamur et ab aliis signatis discernimur. Sed timeant rebelles et in peccatis suis perseverantes, ne signum clementie vertatur eis in signum iracundie" (By the staff of the cross and the blood of Christ we are consecrated and distinguished from those who are signed otherwise. But rebels who persist in their own sins must fear that for them the sign of clemency be turned into a sign of anger).[26] Only those signed with the cross are saved; all others incur God's anger, in this life or at the Last Judgment.

In *Milan*, wrathful interactions between Bishop Turpin and King Charlemagne, before the latter agrees to take part in crusade, testify to the influence of these traditions of *ira dei* and political anger. God's wrath is set up as an authorizing paradigm for Turpin's crusade fervor from the start. The romance opens with the invasion of Lombardy by the forces of a sultan named Arabas. After the lord of Milan, cornered into surrender, comes to Charlemagne and requests his support – "Jesu Criste hase comannde thee / To fare to the felde to feghte for mee, / My landis agayne to gett" (154–56) – Turpin calls the king to action:

> Hafe done! Late semble the folke of thyne –
> Myn hede, I undirnome
> That Gode es grevede at the Sarazenes boste;
> We salle stroye up alle theire hoste. (164–67)

This exhortation establishes military intervention as endorsed by God, whose wrath compels vengeance for the injuries inflicted on fellow Christians. Charlemagne, moreover, had previously received a visit from an angel in a dream, who had designated him as Christ's representative and entrusted him with a sword: "Criste sende the this swerde, / Mase the his werryoure here in erthe, / He dose the wele to weite" (118–20). Yet Charlemagne dismisses both the dream and the churchman's call to crusade, corrupted by "the falseste traytoure" (173) Ganelon, who urges the king to send Roland to Lombardy in his stead. Ganelon's reasons are covetous: married to Roland's mother, he would inherit his son-in-law's lands should the latter die on crusade. Charlemagne, Ganelon argues, must prioritize the defense of his realm – a view that is echoed by the other royal advisors: "Thay prayede the Kynge on that tyde / That he hymselfe at home walde byde, / To kepe that lande right thare" (199–201). Upon hearing of Charlemagne's decision to remain in France, Turpin sets off for the royal household, where, erupting in anger, he accuses the king of living in heresy, being a coward, betraying Christ's sacrifice, and forsaking his faith:

> And here I curse the, thou Kynge!
> Because thou lyffes in eresye
> Thou ne dare noghte fyghte one Goddes enemy! (688–90)
>
> . . .
>
> Nowe arte thou werre than any Sarazene,
> Goddes awenn wedirwyne – (695–96)
>
> . . .
>
> If Cristyndome loste bee,
> The wyte bese casten one the.
> Allas that thou was borne!
> Criste for the sufferde mare dere,
> Sore wondede with a spere,
> And werede a crown of thorne –
> And now thou dare noghte in the felde
> For Hym luke undir thy schelde!
> I tell thi saule forlorne.
> Men will deme aftir thi day
> How falsely thou forsuke thi laye,
> And calle the "Kynge of Skornne." (698–708)

As the top representative of ecclesiastical power in the romance, Turpin excommunicates Charlemagne, who, placing himself outside the Christian community, becomes "Goddes foo" (739), injuring God in the same way as the Muslim enemy had endeavored to do, and thus incurring the same wrathful response. Like the *ira dei* of the Bible and crusade propaganda, Turpin's wrath functions as both a verdict and an instrument of pressure, impelling Charlemagne to reconsider his position. Moreover, the bishop's display adheres to the conventions regulating the expression of righteous human anger: it is triggered by an injustice; it is not impulsive since he travels by horse to see the king after being informed of his resolution; and it contains a pronounced moral judgment and a communicative, political dimension.

Faced with Turpin's wrathful allegations, Charlemagne in turn expresses anger: "Bot then Kyng Charls, withowtten wene, / At the Byschopp was so tene, / A fawchone hase he drawen" (710–12). Here, the nature of the king's anger is markedly set apart from the bishop's: not only is it morally unwarranted insofar as his refusal to wage holy war goes against his oneiric divine appointment, but it is presented as impulsive and rash. The two men are prevented from fighting in the royal hall by Charlemagne's "grete lordes" (721), and Turpin departs, but not before expressing further outrage at the king's transgression of divine will and asserting his intentions to return with an army:

> Goddes byddynge hase thou broken –
> Thurghe the traytour speche spoken,
> Alle Christendom walde thou schende!
> When Criste sent the a suerde until
> Thou myghte wele wiete it was His will
> That thiselfe solde thedir wende:
> Therefore I sall stroye the,
> Byrne and breke downn thi cité
> If thou be never so tende. (746–54)

Only when the bishop's army of clerics is at the point of besieging Paris does Charlemagne, following Duke Naymes's advice to save his "renown" (780), finally consent to embark on crusade. In a ritual act of subordination inaugurating the newfound alliance, Charles falls on his knees and begs forgiveness (791–93). The cessation of hostilities is marked by the conversion of mutual wrath into mutual joy – "Theire joye bygane to newe" (790) – and a celebration "with wyne and welthes at will" (799).[27]

The story of an inward-looking king, who is persuaded by a covetous advisor (Ganelon) to attend to domestic matters at the expense of crusading, would have resonated powerfully for contemporary audiences against the backdrop of the Hundred Years War. Indeed, from the outset of this conflict, English and French kings were enjoined by some to privilege the "defense of their realms" – a rationale invoked by both parties to justify military action[28] – and encouraged by others to make peace and reconquer the Holy Land. Turpin's position in the romance reverberates with the arguments of clerical authors such as Hugo of Lüttich, a priest from Liège who, in a poem entitled *Peregrinarius* (c. 1342), advocates for a redirection of royal energies from inward (the Anglo–French war) to outward (the recovery of the Holy Land) under the aegis of a muscular, unifying Church.[29] A similar agenda was later upheld by the French propagandist Philippe de Mézières, whose crusading order, the Order of the Passion, boasted a significant contingent of English recruits from the gentry and nobility under Richard II.[30] In his allegorical *Songe du vieil pelerin* (1389), Mézières has Queen Truth wrathfully admonish the barons and counts of England – the "grans Sangliers Noirs" – for corrupting Richard II – "le jeune Blanc Sangler couronne" – into privileging dynastic, territorial claims within Christendom over the recovery of Christ's patrimony.[31] As in *Milan*, evil counsel is the cause of detrimental royal policies. Mézières develops this idea in his *Epistre au roi Richart* (1395) with the figure of King Malavisé, who stands for "des roys crestiens qui longuement ont estez malavisez, et encore sont" (the Christian kings who have long been ill-advised, and still are) in their political decisions.[32] Should these kings persist in their ways, Mézières warns, they will incur divine ire:

> En verite je doubte fort que ce vous serez negligens, Dieu le vous monstrera de fait et sentires sa verge, et que fort ly desplaira; de laquele negligence Dieu par sa grace vous vueille garder et vous doint grace que aux consaulz du contraire vous puissies vaillaument resister.

> In truth, I greatly fear that if you prove negligent, God will show His wrath, you will be unpleasing in His sight and will feel His rod of correction. May God spare us this negligence and grant you His grace to valiantly resist adverse counsels.[33]

Mézières's warnings are corroborated by the influential works of Eustache Deschamps in France and those of John Mandeville and John Gower in England. In his "Complainte de l'Eglise," Deschamps remonstrates "tous les empereurs, roys et princes de la religion chrestienne" (all the Christian emperors, kings, and princes), and "leur conseilliers, justiciers, presidens et gouverneurs" (their counselors, judges, and magistrates), whose "convoitise de terres, seignouries et possessions" (covetousness of lands, fiefdoms, and possessions) in Europe had considerably profited Muslims, he laments, and had provoked the "indignacion" (indignation) and "ire" (anger) of God and the Church.[34] Along similar lines, Mandeville's immensely popular travel book chastises the "lordes of the worlde," who, through "covetise," "bien more bisy forto deserte her neyghbores than to chalange and conquere here ryght heritage."[35] The issue is again broached in Gower's *Vox Clamantis*, which decries the domestic disputes that allow Muslims to hold Christian holy places.[36]

Complaints such as these permeate contemporary writings, unsurprisingly soliciting the creative engagement of writers working within the Charlemagne tradition, Europe's imaginative crusade literature par excellence. *Milan* ultimately has Charlemagne submitting to Turpin's wrathful demands and vowing to embark on a crusade. Christian concord is thus attained, but only after the romance offers a critically charged vision of the impediments to realizing this objective. It takes no less than God's wrath, materializing in the bishop's threat to destroy Paris, to convince Charlemagne to reject Ganelon's covetous advice and embrace his divinely appointed role as crusade leader. The romance features as narrative what Mézières, Deschamps, Mandeville, and Gower offer as complaint and expository warning, implicating its audience in a historically evocative scenario where the tensions between Turpin's exemplary commitment and the realities of human failure, embodied by Charlemagne, are acutely rendered.

Collective Sorrow, Vengeance, and Invectives against Heaven

While wrathful displays serve to address *Milan*'s main political conflict of interests, the harmonies and tensions of Christian unity receive their most extensive narrative treatment in the emotion of sorrow, the compassion-arousing character and evaluative potential of which are fully exploited. As in Old French, in which sorrow and anger merge in the terms *doel* and *ire*, used by authors to signify "sad anger" or "angry sadness," the connection between the two emotions is semantically ingrained in Middle English.[37] This is particularly evident in words such as *tene* and *gref*, which can designate anger (as in the depiction of Charlemagne above) but also sorrow.[38] Similarly, sorrow and compassion overlap in Middle English usage, as with the terms *sorwe* and *reuthe*, which can operate as near-synonyms of *compassioun*.[39]

Milan, as we will see, follows an emotional "script" that is widely attested in crusade chronicles, *chansons de geste*, and sermons: sorrow at the injuries inflicted by Muslims underpins military intervention, which is couched in terms of vengeance and/or assistance to other Christians. In the *Chanson d'Antioche*, for example, the impetus for the First Crusade is given when Peter the Hermit, "plains de doeul" (full of grief), requests the pope's support to "Dieu vengier" (avenge God) for the "moult grant damage" (very great wrongs) done to Christians in the Holy Land.[40] Peter the Hermit's response to the predicaments of Christians in the Near East – compassionate grief – is one that crusade preachers also sought to elicit in their audiences. Odo of Deuil describes this process in his account of the Bishop of Langres's preaching campaign for the Second Crusade:

> Tunc religiosus vir episcopus Lingonensis de Rohes, quae antiquo nomine vocatur Edessa, depopulatione et oppressione Christianorum et insolentia paganorum satis episcopaliter peroravit; et de flebili materia fletum plurimum excitavit monens omnes ut cum rege suo ad subveniendum Christianis Regi omnium militarent.

> On that occasion the pious bishop of Langres spoke in his episcopal capacity concerning the devastation of Rohes, whose ancient name is Edessa, and the oppression of the Christians and arrogance of the heathen; and by this doleful theme he aroused great lamentation, while at the same time he admonished all that, together with their king, they should fight for the King of all in order to succour the Christians.[41]

The relation between compassionate grief, the duties of Christian assistance, and violent intervention is thrown into relief. Prior to the Fifth Crusade, Jacques de Vitry likewise framed sorrow as a compulsory reaction to alleged injuries perpetrated by Muslims: "Soli autem gementes et dolentes super abominationibus quae sunt in Hierusalem, a percussore defendentur. Non enim dignus est misericordia, qui pectus terreum habet, et de vituperio patris sui non dolet" (Only those who groan and sorrow over the abominations done in Jerusalem are defended from the striker. For a man who has a heart of earth and does not mourn over the insults to his father does not deserve mercy).[42] Heartfelt sorrow is the *conditio sine qua non* of inclusion into the Christian community, defined in terms of protection against harm in general, and implicitly, against the forces luring humans to damnation. Consumed by "zelus domus Domini" (zeal for the house of the Lord), the crusader must "in praelio succurratis" (hurry to his aid in battle) in remission of all sins.[43] Here, as in Odo of Deuil's account, the elicitation of grief is inherent to the notion of military *auxilium*, which could, and often was, framed as vengeance.[44]

Yet in the lead-up to and aftermath of the Mamlūk reconquest of Acre, crusade apologists increasingly invoked the language of sorrow and compassion to indict Christian inaction. The proceedings of the Second Council of Lyons stressed that no one could be excused from feeling compassion (*compassio*) and sorrow (*dolor*) for the condition of the Holy Land, and therefore none could be exempt from providing succor and seeking vengeance (*vindicta*).[45] Sorrow is inextricable from physical commitment; hence failure to respond militarily is grounds for harsh reproof. In the epilogue to the anonymous "De Excidio Urbis Acconis," a treatise on the loss of the Holy Land that benefited from wide circulation in England and France,[46] Christendom's lack of emotional solidarity is lamented at length:

> Luge, Syon filia, propter tibi dilectam civitatem Acconis ... Luge, Syon filia, tibi presidentes in necessariis rectores, tam summum pontificem et cardinales cum aliis ecclesie prelatis et clero quam reges et principes, barones et milites christianos, dicentes se nobiles generosos, in valle non lacrimarum sed deliciis peccatorum effluenti dormientes, qui solam civitatem populo plenam christiano quasi in vasta solitudine sicut ovem inter lupos reliquerunt indefensam.

> Mourn, daughter of Sion, for the city of Acre, which you hold dear ... Mourn for your rulers, both for the highest pontiff and the cardinals with other prelates of the Church and clergy, and for the kings and princes, barons and Christian knights, who say that they are nobles of high birth,

Sorrow, Vengeance, and Invectives against Heaven 29

who are sleeping not in the valley of tears, but in the valley overflowing with the pleasures of sin, who left this city full of Christian people alone in a great solitude, like a defenceless sheep amongst wolves.[47]

The audience is exhorted to bewail Christian emotional indifference, defined allegorically as "in valle deliciis peccatorum effluenti." Christendom's elite is similarly denounced by conflating human sinfulness with a deficiency of compassion in Philippe de Mézières's account of Peter I of Cyprus's attempts to rouse interest for the Alexandria Crusade of 1365: "Sed heu, peccatis mundi imminentibus ... Non fuit qui terrae sanctae misereretur, nec de opprobrio suo compateretur, proh dolor!" (But alas, the world was sunk in sin ... Nobody, alas, had pity on the Holy Land, or sympathized with its shame). Peter is sent away "ipsum vacuum et lacrimantem" (empty-handed and tearful).[48] Thus, frameworks of emotional solidarity were deployed both to solicit feelings of collective involvement and to signal, criticize, and lament their absence. Drawing on these traditions, sorrowful expression in *Milan* registers a powerful strain between a desire for collaborative, successful crusading and an awareness of both human and providential failure to bring such a desire to fruition.

The author of *Milan* portrays the Muslim attack on Lombardy in terms of various injuries, including the destruction of cities (15), burning of relics (25–27), tormenting of Christians (38), and finally, the taking of Milan. Forced to flee, the lord of the city turns to Christ for guidance: "Than wente that knyghte unto bedde. / For sorowe hym thoghte his hert bledde, / And appon Jesu than gan he calle" (85–87). Falling asleep, "wery forwepe" (89), he receives the visit of an angel who summons him to awaken, go find King Charlemagne, and "say hym God byddis that he sall go / To helpe to venge the of thy foo" (100–101).[49] Weeping, a favorable state for devotion and spiritual communion, enables him to solicit Christ's mercy.[50] Compassion, the romance makes clear through the example of Christ, is the desired response to sorrowful expression, by which individual plight is projected onto collective responsibility. When the lord of Milan arrives in Paris, his account elicits the compassion of Charlemagne's barons and lords, who "mornede and made grete mone" (159) in a collective display that culminates in Turpin's call for vengeance (166–68). Compassionate grief is what binds together the Christian community, as Pope Gregory VIII also emphasized in an encyclical composed prior to the Third Crusade: "Quisquis enim sane mentis in tanta lugendi materia, si non corpore, saltem corde non luget, non tantum fidei christiane, que cum omnibus dolentibus docet esse dolendum, sed ipsius etiam humanitatis videtur oblitus" (Anyone of sane mind who does not weep at such cause for weeping, if not in body at least in his heart, would seem to have forgotten not only his Christian faith, which teaches that one ought to mourn with all others who mourn, but even his very humanity).[51] Noteworthy, here as in *Milan*, is the infectiousness of sorrow, which aligns individuals with groups, crystallizing the boundaries between "us" and "them" – Christians and Muslims.[52] Depictions and authorial interjections of sorrow – such as "Therefore myghte mornne bothe man and maye" (215), "That tornede oure gud men all to gryll, / And many one mo to mene" (224–25), "me rewes sore" (289), "That sorowe it was to see" (339) – then punctuate the account of Roland's campaign in Lombardy, as Christian casualties multiply and the expedition's tragic outcome unfolds. Partaking in the events of the narrative, the author manipulates the rhetorical power of sorrow, calling on the audience's sense of Christian compassion and communal solidarity.

Yet the cause of Roland's grief is double: the devastation wreaked by Sultan Arabas and Charlemagne's initial refusal to engage in crusade. As in the *Chanson de Roland*, the grievous consequences of Ganelon's treason are portended: "His first tresone now bygynnes here / That the lordis boghte sythen full dere, / And to ladyse grete barett bredde" (178–80). After his army is defeated, Roland escapes from Muslim custody and rides to the abbey of Saint Denis, where he encounters Turpin and Charlemagne. Both men are befittingly moved by his fate: the bishop exclaims, "Lordis, morne we may" (529), while "The Kynge myghte noghte a tere holde – / For bale hym thoght he brynt" (576–77). Yet Charlemagne fails to act on his emotions, thereby revealing their emptiness. Whereas Turpin's grief turns into emphatic zeal, as he casts away his monastic attributes and embraces his role as warrior for Christ (542–47), thereafter proclaiming his vengeful intent, Charlemagne again heeds Ganelon's advice to remain in France (589–600). In stark reproof, Turpin asserts: "Was never kynge that werede a crown / So foule rebuytede with relygyon! / Thou sall sone witt of woo" (743–45).

Yet the most dramatic infringement on the community of emotion and martial action petitioned by the romance is not ascribed to Charlemagne or Ganelon, but strikingly, to heaven. During the narration of Roland's offensive, the Christians' grief is fueled by unanswered appeals for divine help. "Of sorowe than myghte thay synge!" (273), exclaims the poet as the Christian vanguard is pierced and human efforts are rendered vain in the absence of God's assistance – "Thare myghte no beryns oure bales bete / Bot the helpe of Hevens Kynge" (275–76). Divine intervention does not

Sorrow, Vengeance, and Invectives against Heaven
31

materialize and, with the exception of Roland and three other knights, the vanguard and middle guard of the Christian army are slaughtered. After Roland is taken captive and the remaining crusaders are attacked, the author interjects a desperate plea for heavenly succor: "Nowe helpe tham the Trynytee!" (348). Yet not a single man survives this last onslaught, the Christian fatalities amounting to forty thousand. Despite responding to the lord of Milan's sorrowful appeal in an exemplary manner – with compassion and retributive zeal – Roland and his army are rewarded with defeat and death. When informed of this news, Turpin, in a prolonged display of grief manifested both verbally and somatically, imputes the blame to no lesser figure than the Virgin Mary:

> "A! Mary mylde, whare was thi myght
> That thou lete thi men thus to dede be dighte
> That wighte and worthy were?
> Art thou noghte halden of myghtis moste,
> Full conceyvede of the Holy Goste?
> Me ferlys of thy fare.
> Had thou noghte, Marye, yitt bene borne,
> Ne had noghte oure gud men thus bene lorne –
> The wyte is all in the!
> Thay faughte holly in thy ryghte,
> That thus with dole to dede es dyghte –
> A! Marie, how may this bee?"
> The Bischoppe was so woo that stownnd,
> He wolde noghte byde appon the grownnd
> A sakerynge for-to see,
> Bot forthe he wente – his handis he wrange,
> And flote with Marye ever amange
> For the losse of oure menyee. (548–65)

Bordering on blasphemy, Turpin's tirade has unsurprisingly arrested critical attention.[53] Maldwyn Mills points out that it is Muslims, not Christians, who are commonly ascribed divinely addressed outbursts in *chansons de geste* and romances, and therefore suggests that Turpin is being presented as non-Christian, thus calling into question his otherwise "unquestionably heroic figure." This, in Mills's view, stems from the fact that he "was in the last resort French, and therefore always a little unreliable."[54] For Suzanne Conklin Akbari, although Turpin's behavior "detracts from the hagiographical motif so prominent in the general characterization of the Archbishop," its significance should not be overstated, given that this type of abuse "in order to elicit more effective intercession ... was not an uncommon practice during the Middle

Ages."[55] Thomas H. Crofts considers this episode a testimony to the romance's "elevation of martial and chivalric imperatives over religious ones," while Stephen Shepherd argues that in light of the contractual relationship of reciprocity binding the crusaders to God, this type of lament is "normative" and "entirely acceptable, if not admirable" in the context of militant crusade discourse.[56]

Yet there exists a significant body of complaint literature and chronicle evidence – thus far unaccounted for in studies of romances and *chansons de geste*, and unexamined as a cohesive corpus by historians[57] – that sheds precious light on the cultural anxieties underlying expressions of divinely addressed reproof, whether attributed to Christians, as in *Milan*, or Muslims, an issue that I discuss in my subchapter on *The Sultan of Babylon*. The traditional justification for crusading defeats is encapsulated in the Latin formula *peccatis exigentibus hominum*, which was widely invoked to explain how people's sins had brought trouble on themselves. In the later years of the Levantine crusades, however, this rationale elicited skepticism: no longer satisfied with carrying the blame, many contemporaries turned an accusatory gaze toward God, Christ, Mary, and the saints themselves.[58] This mindset is powerfully rendered in the grievances of Ricaut Bonomel, a troubadour Templar in the Holy Land when the Mamlūk sultan al-Zāhir Baybars reconquered the city of Arsūf (1265):

> Ire'e dolors s'es dins mon cor asseza
> Si qu'a per pauc no m'auci demanes,
> O meta jos la crotz qu'avi preza
> A la honor d'aquel qu'en crotz fo mes;
> Cor crotz ni lei no'm val ni guia
> Contr'als fels Turcs, cui Dieus maldia;
> Anz es semblans, segon qu'hom pot vezer,
> C'al dan de nos los vol Dieux mantener.

> Anger and grief have so filled my heart that I am close to taking my own life, or to renouncing the cross that I had taken in honor of Him who died on the cross; for neither cross nor faith helps nor protects me against the evil Turks, that God curses; on the contrary it seems, according to all evidence, that God wishes to assist them at our expense.[59]

Ricaut registers bewilderment at God's intentions. If God has complete control over the workings of the world, then why does he not protect those who fight wars in his name? Does he support the enemy? Such doubts were shared by many others. Fifteen years earlier, the Occitan troubadour Austorc d'Aurillac, consumed with "grans dols" (great sorrow), blames God for the Christians' misfortunes following Louis IX of France's defeat

Sorrow, Vengeance, and Invectives against Heaven 33

and capture near the Egyptian town of al-Manṣūra, and voices a similar question to the one addressed by Turpin to the Virgin Mary upon learning of Roland's fate: "[Ai!] Dieus! Per qu'as fa[ch]a tan ma[lez]a / De nostre rey fran[c]es larc e cortes . . .?" (Ah! God! Why did you bring such misfortune to our generous and courteous French king . . .?). The author then proceeds to curse Alexandria, the clergy, and Muslims for their success, declaring that "Mal o fetz Dieus quar lor en det poder" (God was wrong to give them such power) and that "Dieus vol e sancta Maria / Que nos siam vencut" (God and Saint Mary desired their [the Christians'] defeat).[60] Also writing within the Occitan tradition, Austorc de Segret expresses similar sentiments upon hearing of the fate of Louis IX's crusade to Tunis and death in 1270: "Fort esbaÿtz" (utterly bewildered), he knows not whether to hold God or the devil responsible for the Christians' affliction, the destruction of their religion, and the Muslims' well-being.[61]

Such expressions of anger, grief, and bewilderment were not confined to the writings of Occitan troubadours, but also extended to the public, as attested by the chronicle tradition. Matthew Paris's account of popular reactions in France to the news of King Louis's defeat in 1250 yields further insight into the spiritual predicaments faced by Christian Europeans for whom crusades were wars fought on behalf of an all-powerful God:

> Tota Francia dolorem induit et confusionem, et tam ecclesiastici viri quam militares moerore querulo contabuerunt, nolentes recipere consolationem ... omne quoque genus laetitiae in luctum et lamenta commutatur. Et quod pejus est, Dominum de injustitia redarguentes, in verba blasphemiae, quae apostasiam vel haeresim sapere videbantur, prae mentis amaritudine et doloris immanitate desipientes prorumpunt. Et multorum coepit fides vacillare.

> The whole of France was plunged into grief and confusion and both ecclesiastics and knights were consumed with grief and refused to be consoled ... and every sort of enjoyment was converted to sorrow and lamentation. And what was worse, accusing the Lord of injustice, and hysterical in heaviness of heart and enormity of grief, people blurted out blasphemous words which seemed to savor of apostasy and heresy. And the faith of many began to waver.[62]

The monk of St. Albans concludes by asserting that "vix quievit aliquorum, non tamen omnium, indignatio" (the indignation of some, but not all, was with difficulty assuaged),[63] thereby emphasizing the intense and protracted atmosphere of collective despair. The Italian chronicler Salimbene de Adam records a similar emotional uprising after the collapse of the Seventh Crusade, claiming, "Irascebantur ergo Gallici, qui in

34   Royal Emotions, Blasphemy, and (Dis)unity

Francia remanserant, tunc temporis contra Christum, usque adeo ut nomen Christi super omnia nomina benedictum blasphemare presumerent" (The French who had remained at home rose up in anger against Christ – so much so that they dared to blaspheme against the name of Christ, that name blessed above all names).[64] Here, that Salimbene de Adam treats "the French" as a cohesive entity suggests a tendency toward hyperbole. Yet one can glean from his account, and that of Matthew Paris, that such blasphemy was a common, if not unanimous, response to news of the debacle of the crusade.

On the basis of the evidence supplied thus far, it could be argued that these divinely addressed accusations are in large part reflective of the far-reaching expectations vested in the person of Louis IX of France, whose reputation for piety and virtue would lead to his canonization.[65] Yet the fall of Acre prompted similar reactions, as attested, for example, by the letters of the Italian Dominican friar Riccoldo da Monte di Croce, in Baghdad on a preaching campaign at the time.[66] Expressing uninhibited grief, these letters take issue with God, Christ, Mary, and the saints for abandoning the author, and Christians in general, to the advantage of Muslims. God is accused of cruelty (*crudelitas*), for allowing the slaughter of righteous Christians, and ungratefulness to his followers.[67] The author even goes as far as claiming that God and the angels were praying for Muhammad.[68] Lack of divine enlightenment leads Riccoldo to seek Mary's intercession in bewilderment and sorrow:

> Iam pridem literas divine sapientie de mea tristicia et admiracione transmisi, nec usque modo responsionem aliquam, que me instrueret, aut consolaretur, recepi. Et nunc, beatissima regina, eiusdem tristicie et admirationis mee causam per alia verba et raciones presenti litera tibi lacrimabiliter declarare curavi, ut michi misero tua misericordia cito succurrat.

> I have already addressed a letter to the wisdom of God conveying my sorrow and bewilderment, but have not yet received a reply to instruct and comfort me. And now, blessed queen, I have sought to present you in other words with the cause and reasons of this same sorrow and bewilderment so that your mercy can promptly come to the rescue of my misery.[69]

Yet the "queen of mercy" and "advocate of sinners" remains mute: "Ubi sunt misericordie tue atque sollicitudines tue et tui sanctissimi filii pro genere humano ...?" (Where is your mercy, your solicitude and that of your holy son for humankind ...?), the author asks.[70] The last words written to the Virgin Mary take the form of an impassioned appeal for accountability: "Mostra te esse matrem christianorum, quos Sarraceni tam

Sorrow, Vengeance, and Invectives against Heaven 35

multipliciter cruciant et affligunt!" (Show that you are the mother of the Christians whom the Saracens torment and afflict in so many ways!).[71] The pervading sentiment is incomprehension: how could heaven permit such disastrous outcomes of battles waged for God's patrimony and rights? The tone oscillates between supplication and outrage, as the author tries to come to terms with this scandal to the Christian faith. The fundamental question raised by the Christian loss of the Holy Land is asked again in the early fourteenth century by the Austrian chronicler Ottokar von Steiermark:

> Sag, herre got, sag an,
> warumb hâstû daz getân
> und warumb hâstûz vertragen,
> daz sô verderbet und erslagen
> sô manic kristen ist?

> Tell us, God, tell us, why you have done this? Why have you let so many Christians perish and be slain?[72]

These sources are key to understanding the cultural significance of Turpin's castigation of the Virgin Mary for allowing the demise of those who "faughte holly in [her] ryghte" (555). In the episodes leading up to Charlemagne's participation in crusade, *Milan* reflects obliquely on the reasons for Christendom's failures in the Levant, articulating some of the greatest collective anxieties of the post-1291 era. Anxieties about the misdirected priorities of Christian kings find expression in scenes of heated negotiation between Charlemagne and Turpin. Yet even more troubling was heaven's apparent lack of support to expeditions that were, akin to Roland's, conducted in virtuous intent: out of a compassionate urge to avenge the injuries inflicted by Muslims on fellow Christians. After Turpin bullies Charlemagne and the Virgin Mary into supporting the cause of crusade, the double problem of royal and heavenly dereliction of duty reemerges when the king is challenged to a duel and offered territories as an incentive to embrace Islam. Turpin again dramatically questions the king's commitment – "A, Charles, thynk appon Marie brighte / To whayme oure lufe es lentt!" (1041–42) – and aggressively calls on Mary to show her power on earth: "And if ever that thou hade any myghte, / Latt it nowe be sene in syghte" (1043–44). The reassuring image of a cooperative Christendom graced with divine favor materializes thereafter, as Charlemagne wins the duel and the Christians push toward what we can only assume will be a climactic victory (the final lines of the romance are missing). Yet the central questions posed by the romance to contemporary readers (or listeners) well aware of the geopolitical circumstances of the

Holy Land – questions that would have stuck in their minds long after the close of the narration – are anything but reassuring: Could Christian kings change their ways? Why would God and the Virgin Mary allow those who fought wars in their names to persistently be defeated? Did heaven even support the enterprise? *Milan* gives vivid expression to these collective political and spiritual dilemmas, providing a forum where audiences could discuss and debate them.

BLURRING THE LINES: EMOTIONAL PARALLELISM IN *THE SULTAN OF BABYLON*

The Sultan of Babylon (hereafter *The Sultan*), a roughly contemporary Charlemagne romance, offers fruitful correlations with *Milan* in its rendering of emotional displays that test and defy the boundaries of collective identities. Again, what particularly interests *The Sultan* are tensions between Christians and others between the human and divine. Yet if *Milan* strives to establish a strong identification between its audience and the Christian protagonists, with the Muslim characters occupying a background position, the rapport between the audience and the imagined communities is made more complex by *The Sultan*. Indeed, the author dwells at great length on the perspective of Sultan Laban and his soldiers, at times indulging in Orientalist fantasies of alterity, and at others ascribing to them roles and qualities that parallel those of the Christians, causing the audience to consider, compare, and even relate to the predicaments of both sides. Significantly, this concern with Christian–Muslim symmetry is lacking, or at least is far less pronounced, in the romance's sources: the Anglo-Norman *chanson de geste* of *Fierabras* and its prequel *La destruction de Rome*, preserved in the Egerton manuscript, which in turn adapts earlier versions.[73] In what follows, I explore the ways in which *The Sultan*, reworking its sources, attributes to Christians and Muslims emotional displays that unite them in both positive and negative ways. Of special interest are Charlemagne's expressions of wrath against his peers and Laban's tantrums against his "gods," for these displays, I argue, are the locus of the romance's most pronounced anxieties: the fragmentation of crusader armies and the conversion of Christians to Islam.

The Rhetoric of Injury and Retribution

In an influential article informed by Edward Said's *Orientalism* and psychoanalytical theory, Jeffrey Jerome Cohen writes of the Muslims of *The Sultan*:

The Rhetoric of Injury and Retribution

"Embodying an alien, racialized physicality, these Saracens are typically described only in terms of their skin color ... Unintelligible in their customs, language, and vice, they worship senseless idols, torture prisoners, ride strange beasts, murder innocents."[74] There are indeed episodes in which Laban's soldiers are crudely Orientalized and racialized through epidermic, physiognomic, and cultural markers of difference: they have different skin colors, count giants among them, and are ascribed strange customs such as eating serpents and drinking the blood of tigers.[75] Yet equally pronounced throughout the narrative are the author's gestures toward parallelism. Both the Christian and Muslim soldiers of *The Sultan* are pitiless in combat and kill children and women (which is not the case for Charlemagne in the text's source); the insults voiced by Muslim characters mirror those of their Christian counterparts, as "hethen houndes" turns into "Cristen houndes," "Cristen dogges," or "French dogges" (a feature that is also unique to the present version); the authorial interjection "God him spede" becomes "Mahounde him spede" (also a specificity of *The Sultan*); each party expresses a desire to convert members of the other; Christian and Muslim knights are favored equally with adjectives such as "worthy," "myghty," and "doughty" (attributes that are augmented for the Muslims here); there is even a passage where "Mahounde" takes the soul of a fallen Muslim warrior and brings it "to his blis" – which the author explains, noting that "He [Mahounde] loved him wel."[76] The accretion of elements of analogy across the religious divide is striking. In creatively reworking his or her sources, the author blurs the lines between Christians and Muslims not only by ascribing commendable qualities to the latter, but also by imputing reprehensible actions to the former. Saidian Orientalism, premised as it is on binary oppositions, inadequately captures the cultural operations of this romance.

Especially noteworthy for our purposes are the textual manipulations at the origin of a reconfigured emotional rhetoric that causes the audience to oscillate between Christian and Muslim viewpoints as the storyline develops. Before coming to the expressions of wrath that lead Charlemagne to mirror Laban, let us first consider some of the other emotional parallelisms that typify the romance. Like *Milan* and *The Siege of Jerusalem*, analyzed in Chapter 4, *The Sultan* defines itself as a tale of vengeance prompted by injury. This motif permeates crusade sources, as discussed above, and played a key role in promoting the enterprise: Muslims were accused of various crimes, including that of persecuting Christians, whose injuries crusaders were to avenge. In the Egerton *La destruction de Rome*, the emphasis in the opening lines is on the harms done to Rome by Laban, "li soldan maleuré," and on his theft of the relics.

These wrongful acts set the tone for what follows, providing solid moral grounds for reactive measures on the part of Charlemagne, "li fort coroné." The audience is invited to identify with his cause, which acquires collective legitimacy. In *The Sultan*, by contrast, the narrative opens by telling of the righteous vengeance exacted by Laban on Christian Rome for its sins against God:

> For yyfe man kepte Thy [God's] commaundemente
> In al thinge and loved The welle
> And hadde [ne] synnede in his entente,
> Than shulde he fully Thy grace fele;
> But for the offences to God i-doon
> Many vengeaunces have befalle.
> Whereof I wole you telle of oon,
> It were to moch to telle of alle.
> While that Rome was in excellence
> Of all realmes in dignite,
> And howe it felle for his offence,
> Listinythe a while and ye shall see,
> Howe it was wonen and brente
> Of a Sowdon, that heathen was,
> And for synne how it was shente. (9–23)

Laban thus takes on the role, so often held by Christian figures of *chanson de geste* and romance, of agent of divine retribution. This inversion is best understood in relation to historical accounts of crusading defeats, where God's wrath or vengeance against Christian sinfulness is posited as materializing from the hand of the Muslim enemy. Ṣalāḥ al-Dīn's reconquest of Jerusalem (1187) and the ensuing Third Crusade were instrumental in popularizing this representational mode.[77] The English chronicler Roger of Wendover, for example, writes that God, seeing the sins committed by Christians, "haereditatem suam sprevit, et virgam furoris sui, videlicet Salaadinum, in obstinatae gentis permisit exterminium debacchari" (scorned his inheritance, and allowed the rod of his anger, namely Saladin, to vent His anger to the extermination of that obstinate race).[78] A later example, roughly contemporary to *The Sultan*, is Michel Pintoin's account of the Crusade of Nicopolis in 1396, which has the Ottoman sultan Bāyazīd I declare, upon hearing of the lax morals of the crusaders and before crushing their army, that "lento gradu ad vindictam divina procedit ira, et tarditatem supplicii gravitate pensat" (God's anger slowly gives way to vengeance, and compensates for this slowness by the importance of the punishment).[79] Drawing on this tradition in its opening lines, *The Sultan* sets the tone for an ambitious reimagining of its sources, one

The Rhetoric of Injury and Retribution   39

that will accommodate self-criticism alongside more conventional strands of Christian heroism.

Laban is then portrayed as Charlemagne is in so many *chansons de geste* and romances: surrounded by "kinges twelfe" (surrogates of the Frankish king's twelve peers) and barons of whom "worthynesse al may not be told" (37–40). A few lines later, the sultan receives news of the unprovoked attack of his men by Roman soldiers:

> The Romaynes robbed us anone;
> Of us thai slowgh ful many one.
> With sorwe and care we be bygone.
> Whereof, lorde, remedye
> Ye ordeyne by youre barons boolde,
> To wreke the of this vilané. (77–82)

Laban, the "worthy Sowdon" (49), responds to this sorrowful affront in consequence: "Thes tidings make myn herte coolde; / But I be venged, dyen I shalle" (91–92). Yet after Laban claims legitimate vengeance and destroys Rome, the initial framework of sin and punishment is complicated by Charlemagne's introduction into the story as a mirror image of his Muslim counterpart: a "worthy kinge" (583) intent on avenging the "grete sorowe" (574) of his coreligionists, the Romans. Any assumption that Charlemagne will surpass Laban in moral and political virtue is soon dispelled, however. Instead, we witness a double movement toward negative and positive parallelism, with new episodes uniting the Muslim sultan and the Christian king as indiscriminate killers of "childe, wyfe, man," mercilessly ordering their men to "brenne, slo and distroye alle" (note the similar language used at 413–18 and 783–86), and as noble, courtly rulers. Far from presented as incongruous, the sultan's non-Christian identity and oft-asserted worthiness are harmoniously reconciled. In a passage absent from the French source, Laban's worthiness as a conqueror is aligned with his ability to love, a meritorious disposition that underpins his evaluative emotional response to Charlemagne's attack:[80]

> For he was nevere gode werryoure
> That cowde not love aryght;
> For love hath made many a conqueroure
> And many a worthy knighte.
> This worthy Sowdan, though he hethen were,
> He was a worthy conqueroure;
> Many a contrey with shelde and spere
> He conquerede wyth grete honoure. (975–82)
>   . . .

> The Sowdan seyinge this myschief,
> How Charles hade him agreved,
> That grevaunce was him no thinge lese;
> He was ful sore ameved. (991–94)
> ...
> On these Frenche dogges, that bene here,
> Ye moste avenge me nowe.
> Thai have done me vilanye;
> Mikille of my people have thay slayn. (1013–16)

Here, the terms "myschief," "agrevede," and "grevaunce" reflect a quasi-juridical assessment of Charlemagne's previous acts, providing clear justification for Laban's arousal ("He was ful sore ameved") toward vengeance. *The Sultan* is replete with these representational shifts, leading the audience to experience the events from the position of Christians and Muslims in turn. Their emotional responses mirror each other: both display grief engendering retributive violence, anger in battle or when provoked, fear in perilous situations, shame when faced with (the prospect of) dishonor, joy following military success, and love for their God(s).[81] There is no sense of a binary between Christians and Muslims created through depictions of the former as emotionally virtuous and the latter as harmful oppressors. The emotional economy of the romance is instead characterized by blurred boundaries and provocative instabilities.

The motif of the "noble Muslim," converging with that of the "virtuous pagan,"[82] is of course not new to the post-1291 era and is documented in the *chansons de geste* and crusade chronicles of the late twelfth and thirteenth centuries.[83] *The Sultan*, however, brings this motif into unchartered territory by endowing Laban with the same justifications for action as those extensively harnessed in crusade propaganda, chronicles, and literature to promote Christian collective identity and foster feelings of hostility grounded in moral duty. The popularity of the "injury-sorrow-vengeance" script in crusade sermons attests to its rhetorical effectiveness: its ability to win the sympathy, compassion, and support of audiences. While investing Sultan Laban with this type of emotional righteousness is undeniably less conducive to empathic reactivity (for a late medieval English audience) than is the case with the Christian protagonists of *Milan*, for instance, it sets up a narrative structure that stimulates mutual intelligibility and responsiveness.

Wrath and Fratricidal Quarrels

The Christian–Muslim symmetries *The Sultan* establishes not only consist of positive emotional characterizations, but also, as previously noted, negative ones. The most striking element of negative parallelism is that which unites Charlemagne and Laban in displays of unbridled anger. While *The Sultan* supplements its sources with depictions of Laban wrathfully castigating his "gods" for the misfortunes that befall him (passages that I discuss below), it also imputes unchecked anger to Charlemagne, exploiting the *chanson de geste* motif of king–vassal conflict to compelling effect, and probing its militaristic implications.[84] The king's wrath, directed against his peers, is not only overtly admonished, but also exposes the Christian fellowship to risks of Muslim military advantage. The first of two instances in which the dangers of inter-Christian wrath are sharply raised occurs when Roland refuses to champion the Christian cause in combat against Laban's son, Ferumbras, because he had taken offense at Charlemagne's praise of the "old knights" over the "young" (919–30 and 1084–90):

> For that worde the Kinge was wrothe
> And smote him on the mouthe on hye,
> The bloode at his nose oute-goth,
> And saide, "Traitour, thou shalte abye."
> "Abye," quod Roulande, "wole I noughte,
> And traitour was I never none,
> By that Lord, that me dere hath bought!"
> And braide oute Durendale there anone.
> He wolde have smyten the Kinge there
> Ne hadde the barons ronne bytwene;
> The Kinge withdrowe him for fere
> And passed home as it myght beste bene.
> The barons made hem at one
> With grete prayere and instaunce,
> As every wrath moste over-gone,
> Of the more myschiefe to make voydaunce. (1091–1106)

This wrathful exchange features in the Anglo-Norman and Old French texts of *Fierabras*.[85] But it is made more impactful in *The Sultan* through the conversion of indirect into direct speech, and through an interpolated accusation of treachery – a particularly fraught motif in both the Charlemagne tradition and crusade historiography.[86] The author also innovates by adding a moral warning to the importance of conciliation and restraint: Charles's withdrawal is for the best, and "every wrath moste over-gone" to avoid misfortune. The threat to Christian collective integrity nonetheless persists beyond this altercation, since it comes to be up to Oliver, "seke and woundede sore" (1116) at this stage, and thus considerably diminished, to take up Ferumbras's challenge.

In a later episode, Charlemagne's counselors are unable to suppress his anger, as he resolves to send all of his peers as envoys to Laban. The king's wrath is unparalleled in the Egerton *Fierabras*, which instead portrays his decision as a legitimate, composed statement of royal prerogative.[87] By contrast, *The Sultan* has Charlemagne succumbing to fury and spurning all advice toward caution and restraint:

> "Woltowe for angre thy barons sende
> To that tiraunte that all men sleith?
> Or thou doist, for that ende,
> To bringe thy Twelfe Peres to the deth."
> The Kinge was wroth and swore in halle
> By Him that boght him with His blode:
> "On my messange shall ye gon alle,
> Be ye never so wroth or wode."
> Thay toke here lefe and forth thay yede;
> It availed not agayne him to sayne. (1727–36)

Opposed by his most trusted men and warned of the perils of anger (Ogier, "that worthy man," had also previously urged the king to curb his "wroth" [1687–88]), Charlemagne, as in *Milan*, is cast in a distinctly negative light. As warned, the king's decision leads to the peers' capture, imprisonment, and sentence to death (an outcome they ultimately succeed in avoiding). These passages exhibit a purposeful concern with the dangers of wrathful disputes among crusaders. Anger threatens to cripple the Christian ability to function as a united military body.

Thus, while *Milan* invokes wrathful displays between Christians to decry the royal prioritization of domestic politics over crusade commitments, *The Sultan* tackles the no less topical concern of wrath-induced political fragmentation in the course of military engagements with the enemy. In a recent, wide-ranging survey, Stephen J. Spencer shows that "restraining rage" was a major preoccupation of propagandists and chroniclers from the First Crusade to the fall of Acre.[88] The sources I have consulted, from this period and from the fourteenth century, bear out Spencer's assessment. If, as discussed above, some authors viewed anger as desirable when expressed correctly, many others saw it as a dangerous emotion, likely to cause inter-Christian discord and hinder collective crusading efforts. Odo of Deuil's account of the Second Crusade, for instance, while imputing the failure of the expedition to the treachery of the Greeks, traces their ill will toward the French troops of Louis VII to the wrath (both *furor* and *ira* are used) of the Germans, guilty of having killed a number of Greeks outside the town of Philippopolis.[89] *De expugnatione*

Lyxbonensi, an eyewitness report of the siege of Lisbon at the inception of the Second Crusade, explicitly denounces anger as a component of crusading: "Zelo iusticie, non felle ire, iustum bellum committite" (Engage in a just war with the zeal of righteousness, not with the bile of wrath).[90] Remedy against wrath can, however, be found in Christ: "Que iracundia, si Filii Dei patientia non sanatur?" (What proneness to anger, if it be not cured by the patience of the Son of God?).[91] Indeed, although the later stages of the siege find the Christian forces immersed in wrathful quarrels, such that these "intractabilibus discidiorum causis" (uncontrollable causes of discord) prompt their leaders to lose control of their tempers, God reestablishes harmony and the Christians prevail. Yet concord is only achieved after the author elaborates on the risks of disunity and the importance of conciliation, a position championed by the army's elders (*senioribus*).[92] Direct warnings against the detriments of the emotion, similar to those in *The Sultan* and *De expugnatione*, were also voiced by propagandists invested in laying out the prescribed conduct of (future) crusaders. Drawing upon scripture in one of his *sermones ad status*, Jacques de Vitry alerts his audience to the perils of wrath as a source of dissent among crusaders.[93] In the early fourteenth century, the Italian propagandist Marino Sanudo likewise stresses the importance of avoiding *ira* in his discussion of the qualities of a prospective Christian ruler in the Holy Land.[94]

Despite the existence of a form of praiseworthy anger in historical and literary crusade sources, these examples, among numerous others available, register acute awareness of the self-damaging potential of the emotion. Ludolph of Suchem's account of the Mamlūk siege of Acre in his *De itinere terrae sanctae liber*, a work composed after a visit to the Levant from 1336 to 1341, bears broad resemblance to *The Sultan* in the Christian–Muslim dynamics it establishes. The city's fall, the author asserts, was the result of its citizens' wrathful quarrels, which served as a cue for the Mamlūk sultan al-Ashraf Khalīl, "vir sagacissimus, in armis potentissimus et multum strenuus et sciens" (an exceedingly wise man, most potent in arms and bold in action). The author juxtaposes the Christians' disarray with the order that reigns in the Muslim camp, as the wise sultan summons his counselors and holds a parliament before besieging the city.[95] In *The Sultan*, too, Christians are the ones who quarrel, while Muslims maintain political unity under the leadership of Laban, a "worthy conqueroure" who places unwavering trust in the "trewe and good" counsel of his advisors (see, for example, 1739–74, an episode that directly follows Charlemagne's wrathful admonishment of his peers). Yet Laban does not achieve final victory, for, whereas the Christians' pleas to "Lord

44 Royal Emotions, Blasphemy, and (Dis)unity

God in Trinite" are answered by the intervention of angels, his appeals to his "gods" are to no avail.

The Motif of the Afflicted Muslim

As is well known, within the genres of *chanson de geste* and romance, Islam is constructed as both a distorted image of Christianity and a manifestation of ancient Greek and Roman polytheism.[96] The Christian Trinity and statues of saints are mirrored in a Muslim "counter-Trinity," composed of Muhammad, Tervagant, and Apollo (but sometimes supplemented by other "gods") worshiped in the form of idols. Thus, the very aspects of Christianity – a Triune God and the use of statues and images as monuments of faith – that were denounced by Muslim poets and polemicists of the crusader era as *shirk*, the sin of polytheism and idolatry, lie at the heart of this misrepresentation of Islam.[97] In *The Sultan*, Laban, like other Muslim characters of crusade literature, rebukes his gods in anger or sorrow following military setbacks and defeats. What is noteworthy, however, is that, in reworking his or her sources, the author added altogether new scenes where Laban acts in this way: of no less than seven such instances in *The Sultan*, only one is matched in the Egerton manuscript.[98] Significantly, this tendency extends across the Middle English romance tradition: episodes of divinely addressed frustration were also interpolated in the adaptation of *Otuel and Roland* and *Guy of Warwick* and feature prominently in other romances, such as *The King of Tars* and *Richard Coeur de Lion*, which have no extant French source.[99] Whether we are dealing with translations of earlier texts or narratives for which there is no extant source material, the evidence suggests a strong authorial interest in the motif of the "afflicted Muslim" in late medieval England. Why was this motif so popular?

In *Idols in the East*, Suzanne Conklin Akbari argues that *chanson de geste* and romance scenes featuring Muslims railing against their gods served to signal to contemporary audiences the "waning power" of Islam, showing them "what they are *not* so that they may understand what they *are*."[100] Yet in the real world, as we have seen, the thirteenth and fourteenth centuries were a time when Christians, not Muslims, rebuked the holy figures of their religion after military defeats. This context is indispensable for understanding the cultural work performed by the "afflicted Muslim" motif after 1291. In an insightful article drawing on Freudian psychology, Gerald J. Brault sets out theoretical premises for considering negative depictions of Muslims in *chansons de geste* in terms of how they

The Motif of the Afflicted Muslim

subconsciously project Latin European insecurities and shortcomings (without, however, exploring how these premises might apply to specific motifs and characterizations, beyond general references to moral flaws such as pride and deceitfulness).[101] Brault's assessment is highly relevant for our purposes. Whether we are dealing with a subconscious or – as I would suggest – a very conscious impulse on the part of the authors, projection seems to me a persuasive explanation for the proliferation of depictions of Muslims venting their military frustration on their gods in Middle English romance.

Turning again to some of the works discussed above in relation to Turpin's admonishment of Mary in *Milan* is useful at this stage. Two of the most characteristic components of the "afflicted Muslim" motif – the accusation of divine negligence, commonly couched in terms of "sleep," and the threat of religious apostasy – warrant special mention because of how prominently they also feature in Christian complaints against heaven after crusading defeats. Representative in this regard is Laban's expression of wrath against the Muslim "counter-Trinity" following an unsuccessful siege on a Christian-held tower:

> King Laban turnede to his tentes agayn.
> He was nere wode for tene.
> He cryede to Mahounde and Apolyne
> And to Termagaunte that was so kene
> And saide, "Ye goddes, ye slepe to longe;
> Awake and helpe me nowe
> Or ellis I may singe of sorowe a songe
> And of mournynge right i-nowe.
> Wete ye not wele that my tresoure
> Is alle withinne the walle?
> Helpe me nowe, I saye, therfore
> Or ellis I forsake you alle."
> He made grete lamentacion. (2103–15)

The letters of Riccoldo da Monte di Croce attest to how closely such sentiments reflect those experienced by Latin Christians when faced with Muslim victories. Riccoldo's lament is punctuated by references to God, Jesus, and the Virgin Mary sleeping, followed by impassioned pleas for them to arouse. The most striking of these is that which sees the author suggesting that Mary has fallen asleep in a wine cellar.[102] The urge of fictional Muslims to compel their gods to action by physical means (notably by hitting them with sticks) is paralleled, though downplayed in intensity, in the author's impulse to stir God's vigilance by shaking the

46   Royal Emotions, Blasphemy, and (Dis)unity

pillow upon which he sleeps.[103] The Templar Ricaut Bonomel's afore-mentioned poem likewise invokes the language of sleep to complain of divine inaction, proof of which appears in Muslim victories: "E nos venzon sai chascun dia, / Car Dieus dorm, qui veillar solia, / E Bafometz obra de son poder" (And here every day they are victorious / For God, who used to watch, now sleeps, / And Muhammad acts in full strength).[104] If the metaphor of sleep was a natural choice for these authors and for writers of *chansons de geste* and romances, it is in part because of its presence in the Bible: passages where God is urged to awaken from sleep and contend for his people are found in the book of Psalms, for example.[105]

Laban's threats of apostasy, too, resemble those voiced by real-life Christians. In response to the debacle of Louis IX's second crusade, Austorc d'Aurillac writes:

Crestiantat vey del tot a mal meza,
Tan gran perda no cug qu'anemais fezes,
Per qu'es razos qu'hom hueymais Dieu descreza,
E qu'azorem Bafomet lai on es,
Tervagan e sa companhia,
Pus Dieus vol et sancta Maria
Que nos siam vencut a non dever,
E·ls mescrezens fai honratz remaner.

I see that Christianity is undermined; I do not believe that we have ever suffered such a great loss. It is therefore reasonable that we cease to believe in God, and that we worship Muhammad, Tervagant, and his company, since God and Saint Mary desire that we be vanquished against all right, and that the misbelievers be awarded all of the honor.[106]

Austorc's outrage was transient (as is Laban's in *The Sultan*).[107] Yet it reflects a mode of thought in which the relation between human and divine is one of mutual reciprocity: if the Christian God does not protect his followers, then why should they worship him? In a similar vein, the troubadour crusader Ricaut Bonomel claims that if God gets his way and the Christians continue to be overpowered, not only will the author renounce the cross, but "nuls hom que en Jhesu Crist creza / Non remandra . . . en est paes" (not a single man that believes in Jesus Christ / will remain . . . in this country).[108] By failing to uphold his side of the contract, God quite simply relinquishes the right to be served, militarily and spiritually.

References to the conversion of Christians to Islam permeate Riccoldo's divinely addressed letters. Whether Muslims prevail through God's negligence or active support to Islam, the consequence is that numerous Christians relinquish their faith:

The Motif of the Afflicted Muslim

> Quid nobis accidit doloris et tristicie, quia ubique perdimur, ubique succumbimus cum Sarracenis non solum in bello corporali, sed eciam in pugna spirituali! Nam Sarraceni multos christianos occidunt, et multi alii christiani, qui relicti sunt, legem ymmo perfidiam Sarracenorum suscipiunt.
>
> What pain and sorrow have befallen us, everywhere we are put to ruin, everywhere we succumb to the Saracens, not only in bodily war, but even in spiritual combat! The Saracens kill the Christians in great number, and a great number of other Christians who survive embrace the faith, or rather the perfidy, of Muhammad.[109]

Riccoldo even goes as far as to question whether Christ's support to the enemy is "preludia, quod ipse vere efficietur Sarracenus" (the prelude to his true conversion to Islam). The saints, he later suggests, have already changed sides: "O sancti patriarche, o patres antiqui Veteris Testamenti, quare facti fuistis Sarraceni et imitatores Machometi?" (Oh saintly patriarchs, oh ancient fathers of the Old Testament, why have you become Saracens and imitators of Muhammad?).[110] Riccoldo repeatedly beseeches heaven to confirm him in his faith, lest he follow the example of the great multitude (*maxima multitudo*) of Christians in the Near East who have converted to Islam: "Si tibi placet, ut regnet Machometus, indica nobis, ut veneremur" (If it pleases you that Muhammad should rule, tell us so that we may venerate him).[111] According to Matthew Paris, threats of apostasy (*apostasiam*) were common in France at the time of the Seventh Crusade, and would have materialized were it not for the comfort provided by priests.[112] Salimbene de Adam claims that this same crusade caused Christians in France to declare in anger (*irascebantur*) that Muhammad was more powerful (*potentior*) than Christ.[113]

Thus, crusading defeats prompted Christian laypeople, clerics, and crusaders in Europe and the eastern Mediterranean to question divine justice, voice religious doubt, and threaten to apostatize. Did contemporaries act on such threats? In areas of Europe remote from Muslim lands, practical considerations prevented large-scale apostasy of the kind suggested to be possible by Matthew Paris and Salimbene de Adam.[114] Yet, if the crusader Ricaut Bonomel and the missionary Riccoldo da Monte di Croce did not convert to Islam while in the Near East, numerous Christian Europeans did. Latin and Arabic accounts spanning the core period of the Levantine crusades (1096–1291) tell of repeated instances of crusaders who, during military altercations or following defeats, crossed the lines for the purpose of converting to Islam, often reporting numbers in the thousands.[115] While the motives of those who converted under such circumstances are often difficult to ascertain based on the extant evidence, and no doubt comprised a range of practical and spiritual considerations, it is not unlikely that many saw Muslim victories as evidence of God's favor to Islam. Indeed, as scholars working outside the confines of crusade history have shown, this was a common rationale for conversion from the early Muslim conquests to the rise of the Ottoman Empire.[116] What greater proof was there of the truth of Islam than the worldly successes that God granted its followers?[117]

The high degree of interplay between the historical predicaments of Christians and those of fictional Muslims is evident in light of the sources analyzed above. If the "afflicted Muslim" motif was so popular in late medieval England, it is, I believe, because it fulfilled the projective needs of a post-1291 society harboring deep collective anxieties about the workings of God's will, divine support to the crusading enterprise, and the conversion of Christians to Islam. Middle English crusade romances were by no means adverse to self-criticism, as demonstrated in this chapter, and as will be further discussed in what follows. But not all texts engaged as directly as *Milan* with the providential anxieties that generations of crusading defeats had engendered. These uncomfortable feelings found compensation by means of projection, in a similar way that medieval Christianity's fixation on images and relics is counteracted by *chanson de geste* and romance renderings of Muslim idolatry.[118] Even the iconoclasm that Christian characters of fiction perform against the statues of Muhammad, Tervagant, and Appollo mirrors what Muslims were accused of in historical reports, such as Fidenzio of Padua's on the fall of Tripoli in 1289:[119]

> Ipsi etiam Sarraceni multum abhorrent ymagines, et picturas destruunt, et sibi substernunt, et in loca inmunda proiciunt. Intellexi ergo, quod nuper post captionem civitatis Tripolitane Sarraceni trahebant crucem Xpisti ad caudam asini, et omnia vituperia que poterant ymaginibus inferebant.

> These very same Saracens greatly abhor images, and they destroy pictures, and trample them, and fling them into filthy places. Indeed I heard that recently, after they captured the city of Tripoli, the Saracens dragged a crucifix on the tail of an ass, and threw all the foul things they could on the images.[120]

The same story is recounted by Riccoldo da Monte di Croce, who adds that throughout Galilee, Judea, and in Jerusalem, almost all of the images of God and Christ that fell in Muslim hands were mutilated by spears, swords, and sticks.[121] These testimonies should not be taken at face value. Yet they are important to the present discussion because they further

The Motif of the Afflicted Muslim   49

illustrate the complex ways in which crusade literature engages the historical record, at times mimetically and at others projectively.

This chapter has elucidated the ways that *Milan* and *The Sultan* deploy representations of anger, sorrow, and vengeance to engage their audiences' responses and reflections on post-1291 concerns about royal politics, covetous counsel, Christian infighting, divine support to the crusaders, and religious apostasy. *Milan* directs its polemical energies against Christendom's royalty for prioritizing domestic over crusade duties. Both the critique and the solution to the problem are carried by Turpin, upon whom the power to enact divine anger is conferred. Yet a much more fraught impediment to successful crusading, and a source of profound unease as expedition after expedition dashed the hopes of contemporaries, was God's perceived neglect of the crusaders' fate. Whether European kings cooperated or not, the question remained: how could God refrain from rewarding Christians for their persistent efforts? The conventional answer to this question was that God was angry at the Christian community for its sins – the logic invoked by the author of *The Sultan* to frame Laban's destruction of Rome. But, from the time of Louis IX's crusades to Egypt and Tunis, dissatisfaction with this rationale was increasingly felt, and many turned to God for accountability, accusing him of failing his Christian followers and threatening to abandon (or actually abandoning) their faith. In *Milan*, these providential anxieties, voiced by Bishop Turpin, are confronted head-on. In *The Sultan*, they are projected onto the Muslim Other, who closely resembles the Christian self.

CHAPTER 2

Hopes and Anxieties of Conversion
in the Otuel Romances

In the previous chapter, I discussed how the Middle English Charlemagne romances articulate anxieties related to the crusades through such culturally resonant characters as the inward-looking king, the blasphemous bishop, and the worthy sultan. Here, I turn to another central figure of this corpus: the heroic convert. Of the nine verse Charlemagne romances to have reached us, six feature a Muslim warrior who, after demanding the surrender of Christian lands and challenging the most valorous Frankish knights to meet him in combat, converts to Christianity and fights for his new religion.[1] These texts fall into two traditions, those of *Fierabras* and *Otinel*, named after the *chansons de geste* they freely adapt.[2] My concerns in this chapter are with the three romances of the *Otinel* tradition: *Otuel* (before 1330; the Auchinleck version), *Otuel and Roland* (c. 1330; the Fillingham version), and *Duke Roland and Sir Otuel of Spain* (c. 1400; the Thornton version).[3] I explore how these romances, building on the potential of their French sources, use the figure of the Muslim challenger-turned-convert to grapple with and invite their audiences' reflections on post-1291 concerns about Christendom's beleaguered state, the power of non-Christian empires, the human ability to enact divine will, and the reckless behavior of crusaders.

Like the author of *The Sultan of Babylon*, the authors of the *Otuel* romances reworked their sources to engage with broader traditions of crusade writing and drew extensively on the repertoire of emotions. From the thirteenth to the fifteenth centuries, fear pervaded the rhetoric of many responses to the rise of the Mongol Empire, the Mamlūk campaigns culminating in the fall of Acre, and Ottoman advances into Byzantine Anatolia and southeastern Europe. Yet these territorial (re) conquests also raised hopes that a prominent non-Christian leader would, through religious conversion, infuse the Christian community with much-needed strength. This dialectic of fear and hope captured the imagination of the writers to whom we owe the Middle English *Otuel* romances. The

Fear and Hope in Europe's Dream of Conversion   51

alterations they made to the *chanson de geste* of *Otinel* have two principal effects: (1) a heightened sense of Christian apprehension, powerlessness, and inadequacy in response to the threat posed by the eponymous character, which gives way to newfound confidence when he converts; and (2) the amplification of his chivalric and moral qualities, first as a Muslim and then as a Christian. After he embraces Christianity, in scenes unparalleled in the French tradition, Otuel is made to embody values of fellowship and mutual solidarity sorely lacking in Charlemagne's closest peers (Roland, Oliver, and Ogier), whose pride, envy, and excessive competitiveness he condemns.

I elucidate these postconversion scenes in light of a representational mode that is thinly documented in modern scholarship but was immensely popular in late medieval crusade culture: "reverse Orientalism," in which Muslim figures, typically portrayed as wise and righteous, look down on and offer damning critiques of Christians.[4] This mode was widely invoked following the Mamlūk siege of Acre and the Ottoman victory at Nicopolis (1396) – events that, in the eyes of contemporaries, signaled divine dissatisfaction with the Christian community and the urgency of moral reform. While most of the righteous, admonitory Muslims of crusade writing are nonconverts, Otuel's position as a convert and bearer of Christian victory makes his rebukes all the more fraught: could Christians change their ways without the intervention of a strong, morally principled ally?

Fear and Hope in Europe's Dream of Conversion

Benjamin Kedar has shown that religious conversion was not an avowed goal of the First Crusade.[5] Yet pleas to convert non-Christians became increasingly common as Christian defeats and territorial losses in the Levant multiplied. The perception that crusading should be accompanied by efforts to evangelize prominent Muslim leaders emerged most powerfully during the Fifth Crusade, with Oliver of Paderborn and Francis of Assisi's notorious failed attempts to convert Sultan al-Kāmil of Egypt.[6] It is also during this expedition that reports of the inroads of the Mongols (commonly called Tartars) surfaced in the form of prophecies predicting that aid to Christendom would come from a mysterious "King David," whose reported conquests mixed components of the legendary Prester John with the actual campaigns of Chinggis Khān, the founder of the Mongol Empire. These accounts, initially propagated by Oliver of Paderborn and Jacques de Vitry, sparked long-standing hopes for a Christian–Mongol alliance against a common enemy, first the Ayyūbids and then the Mamlūks in the Holy Land. The Mongols' ostensibly

52   Hopes and Anxieties of Conversion

enthusiastic subscription to this collaboration prompted years of diplomatic correspondence and negotiations, often involving appeals for the īlkhāns to embrace Christianity. For over a century, rumors circulated that a high-ranking Mongol leader would join the religious and political community of Latin Christendom.[7] Yet during these years the Mongols' open claims to world domination also materialized in dramatic encroachments into Europe, starting with attacks on Poland, Hungary, eastern Germany, and the Austrian border in the 1240s.[8] The rhetoric of destruction and terror is ubiquitous in contemporary responses to these advances. Matthew Paris characterizes the Mongols as "feralis" (brutal) warriors, who struck "timorem et horrorem" (fear and terror) throughout Europe. Frederick II evokes the "timor ac tremor" (fear and trembling) roused by their "furore" (fury) and desire to ruin Christendom. And the canons of the First Council of Lyons elaborate on the "crudelitate horribili" (dreadful barbarity) with which they "devastarit" (ravaged) Christian territories.[9] Reports such as these were integral to the formation of Latin Christendom's "dream of conversion" (a phrase I borrow from Robert I. Burns): that a fearsome, menacing non-Christian opponent would be baptized and help redress the crusaders' fate in the Levant.[10]

The fall of crusader Acre lent renewed urgency to this cooperative agenda, promoted by figures such as James II of Aragon, Edward I of England, and Pope Clement V even after the formerly shamanistic īlkhāns adopted Islam at the accession of Ghāzān Khān in 1295.[11] As put by Riccoldo da Monte di Croce, "Tartari facti sunt Sarraceni" (The Tartars became Saracens).[12] Ghāzān's change of faith did not, however, curb his enmity against the Mamlūks, and his invasion of Syria and capture of Damascus in 1300 marked the apotheosis of Christendom's aspirations for assisted reconquest of the Holy Land.[13] But these hopes were dashed when, a few months later, the Mongols were forced to withdraw. Despite the subsequent defeat of Ghāzān's army by the Mamlūks at Marj al-Ṣufr in 1303, the project of a Christian–Mongol coalition persisted in later years, featuring in various early fourteenth-century treatises that offered advice on how to reconquer the Holy Land. Hayton of Korykos emphasized the Mongols' credentials as possible converts in his *Flos historiarium*, which espoused the idea of a military alliance between the two powers.[14] Marino Sanudo's *Liber secretorum fidelium crucis* (1307) placed hope in collaborative action, as did William of Adam's *Tractatus quomodo Sarraceni sunt expugnanti* (c. 1317). The resilience of the idea was such that, even after the Mongols and Mamlūks signed a peace treaty in 1323, it reemerged in the writings of two later propagandists: Garcia

Fear and Hope in Europe's Dream of Conversion

d'Ayerve, the bishop of Leon, and the anonymous author of the *Directorium ad passagium* (c. 1332).[15]

The rhetoric of peril and ruin, so pervasive in responses to the rise of the Mongols, also permeates writings on the Mamlūk countercrusading campaigns that culminated in the siege of Acre. The decrees of the Second Council of Lyons portrayed the Holy Land as fearlessly laid to waste (*intrepide devastatur*), while Rutebeuf's *Lament* (c. 1266) described it as burned and destroyed from all sides.[16] "Que nuyl temps la Cristiandat no fo en maior peril que en est temps era" (Never before has Christianity been in such peril than it is at this time), declared the General Cortes of Aragon in 1291.[17] This sense of a hard-pressed, beleaguered Christendom prompted crusaders and their apologists increasingly to integrate the conversion of high-ranking Mamlūks, as well as Mongols, into their agendas. Of particular interest for our purposes are attempts to convert Muslim princes and military leaders, either to neutralize the threat they posed, appropriate their military strength, or ensure lasting possession of freshly conquered territories. In his *Liber de fine* (1305), a treatise advocating recovery of the Holy Land, Ramon Llull argued that preachers should be dispatched to Muslim rulers alongside crusade armies with offers of castles and territories if they accepted Christianity.[18] The French propagandist Pierre Dubois proffered an original alternative to material incentives. His *De recuperatione Terra Sanctae* (c. 1307), addressed to Edward I, proposed that European women undergo instruction in Arabic and be offered in marriage to Muslim men of status so that they might eventually convince the latter to convert.[19] While Lull and Dubois differed in their approaches, they shared the conviction that, in view of Christendom's past failures in the East, conversion was an indispensable complement to traditional warfare.

A similar dual perception of non-Christians as both a fearsome military threat and potential ally emerged in response to the Ottoman conquests of the fourteenth and fifteenth centuries, although at first, the element of peril seems to have markedly taken precedence over that of cooperation.[20] In the 1330s and 1340s, Ottoman piracy in the Aegean gave rise to a series of relatively small-scale crusade operations, but only the capture of Smyrna in 1344, by an army of Italian, English, and French knights, led to the enduring occupation of an important strategic location.[21] In the 1360s, Ottoman forces took possession of Thrace, escalating the threat to Europe. After invading Bulgaria and Serbian Macedonia, the Ottomans expanded into the Balkans after the Battle of Kosovo in 1389, and defeated an international army of crusaders at Nicopolis in 1396.[22] The Ottoman threat was couched in similar emotional terms as the Mongol conquests in the previous century. Pope Clement VI, in decreeing crusade measures in 1343, depicted the Ottomans as "attrociter sevientes" (raging atrociously) against Christian populations, "dampnificantes et depopulantes" (despoiling and depopulating) settlements in their raids. Appealing for the defense of Smyrna in 1389, the Avignon antipope Clement VII lamented the fall of Christian lands to "Turchorum potencie et furori" (the strength and fury of the Turks).[23] The Middle English sermon "De Sancta Maria," dated circa 1380, eloquently speaks to contemporary perceptions of Christian–Muslim power dynamics: "þe lordeshippes of hethen men groweþ vpward and in-creseþ; for seuerly oure Cristen prynces with-in þis xl ʒere and lasse haþ lost more þan þe þirde parte of Cristendom."[24]

But distress at Ottoman military successes was accompanied by collaborative aspirations, just as with the Mongols and Mamlūks. In his *Songe du vieil pelerin*, Philippe de Mézières invoked beliefs in the common Trojan ancestry of the French and Ottomans to urge Charles VI to seek the *amour* and *amitie* of "tous les princes et seigneurs des Sarrazins et Crestiens" (all the Saracen and Christian princes and lords), relations that he posits as prerequisites for launching a *saint passage* to recover the Holy Land.[25] Ottoman–Christian collaboration was not just encouraged but was actively sought out by crusaders. The anonymous *Livre des fais* reports that Jean II le Maingre, Marshal Boucicaut (to whom I return in Chapter 3) traveled to Adrianople to fight alongside Sultan Murad I against the Mamlūks.[26] The Frenchman Jacques de Helly is also said to have served under the Ottoman sultan against the Mamlūks.[27] These cases testify to the enduring potency of beliefs that joining forces with powerful non-Christians could help remedy Christendom's misfortunes in the Levant. The inclusion of religious conversion in agendas touting political collaboration resurfaced in the aftermath of the siege of Constantinople by Mehmed II in 1453, the effects of which reverberated across Europe. The attitude of Pope Pius II toward the Ottoman Sultan captures the emotional rhetoric under consideration: Mehmed, initially painted as a fearsome agent of destruction, is wishfully reimagined by Pius II as a new Constantine or Clovis, whose defection from Islam would bring the Ottomans into the Church's embrace. Pius's delusion was shared by several contemporaries, and rumors surrounding Mehmed's conversion were rife.[28] The "dream of conversion" had taken more time to crystallize than it had with the Mongols, but its ideological basis was consistent: Christendom was, more than ever, in danger and in dire need of an ally.

During the thirteenth to fifteenth centuries, there emerged a substantial body of *chansons de geste* and romances featuring Muslim warriors who convert to Christianity. In the *Chrétienté Corbaran*, grafted to the Old French epic cycle of the First Crusade near the end of the thirteenth century, the Muslim king of Oliferne, Corbaran, transitions from the status of foe to friend after his overlord, Soudan, is defeated by Godfrey of Bouillon. Upon embracing Christianity and returning to Oliferne, Corbaran has his subjects choose between conversion and death before engaging in battle with Soudan, whom he ultimately defeats in concerted action with Godfrey.[29] In the *Fierabras* story, *Otinel*'s counterpart in the Charlemagne tradition, conversion is also the result of Christian victory in combat. Reworking its French sources, the Middle English *Sir Ferumbras* repeatedly stresses the eponymous character's vast political power, fearlessness, and chivalric fame, which are assimilated to the Christian cause after his defeat by Oliver and embrace of Christianity: "Y schal scaþye hem niȝt & day þat bileueþ on Mahounde; / Cristendom by me schal encressed be."[30] An alternative to conversion through force of arms is envisioned in what Dorothee Metlitzki calls the "marriage theme," popularized in England by *The King of Tars* and the tale of Constance, told by Trivet, Gower, and Chaucer. *The King of Tars* finds a historical basis in the Mongol leader Ghāzān Khān's aforementioned victories in Syria in 1299 and 1300, which English chroniclers attributed to the miraculous conversion of the īlkhān's brother.[31] In this romance, the sultan of Damas (the brother's counterpart) comes to accept Christianity after he marries the King of Tars's daughter, and their child, born a lifeless lump of flesh, is miraculously healed by God. Like Corbaran, the sultan forces his barons to opt for conversion or death, and unites with the Christians to wage war against a coalition of resisting Muslim kings. The tale of Constance, finally, dissociates conversion from crusade, upholding aspirations for peaceful assimilation even as it signals the unlikeliness of their realization: Constance's union with the sultan of Syria was to bring about the "destruccioun of mawmettrie" and the "encrees of Cristes lawe" without any recourse to violence, but is rapidly thwarted by the latter's mother.[32] Offering variations on the modalities of Christian–Muslim union, these stories converge in presenting a view of religious conversion as indispensable to Christendom's ability to compete with powerful Muslim empires.

Converting Fear and Shame into Self-Assurance

The *chanson de geste* of *Otinel* provided the authors or adaptors of the Middle English *Otuel* romances with a propitious framework in which to explore the anxieties and tensions in late medieval Europe's "dream of conversion." In the initial scenes, the Auchinleck and Thornton versions in particular substantially depart from the Old French and Anglo-Norman *Otinel*, supplementing the emotional repertoire of their sources to describe the alarm and disarray caused by Otuel's presence at Charlemagne's court. The Auchinleck prefaces Otuel's arrival with five stanzas of mostly new, interpolated material, presenting his lord and emperor, Garcy, at the head of a force of "heþene kinges" whose sole desire is "al cristendom ... to maken heþennesse" (41–42).[33] Portrayed as "a sarazin ful of rage" (71), "of no man a-fered he nas" (76), following his introduction into the romance, Otuel expresses and provokes anger, couched in terms of threats, violence, and injury (149, 163, 277, 282–83), so that a tone of antagonism and peril is set from the start. At this point, however, the Christians' wrath is infused with other emotions: fear and shame. Despite Charlemagne's orders that Otuel be granted the protection befitting a royal envoy (reiterated in this version, see 141–43, 193–96, 205–8, and 329–32), his knights are unable to suppress their anger – "þe kinges kniȝtes hadden tene, / Of otuwel wordes kene" (149–50) – and after one attacks the Muslim warrior from behind and is promptly killed, their reaction mingles wrath and shame:

> þe kinges kniȝtes were agramed,
> & summe of hem were ashamed,
> þat Otuel in þe halle,
> Slouȝ a kniȝt among hem alle. (169–72)

The emotions roused by Otuel's threatening presence, unspecified in the French texts,[34] highlight the lack of self-control and disruption of unity inherent in the man's unsanctioned assault, and the ensuing humiliation caused by the Muslim knight's ability to slay him in Charlemagne's royal hall. In the parallel episode of the Thornton manuscript, reprehensible chivalric behavior is similarly defined when Otuel's assailant bluntly disregards Roland's warning to keep his emotions in check: "For-thi, gud sir, par charyte, / thyn hert þat þou wolde stere" (161–62).[35] When Charlemagne then reiterates his command that Otuel be left alone, his men's response, as rendered in the Auchinleck version, conveys fear-induced relief:

> Kniȝtes & sweines in þe halle,
> Were wol glade þer of alle,
> þat þe king so bad,
> For mani of hem was sore adrad,
> & þei wiþ drowen hem echone. (197–201)

This sense of Christian frailty is reinforced through an emphasis on Otuel's insults of weakness and old age leveled at Charlemagne, generative yet

Converting Fear and Shame into Self-Assurance 57

again of reactions of wrath and shame in the Auchinleck (277–78), and marked by "ferde" – signifying "fear" but also the state of being in "danger"[36] – in the Thornton: "Cherlles, with thi longe berde, / þat Emperoure [Garcy] schall make þe full ferde / With his stronge powere" (277–79). Charlemagne's advanced years are called upon to suggest Christian inadequacy in face of Muslim power. Emotional rhetoric in these initial scenes thus participates in a double, mutually enforcing rationale: it heightens the threat posed by Otuel, while foregrounding the Christians' inability to respond.

In all three Middle English versions, an atmosphere of imminent peril is maintained throughout the episode of combat between Roland and Otuel. A representative passage that exploits emotional language in the Auchinleck describes Charlemagne's distress when Roland accepts the Muslim knight's challenge:

> Littel slep þe king þat niȝt,
> For ferd of roulant þat gode kniȝt
> Of þe bataille he hadde inome,
> Leste he were ouer-come,
> For þe king hadde sein fol wel,
> þe kuntenaunse of otuel:
> þe king wiste wel a fin,
> Hit was a bold sarazin,
> For he sauȝ hit wel by siȝt,
> þo he sauȝ him slen his kniȝt. (377–86)

No mention is made in the French texts of the king's insomnia and feelings of apprehension.[37] Subsequent passages confirm that this use of the semantic field of fear was part of a deliberate authorial design:

> King charles sauȝ þere he stood,
> & was fol dreri in his mood,
> & was swiþe sore afriȝt,
> To lese roulond his gode kniȝt.[38] (555–58)

In the Thornton version, the king's pleas to God for help during the duel, while present in the French texts, are tweaked for a sense of greater urgency with the interpolation of the emotion of shame: "Fro schame ȝe Rowlande schelde!" (492, 510). The Fillingham manuscript, moreover, has Roland admitting that he was "neuer so sore a-schamed, / by-fore in no batayle" (486–87). The possibility of Roland prevailing diminishes as the duel progresses. The notion of divine endorsement through victory – a cornerstone of crusade ideology – does not materialize, and it is only after a communal appeal for God's help that Otuel, clearly presented as having the upper hand, is struck by an epiphany and surrenders, accepting Roland's offer to convert to Christianity, become his companion in arms, and marry Charlemagne's daughter Belisent. While this episode sees God showing his support through direct intervention, the necessity of this intervention highlights the failure of Christian knights to act as divine agents on earth. Overall, it appears quite clearly, particularly in the Auchinleck and Thornton versions, that the Middle English adaptors invoked the language of fear and shame to imbue the narrative with a heightened sense of Christian unease and ineptitude in relation to Otuel's hostile presence and the threat he embodies.

A purposeful emotional rhetoric is then mobilized, as Otuel's incorporation endows the Christian army with the qualities required for a successful offensive against the Muslim forces of Garcy. The Fillingham text stages a courtly dialogue between Otuel and Belisent to expose the new dynamics established through the former's inclusion as one of them:

> Quod Otuel, "ȝyf ȝe loue me wel,
> ȝe ne dur drede neuer a del
> Off Garcins grete power."
> the mayde ȝaf aȝen andswere:
> "syr," sche sayd, "haue thou no care,
> by goddys moder dere!
> y loue the more in hert myn
> thanne y do my fadyr and al my kyn
> that me to womman bere." (605–13)

Implicit in Belisent's statement, unique to the Fillingham version, is that Otuel is much more able to offer protection against Garcy than are other Christians who, lacking their new ally, would indeed have reason to fear. In the Auchinleck manuscript, after Roland and Otuel make peace, Charlemagne's repeatedly emphasized fear gives way to newfound confidence. His transition from the status of fearful to fear-inspiring king is marked by a boast: "In all þe world in lenkþe & brede, / þer nis king þat nolde me drede" (627–28). Otuel's conversion, brought about not by Roland's prowess but by direly needed divine intervention, thus enables the Christians to convert fear and shame into self-assurance – and military success.

The reconfigured emotional rhetoric of these narratives in episodes surrounding Otuel's conversion is an eloquent testimony to the imaginative force inherent in the absorption of a powerful oppressor, transformed into a defender of Christendom. In the late thirteenth and early fourteenth

Converting Fear and Shame into Self-Assurance 59

centuries, this search for allies was grounded in realistic knowledge of the strength of the Mamlūk Empire and the vastness of its army.[39] The loss of the last crusader territories in the Levant led contemporaries to ponder in practical terms over the reasons for Christian military failure. The inapposite response of Charlemagne's men to Otuel's presence, and the urgency of appropriating his titanic strength, dramatically enact the conclusions of crusade apologists such as Fidenzio of Padua and Thadeo of Naples, who emphasize the Mamlūks' military muscle and discipline, which they contrast with the weakness and imprudence of Christians.[40] Similarly, the English Hospitaller Roger Stanegrave's crusade treatise *Li charboclois* elaborates on the qualities and size of the Mamlūk army, and then expresses preoccupation with Christian frailty and the prospect of dishonor in battles to come.[41] This view finds further confirmation in Marino Sanudo's *Liber secretorum fidelium crucis*, which pinpoints military ineffectiveness and lack of caution when faced with more experienced and stronger enemies as a principal reason for the collapse of previous Levantine expeditions.[42] According to Riccoldo da Monte di Croce, the military failures of the past inspired fear (*timor*) in Christians and weakened their faith.[43] In the *Otuel* romances, if the Christians' trust in God does not seem to be questioned in the lead-up to Otuel's conversion, the threat of Muslim military superiority, and the fear it entails, are afforded special treatment.

Shame is an emotion that also permeates responses to the Mamlūk reconquests and, subsequently, to the rise of the Ottomans. In a report prepared for the Second Council of Lyons in 1274, Gilbert de Tournai describes how the shame of past endeavors extends into the present, begging for rectification:

> Iam haereditas nostra versa est ad alienos, domus nostra ad extraneos; terram enim illam, quam Dominus proprio sanguine consecravit, amisimus. Nec eam eripuit crucis signatus charactere, iam pluries suffusus verecundia populus christianus.

> Our inheritance has passed to others, our house to strangers; we have lost the land our Lord consecrated with his own blood. Nor have the crusaders, Christians now several times stained with shame, taken it back.[44]

References to the shamefulness of Christendom's fate punctuate Riccoldo da Monte di Croce's letters responding to the fall of Acre, as well as Ramon Llull's aforementioned crusade treatise, the *Liber de fine*.[45] Roger Stanegrave declares that Christians are "saunz vergoine" (without shame) because they delay to reconquer the lands of which they were "hounteusement desheritez" (shamefully disinherited).[46] In the late four-teenth century, Christendom's "vergoingne magnifeste et honteuse" (blatant and humiliating shame) continued to be decried, with regard to both the Mamlūk occupation of the Holy Land and Ottoman successes, as attested by Philippe de Mezières's *Epistre au roi Richart* (1395), his *Epistre lamentable et consolatoire* (1397) on the Battle of Nicopolis, and Honorat Bovet's *Apparicion maistre Jehan de Meun* (1398), which responds to the same event.[47]

In *Empire of Magic*, Geraldine Heng argues for an understanding of romance as a genre that transforms historical humiliations and crises into success, celebration, and triumphalism.[48] The *Otuel* romances (which Heng does not discuss) complicate this claim: Christian shame and fear are certainly redressed, but in a way that is deeply critical of crusaders, rather than celebratory. Their deficiencies in matters of discipline and internal cooperation are thrown into relief. And, as evinced by Roland's limitations when faced with his superior Muslim opponent, the solution transcends human agency, which proves inadequate to the situation, and is contingent on God's will to substantiate his support through direct, unmediated intervention. This concern with the blunders and limitations of crusaders will be further developed in postconversion scenes that contrast Otuel's exemplary chivalric and religious ethics – not "new" to his Christian life but carried over from his "old" Muslim life – with the disruptive actions of Charlemagne's closest peers, driven by pride and envy.

Envy, Pride, and Rash Crusader Conduct

In high and late medieval Europe, a vastly influential pastoral tradition disseminated views of pride (*superbia*) and envy (*invidia*) as prejudicial to the order and proper functioning of society. Variously described as a disordered desire (*desiderium*) for excellence, or a lust to dominate (*libido dominandi*), pride was, according to the English Cistercian Aelred of Rielvaux, the worst passion (*pessima passio*) of all.[49] Like other emotions, it was commonly portrayed in Middle English literature as "rootyd in" and effecting "sterynges of" the "herte."[50] Pride, moreover, could take various forms.[51] Of interest for our purposes is the branch of "presumpcion," which, as Chaucer's Parson explains, "is whan a man vnder-taketh an Emprise þat hym oghte nat do, or elles þat he may nat do; and this is called surquidrie" – or, as defined by the Middle English translator of Frère Laurent's influential *Somme le roi*, "arrogaunce" or "ouerboldenesse."[52] The "proude and þe surquidous man" imperils himself and others by

Envy, Pride, and Rash Crusader Conduct

striving at all cost to "be of more my3t or be worþier than oþere."[53] Due to its array of manifestations and prejudicial effects, pride was widely considered the most displeasing of all sins to God. In Richard Lavynham's *A Litil Tretys on the Seven Deadly Sins*, one of the most popular vernacular manuals in circulation in late medieval England, it is characterized as "a synne þat distroyth alle vertewis & most greuyth god of alle oþer vicys."[54]

Only envy rivaled pride in this regard, being likewise regarded by some as "contrarye to all vertuys & to alle goodnessis," but most commonly opposed to the highest theological virtue of *caritas* – the love of one's neighbor in the name of God (which will be discussed in Chapter 3).[55] Envy, often described as an agitation of the soul (*animus*),[56] was considered a "public" emotion, produced by feelings of competition that precluded social collaboration and undermined communal solidarity.[57] According to Thomas Aquinas, envy was a response to the possibility or fact that one was not the favorite, the most esteemed, the most loved.[58] Middle English authors, following Augustine, commonly elucidated "enuye in herte" as a deviation of sorrow: a form of sorrow in another person's success, wellness, or "goodness."[59] In Gower's *Confessio Amantis*, Amans details envy's physiological effects: "Envie makth myn herte change, / That I am sorghfully bestad / Of that I se another glad."[60] Mireille Vincent-Cassy argues that the thirteenth to fifteenth centuries witnessed an increase in references to envy as an explanation for conflicts in Europe, a rise she traces to the Fourth Lateran Council of 1215, which imposed annual confession on the laity and enjoined the faithful to put aside any "rancore ac livore a se penitus relegatis, ut sic spiritualibus et materialibus armis muniti, adversus hostes fidei securius praelientur" (bitterness or envy, so that thus armed with spiritual and material weapons they may the more fearlessly fight against the enemies of the faith).[61] Like wrathful quarrels, chivalric actions spurred by pride and envy were viewed as provoking misfortune in war, for, as Gower reminds us, "Moribus arma vigent, aliter fortuna recedit" (Feats of arms thrive upon good morals; otherwise, good fortune vanishes).[62] With the succession of Muslim victories leading to the fall of Acre, and against a backdrop of frustrated Christian recovery efforts and disappointing expeditions, it comes as no surprise to witness the proliferation of accusations of envy and pride in contemporary crusade documents.

In the *Otuel* romances, Charlemagne's ability to assume the role of successful crusader-king upon Otuel's conversion is contingent on the latter's military and moral merits. These, already on display during his duel with Roland, are what made his assimilation desirable in the first place. The Thornton version, for example, departs from its sources in having Charlemagne extol the Muslim knight's qualities in a divinely addressed appeal:

> And conuerte vs ȝone gentill knyghte
> þat es so hardy and so wighte,
> For elles it were grete wathe.
> He es so ferse in armes to fyghte
> And a man of mekill myghte. (511–15)

Otuel, a Muslim, embodies knightly ideals to which Roland can only aspire. Indeed, when Otuel consents to become Christian after a dove settles on his helmet, in a statement that finds no counterpart in the French texts, Roland admits to having "foghten with þe beste knyghte, / In alle this werlde es none so wighte" (595–96). Otuel's conversion to Christianity has no influence on his knightly merits and religious devotion, which were already portrayed in exemplary terms. Adjectives such as "douȝti," "noble," and "wighte" characterize Otuel before he embraces Christianity and after; his love for Garcy and dedication to the Muslim fellowship shift to Charlemagne and the Christian army; and his unwavering devotion to "Mahoun," foregrounded in the lead-up to his change in faith, is transferred unto God.[63] Thus, Charlemagne appropriates the martial energy of a Muslim knight with already unimpeachable ethics. Following his conversion, Otuel replaces Roland in the role of primary defender of Christendom and agent of God. He enables the Christians to multiply their victories and challenges Clarel, Garcy's new champion, to a final duel, the outcome of which is set to determine, to quote from the Auchinleck manuscript, "wheþer is more of miȝt, / Ih'u, þat is louerd min, / Or mahoun & apolyn" (1266–68). In contrast to Roland, who, despite proclaiming Jesus's "miȝt," is unable to back his religion with victory in combat, Otuel expeditiously defeats Clarel, unassisted by divine supernatural interference, proving Christ's superior "miȝt" through force of arms alone. Overall, Otuel is portrayed as championing Christianity on the battlefield far more effectively than Roland and other Christians, and as the narrative makes clear, his chivalric merits, moral values, and spiritual devotion are what tip divine providence in the crusaders' favor.

If Otuel is presented as embodying the ideals of chivalry, the same cannot be said of the most valorous warriors of the Charlemagne tradition. Spurning the very principles of fellowship and community that he had advocated in his attempt to persuade Otuel to convert,[64] Roland sneaks away from camp "full preualy" accompanied only by Oliver and Ogier in search of "awnters" to reassert his wounded chivalric honor.[65] This

Envy, Pride, and Rash Crusader Conduct

escapade, driven by competitive concerns of chivalric standing, sees Ogier injured and held captive, while Roland and Oliver are forced to flee for their lives, pursued by Muslim forces. The French narratives only allude in passing to the implications of this venture when Otinel, preoccupied by the insult of having been excluded from this opportunity for chivalric prowess, raises the question of who will take the blame if the three peers come to harm. But this thought is promptly dismissed in favor of antici-patory pronouncements of enthusiasm at the pleasures of battle to come.[66] The Middle English versions, on the other hand, adopt a far more judgmental outlook, denouncing the peers' transgressions of the values of community and service to one's king.[67] Again, this evaluative dimension is assimilated through the interpolation of emotional representations, in this case involving envy and pride. The Otuel of the Auchinleck, upon learning of the peers' absence, rebukes them for their envious response to his recent chivalric successes: "Beþ went for envie of me, / To loke wher þei miȝten spede, / To don any douȝti deede" (1020–22). Otuel then provides a clear counterexample to their selfish behavior, as he dismisses their affront and conforms to the very standards they fail to live up to:

> þouȝ þei habben envie to me,
> Ich wille for þe loue of þe [Charles],
> Fonden whoþer i miȝte comen,
> To helpen hem ar þei weren inomen. (1027–30)

He acts out of "loue" for Charlemagne and God (1071), upholding values of collective effort and mutual solidarity, and upon finding Roland and Oliver, laments Ogier's capture: "'Allas! allas!' quaþ otuwel, / 'þis tiding likeþ me nout wel'" (1067–68). The Fillingham manuscript has Otuel scold ("he gan to Chyde" [1055]) Roland for succumbing to pride, rather than envy:

> Roulond, for thy pryde,
> Thy lyfe þu wylt for-lete!
> What! wenes tou and Olyuere alone
> To sle þe sarysyns euerchone,
> and thus to grounde hem bete?
> Nay, þouȝ þou and y & Olyuer,
> hadde ben þere al in fer
> Aȝeyns þe hethyn lawe, –
> And ek charlys, the conquerour,
> Thouȝ he Brouȝt alle hys power, –
> ȝyt schuld they be nouȝt alle slawe.
> Ac turne a-ȝeyn with me a-none,
> And venge we ous of godys sone. (1056–68)

64   Hopes and Anxieties of Conversion

Collective action is promoted as vital to successful holy warfare, whereas pride leads to defeat and death. The Thornton version elaborates along similar lines, with Otuel "þat was so wighte" (1009), upon seeing the peers "alle blodye / With woundes Many one" (1046–47), reproving them "with steryn chere" (1042) and "full velanslye" (1045) for their presumption and folly ("ȝoure boste and ȝoure folye" [1049]). The rashness of the operation is underscored as Otuel, through his unimpeachable stance, is enabled to speak for Charlemagne and the whole group in asserting that the king will condemn their enterprise as overambitious (1051–52). These rebukes assume their full significance when considered in relation to the corresponding passages of the French texts, which instead see Otinel humorously voicing dismay at having nearly missed out on such a feast of Muslims.[68]

The Middle English narratives are thus distinctive in contrasting the dangers of individual chivalric action, prompted by selfish, competitive passions, with the importance of remaining "al in fer," sustaining a unified Christian body buttressed by ties of "loue." Emotions are in this way drawn upon by the adaptors of the Middle English versions to define the standards held up for emulation – sorely lacking in Otuel's absence – and to highlight antithetical, disruptive chivalric conduct. It is significant – and must be stressed – that this subversive behavior is assigned to medieval Europe's paragons of chivalry, Roland and Oliver, and that it devolves to the figure of the religious convert, fantasized as an agent of Christian regeneration, to remedy the peers' shortcomings. Otuel's praiseworthiness is set forth as a catalyst to critical self-analysis, as the quintessential Christian knights' conduct falls short of the exemplary crusading values he personifies.

Sinful Christians and Righteous Muslims

Matthew Paris's *Chronica majora* offers an interesting parallel to the *Otuel* romances in also contrasting the values of unity and collective solidarity with the passions of pride and envy to dispense blame in its account of the debacle of the Seventh Crusade under the command of Louis IX of France. Narrating the later stages of the expedition, the English chronicler chastises the French crusaders for their *innata superbia* and for the *invidia* they harbor toward their English coreligionists on account of the latter's success in capturing an important strategic tower.[69] These passions or sins are the grounds for Christian failure; as asserted by Saint Louis, who is irreproachable in the eyes of the author: "Formido vehementer, ne nos nostra confundat cum aliis peccatis superbia" (I greatly fear that pride, with other

Sinful Christians and Righteous Muslims

sins, will cause our downfall).[70] Responsibility for the failure of the expedition is ultimately ascribed to the French king's brother, Robert of Artois, who, in a decision much like that of Roland discussed above, is portrayed as covertly launching an assault, driven by pride, arrogance, and a selfish desire to receive sole credit for the victory:

> Robertus autem frater regis, comes videlicet Atrabatensis, assumptis secum multis nobilibus, quorum unus erat Willelmus Longa-spata, nesciente rege fratre suo, ad ulteriora litoris se contulit. Cujus erat intentio pro omnibus solus triumphare et titulos asportare, et ut ei soli victoria ascriberetur. Erat namque superbus nimis et arrogans, atque vanae gloriae appetitivus.

> The king's brother, namely Robert, count of Artois, taking with him many nobles, one of whom was William Longespee, crossed over to the opposite shore unknown to the king his brother. His intention was alone to triumph and carry off the honor, instead of everyone, so that the victory would be ascribed to him alone, for he was extremely proud and arrogant and was filled with vainglory.[71]

Warned by the Master of the Templars to act out of "modestiam" (moderation) and "prudentiam" (good sense), and to retreat so that "uniti" (united) with the army of the king they may pursue the attack in full strength, the count of Artois, "superbia turgidus et inflatus" (excited and flushed with pride), declines with a stream of invective.[72] Moderation and good sense are instead the prerogative of the Ayyūbid sultan al-Mu'aẓẓam Tūrān Shāh, whom Matthew Paris has declare, in anticipation of final victory: "Divisi sunt Christiani, nec frater fratri jam adhaeret . . . Dati sunt nobis in praedam et direptionem" (The Christians are divided so that one brother no longer supports another ... They are ours for booty and plunder).[73] Of course, the *Otuel* romances' renderings of cognate scenarios redress disunity and human sinfulness, reversing the situation into Christian military victory. But this is only achieved through the ambivalent persona and exemplarity of the recently assimilated convert.

Like Matthew Paris's *Chronica majora*, Jean de Joinville's *Vie de Saint Louis* (completed in 1309) enlists the opinion of a Muslim figure to criticize Christian rivalry, also identified as the cause of crusading failures and articulated through the medium of emotions and sin. This figure is an old man in the market of Damascus:

> Mout vous devez haïr entre vous crestiens; que j'ai veu tel fois que li roys Baudouins de Jerusalem, qui fu mesiaus, desconfist Salehadin; et n'avoit que trois cens homes à armes, et Salehadins trois milliers: or estes tel menei par vos pechiés, que nous vous prenons aval les chans comme bestes.

> You Christians must really hate each other, for I witnessed a time when King Baldwin of Jerusalem, who was a leper, defeated Saladin even though he had only 300 armed men while Saladin had 3,000. Now your sins have reduced you to such a state that we round you up in the field like cattle.[74]

The progressive loss of Christian-held territories in the Levant was a powerful catalyst to criticism. Gilbert of Tournai's *Collectio de scandalis ecclesiae* (1274) assigns contemporary crusading defeats to the Military Orders' pride and envy, sins that John Bromyard's later *Summa praedicantium* (c. 1330–48) ascribes to the Christian community at large to explain the loss of the Holy Land.[75] In Roger Stanegrave's aforementioned recovery treatise, it is again through the voice of a Muslim agent – a "sage amerail" (wise emir), "lequel estoit plus noble et soveraigne de tout Paynime après le soudan" (who was the most noble and powerful of the infidels after the sultan) – that the author denounces the "defautz saunz nombre et les cruels peschietz" (innumerable faults and cruel sins) that caused the Christians' eviction from the Holy Land. For Stanegrave, true chivalry was all but lost, replaced by a generation of prideful and boastful knights, lacking any emotional restraint.[76] In his immensely popular travel book, John Mandeville reached a similar verdict, also expressed by means of a discerning Muslim man (the sultan of Egypt) in an alleged conversation with the author: the Christians had been expelled through sin – notably the sin of pride – and there was no chance of recovery at present since "God wole noght help hem."[77]

The idea that crusading defeats were manifestations of divine anger against Christian pride, envy, and other transgressions – the concept of *peccatis exigentibus hominum* – has a long history in crusade culture, going back at least to the Second Crusade (1145–49).[78] In the lead-up to and aftermath of the Mamlūk reconquest of Acre, however, it became increasingly common to attribute such critiques to Muslim figures. Why did authors do so? One reason is that in the eyes of many Christians, the military successes of Muslims endowed them with a form of moral authority. In his widely disseminated *Summa praedicantium*, John Bromyard presents the occupation of the Holy Land as a divine verdict on the relative merits of Christian and Muslim believers: if the former were allowed to occupy it when they were virtuous and faithful to God, the latter now possess it because they are less evil (*minus malis*).[79] This providential logic underpins the author's analogical approach to Islam. He focuses on moral codes and religious practices that he sees uniting, rather than separating, Islam and Christianity – being charitable to the poor, assisting one's neighbors, refraining from blasphemous language, avoiding adultery – and admonishes Christians for failing to live up to the good works (*bona opera*) of Muslims, to whom he ascribes pointed critiques of the former.[80] Indeed, his handbook features several episodes where Christians are criticized by an imagined Muslim speaker or the Muslim community as a whole.[81]

A similar connection between Muslim victories, discipline in following rules of conduct that bridge Christianity and Islam, and admonitory authority is on display in the oeuvre of Riccoldo da Monte di Croce, which illustrates the complex interplay between providential beliefs and firsthand experience that underpins so many accounts of European travelers. In his divinely addressed letters, discussed in Chapter 1, Riccoldo blames heaven for the Mamlūk victory at Acre; yet he also assigns responsibility to Christians, who have the law of God but "sine perfectione operis," ("without the perfection of works").[82] His choice of words is revealing, for in the *Liber peregrinationis*, a travel account produced around the same time as his letters, he asserts that while adhering to a "lege mendacissima" (false law), Muslims are the ones who possess the "opera perfectionis": studiousness, devotion in prayer, mercy toward the poor, reverence for the name of God, dignified behavior (*grauitas in moribus*), friendliness to foreigners, and mutual love.[83] He extols these *opera perfectionis*, dwelling at length on their "concordia et amor ad suos" (concord and love of theirs), to which he ascribes their military successes, concluding: "Ipsi Sarraceni dicere Christianis: 'erubesce'" (The Saracens are entitled to tell the Christians: blush for shame).[84]

The moral and providential rationale underlying the motif of the righteous Muslim critic of Christians is further elucidated by the early fifteenth-century *Reisebuch* of the German Johann Schiltberger, who remained in servitude under Ottoman and Turko-Mongol rulers for over three decades after his capture at the Crusade of Nicopolis. In this travel book, Schiltberger writes that Muslims are taught that when they are obedient to their superiors and charitable to each other, "so git in der allmächtig got crafft und macht gegen iren vinden" (then God Almighty gives them strength and might against their enemies).[85] He then asserts that Muslims say of Christians that they have lost wars and territories because they fail to uphold the doctrine of the Messiah (*Messias*), treat one another with injustice and vileness (*ungerechtigkeit und widerwärtigkeit*), and live a generally disordered life (*unordenlichem leben*).[86] The internal logic of Schiltberger's *Reisebuch* is consistent with that of Bromyard's *Summa praedicantium* and Riccoldo's *Liber peregrinationis*: it is the

68   Hopes and Anxieties of Conversion

Muslims' status as victors in wars whose outcomes are morally and providentially determined that grants them the right to rebuke Christians for their failures and that makes their opinions worthy of attention. As these authors knew, Muslim figures, through their accomplishments and criticisms (whether truthful or imagined), could so effectively elicit feelings of shame and humility in European audiences because they were successful in holy war where Christians were not. In the *Otuel* romances, the eponymous hero's conversion permits an assimilation of his virtues. Yet the implications are all the more shameful: had Christendom reached a state where hopes for external help trumped beliefs in its ability to implement internal moral reform?

By the time the Thornton version was composed (c. 1400) and circulated, Roland, Oliver, and Ogier's dismissal of collective action in favor of individual prowess had a striking counterpart in contemporary crusade events. The outcome of the Battle of Nicopolis against the forces of the Ottoman sultan Bāyazīd I in 1396 was, according to the well-informed chronicler of Saint-Denis, Michel Pintoin, decided by the pride, presumption, and recklessness of the French knights, who, "cor facile sequebantur" (heedlessly following their hearts), are reported to have deliberately spurned King Sigismund of Hungary's warnings that they stay united and "non dirigantur impetus" (resist the impulses of passion).[87] The Nicopolis expedition offered fertile ground for the flowering of the motif of the wise, admonitory Muslim. Pintoin presents Bāyazīd as a "vir providus et discretus" (prudent and wise man), righteously chastising the Christians for their moral corruption.[88] Similarly, though more wide-ranging in scope, the French lawyer Honorat Bovet's reformist poem the *Apparicion maistre Jehan de Meun* meditates on the divinely permitted "avancement" (progress) of the "annemis de nostre foy" (enemies of our faith) through the voice of one of Bāyazīd's courtiers. This "hardy et sage parlier" (brave and wise orator), praised by the narrator for his intellect and moral discernment, ascribes the Ottomans' triumph at Nicopolis to the "charité" (charity) that unites them, saying of the French: "Pour dessourdre et par orgueil / Sont souvent venus a leur dueil" (Through disorder and pride / Many have come to grief).[89]

Nicopolis, one of the most important crusading defeats since the fall of Acre, yet again disproved Christendom's ability to cooperate militarily against Muslim forces. Though the original crusade plan for joint Anglo-French leadership was compromised by political complications in England and Gascony, the presence of English crusaders is attested by several sources.[90] Significantly, the crusaders' much-decried rashness came to be

Sinful Christians and Righteous Muslims

viewed by contemporaries in correlation with Roland's legendary *démezure*. Jean Froissart imputes Bāyazīd's victory to the "fole oultrecuidance et orgueil" (mad audacity and pride) of the "françois, anglois et allemans" (French, English, and Germans): "Et le dommage que ils recheuprent, si grant que depuis la bataille de Ronchevauls où les douze pers de France furent mors et desconfis, ne receuprent si grant dommage" (And the damages they incurred were so significant that not since the battle of Ronçevaux, which saw the defeat and death of the twelve peers of France, were such damages incurred).[91] This identification is corroborated by Philippe de Mézières, whose *Epistre lamentable et consolatoire* invokes Roland and his peers as negative models of pride and audacity:

> Et toutesfoiz par l'orgueil qu'ilz se fioient trop en leur force et par oultrecuidance, ilz furent mal regulé, car Roland ne voult oncques souffrir que on alast querre le secours a Charlemaine qui estoit a IIII lieues pres de Roncevaulx.
>
> However by the pride which led them to overly rely on their strength and by their audacity, they were poorly guided, for Roland refused to suffer that they seek the help of Charlemagne who was but four leagues away from Roncevaux.[92]

The conflation of the Nicopolis crusaders' behavior with that of the peers is an eloquent testimony to the degree to which the Charlemagne material informed – and was informed by – contemporary crusading events. The *Otuel* romances were reworked by adaptors to address the concerns that contemporary crusading activity had brought to light; and they were interpreted accordingly by audiences.

This chapter has explored the ways in which the *Otuel* romances bring together, dramatize, and adapt diverse elements of contemporary political discourse: fears about Christendom's beleaguered state and non-Christian territorial (re)conquests, hopes of conversion, critiques of Christian pride and envy, and what I have called "reverse Orientalism," a mode in which Muslims occupy the moral high ground vis-à-vis Christians, whose transgressions they righteously condemn. Deeply implicated in the political events and cultural currents of their time, these romances uphold ideals of crusading while expressing anxieties about the power of the Islamic world, the vulnerability and divisions of the Christian community, and the intemperance and individualism of knights, who, time and again, proved incapable of serving as divine providential agents. These texts offer a solution to Christendom's predicaments, but an uncomfortable one: the infusion of Muslim strength and moral discipline. Contemporary readers and audiences would have had much to reflect upon, discuss, and debate.

CHAPTER 3

Women, God, and Other Crusading Motives in Guy of Warwick

Like the Middle English Charlemagne tradition, the immensely popular romance of *Guy of Warwick* (hereafter *Guy*) served as a vehicle for the expression of crusade-related concerns and critiques. But while the Charlemagne romances are mainly interested in the communal politics and providential dilemmas of crusading, *Guy* tackles questions of motivation and intentionality. Thus, whereas the Charlemagne texts elucidate emotions as responses or appraisals with collective and political implications, *Guy* explores the notion of emotion as personal, private motivation. In this chapter, I read *Guy* against the fourteenth-century development of an ideology of "chivalric crusading," predicated on the values of knight-errantry, courtly love, and social advancement. Many contemporaries viewed this ideology as unproblematic. For others, however, it was a source of profound unease. I consider the significance of this debate in late medieval crusade culture, ranging over biographical, chronicle, and didactic evidence, but focusing in particular on the romance of *Guy*. As a substantial piece of narrative literature, *Guy* intervenes in this debate by probing and inviting reflection on the practical and experiential implications of fighting for worldly and devout motives.

Guy, like the *Otuel* romances, adapts an earlier Anglo-Norman source, in this case *Gui de Warewic*, composed circa 1205.[1] The romance's elemental plot, structured around the conversion of its protagonist from glory-seeking knight to *miles Christi*, is modeled on a foundational image of the crusading movement, and would thus have already appealed to the crusading sensibilities of earlier generations. Having successfully dedicated his youth to becoming the most renowned of knights – a condition stipulated by the woman he loves, Felice, for her consent to wed him – Guy/Gui is struck by an epiphany that reveals the sins of his way of life and the need for immediate atonement. He determines to do penance by becoming a pilgrim and participating in further martial ventures, but anonymously and for God's sake. This "conversion" motif features in

Urban II's speech at Clermont at the inception of the First Crusade as rendered by Fulcher of Chartres, according to whom the pope compared the "new knight," who devoutly took the cross out of love for God and his Eastern Christian brothers, with the "old knight," who followed his own ambitions.[2] Bernard of Clairvaux famously took up the theme in his *De laude novae militae*, which stressed the required disposition or affection of heart (*affectum cordis*) for holy warfare, defined through the love of God (*caritate Dei*), in contrast to the sinful thirst for vainglory (*frustra gloriaris*), which leads to homicide.[3] From the outset and over the course of centuries, crusaders were encouraged to conceive of themselves as penitent soldiers of Christ who expressed their love for him through martial service.[4]

Despite its origins in the early 1200s, *Guy* reached its heyday in the following century. The romance's fourteenth-century vogue is not only indicated by an increase in manuscript production and dissemination, both in Anglo-Norman and Middle English versions, but also by an appropriation of the eponymous hero in chronicles and didactic texts, and as a visual image in manuscript illuminations and carvings on misericords.[5] *Guy*'s acute relevance to contemporary crusade culture goes a long way in explaining this spurt in popularity. The protagonist's rebirth as a *miles Christi* in renunciation of earthly knighthood spoke to the tensions of a culture torn between acceptance of an increasingly widespread form of crusading motivated by the rewards of honor and chivalric prestige, and a desire to return to former, "purer" values. This debate came into the purview of romance through the novel appropriation, by authors of propaganda, poetry, and chivalric biographies and handbooks, of the conventions of knight-errantry and love-service to frame and promote crusading activity. Works such as Guillaume de Machaut's *La prise d'Alixandre* and the anonymous *Livre des fais* of Jean le Maingre, Marshal Boucicaut, drew on the repertory of Arthurian romance, depicting crusade expeditions as ventures that knights undertook not only for the sake of honor and renown, but also to win the favors of women.[6] This appeal to the amorous ethics of romance emerged out of authors' desires to associate their protagonists with the heroes of the Arthurian world, who were spurred by love to attain glorified chivalric heights. Love thus functioned as an ideological buttress for the secular aspirations of knights, a mainspring for their competitive drive to surpass their peers in honor, reputation, and social standing.

Yet the absorption of crusading within this fundamentally individualistic, worldly value system was bound to be controversial. Indeed, concerns with the moral predicaments of Christians engaged in "God's wars" for worldly love and fame permeate contemporary sources. Treatises for the recovery of the Holy Land composed at the beginning of the fourteenth century stressed the importance of the crusaders' pure intentions and abandonment of personal ambitions.[7] For authors such as Philippe de Mézières and John Gower, the notion of crusading for the love of a woman, inextricably linked to self-advancement, represented the height of vainglorious chivalric endeavor.[8] The antidote to this type of "fole amour" (vain love) is the "vraye amour" (true love) that unites humans to God, the foundational premise for Mézière's Anglo-French crusading society, the Order of the Passion of Jesus Christ, the main purpose of which was to reconquer the Holy Land.[9] This atmosphere of chivalric reform is given equally important testimony by the devotional treatises of the English crusader-knights Henry of Grosmont, who fought in religious wars in Iberia, North Africa, and the Baltic,[10] and John Clanvowe, who took part in the Barbary Crusade of 1390.[11] Both men devised their works as confessional exercises, animated by an urgent desire for atonement and true self-realization in God's service.[12] During a period when perceptions of the decline of chivalry were at the forefront of political thought, the sins of Christendom's knighthood were repeatedly configured as misdirected love, rectifiable only through the regenerative power of Christ's suffering and love. This tendency evolved, in part, out of the growing influence of pastoral teachings such as William Peraldus's *Summa de vitiis* and Thomas Aquinas's *De malo*, which related "affectio virtutis" (virtuous affect) to "amore ordinato" (ordered love) and "affectio peccati" (sinful affect) to "inordinato amore" (disordered love).[13]

This chapter considers *Guy*'s rise in currency in the post-1291 era against the emergence and crystallization of these conflicting crusade ideologies, which acquired central importance in literature and political thought. Despite *Guy*'s exploitation of the ideals of *amour* and *armes* to grapple with contemporary chivalric ethics, and the crucial role of crusading in elucidating the narrative's moral tensions, little scholarly attention has been paid to the romance's engagement with love and crusading as such; and the historical writings, practices, and ideals that informed the text's adaptation and dissemination have been entirely overlooked.[14] To address this gap in scholarship, I examine a series of developments in post-1291 crusade culture that invested *Guy* with unprecedented relevance: the geographical expansion of crusading, and how it was subsumed into larger structures of international careerist pursuit; the use of love-service to describe, promote, or criticize real-life crusading practices; and

The growing importance, in late medieval chivalric biographies and manuals, of a form of homosocial friendship or love, inherently bound up with individual worth and reputation.[15] I then explore how *Guy*'s rhetoric of love – both heterosexual and homosocial – solicits reflection on the practical challenges and ideological shortcomings of a value system that reconciled wars fought on behalf of God with the pursuit of glory; and how this rhetoric illuminates the desired temporal manifestations of an unwavering devotion to Christ.

As is the case with the romances considered in Chapters 1 and 2, *Guy* was freely adapted in the post-1291 period in such a way as to engage with the prevailing preoccupations of its time. But rather than reconfigure the dynamics of interreligious conflict by enhancing problematic Christian behaviors (as in *The Sultan of Babylon* and the *Otuel* romances), the Middle English Auchinleck *Guy* (c. 1330) heightens the early thirteenth-century *Gui*'s critique of the protagonist's worldly ethos through a prescriptive reworking of his postconfessional, God-serving life.[16] While many critics have distinguished the Auchinleck *Guy* from its Anglo-Norman counterparts in terms of its emphasis on Englishness, I instead document the adaptor's pervasive interest in and elaboration on the spiritual, emotional, and practical implications of the hero's conversion.[17] Previous scholarship has remained skeptical of Guy/Gui's sincerity as a martial pilgrim, viewing his piety as a narrative ploy to extend his adventures, an attribute of secular heroism, or merely a morally enhancing motif of insular romance.[18] These conclusions rest on the belief that very little separates his acts and decisions as a worldly knight and a *miles Christi*. I argue, however, that this distinction occurs in the realm of friendship: its nature, motivations, and modalities of expression. In exploring the practical manifestations of the protagonist's worldly and devout motives, the romance constructs a discourse – informed by theoretical literature and further developed in the Auchinleck manuscript – opposing self-promoting friendship and charitable love, the biblical corollary for love of God. If the success of Guy's love-driven ambitions relies on the "ennobling" friendship/love, praise, and worship of chivalric peers and social superiors,[19] his quest for divine love translates Christian spirituality into chivalric practice through martial acts of "brotherly" *caritas*.

The Topography of English Military Careers

Guy's chivalric career in the first half of the romance consists of tournaments and secular conflicts in various European countries, followed by a crusade expedition to Constantinople and more battles in Europe before a triumphant return to England, where he kills a dragon on behalf of King Athelstan. His martial pilgrimage is then structured around three single combats: in the Holy Land against the Muslim giant Amoraunt as part of a contractual agreement to ensure safe passage to all Christian travelers; in Germany against the steward Berard in defense of his sworn brother Tirri; and finally in England against the African giant Colebrond, warrior of the Danish pagan invaders. Scholarly reluctance to consider *Guy's* exploration of knightly ethics in relation to the crusading movement can to some extent be explained by the narrative's inscription of religious warfare into a wider spectrum of diversified military pursuits.[20] Yet this framework of knight-errantry is precisely what would have made Guy's crusading experience relevant and relatable to a fourteenth-century English audience. Timothy Guard, building on the work of Christopher Tyerman and Maurice Keen, has mapped out the topography of late medieval English crusading in close connection to knightly involvement in other secular battlegrounds.[21] Crusading not only expanded its geographical horizons after 1291, but also witnessed increased professionalization and became bound up with the other military duties of the fighting classes. The records of the *Scrope v. Grosvenor* case are particularly illuminating in this regard, providing us with a wealth of chivalric biographical information spanning circa 1330 to the late fourteenth century.[22] The depositions given by the several hundred witnesses of the two claimants illustrate the remarkable range of contemporary English military careers. The veteran knight Maurice de Bruyn, for instance, claims participation in campaigns in Scotland, France, Gascony, Brittany, and Normandy, alongside crusade expeditions to Spain, the eastern Mediterranean, and Prussia.[23] Lower on the social ladder, the unknighted soldier Nicholas Sabraham combined service in several theaters of the Anglo-French war with a diverse crusading record: in Alexandria, "in Prussia, in Hungary, at Constantinople, at the Bras de St Jorge [Gallipoli], and at Messembria [Nessebar in Bulgaria]."[24] De Bruyn's and Sabraham's experiences are corroborated by numerous other cases across the gentry classes and the nobility. This intertwinement of engagement in royal and religious wars was typical in a period when crusading activity hinged on the ebb and flow of the Hundred Years War.[25]

Similar chivalric trajectories are attested for the Beauchamp earls of Warwick, noteworthy for our purposes because they are known to have shaped their familial identity through association with the romance of *Guy*.[26] Thomas Beauchamp, who went as far as naming his own sons

Guy and Reinbrun (Guy's son in the romance), gained a fierce reputation for martial prowess in Scotland and France, becoming one of Edward III's most distinguished companion in arms. After the peace of Brétigny, Thomas arranged to join the Alexandrian crusade of 1364 along with a large part of his military household and an entourage of English knights, but when Peter of Cyprus's forces were delayed, he withdrew and decided to engage in crusade alongside the Teutonic knights in Prussia.[27] His grandson Richard Beauchamp, who is likely to have commissioned the French *Prose Guy* as part of his literary and material efforts to foster connections with the romance,[28] also perpetuated the familial crusading tradition alongside service in national wars. From 1408 to 1410, Richard traveled to the Holy Land, where reports of his shared bloodline with the legendary romance figure are said to have prompted admiration from the vizier to the sultan.[29] He then returned to England via "Russy Lettowe Poleyn and Spruse Westvale," according to the Warwick pageant, in emulation of his grandfather: "And in this Jurney Erle Richard gate hym greet worship at many turnamentes and other faites of werre."[30] Richard thus merges pilgrimage, tournaments, and other unspecified chivalric deeds under the banner of itinerant knightly pursuits. These examples, among many others available, offer insight into the geographical breadth of the secular and religious war experiences against which *Guy* would have been read.

For Love, Praise, and Glory

Like the paradigmatic heroes of Arthurian romance, Lancelot and Tristan, Guy attains exceptional chivalric heights under the auspices of a woman.[31] The beginning of the romance casts its protagonist in a state of love-longing, manifested somatically by extreme spells of "hete" and "chele," and culminating in frequent swooning – a condition, as underscored by the fruitless efforts of the court physician, that only Felice has the power to cure.[32] But as in most romances of *innamoramento*, the social barriers separating Guy, a steward's son of unproven merit, from Felice, the daughter of his liege lord (the Earl of Warwick), are sharply drawn.[33] Felice's other suitors, the "best" and "richest" earls and dukes "in þis world," establish the standards to which Guy must rise to find amorous fulfilment. Her requirement that he be held "best doinde / In armes þat animan mai finde, / þat vnder heuen þi beter no be" (1157–60) awakens Guy to the possibilities of worldly self-realization afforded by the knightly profession: "God to gode hauen me sende! / Time it is þat ich fond / To winne priis in vncouþe lond" (1190–92). The parting words addressed to his father establish his social ambitions: "mirþe & ayse" in old age, Guy asserts, are the natural payoff for a career dedicated to garnering "pris" and "los" "ouer þe se" in youth (1219–32). The hero's all-prevailing concern with glory and fame is repeatedly affirmed, first on the European tournament scene, and then in the lead-up to the first two major conflicts in which he participates: the battle of Segyn, Duke of Louvain, against the German emperor Reiner; and the defense of Emperor Hernis of Constantinople against the Muslim forces of an unnamed sultan.[34] His worldly success, viewed by many (himself included) as a sign of divine favor,[35] is enabled and validated by the "loue," "frendshipe," "worþschipe," and "preyse" of dukes, kings, and emperors. The romance mobilizes an economy of love-as-praise. Winning friends and praise are commensurate in the narration of his chivalric feats in Rouen, Spain, Germany, and Lombardy; Duke Reiner, "þat him loued and held dere," showers him with "worþschipe," "manschipe," and "praise" upon his arrival in Saxony; similarly, the Byzantine emperor Hernis asserts his love, friendship, and affection for Guy, buttressed by promises to do him "miche honour."[36] Opportunities for social advancement afforded by the hero's prowess are substantial. His upward trajectory culminates in a crusade expedition that sees him offered Hernis's daughter in marriage, half of the emperor's lands, and the imperial title after the emperor's death. Guy ultimately declines the reward and returns home to claim Felice as his wife, and the associated noble title – "þan was sir Gij of gret renoun / & holden lord of mani a toun" (20:1–2).

The romance's inscription of religious warfare within a framework of love-service – performed by acquiring social recognition in the form of homosocial love, praise, and fame – would have powerfully resonated with perceptions of the place and appeal of crusading in fourteenth-century chivalric society. With the increasing elusiveness of the movement's traditional material incentives (such as spoils of war and fiefdoms in the Levant), the rewards of honor and renown became commensurately more important. The enduring popularity of crusading was integral to the full flowering of chivalry.[37] The cult of chivalry, most fully elaborated after the fall of Acre, was institutionalized through the creation of a multitude of secular orders, many of which combined devotion to crusading with an indebtedness to romance models.[38] The Order of the Garter in England, imbued with the allures of the Arthurian world and a strong culture of chivalric fame, boasted a significant number of crusaders.[39] Crusade propaganda capitalized on the stimulus of secular chivalric ideals. The Teutonic Order in particular fostered an image of the Baltic crusades that appealed to the self-aggrandizing aspirations of Christian soldiers. This effort crystallized in the institution of a "table of honor," reserved for the most valorous warriors.[40] In a competitive environment where knights and squires strove for distinction, the special prestige of crusading was of considerable motivational influence.

The honor and recognition afforded by fighting non-Christians could also translate into opportunities for social and political advancement. Crusading, as noted by Christopher Tyerman, "acted as a means of entry to the ranks of the knightly and respectable for parvenus, a ticket of admission into the secular social elite."[41] The illegitimate son of John of Gaunt, John Beaufort, acquired a reputation for chivalric valor by crusading in North Africa in 1390, Prussia in 1391 and 1394, and perhaps against the Ottomans at Nicopolis in 1396. Though he was already an eminent member of the nobility, his career prospered remarkably in these years: he was put on the royal payroll as a king's knight in 1392 and was made earl of Somerset and knight of the Garter in 1397. Lower-ranking soldiers also stood to gain from fighting on Christendom's frontiers. Henry Scrope of Masham's participation in the Barbary Crusade of 1390, for example, saw him knighted and promptly employed in Richard II's service upon his return.[42] Similar patterns are discernible at the county level. Guard describes the composition of Thomas Beauchamp's 1364 crusading retinue as "a mixture of fee'd retainers, territorial clients and the cadets of lesser noble families seeking means for advancement and a stable income."[43] The notion that crusading could take the form of a rite of passage is epitomized by the tradition in the Prussian *reysen* of dubbing squires who had proven their merit.[44] As summed up by Froissart, crusading in "Prusce," "Constantinople," or "Jhérusalem" was of primary importance for "tout chevalier et escuier qui se désirent à avancier" (every knight and squire who wishes to advance himself).[45]

A work that encapsulates the culture of chivalric careerism that *Guy* would have evoked is the anonymous *Livre des fais* of Jean le Maingre, Marshal Boucicaut. The *Livre des fais* is an exemplar of the heroic biography, an increasingly popular genre that, in its very conception, attests to knights' growing concern with their reputations and the posterity of their achievements. Boucicaut's career consists of a dizzying array of tournaments; Hundred Years War campaigns in Normandy, Flanders, and Toulouse; and battles against Cyprus, Venice, Milan (and the list goes on). But several interspersed crusade expeditions proved his greatest claim to fame: in the Baltic, the Iberian peninsula, the eastern Mediterranean, and the Balkans.[46] The work is replete with references to the importance for knights of *vaillance, fais de guerre, ardeur d'armes*, and *poursuite chevalereuse*, driven by desires to *accroistre leur pris* and seek *avancement*.[47] While situated within a framework of divine service, Boucicaut's motivations, the *Livre des fais* suggests, transcend the secular or religious nature of the conflicts in which he partakes: his primary concern is "pour tous jours son honneur accroistre en voyagent et voyant de toutes choses" (to continually increase his honor by travelling and seeing many things).[48] He dedicates his "belle jeunece" (youthful years) to crusading because its inherent virtue endows it with unequaled prestige.

Underlying the system of chivalric values epitomized by Boucicaut's biography is an ideology of love inspired by Lancelot, Tristan, and "plusieurs autres que Amours fist bons et a renommee attaindre" (many others that love made valorous and famous).[49] *Amours* and *poursuites d'arme* are portrayed as inextricable. The grounds on which love permits men to reach *vaillance* are expounded at length in two chapters, the second of which concludes by crediting Boucicaut's chivalric career to the incentive provided by women.[50] The narrative does not elaborate on any amorous relationship at this stage, but instead focuses on the social function of love as a practical buttress for chivalry.[51] Love stimulates knights to fight courageously and achieve renown, which results in an enhancement of their standing in society. The connection between love and social improvement is underscored when, upon being named marshal of France at the age of twenty-five, Boucicaut is compared to the *chevalereux Rommains* of old, whom love had driven to achieve *maintes choses honorables*: "Et pour ce les Rommains ne laissoient point, pour la grant jeunece d'iceulx, a les mettres es grans offices de la chevalerie, si comme les faire ducs, connestables et chevetains de tres grans ost" (And for this, the Romans did not let the great youth of these men interfere with their appointment to the high offices of chivalry, such as making them dukes, constables, and commanders of great armies).[52] The author advocates a model in which social rank is no longer solely a prerogative of birth, but can also be achieved through chivalric merit and reputation, spurred from a young age by the emotion of love.

Inherently bound up with this economy of heterosexual love is one of homosocial friendship. If the love of women prompts and rewards knightly endeavor, it is, as in *Guy*, through the love and favors of high-ranking men that chivalric fame is measured and social advancement achieved. By outshining others in valor, Boucicaut incurs the *bonne amour* and *doulce amistié* of some of the most influential aristocrats of France, resulting in various honors, appointments, and promotions.[53] The love of powerful men stands as a gauge of respect and honor, a token of high

For Love, Praise, and Glory

favor that comes with social benefits. This form of love underlies Boucicaut's participation in the Nicopolis Crusade of 1396. King Sigismund of Hungary couches his appeal of assistance to Philip of Artois against the political expansionism of the Ottomans in terms of *honneur, amistié,* and *amour*. Pitched as an opportunity for French knights to "accroistre leurs honneurs et leur vaillances" (increase their honor and valiance), this expedition appeals to Boucicaut for three particular reasons: the prestige of fighting Muslims, the honor and affection granted him by Sigismund during an earlier visit to Hungary, and his *grant amour* for Philip of Artois.[54] Crusading thus provides opportunities for meritorious martial achievements, while contributing to structures of mutually exalting love that ensure knights' social recognition and advancement in society.

The chivalric values embodied by Boucicaut were theorized by Geoffroi de Charny, also a celebrated professional soldier and crusader. His *Livre de chevalerie* situates the practical edification of the knights of his time within the tradition of other vernacular manuals of chivalry while assimilating the amorous ethics of Arthurian romance.[55] Like Boucicaut's biographer, Charny insists on the "utility" of love, invoking the example of naïve men who would have remained oblivious to their chivalric potential were it not for the fruitful exhortations of women. Charny envisages love-service as beneficial to both sexes, inspiring men to "aler oultre ce que par avant n'en avoient eu nulle volenté" (reach beyond any of their earlier ambitions), while also prompting them to protect and defend the honor of women. The strength and durability of love is in turn dictated by the levels of worldly success to which the knight aspired: a woman's love for him should be commensurate with the love and esteem bestowed upon him by his peers.[56] Through honorable feats of arms, knights elicit the love, admiration, and praise of other men, in turn gaining "cognoissance, avansement d'estat, profit, richesce et acroissement de tout bien" (recognition, rise in status, profit, riches and increase in all benefits).[57]

Thus, given the social prestige of crusading and the perceived role of love in stimulating chivalric achievement, it comes as no surprise to find the two increasingly connected in fourteenth-century historical and literary sources. The prevalence of this link is further attested by the works of Guillaume de Machaut and by German chronicles and poetry of the Prussian *reysen*. Machaut's *Le dit dou Lyon* (1342) extols the merits of men who fight for love's sake in such places as Cyprus, Alexandria, and Prussia,[58] while his later verse biography of Peter of Cyprus, *La prise d'Alixandre*, prefaces the account of the Alexandrian Crusade of 1365 with a fictional introduction of mythological inheritance whereby Venus instructs the protagonist in the affairs of love and Mars in the art of war.[59] The moral and chivalric education underpinning Peter's career as the most illustrious crusader of his generation commences at the age of nine, when "tuit si penser tuit si desir / furent en faire le plaisir / de dames et de damoiselles" (all his thoughts, all his desires / Were directed toward what would afford pleasure / To ladies and young women).[60] As in the *Livre des fais*, there is no apparent tension between the protagonist's earthly aspirations and his service to God. Peter affirms the pursuit of honor, glory, and love within a crusading framework, but is also depicted as a fervent *miles Christi*.[61] Religious ideals are similarly refracted through the romance conventions of love in Nicolaus of Jeroschin's *Krônike von Prûzinlant*, a history of the Teutonic Order's Baltic activities written circa 1341, and Peter Suchenwirt's *Von Herzog Albrechts Ritterschaft*, which tells of Duke Albert III of Austria's journey to Lithuania in 1377 "to achieve knighthood." In its reworking of Peter of Duisburg's *Cronica terre Prussie*, the *Krônike* not only refigures Baltic crusading as a project in defense of the Virgin Mary, cast as a "zarte mait" (tender maiden), but also punctuates its report with damsels in distress.[62] Even more heroic in tone, Suchenwirt's *Von Herzog* presents crusaders racing joyfully into combat wearing lavish love tokens.[63] These authors capitalize on the allure of an enterprise in which spiritual salvation, the favors of women, and worldly praise could be concurrently obtained.

It is thus against the efflorescence of these crusading ideals, colored by amatory precepts and their associated worldly ethic, that Guy's earthly *vita* would have been understood. Love-service had entered the realm of reality to support a chivalric philosophy of devotion to the values of honor, glory, and reputation. Crusading's prestige gave ample grounds for its appropriation as the main constituent of this ethos. Proponents of this ethos strove to blend religious and worldly motivations in a harmonious way, fostering an image of crusading as both temporally and spiritually rewarding. The appeal of crusading was broadened by the fact that an honorable record could facilitate upward mobility, or strengthen the case for a promotion well suited to one's rank. For the authors of heroic biographies and manuals of chivalry such as the *Livre des fais* and the *Livre de chevalerie*, social ambitions were realized by earning the friendship and affection of fellow knights and social superiors. The love of these men was to be gained, nurtured, and upheld through meritorious martial achievements, for it was seen as determining one's worth and status in society. The emerging discourse of love – both romantic and political – is thus inherently instrumental. Guy capitalizes on both types of love in eminently successful ways, yet their inscription within a context of religious warfare proves fundamentally problematic. Worldly love devolves into a code of ethically ambivalent chivalric pursuit profoundly at odds with the Christian precepts of divine and neighborly *caritas*.

Problematizing Love-Service and Crusading

Guy's crusading expedition in defense of the Byzantine emperor Hernis subsumes the traditional crusading pattern of aid to Christian "brothers" in the East into a framework of careerist pursuit. At the opening of this crusading episode, Guy announces his desire "to help þemperor of his wo" (2850) and rallies his men to battle "for godes loue" (2930). But fighting for the faith is also the apotheosis of his quest for worldly "worþschipe" (2856), and his service rests upon temporal compensation: "3if þou mi3t me of hem wreke," pledges Hernis, "Mine feyr douhter þou schalt habbe, / & half mi lond, wiþ-outen gabbe" (2885–88). Religious and secular incentives are fused, setting the scene for an exploration of the tensions at play: were wars founded upon the doctrine of *caritas*, comprising both love of God and fellow Christians, reconcilable with the selfish ambitions that crusading so often satisfied? If the instrumental garnering of homosocial love, praise, and worship is a stipulation of Guy's amorous quest, it becomes, in the course of this pivotal episode, so all-consuming that it not only effectively trumps his love for Felice, but also his devotion to the Christian faith. The cycle of always higher social and material expectations in which the protagonist finds himself engulfed is only broken when he explicitly dissociates love – heterosexual and homosocial – from self-advancement, in a prefiguration of the central confessional scene, in which "true," marital love is in turn surpassed in the hierarchy of human pursuits by love of God. Through its demythologizing critique of chivalric love-service, the romance invites its audience to reflect on the practical and ideological shortcomings of an increasingly popular crusade ethos combining service to God with the pursuit of glory. It shows that social and material aspirations are self-perpetuating and can never be fully satisfied, that they are constantly at risk of prevailing over all else (especially one's devotion to God), and that given the transient nature of earthly recompense, they are pointless.

Although perceived by many as a favorable spur for martial prowess, fully compatible with knights' duties to God, the Arthurian dictates of love had long been viewed by others as inimical to the chivalric vocation and generative of sinful behavior. This negative evaluation originated in the

82   Women, God, and Other Crusading Motives

distinction, fundamental to theological thinking in the high and later Middle Ages, between spiritual love (*amor spiritualis*), leading to virtue, and carnal love (*amor carnalis*), through which humans are tempted to vice.[64] Erotic love's potential to corrupt was in fact inscribed into one of the most extensive codifications of the emotion in the medieval period, Andreas Capellanus's *De amore* (c. 1186–90). In structuring his work, Capellanus appears to have invoked the principle of *duplex sententia*: books 1 and 2 glorify sexual love, whereas book 3 condemns it as a sin that disrupts social harmony, leads to devastating wars and pointless deaths, and deprives humans of God's grace.[65] The Arthurian tradition itself had challenged the inherently individualistic worldly value system promoted in its use of the terms of love. In the Vulgate cycle's penultimate romance, *La queste del Saint Graal* (c. 1215–30), erotic love is denounced as an impediment to moral judgment and social concord. Lancelot's obsession with garnering Guinevere's favor at all costs makes him act for the wrong reasons – worldly worship – which impairs his ability to prioritize just over unjust wars.[66] Within the formative traditions on the subject, there had already emerged a counterdiscourse rejecting the benefits of heterosexual love, underpinned by a belief in the emotion's tendency to detract from chivalry's core values.

Various didactic and theological writings testify to the currency of such critiques during the fourteenth and fifteenth centuries. Honorat Bovet's *Arbre des batailles* equates fighting for women with the sin of vainglory.[67] Similarly, *The Book of the Knight of the Tower* accuses knights of misleadingly ascribing the "honour" and "worshyppe" accrued during their "vyages" to their paramours, when in fact "they done it only for to enhaunce them self / and for to drawe vnto them the grace and vayne glory of the world."[68] An equally disenchanted perception of knights' exploitation of amorous motives is espoused by Christine de Pizan's *Livre des trois vertus*: when men engage in chivalric endeavors under the pretense of love, she contends, "ilz servent eulx mesmes, car l'onneur et le preu leur en demeure et non mie a la dame" (they are serving only themselves, for the honor and the benefit remain with them and not with the lady). Love's appropriation for self-interested purposes is compounded by the emotion's inherently transient nature: even when love is true and faithful, Pizan asserts, it invariably subsides.[69] Other authors went even further and refuted the very premise of love's connection to chivalric achievement. Thomas Bradwardine's "Victory Sermon" after the Battle of Crécy in 1346, for instance, denounced the notion of love's positive influence on military valor and success as erroneous on the grounds that

Problematizing Love-Service and Crusading   83

victory and defeat were God's sole prerogative.[70] Roughly a century later, Ghillebert de Lannoy's *Enseignements paternels* altogether debunked the link between amorousness and prowess, asserting that women were in fact detrimental to knights' worldly careers, causing them to lose "honneur, terres et seignouries" (honor, lands, and power).[71] This countercurrent of opposing voices, while further testifying to love's entrenchment in contemporary chivalric mores, raised serious questions about its moral and political perils. Among the most recurrent counterarguments were love's damaging effects on moral judgment and sociopolitical bonds; its transitory nature, making it unworthy of serious investment; its appropriation as a front for vainglorious chivalric pursuit; and its irrelevance to or prejudicial impact on military outcomes, which God alone controlled.

Guy's superficial adherence to love's inspirational power belies a profound skepticism of the interdependence of *amour* and *armes*, which suffuses the narrative and provides an underlying rationale for the protagonist's conversion to God's service. Echoing a complaint frequently voiced in didactic writings, *Guy* constructs a discourse of opposition between heterosexual love and harmonious chivalric relationships, the significance of which is enhanced (as we will see in the next section) by the narrative's rhetoric of charitable friendship as a means of reclaiming divine favor. The most explicit manifestation of this tension, interpolated in the Anglo-Norman *Gui* tradition at the end of the thirteenth century and foregrounded in the Auchinleck manuscript, occurs in the aftermath of an ambush in Lombardy, which costs the eponymous hero the lives of two of his most cherished friends: "For þi loue, Felice, the feir may, / þe flour of kniȝtes is sleyn þis day" (1559–60). Guy continues by asserting the prevalence of love's chivalric casualties: "For þe last no worþ y nouȝt / þat wimen han to grounde y-brouȝt" (1563–64).[72] The Auchinleck version further cements the connection between romantic love and unwarranted wars and/or deaths in the narration of the battle of Sir Tirri of Gormoise against Duke Loher. Tirri's attempted elopement with Loher's daughter Oisel, like Guy's service to Felice, results in the loss of his closest companions: "Alle þai slouȝ mine feren, / þat swiþe gode kniȝtes weren" (4631–32).[73] Love's socially disruptive power is perhaps most sharply raised in the acts of betrayal and breaches of agreement perpetrated by the romance's villains. Love of Hernis's daughter, promised to Guy, prompts Steward Morgadour to plot the protagonist's demise, in violation of his emperor's trust and the Christian faith (3161–390); Duke Otes of Pavia's treacherous actions against Guy and Tirri of Gormoise originate in an amorous conflict with the latter over Oisel (5635–732); and the

84   Women, God, and Other Crusading Motives

Muslim warrior Amoraunt's failure to uphold a contractual agreement during his duel with Guy is imputed to his amorous enthusiasm (122:2–10). Thus threaded throughout the romance, in the lead-up to and aftermath of the conversion episode, we witness the articulation of a subtext of evaluation (implemented through primary and secondary characters) of love's damaging effects on homosocial relationships and chivalric morals, in consonance with contemporary didactic literature on the subject.

Within a context of crusade, *Guy's* interrogation of love comes to bear on the intrinsic questions of the chivalric vocation: its underlying motives and expected rewards. Love-service, conceived as a shorthand for knights' "loue of þe world," is invoked to comment on the inconstancies and vanity of earthly chivalric pursuits. Reminiscent of Chrétien de Troyes's Yvain, the eponymous hero becomes so enthralled by the possibilities of self-enhancement afforded by chivalry that he temporarily forgets the end goal of Felice's love. By having Guy repeatedly and enthusiastically consent to marry Emperor Hernis's daughter Clarice – as part of a package deal of lands, power, and social status in compensation for his military assistance against a Muslim army – the romance offers a dual critique of worldly motivations: not only are they exposed as transient and susceptible to corruption and change, but they are also shown to cultivate a cycle of escalating expectations of social and material recompense. For Herhaud, cast as the guarantor of Guy's worldly success, love-service is in fact divorced from the emotion of love, serving only to enhance knights' reputation and status.[74] The natural culmination of his protégé's quest – which, as he is fully aware, was undertaken to win over Felice – is to marry Clarice and thus acquire unrivaled rank and power: "In þe world ne worþ man of so gret miȝt, / No of so gret pouer, y pliȝt" (4263–64). Herhaud's surprise at Guy's reasserted feelings for Felice – "þat þou hir louedest wist y nouȝt" (4275) – affirms the subordination of amorousness to worldly ambitions within a system that commodifies women as one among other forms of chivalric "pris." Guy rejects this ideology at the end of the crusading episode by disconnecting love from self-advancement, proclaiming his preference for Felice over "alle oþer þat were o liue / Wiþ alle þe gode men miȝt him ȝiue" (4203–4). This realization prompts him to abandon his pursuit of "pris" and "los," in anticipation of his subsequent epiphany and rebirth as a *miles Christi*.

Equally central to the romance's evaluation of worldly motivated crusading, effected through its critique of love-service, is the notion that temporal rewards, unlike spiritual ones, are uncertain and ephemeral. On his way back to England, Guy encounters Tirri, whose love-spurred

Problematizing Love-Service and Crusading

85

expedition to the frontiers of Christendom finds Oisel in the meantime promised to Duke Otus of Pavia. It is only by waging a destructive war against Otus and Duke Loher that Tirri is able to rectify the damages incurred during his absence and claim the object of his desire. The futility of worldly inspired pursuits and the transitoriness of worldly rewards are of course thrown into sharpest relief by the protagonist's conversion in an episode that brings these critical strands to didactic fruition. Despite Felice's expectations of undying love, Guy's reputation, social status, and newly found marital bliss can in no way compete with the joys of heaven granted to those who fight for divine rather than worldly approval – a juxtaposition that the Auchinleck version, deviating from its Anglo-Norman counterparts, couches in terms of love: [75]

> Ac 3if ich hadded don half þe dede
> For him þat on rode gan blede
> Wiþ grimly woundes sare,
> In heuene he wald haue quite mi mede,
> In joie to won wiþ angels wede
> Euer-more wiþ-outen care.
> Ac for þi loue ich haue al wrou3t;
> For his loue dede y neuer nou3t.
> Iesu amende mi fare! (25:1–9)

If amorous passion spurs the pursuit of fame and self-enhancement, God's love and the associated promise of eternal salvation demand atonement through the espousal of a lifestyle of humility and self-denial: "For his loue ichil now wende / Barfot to mi liues ende, / Mine sinnes for to bete" (26:4–6). Guy's asceticism, devotion to Christ's Passion, and piety, though integral to the early thirteenth-century *Gui*, were intensified in the course of the romance's translation in the Auchinleck manuscript. Expanding on his or her sources, the adaptor elucidates the implications of Guy's rebirth as a soldier of Christ: he walks "barfot," "in pouer wede," and begs for his food; his rejection of material wealth is more emphatic; he repeatedly expresses "wo," "care," and "sorrow" at the magnitude of his earlier transgressions; his devotion to the Passion of Christ and reliance on divine help are enforced; and the crusading language of penitential pilgrimage, "for godes loue" and in remission of sin, is more pervasively employed in the narration of his travels and combats in the Holy Land and Europe.[76] It appears quite clearly that the fourteenth-century refiguration of Guy's God-serving life infuses the previously produced text with a powerfully ascetic thrust, in marked contrast to the worldly value system of the protagonist's youth.[77]

86 Women, God, and Other Crusading Motives

At a time when the sins of Christian knights dominated moral discourse on the crusades, the polemic surrounding crusaders' motivations played out through a rebuke of the movement's exploitation of the ethics of *amours* and *armes*. One of the most outspoken objectors to the waning pious sensibility of which love-service was perceived as symptomatic was Gower, whose principal works in French, English, and Latin broach the issue with characteristic verve. His *Mirour de l'Omme* assigns contemporary enthusiasm for crusading in "Espruce" and "Tartarie" to three reasons, the first two of which "ne valont une alie" (are not worth a sorb-apple): "pour loos" (for praise); "pour m'amye, / Dont puiss avoir sa druerie" (for my beloved, so I may have her affection); and for God, who should be served "Devant tous autres" (before all others).[78] Like *Guy*, Gower calls upon love-service to denounce the unpropitious nature of worldly motivated pursuits and the transitory nature of earthly rewards:

> Et nepourquant a mon avis,
> Si plainement a ton divis
> De l'un et l'autre q'ai nomé
> Ussetz le point en toy compris,
> Primer que du loenge et pris
> Sur tous les autrez renomé
> Fuissetz et le plus honouré,
> Et q'ussetz a ta volenté
> Le cuer de tes amours conquis,
> Trestout ce n'est que vanité;
> Car huy es en prosperité
> Et l'endemain tout est failliz.

> And yet, in my opinion, even if you had accomplished either one or the other of the two purposes that I name, that is, first that you were renowned for being praised, lauded and honored above all others, and even if you had conquered the heart of your love to your will, still this is only vanity. For today you are in prosperity, and tomorrow everything is lacking for you.[79]

The uncertainty of worldly recompense is reaffirmed in *Confessio Amantis* through a rhetorical question reminiscent of Tirri's plight – "What scholde I winne over the se, / If I mi ladi loste at hom?"[80] – while in *Vox Clamantis*, Gower again exposes the futility of such endeavors, even when (as is the case with Guy) they yield desired results: love and worldly fame, he declares, pass away in vain "diuine laudis merito vacuus" (without the reward of divine commendation). Love, according to the author, is both endemic to the chivalric stratum and profoundly detrimental to its morality, engendering inconstant behavior, breaches of judgment, irrationality,

Problematizing Love-Service and Crusading 87

and folly. In sum, love "vere probitatis miliciam extinguit" (veritably extinguishes all chivalrous virtue). Knights are chastised for espousing this ethos, as are women for perpetuating it.[81] Chaucer's *Book of the Duchess* echoes Gower's *Vox Clamantis* by admonishing women who send men to "Walakye," "Prusyse," "Tartarye," "Alysaundre," and "Turkye" for promoting "half word" and "contenaunce"; good women, Lady White asserts, avoid such "knakkes smale."[82]

Gower and Chaucer were not alone in deploring love's morally detrimental hold on fourteenth-century chivalric society. The urge toward chivalric spiritual revival that underpinned such critiques was championed most vehemently by Philippe de Mézières; and the influence of such ideals on contemporary chivalric introspective thought is witnessed by the penitential treatise of Henry of Grosmont, duke of Lancaster (and John of Gaunt's father-in-law), and a veteran of crusades in Spain, North Africa, and the Baltic. Mézières's order was, in its very conception, the most tangible embodiment of contemporary aspirations to renew knights' devotion to Christ.[83] Its original purpose, as described by Christopher Tyerman, was "to inspire repentance and piety through the cult of the Passion which would then lead to assistance for Christians in the East, the recovery of the Holy Land, and the strengthening of the church."[84] In his *Songe du vieil pelerin*, Mézières not only accuses English knights of being "enyvrez d'oultrecuidance et animez en la doctrine des belles bourdes, contenues et manifestees en vaillance mondaine de Gauvain et de Lancelot" (drunk with audacity and spurred by lying ideologies manifested in the worldly valor of Gawain and Lancelot), but defines his "sainte de chevalerie" (holy chivalry) in opposition to "ceulx qui veulent devenir preux comment qu'il aille, et font leurs moyens d'amer par amours pour parvenir a vaillance" (those who want to become brave by any means, and go through courtly love to reach valor).[85] The theme takes on a distinctly pastoral dimension in his *Sustance de la chevalerie de la Passion de Jhesu Crist*, which laments the prevalence of wars waged for the sin of lechery: knights, he asserts, all too often "destruient l'un l'autre pour acomplir leurs folz delis charnelz" (destroy one another in order to consummate their foolish carnal desires). Thus "pour les pechies dessusdis noz chevaliers d'occident, hardis entre lez dames, helas, ont perdu l'amour et charite de Dieu et de la foy" (for the above-mentioned sins, our western knights, brave among women, alas, have lost the love and charity of God and the Christian faith).[86] Grosmont's *Livre de seyntz medicines* offers an experiential corroboration of Mézières's trenchant views. Confessing to a lifelong martial career driven by lecherous passion, the duke of Lancaster contrasts

88 Women, God, and Other Crusading Motives

his unwillingness to go "nuz pieez en pelerynage" (barefoot on pilgrimage) to earn God's love to the lengths to which he went to gain "le pris, le gree et l'amour" (the esteem, the favor, and the love) of foolish men and women.[87] Love-service thus stands within these writings as a rival moral code to Christianity, symptomatic of the moral degeneracy of the "chevalerie mondaine du jourduy" (worldly chivalry of the day), whose obsession with self-enhancement thrives off the vain love and accolades of chivalric peers and women.[88]

Correspondingly, Guy's postconfessional *contemptus mundi*, markedly enforced in the Auchinleck version, aligns with Grosmont's and Mézières's belief that moral reform was to be enacted through humility and divestment from self, founded on what Andrea Tarnowski has called "knighthood's fundamental connection to suffering and love – that of the Saviour for man, and, as the author hoped, that of man for his Saviour."[89] But whereas Grosmont, writing for confessional purposes, focuses predominantly on his own moral failures, Mézières, whose intentions are socially prescriptive, elaborates at length on the behavioral remedies to the sins of his day.[90] As in *Guy*, Mézières considered the outward appearance and material values of his order of primary importance in reflecting the desired inner disposition of piety and dedication to Christ. Members were thus required to renounce "lez grans honneurs, richesses et delis du monde occidental" (the honors, wealth, and pleasures of the western world); to wear nothing more extravagant than "une robe honneste de drap de simple couleur" (a fitting fabric mantle of simple color), in the image of Christ; to abstain from eating copiously on Fridays, as an act of penitence "par compassion de la Passion de Nostre Segneur" (out of compassion for the Passion of our Lord); and to be "bien regulee, pour avancier le tamps de la sainte conqueste et recommencier saintement et vaillaument la bataille de Dieu" (well regulated, in order to advance the time of the holy conquest and piously and valiantly relaunch God's war).[91] Successful crusading, in the author's view, hinged upon an ambitious program of individual moral reform, enforced by ascetic discipline and the rejection of all material overindulgence, in emulation of Christ.

Yet while proponents of this ascetic crusade ethos saw humble awareness and the shunning of material values as antidotes to chivalric vainglory, they followed Christian theology in positing brotherly *caritas* as the foremost way of performing divine love on earth. If the love of fellow knights and social superiors serves as a benchmark for Guy's reputation prior to his renunciation of worldly glory, it is thereafter through charitable martial assistance, devoid of self-interest, that the protagonist enacts penance for his earlier sins.

Selfish and Selfless Friendship

As shown by the work of Albrecht Classen and Klaus Oschema, among others, medieval Christian understandings of selfish and charitable friendship relied on ancient philosophy.[92] Aristotle's *Nicomachean Ethics* ascribed human mutual affection to three motivations: utility, pleasure, and "good" in abstract terms. His threefold division, predicated on the distinction between transitorily based friendships and "true" *philia*, was in turn appropriated by Cicero, whose immensely influential *De amicitia* opened the way for Christian redefinitions of a secular concept according to the demands of a new religion.[93] New Testament writers and Old Testament translators narrowed the vocabulary of unselfish love to the terms *agape* and its Latin equivalent *caritas*, which was intimately bound up with the paradigm of "brotherhood," a central guideline of Christian doctrine.[94] The notion that God was the source, inspiration, and goal of true friendship was formulated by Augustine and further elaborated by Aelred of Rielvaux, who argued for an understanding of benevolent, charitable friendship as a worldly manifestation of piety and a route to the knowledge of God.[95] Friendship's spiritually exalting ability was reaffirmed by Thomas Aquinas, as was the distinction between *caritas*, performed by doing good to others, and a form of tainted love, rooted in personal benefit or pleasure.[96]

These theories were instrumental in establishing the devotional framework for the crusades. From the movement's inception, Christ's Passion was posited as irrefutable proof of God's love, requiring charitable reciprocation through aid to fellow Christians in the East. Pope Innocent III, proclaiming the Fifth Crusade, grounded this responsibility in scripture: "Nam et quomodo secundum preceptum divinum diligit proximum suum sicut se ipsum, qui scit fratres suos, fide ac nomine christianos, apud perfidos Sarracenos ...?" (For how can a man be said to love his neighbor as himself, in obedience to God's command, when, knowing that his brothers, who are Christians in faith and in name, are held in the hands of the perfidious Saracens ...?).[97] Eudes of Châteauroux, drawing on Augustine, presented brotherly charity as a natural extension of divine love, implying a rejection of worldly honors for the salvation of one's soul: "Sic ergo hec conversio fit per amorem. Et ex quo convertit se quis ad Dominum per amorem, mundum et ea que in mundo sunt derelinquit, ut non amet ea" (This conversion thus happens through love. And when someone converts to the Lord through love, he renounces the world and everything that is of the world, so that he may not love them).[98] The

90   Women, God, and Other Crusading Motives

temporal sacrifices inherent in crusading were repeatedly set against the much higher spiritual rewards conferred upon the charitable, devout, and penitent.[99] In its purest form, brotherly *caritas*, as theorized by propagandists, was to be devoid of any worldly considerations, and served as a means of obtaining God's love.

But in practice the spiritual benefits of crusading were often supplemented by temporal ones. Sermons stressed the importance of self-denial, fraternal charity, and devotion to God, and yet the possibilities of political and economic advancement came to be recognized and accepted from an early stage. Abbot Martin of Pairis, preaching the Fourth Crusade, offers a strikingly direct assertion of the good fortune likely to reward pious crusaders: "Nunc videte, fratres, quanta sit in hac peregrinatione securitas, in qua & de regno celorum promissio certa est, & de temporali prosperitate spes amplior" (See now, brethren, what assurance there is in this pilgrimage, which holds out both a sure promise of the kingdom of heaven and a greater hope of temporal prosperity).[100] Such perceptions hinged on the belief that divine favor could be manifested not only in transcendent but also in worldly terms. Crucially, however, this acceptance depended on the crusaders' motivations. Apologists admonished those whose primary motives were worldly, rather than pious. The Clermont decree of 1095 restricted the remission of sins to those who took the cross "pro sola devotione, non pro honoris vel pecunie adeptione" (for devotion alone, not for the acquisition of honor and money). Before the Third Crusade, Gregory VIII enjoined participants from going to the Holy Land "ad lucrum vel ad gloriam temporalem" (for wealth or worldly glory).[101] Thus temporal honors could come as a divine reward – a bonus to the much more important prize of heavenly salvation – but only if the crusaders' motivations were charitable and devout. The key criteria in this subtle yet critical distinction were right intent and purity of motive, the legal stipulations of penance and just war.[102]

Guy engages with the fraught issue of crusaders' mixed motivations by inviting scrutiny of the eponymous hero's relationship with the Byzantine emperor Hernis, joining a group of noncrusading Middle English romances such as *Amis and Amiloun*, *Athelston*, and the alliterative *Morte Arthure* in which friendship, as shown by Christine Chism, is "a site of questioning."[103] As suggested above, Emperor Hernis's love for Guy is constructed as a gauge of the protagonist's worldly status and achievements: within this framework, the narrative makes clear, love is the currency by which reputation is measured and social success made possible. Yet Guy's desire to garner the love and praise of other men is also shown to be his greatest moral weakness. Love's potential to exalt, and thus flatter, is manipulated by the emperor's steward Morgadour to plot Guy's demise. Morgadour lures the protagonist into a trap by appealing to the language of friendship ("mi frende dere, / Y þe loue in gode manere" (3163–64)) and offering him "Castels," "mani feir tour," and "Riche cites" (3170–71) – in other words, by exploiting the very social and material ambitions shoring up his initial participation in crusade. Tricked into believing the emperor has betrayed him, Guy laments the affront and wrathfully revokes his pledge of martial assistance to the Eastern Christians, resolving no less than to defect to the Muslim enemy:[104]

> An arnemorwe, when he out ȝede,
> Miche he me o loue bede;
> Hou schuld ich euer siker be
> Of ani bi-hest men hotes me?
> For þemperour me seyd þo,
> And trewelich me bihete þerto,
> þat he me wold gret worþschipe,
> & now he me wil sle wiþ schenschipe (3287–94)
>
> . . .
>
> "Lordinges," he seyd, "to armes snelle!
> Here wil we no longer duelle:
> To þemperour y-wraid we beþ,
> Alle he wil don ous to þe deþ.
> Bi þe treuþe y schal our lord ȝeld,
> þat heuen and erþe haueþ in weld,
> Er þan we be nomen & ded,
> So mani schal dye of her ferred,
> þat it worþ abouȝt wel strong
> þat ich am bi-wrayd wrong!"
> To armes þai went wiþ þat ichon;
> Out of þe cite þai ben y-gon,
> & went toward þe heþen men,
> Wiþ þem to holden & to ben,
> To help þe heþen men ichon. (3301–15)

Guy's misdirected priorities are thrown into relief: the promise of "gret worþschipe" inherent in the emperor's "loue" takes precedence over his religious identity, to the extent that he is ready not only to abandon his fellow crusaders but to join the Muslim forces in defeating them. Confronted by Hernis, Guy somewhat ambiguously denies then confirms the emperor's (justified) assumption that his friendship is a commodity that can be bought, declaring that he was never a "traitour" yet confessing to a prevailing desire to fight for someone "þat mi seruise ȝeld me wold" (3356 and 3368). Realizing that Guy's decision to change sides was prompted by a perceived breach of love, implying a setback to his rise in chivalric eminence, Hernis responds in consequence: he proclaims his unrivaled love for the protagonist ("& topon al oþer y loue þe" [3346]), swears to love only those who treat him well, takes his "dere frende" into his arms, and reaffirms Guy's rights over "alle þat min is" (3372–82). The protagonist's attempt to capitalize on crusading to further his own personal interests thus culminates in him not only defaulting on his amorous vow to Felice, temporarily revoked by the very ambitions she served to rouse, but nearly deserting the Christian cause, blinded by his obsession with the "pris" and "los" to be gained through the love and worship of high-ranking men.

After Guy renounces his quest for worldly glory, the romance's economy of self-advancing love gives way to one of charitable friendship, especially pronounced in the Auchinleck manuscript. Taking leave of the Byzantine emperor, Guy encounters Tirri, who poignantly laments Oisel's abduction and the loss of his comrades to the forces of Duke Otous. While the early thirteenth-century *Gui* grounds the protagonist's solicitude in the man's chivalric identity as "Terri," "le preux, le vaillant, le hardi," the Auchinleck version, by contrast, portrays Guy's response as heartfelt, free of worldly concerns, and elicited by Tirri's misfortunes: "Wel depe in hert he haþ y-siȝt. / Grete pite he haþ of þat kniȝt: / He knewe Tirri for his frende" (4683–85).[105] A similar elision of worldly considerations characterizes the romance's rendition of the two men's oath of sworn brotherhood. Both versions present Guy/Gui taking the initiative in establishing the bond, but the Anglo-Norman text suggests that he is prompted by a return on investment (principally in the symbolic form of gratitude) for the "mult grant honur" conferred upon Tirri by his presence and help, whereas the Middle English romance omits reference to any such expectations. Instead, it introduces Guy's proposal simply with the statement "Miche loue was bitven hem to" (4904).[106] Particularly noteworthy for an oath premised on the agreement to "no faile oþer while he liues is" (4912) is the degree of worldly disinterest operative in Guy's conception of the union, the profits of which go almost exclusively to Tirri.[107] While scholars often disagree on the animating motives of such covenanted associations (which were often too diverse for systematic codification), Guy's altruistic devotion to Tirri, pervaded by a growing spiritual consciousness, aligns with theological understandings of "true" friendship as a fundamentally ethical value in agreement with divine will.[108] The

Selfish and Selfless Friendship

paradigm of fraternal charity is thus already introduced in the lead-up to the protagonist's epiphany, as a determining catalyst in his journey toward God.

The romance's rhetoric of brotherly *caritas* is subsequently borne out in the three battles the protagonist undertakes during his penitential pilgrimage in the Holy Land, Germany, and England. After visiting the holy sites of Jerusalem and Bethlehem, Guy falls upon a grief-stricken crusader named Jonas, whose failed attempt to recover Jerusalem from Muslim forces threatens to cost him his life and those of his fifteen sons – a verdict that can only be reversed through the intervention of a champion willing to duel against the Muslim giant Amoraunt. Guy expresses "rewþe" at the man's sorrows and anonymously accepts to take on the combat out of "loue" for him.[109] Like his earlier assistance of Hernis, Guy's one-man crusade in support of Eastern "brothers" is buttressed by a contractual agreement. But rather than resting on the rewards of status, power, and reputation, his intervention bears the promise of freedom to all Christian prisoners in Alexandria and safe passage to Christian pilgrims in the Levant (88:1–9). The protagonist's sphere of charitable influence thus extends beyond Jonas and his sons to encompass not only a significant group of persecuted Christians in the East, but also the Christian community as a whole through the spiritual benefits afforded by the restored possibilities of pilgrimage to the Holy Land. Fraternal charity and divine love are in fact conflated in the Auchinleck manuscript, when Guy, charged with serving a "feble lord" on account of his humble attire, describes his martial pilgrimage for God using the imagery of feudal friendship: "& þer-fore icham þus y-diȝt, / To cri him merci day & niȝt, / Til we ben frendes same" (85:7–9).[110] As is widely documented, couching the charitable framework of crusading in terms of a feudal obligation was one of the most common and presumably effective motifs of crusade propaganda.[111]

The language of penitential pilgrimage is finally maintained during Guy's adventures in Germany and England, where he single-handedly reestablishes Western peace and harmony through acts of charitable martial assistance. His charitable intentions are underscored in the Middle English text as he instates Tirri to the position of steward to the Western Christian emperor in place of the "prout" villain Berard: "Y no fiȝt for to win no þing, / Noiþer gold no fe, / . . . Bot for mi felawe y loued so wel" (197:5–8).[112] Similarly, when King Athelstan, faced with the invading pagan Danes and their African giant Colbrond, implores Guy to "take þe batayle now on hond, / & saue ous þe riȝt of Inglond, / For seynt Charite," the protagonist expresses "care" at the great "sorwe & sikeing sare" of the

English, and accepts "for god in trinite" (246:10–248:6).[113] The Auchinleck *Guy*'s concern with the spiritually exalting nature of brotherly love is finally perhaps most evident in the adaptor's reworking of the protagonist's funerary arrangements after his death as a solitary hermit. While in both *Gui* and *Guy* the hero is provided with a humble burial outside his hermitage, the Middle English romance interpolates a final stanza in which Tirri brings his sworn brother's body "into his owhen cuntray," Lorraine, where he builds an abbey in his honor (298:1–12). In death as in life, the devotion shared by the two men is celebrated as an expression of piety and love of God.[114]

Caritas and Chivalric Piety

Clear evidence that Guy's martial pilgrimage was understood in the fourteenth century as promoting the virtue of brotherly *caritas* is provided by contemporary writings that appropriated the romance hero for didactic instruction. The *Gesta Romanorum*, a collection of stories and anecdotes in Latin compiled in England for pastoral use, presents a much-abridged, free adaptation of Guy's penitential life, showcasing the importance of crusading and friendship as complementary means of spiritual self-realization. The tale conflates themes of crusading as both vengeance and compassionate love with an elaboration on mental constancy in friendship, where Guido's self-denying devotion to his companion Tyrius serves to allegorize Christ's loving sacrifice for humankind.[115] The doctrine of *caritas* also underlies the *Speculum Gy de Warewyke*, a Middle English didactic treatise based on Alcuin's *Liber de virtutibus et vitiis* and framed as a dialogue between the author and Guy, but commonly dismissed by critics as bearing little relation to the romance.[116] The opening exhortation for the reader to "loue god ouer alle þing" to "heuene winne" is a generic commonplace, yet the treatise's repeated emphasis on divine love's practical application – "If þou louest god ful iwis, / þu [wolt] louen alle his" – is intertextually illuminating.[117] This "verray charité" is underpinned by "humilite" and a rejection of "þis worldes blisse" – of the "worldes honour," and "gret los and pompe and pride." Guy, who "forsook" the world, serves both as a pupil for moral edification and as an exemplar held up for emulation.[118]

While the rhetoric of *caritas* was bound up with the crusading movement from the beginning, Mamlūk reconquests in the Levant and the rise of what I have called "chivalric crusading" invested God's two "greatest" commandments with renewed urgency. The French poet Rutebeuf's

Lament warns of the impending universal uprising of non-Christians caused by Christian lack of charity.[119] Treatises offering advice on how to reconquer the Holy Land proposed ambitious programs of logistical, structural, and strategic improvement, and yet all agreed that these measures would be to no avail lacking God's support, which could only be secured through the individual efforts of inward moral regeneration of knights. Fidenzio of Padua imputed the fall of Acre to the crusaders' breaches of *caritas*, *unitas*, and *fidelitas* – qualities that he posits as indispensable for the recovery and subsequent preservation of Christian holy sites in Syria and Palestine.[120] The resulting agenda of chivalric reform was perhaps most influentially championed by the Spanish writer Ramon Llull, who himself experienced a transformative conversion in 1263, relinquishing the worldly lifestyle of his youth – a period when, according to his biographer, he delighted in composing worthless songs (*uanis cantilenis*) of foolish love (*amore fatuo*) – to become one of the staunchest supporters of a purged, Christianized ethic of knighthood.[121] His *Book of the Order of Chivalry* – narrated by a veteran knight hermit rather like Guy (and literally Guy in Joanot Martorell's *Tirant lo Blanc* [c. 1460–64], which conflates *Guy* and Llull's *Book*) – founded its prescribed code of chivalric behavior on "charyte in God / and in [one's] ney3bour": for "charite is a vertu aboue other vertues" which "departeth euery vyce."[122] His *Book*, a work of immense popularity across western Europe, became the crux of his subsequent ambitions to recover the Holy Land, which hinged upon the organizational attributes of *sapientia* and *potestas*, and their spiritual sine qua non – *caritas*.[123] Later in the fourteenth century, Mézières' Order of the Passion mobilized similar spiritual guidelines. To rectify "le monde qui fort va a declin," his "sainte Chevalerie" was to provide a model of penitential and compassionate unity among themselves and toward the "crestiens d'orient," which would renew Latin Christendom's love for "Nostre Segneur Jhesu Crist" and establish peace "entre les crestiens" at home.[124] Individual chivalric moral regeneration from the ground up was thus viewed as key to both successful crusading in the eastern Mediterranean and peace and harmony in Europe. Mézières's ideas imbricate with *Guy*'s premise that individual acts of charitable friendship can effect sociopolitical change for the Christian common good in the West, as in the East.

The practical influence of such notions of charitable friendship and penitential martial pilgrimage as the chosen route to chivalric spiritual fulfilment is reflected in a number of English fourteenth-century knightly trajectories. Most illustrative for our purposes are those of John Ryvere (c.

96   Women, God, and Other Crusading Motives

1313–64) of Gloucestershire, where the story of *Guy* is known to have circulated, and John Clanvowe (c. 1341–91), one of the so-called Lollard knights and a friend of Chaucer, who was well acquainted with the romance.[125] Ryvere dedicated his early martial career to serving Edward III, particularly in the Scottish wars, but is reported to have developed an aversion to killing fellow Christians. Hoping, as put by Guard, "to expiate crimes committed during his former soldiering career," Ryvere received a papal safe conduct and embarked to the Holy Land "in subsidium fidelium" (in aid of the faithful) against the Mamlūks, accompanied only by two long-serving members of his household. He fought in Romania (western Anatolia) before spending several months traveling as a pilgrim and spy in Syria, Egypt, and Jerusalem, where he became a patron of the Order of the Holy Sepulchre, an international knightly brotherhood vowed to the rules of poverty, charity, and obedience. In the year of his death, he gained papal permission to become a Dominican friar in London.[126]

Clanvowe's life also bears broad resemblance to Guy's, showcasing a mixture of crusading, pilgrimage, and devotion to fellow Christians as the privileged means of translating penitential piety into knightly practice. He served as a soldier for the crown when the spoils of the Anglo-French war were notably rich, and as a courtier under Richard II, but rejected the worldly values of praise, fame, and glory in his devotional tract, *The Two Ways*, written at the end of his life. *Caritas*, the key concept in this work, is ascribed a position of unrivaled prominence in the hierarchy of human endeavors: "Alle þoo þat louen so God and here neiȝebour as hem self þei been in the nargh wey þat leedeþ to þe blisse þat euere shalle lasten."[127] These words were reportedly composed after the author's participation in the Barbary Crusade of 1390, an expedition that culminated in the unsuccessful siege of the Tunisian coastal city of Mahdia, and shortly before his death on a pilgrimage to Jerusalem the following year, accompanied by his sworn brother and crusading associate, William Neville.[128] *The Westminster Chronicle* couches the two English companions' quasi-concurrent deaths near Constantinople in terms of fraternal love:

> Item xvij. die Octobris dominus Johannes Clanvowe miles egregius in quodam vico juxta Constantinopolim in Grecia diem clausit extremum: quam ob causam dominus Willelmus Nevyle ejus comes in itinere, quem non minus quam se ipsum diligebat, inconsolabiliter dolens numquam postea sumpsit cibum, unde transactis duobus diebus sequentibus in eodem vico lamentabiliter expiravit.

It was also on 17 October that in a village near Constantinople in Greece the life of Sir John Clanvowe, a distinguished knight, came to its close, causing to his companion on the march, Sir William Neville, for whom his love was no less than for himself, such inconsolable sorrow that he never took food again and two days afterwards breathed his last, greatly mourned, in the same village.[129]

As in *Guy*, their mutual devotion, rooted in a common love for God, was commemorated in special funerary arrangements. The men were buried in a shared tomb bearing a double epitaph and their impaled arms, symbolizing the strength of their affection.[130]

The brand of chivalric piety purveyed by *Guy* was in vogue in fourteenth-century England, as attested by pastoral literature, chivalric manuals, penitential treatises, and biographical trajectories. Even the written testaments of contemporaries supply evidence of the purchase held by this form of humble, penitential awareness. In his will, Lewis Clifford (c. 1330–1404) – also a Lollard knight, a friend of Chaucer, a participant in the Barbary Crusade, and, moreover, a member of Mézières's Order of the Passion – commends his "wretched and sinful soul" to God and instructs that his "stinking carrion" be buried in an unadorned, anonymous grave in the furthest corner of the local churchyard.[131] With these directions, Maurice Keen remarks, Clifford "struck out at the flamboyance that was the outward symptom of chivalry's vainglory."[132] Chaucer himself modeled aspects of his Squire and Knight in *The Canterbury Tales* on the conflicting chivalric ideologies of his time. The Knight, clothed in humble attire (a travel-stained doublet of simple fustian), is characterized by his love of "chivalrie," framed as integral to his dedication to "oure faith." His son, by contrast, is lavishly dressed in the latest fashion (a short gown with long, wide sleeves, embroidered in fresh-cut flowers), and fights primarily "to stonden in his lady grace."[133] The Knight is by no means representative of an outdated ethos – as critics long believed – but is best understood as an exemplar of the increasingly widespread pious sensibility explored in this chapter, which defined itself against an equally important, concurrent movement toward chivalric secularization. Knights' "loue of þe world," viewed by many as endemic, was rejected in multifarious ways: through a critique of the ideology of *amour* and *armes*; the associated values of praise, fame, and social advancement; the garnering of homosocial love to further one's own selfish ends; and all forms of material excess. *Guy* invites its audience to reflect on the conflicting crusading values of the time, exposing the practical dangers and futility of waging religious wars for earthly glory, while suggesting that as an antithetical code of conduct, brotherly *caritas* held unequaled practical applicability: as Christianity's prescribed temporal manifestation of love of God, it enabled pious knights to carry out their spiritual mission through virtuous martial action. It is within this nexus of tensions that *Guy* would have been understood in late medieval England.

CHAPTER 4

Therapeutic Crusading and Excessive Violence in The Siege of Jerusalem *and* Richard Coeur de Lion

In this final chapter, I consider a key tension of post-1291 crusade culture: between beliefs in the benefits of crusading for the "good health" of Latin Christendom and anxieties about the morality of religious violence. My discussion begins with the work of John Gower. As already seen in Chapter 1, Gower's *Vox Clamantis*, lamenting the evils of inter-Christian warfare, prescribes a redirection of martial energies toward the Holy Land.[1] Similarly, *In Praise of Peace*, written for Henry IV, posits crusading as an outlet for excessive chivalric "wrothe," which threatens to destroy Christendom from the inside: "And if men scholde algate wexe wrothe, / The Sarazins, whiche unto Crist be lothe, / Let men ben armed agein hem to fighte."[2] Yet when it comes to a moral consideration of the act of killing as such, the poet unequivocally condemns it as antithetical to biblical teaching. Book 3 of *Confessio Amantis* on "Wrath" has Amans asking, "To passe over the grete see / To werre and sle the Sarazin, / Is that the lawe?" to which the confessor responds: "To preche and soffre for the feith, / That have I herd the Gospell seith; / Bot for to slee, that hiere I noght."[3] In book 4, Gower explains why missions for peaceful conversion supersede military action: "A Sarazin if I sle schal, / I sle the soule forth withal, / And that was nevere Cristes lore."[4]

Criticism of crusading on moral or scriptural grounds, while voiced in the twelfth and thirteenth centuries,[5] appears to have been particularly rife in fourteenth-century England. The tensions between crusading and Lollard doctrine are well known. John Wyclif himself held contradictory views, accepting the idea of fighting enemies of the faith in some writings while in others rejecting it through such statements as "sleeyng [Christ's] tormentoures is odiouse to God."[6] Walter Brut denounced campaigns against both Christians and Muslims, as did William Swinderby.[7] And the Lollard manifesto nailed to the doors of Westminster Abbey and St. Paul's Cathedral in London in 1395 associates crusading with manslaughter: "Knythtis, þat rennen to hethnesse to geten hem a name in sleinge of men, geten miche maugre of þe king of pes."[8] Mounting criticism of war, secular and religious, among Lollard thinkers is perhaps what led some Wycliffite sympathizers who were also crusaders to express moral compunction late in life, as Celia M. Lewis suggests.[9] John Clanvowe's *The Two Ways*, for example, presumably based on firsthand experience, laments the slaughter and destruction caused by knights in search of conquests in "manye loondis."[10] Yet penitential treatises were not the sole prerogative of those bearing Lollard affinities; other veteran crusaders expressed remorse. In his *Livre de seyntz medicines*, Henry of Grosmont ascribes to the sin of anger an appetite for bloodshed that had defined his chivalric career.[11]

Concerns about knights' lust for killing were also voiced by preachers and theorists who, while in favor of crusading, sought to define its parameters and curb excesses. In his influential guide for preachers, John Bromyard bemoans the degeneracy of Christian knights and the pleasure they take in pillage and murder.[12] This position is reflected in his treatment of crusading, which he views as a fallback to missionary activity. He instructs preachers to enjoin the liberation of the Holy Land and the defense of the Church, while prohibiting them from encouraging homicide (*provocare ad homicidium infidelium*). For Bromyard, if missionizing efforts failed, a new Levantine crusade could be launched, provided it was waged with charitable motives and in a manner that did not indecently flout Christian morality.[13] Even Philippe de Mézières, one of the most diehard crusade enthusiasts of the day, warned of the moral perils of violence against non-Christians. In laying out the behaviors to be adopted by the members of his Order of the Passion, he stressed the importance of avoiding inhumane warfare and treating Muslim prisoners compassionately.[14] The post-1291 era thus witnessed the emergence and dissemination of writings, both at the margins and within the social and political mainstream, that placed religious violence under moral scrutiny, in some cases condemning it outright and in others attempting to circumscribe it.[15]

This chapter probes the boundaries between legitimate and morally transgressive religious violence in two Middle English crusade romances, *The Siege of Jerusalem* and *Richard Coeur de Lion* (hereafter *The Siege* and *RCL*). Both romances situate Jerusalem as the object of crusader aspirations and the acme of Christian collective regeneration. They literalize the regenerative power of crusading by framing the physical restoration of their leading protagonists through emotional and physical violence, drawing on notions of armed and unarmed pilgrimage as medicine for body and soul.

Therapeutic Crusading and Excessive Violence

During the fourteenth century, crusading was understood by many as a cure for the ailments of individual Christians but also of Latin Christendom as a political entity.[16] Yet despite promoting views of crusading as "healthy" and salvific, these romances deploy representational strategies that preclude readings of the depicted violence as normatively meritorious. Christians are portrayed as bloodthirsty, merciless, and cruel. Non-Christians are ascribed compassion-arousing sorrow and/or righteous anger. The perspective of aggrieved civilians and bereaved family members is foregrounded. In *The Siege*, empathic authorial pronouncements abound. These romances, I argue, inscribe ideological tensions between the redemptive, "necessary" character of crusading and the attendant atrocities, the merits of the enterprise and its moral dangers.

Given the absence of a rule of consensus to distinguish between depictions of violence as praiseworthy and reprehensible, any attempt to elucidate the authorial stances behind such representations must rely on narrative tone: the ways in which events, actions, and behaviors are characterized and framed. Examining authorial modes of evaluation in an array of war accounts spanning the high and later Middle Ages reveals certain representational patterns. In my discussion of *The Siege of Milan* in Chapter 1, I showed that casting Christian characters as sorrowful victims of violent injuries was a way of asserting the legitimacy of their cause, their entitlement to righteous vengeance. Conversely, as we will see, lengthy elaborations on the grief and suffering of enemies often served to raise questions about the nature and effects of the violence inflicted on them. Studying the ways in which *The Siege* and *RCL* reconfigure their sources reveals a common concern, on the part of the authors or adaptors, with a lust for violence that crusading could satisfy and the human costs of war. *The Siege* grounds its rhetoric of crusader vengeance in the "curative" compassion its protagonists feel for the Passion of Christ. Yet compassion is also the response it elicits toward the non-Christians upon whom this vengeance is mercilessly enacted. The audience is thus invited to partake in the romance's vindictive crusading impetus *and* decry its human implications. In *RCL*, the ethos of crusade is overstated by the eponymous king's cannibalism, which, as scholars have noted, stands as a symbol of expansionist ideology.[17] Yet at the same time, I argue, cannibalism is the locus of anxieties about the dehumanizing potential of crusading. I support this reading of *RCL* as ambivalent by reassessing the long historiographical and literary tradition of crusader cannibalism that originated in events at the siege of Ma'arra (1098) during the First Crusade, arguing that, by the time the romance was produced, cannibalism was widely understood as an

102 Therapeutic Crusading and Excessive Violence

expression of the darkest side of the enterprise: an extreme form of violence that was fiercely effective and yet symptomatic of brutality and excess.

CURATIVE VIOLENCE AND EMPATHIC RESPONSE IN *THE SIEGE OF JERUSALEM*

The Siege, estimated to have been composed in the late fourteenth century, draws freely on several sources, including the apocryphal *Vindicta salvatoris*, Jacobus de Voragine's *Legenda aurea*, Roger of Argenteuil's *Bible en françois*, Ranulph Higden's *Polychronicon*, John of Tynemouth's *Historia aurea*, and Josephus's *De bello Iudaico*.[18] It is preserved in nine manuscripts alongside other crusade-oriented romances such as *RCL*, *Duke Roland and Sir Otuel of Spain*, *The Siege of Milan*, *Octavian*, and *Sir Isumbras*.[19] Like Charlemagne, the Roman generals Titus and Vespasian, protagonists of the romance and leaders of the siege of Jerusalem in 70 CE, were icons of the crusading movement. Accounts of the First Crusade – such as William of Tyre's *Historia Ierosolimitana*, adapted into the immensely popular Old French *Eracles*, and Albert of Aachen's chronicle – situate the expedition in the trajectory of the Roman conquest of Jerusalem from Jewish occupation.[20] This view persisted in the later Middle Ages. Marino Sanudo's *Liber secretorum fidelium crucis*, writing in a section on historical precedents designed to provide direction for present and future generations, offers a lengthy report of the taking of Jerusalem and the expulsion of the Jewish population by Titus and Vespasian.[21] Pierre Dubois's crusade treatise draws a connection between the recovery mission it promotes and the events of 70 CE.[22] In Philippe de Mézières's plea for peace in Christendom and a crusade to the Holy Land, Richard II is encouraged to emulate Titus's actions.[23]

Scholars of *The Siege* have adopted different positions with regard to the identities of its characters. Some argue that given its ample use of crusade imagery, the romance is best understood as a piece of polemical writing or recruitment propaganda in which Jewish characters essentially function as placeholders for Muslims.[24] Others posit a literal understanding of the Jews *qua* Jews,[25] and yet others see Jewish and Roman identities as variable.[26] Suzanne Conklin Akbari, who considers the poem alongside First Crusade chronicles, argues that the Jews are likened to Muslims in scenes that depict them "with malicious pleasure at their plight" and to Christians in episodes that portray them "with compassion."[27] Suzanne M. Yeager adopts a similar stance toward the Romans in her exegetical study of *The Siege*, viewing them on the one hand as "depraved persecutors of the faithful" who take on an antagonistic, Antichristlike role, and on the other, "as victorious warriors for Christ," who are described using the conventions of crusade literature.[28] Thus, for Akbari and Yeager, understandings of the Jews as Muslims and the Romans as crusaders mutate into other modes of identification when the narrative elicits compassion for the Jews and presents the Romans as "depraved." Yet in post-1291 crusade culture, the image of Titus and Vespasian was closely tied to dilemmas of excessive violence and compassion or lack thereof, as I will illustrate drawing on works by Marino Sanudo and Philippe de Mézières. Moreover, the event implicitly evoked by *The Siege* – the conquest of Jerusalem during the First Crusade – had raised troubling questions about the corruptive potential and human toll of crusading. Before discussing these issues, however, I will consider two central ingredients of the romance's crusade rhetoric: the themes of compassionate vengeance and "curative" violence.

The Emotive Underpinnings of Religious Violence

The narrative impetus of *The Siege* is given when Titus, afflicted with cancer of the mouth, is healed upon lamenting Christ's Passion at the hands of the Jews (173–76). His newfound health, both physical and spiritual, is predicated on the connection between emotion and action: "A, corteys Crist! . . . / Was neuer worke þat Y wroȝt worþy þe + t[i]lle, / Ne dede þat Y [d]on haue bot þy deþ mened" (181–83). Titus pledges "to stire Nero with noye and newen his sorowe" so that he may be granted permission to set off to Jerusalem "to do the develes of dawe and þy [Christ's] deþ venge" (186–88). Sorrow stands as a physiological manifestation of injury and thus an essential buttress for retributive violence. The perspective then shifts to Titus's father, Vespasian, who, also severely ill (with leprosy), swears to avenge Christ's death if he is granted good health (201–4). Vespasian is effectively cured when, on the advice of St. Peter, he sends for a veil upon which Jesus had left his image and invested with healing powers (the Veil of Veronica); he is restored to health through Christ's "bitter woundis," a devotional setting that gives rise to collective "wepyng and wo and wryngyng of hondis / With loude dyn and dit for doil of hym one" (251–52). The spiritual healing of humankind, effected through the crucifixion of Christ and marked here by the Roman leaders' conversion to Christianity, is manifested in physical terms, drawing on medieval medical notions of interdependence between moral state and physical symptoms. Sickness of the body was understood to correlate with moral failure, and could thus be remedied through penitence according to the precepts of Christ the physician.[29] The spiritual and physical regeneration of the two Roman leaders takes the form of a penitential crusade to avenge Christ, whom they "mychel ... loued" (277): they are reborn as Christian kings "þat for Crist werred" (194, 954).

The theme of affective vengeance has received little attention among scholars interested in *The Siege*'s crusade imagery.[30] Yet the image of Titus and Vespasian compassionately avenging Christ's Passion was foundational to the crusading movement. Two sources are particularly illuminating: the eleventh-century pseudoencyclical of Sergius IV, which appears to have been composed by the Cluniac monks of Moissac prior to and in support of the First Crusade;[31] and the twelfth-century semihistorical narrative of the First Crusade known as the *Chanson d'Antioche*, which circulated in versions spanning the thirteenth and fourteenth centuries.[32] The encyclical of Sergius IV grounds its promotion of a *passagium* to Jerusalem in the crucifixion of Christ on Mount Calvary, "in co nos suo sanavit libore" (where he healed us by his own wounds). The act of retribution that the author calls for in response to the Holy Sepulchre's destruction – for which "universa aecclesiam vel urbe Roma turbata est et in [im]mensa lamentatione posita est" (the universal church and the city of Rome are deeply troubled and put in a state of great lamentation) – is situated in the line of Titus and Vespasian's vengeance for Christ's death: "Spero, credo et certissime teneo qui, per virtutem Domini nostri Jesu-Christi, nostra erit victoriam, sicut fuit in diebus Titi et Vespasiani, qui Dei Filii morte vindicaverunt" (I hope, I believe, and most certainly I hold true that through the virtue of our Lord Jesus Christ victory will be ours as it was in the days of Titus and Vespasian, who avenged the death of the son of God).[33] The *Chanson d'Antioche* likewise traces the First Crusade back to the Roman generals, cast as embodiments of the crusading ideal. One of its opening scenes is of Christ on the cross prophesying the coming of the crusaders "oltremer" to take "venjement" of his death.[34] The author gives further prophetic force to the enterprise by invoking the image of Titus and Vespasian lamenting Christ's injuries before taking Jerusalem: "Dont fu vengiés Nos Sire et encore sera" (And thus our Lord was avenged, and will be again). The protagonists of the *chanson* are urged to emulate the Roman leaders' example if they are to earn the reward of "jovente" (youthful vigor) and a crown in paradise.[35] Redemption, enabled by Christ's Passion and assuming a bodily dimension here, depends on the reciprocation of his sacrifice through compassionate vengeance.

If the theme of affective vengeance is a key component of *The Siege*'s crusade rhetoric, so too is that of "salutary" violence. In the post-1291 era,

The Emotive Underpinnings of Religious Violence   105

connections between crusading and the good health of Christian individuals, the Latin West, and the Holy Land were frequently drawn. Sanudo devised the whole of his monumental treatise as three remedies for the infected body of the Holy Land.[36] More relevant to *The Siege*, however, is Mézières's notion of the passage of *outremer* as a medicine for the malady of warfare within Europe, detailed at length in his *Epistre au Roi Richart*. The author exhorts the English and French kings to present themselves before God, ready "pour vengier son injure" (to avenge His wrongs), lest they be struck down by leprosy, like Miriam.[37] The curative power invested in crusading is allegorized in the author's conception of the Order of the Passion, which he holds responsible for administering a "petite medecine preparative" (simple preparatory medicine): a *passagium particulare* to pave the way for the *passagium generale* to follow.[38] This order, as spelled out in his *Sustance de la chevalerie de la passion de Jhesu Crist*, is named thus to "rafressir et renoveler la piteuse memoire de la Passion du doulz Jhesu Crist entre les crestiens" (refresh and renew the piteous memory of the Passion of Jesus Christ among Christians).[39] For Mézières, Christian self-destructiveness is a body-political disease that finds remedy in compassionate vengeance for the injuries inflicted on God and Christ.

The Siege mobilizes a similar agenda to that of Mézières. As the siege on Jerusalem is prolonged, Titus and Vespasian receive news from Rome of how Emperor Nero had killed his mother, his wife, and many "Cristen fele þat on Crist leued" (902). Nero opts for suicide over execution when Roman citizens and senators rise up in anger. Intense political turmoil over his succession ensues, as emperors come and go in a series of political coups spurred by hatred, vengeance, and conflicting claims. Eventually, Vespasian is elected to the imperial crown by the senate and must return to Rome. Conforming to legal crusading stipulations, his vow to avenge Christ of his injuries is passed on to his son Titus, who thus bears sole responsibility for the mission.[40] At this point, Titus's health suddenly deteriorates when he averts his attention from the external enemy – the Jew – and toward the internal, domestic concerns of Rome, as he expresses joy at his father's coronation: "And Titus for þe tydyng ha[þ] take [so] mychel ioye / þat in his synwys soudeynly a syknesse is fallen" (1027–28). The only person capable of healing him, Josephus (a Jew), presents him with a Jewish man whom Titus hates with such intensity that the "hote yre" that so quickly rises upon seeing him makes the blood spread in his veins, and his sinews return to their proper state:[41]

106   Therapeutic Crusading and Excessive Violence

> And he ferkiþ hym forþ, fettes ful blyue
> A man to þe mody kyng þat he moste hated
> And yn bryngeþ þe burne to his beddes syde.
> Whan Tytus saw þat segge sodeynly with eyen,
> His herte in an hote yre so hetterly riseþ
> þat þe blode bygan to [b]red[e] abrode in þe vaynes
> And þe synwes resorte in here self kynde. (1046–52)

Titus's misdirected joy creates an imbalance of his bodily humors, which manifests in coldness (1030) and lethargy (1032), in accordance with medieval humoral theory. Medieval medicine ascribed to emotions the ability to both cause and cure imbalanced humoral states; Titus's anger causes the vital spirit and natural heat to move from his heart to his extremes, thus rectifying the imbalance.[42] The proliferation of works on the influence of emotions on disease and recovery would have ensured the rhetorical efficacy and ideological potency of this image. It is significant, moreover, that Titus's recovery is made possible by a combination of anger and *hate*, an emotion with strong connotations of durability. Richard Lavynham's treatise on the sins defines "hate of herte" as a subcategory of anger that endures in silence and bides its time.[43] Thomas Aquinas opposes hatred, a stable desire for another's evil, with anger, which can be harnessed in the service of justice and assuaged by revenge.[44] This opposition between the release that vengeance provides for anger and the resilience of hatred is also highlighted by the author of the anonymous *Fasciculus morum*, a fourteenth-century preacher's book that circulated in England, and by Giles of Rome in his *De regimine principum*.[45] Giles, moreover, distinguishes the two emotions in terms of their scope: hate can be cultivated toward an entire group of people, whereas anger has a more limited reach.[46] Thus, what *The Siege* seems to be suggesting is that, for the good health of Christians – and by extension, Christendom – a perennial "external" enemy upon which to focus violent energy is needed. Invoking both contemporary and earlier ideas about emotions and holy war, *The Siege* grounds its narrative in a logic of curative, salvific crusade, underpinned morally and rhetorically by the compassion its protagonists and readers are invited to partake in for Christ's Passion.

Christian Brutality, Self-Inflicted Death, and the Compassionate Voices of the Enemy

Despite the carefully crafted moral, ideological, and diegetic structures set up by *The Siege* to exalt the necessities of Christian religious violence, the narrative makes an unexpected shift in its ambivalent rendering of the realities of war. Through increasingly complex and nuanced aesthetics of violence, the romance poses probing questions about the morality and effects of religious violence. The notion that the horrors inherent in even the most doctrinally sanctioned type of warfare should be deplored with anguish of soul (*animi dolore*) stems from the origins of just war theory, with Augustine's *De civitate dei*:

> Sed sapiens, inquiunt, justa bella gesturus est. Quasi non, si se hominem meminit, multo magis dolebit justorum necessitatem sibi exstitisse, bellorum ... Haec itaque mala tam magna, tam horrenta, tam saeva quisquis cum dolore considerat, miseriam fateatur. Quisquis autem vel patitur ea sine animi dolore, vel cogitat, multo utique miserius ideo se putat beatum, quia et humanum perdidit sensum.

> But the wise man, they say, will wage just wars. Surely, however, if he remembers that he is a human being, he will be much readier to deplore the fact that he is under the necessity of waging even just wars ... Let everyone, therefore, who reflects with pain upon such great evils, upon such horror and cruelty, acknowledge that this is misery. And if anyone either endures them or thinks of them without anguish of soul, his condition is still more miserable: for he thinks himself happy only because he has lost all human feeling.[47]

For Augustine, just wars are necessary in the face of iniquity, and yet the evils within them are to be condemned, lest we devolve into a subhuman state. It is likewise the humanity of Christians, and thus their inherent sinfulness, that forms the premise for an analogous position upheld by the anonymous chronicler of the siege of Lisbon during the Second Crusade. Christians are enjoined to feel sorrow and pity for the enemy because they too are sinners, also exposed to the scourge of divine vengeance.[48] Thus, "Dolendum et gaudendum est. Nam cum perversos quosque Deus omnipotens percutit, pereuntium miserie condolendum et iusticie iudicis congaudendum" (There is a necessity for both sorrow and rejoicing. For when the omnipotent God strikes down sinners, whoever they be, one must grieve for the sufferings of the perishing yet rejoice at the justice of the judge).[49]

Similar tensions transpire in Sanudo's and Mézières's treatments of the siege of Jerusalem by Titus and Vespasian, testifying to the currency of such questions in the context of the events of 70 CE. Drawing on Josephus's *De bello Iudaico*, Sanudo presents the destruction of the holy city as an act of divinely ordained vengeance for Christ's injuries in the same light as the crusaders' massacre of the inhabitants of Jerusalem in 1099.[50] Yet after describing in highly affective terms the suffering of the

108   Therapeutic Crusading and Excessive Violence

Jews – "ubique pauor, morientium gemitus, viventium desperation" (everywhere there was terror, the groans of the dying, the desperation of the living) – the author has Titus decrying the enterprise's human costs: "Proiecta tandem multitudine cadaverum per muros Ciuitatis, Titus alte ingemuit; & manum ad coelum elevans, protectabatur illud nunquam sibi ascribi: quia veniam dare voluit, si assuisset deditio, & armorum deposition" (At last with many of the corpses thrown from the city walls, Titus groaned aloud and raised his hand to heaven, he protested that this should never be ascribed to him since he had wished to show lenience if surrender and the surrender of arms had been agreed).[51] The violence, required by God, is bemoaned as lamentably excessive. A comparable image of Titus, a "large et piteux" (magnanimous and pitiful) leader, having great "compassion des mors" (compassion for those who died), is given by Mézières:

> Et quant le tresvaillant et debonnaire Titus vit si grant mortalite de ses propres anemis et anemis de sa loy ... et vit que les Juyfs de Jherusalem jetoient les mors sans nombre par dessus les murs, en emplissant les fosses, le tresdebonnaire Titus, ce veant, ot si grant compassion qu'il leva les yeux et les mains au ciel et ploura tendrement, disant a Dieu, Sire Dieux, tu vois bien ma douleur que je de ceste gent, car c'il se voussissent estre rendus a l'empire de Romme et le recognoistre comme il faisoient devant, un tout seul n'en fust mors.

> When the valiant and worthy Titus saw the great mortality of those who were the enemies of his religion ... and saw, too, how the Jews of Jerusalem cast their dead, who could not be numbered, over the city walls into the ditches, the good Titus, seeing all this, was so overcome by pity that, raising his eyes and hands to Heaven, with tears he cried to God, Lord God, thou seest how much I grieve for these people, for had they been willing to submit to Rome and recognize her as they had done in times past, not a single man would have died.[52]

It is noteworthy that for Mézières, the object of Titus's campaign, to confront the "anemis de sa loy," does not conflict with the purpose for which the episode is invoked: to warn of the moral dangers of war and spur compassion for the slain.[53]

The prescribed response to the atrocities of war, as illustrated by Sanudo's and Mézières's accounts, is compassionate grief.[54] In both texts, Titus laments the human toll of the slaughter that he, as agent of divine judgment, had no choice but to commit. The *Siege*-poet's choices when depicting Titus and Vespasian during and after the scenes of graphic violence are, however, different: their actions are invested less with a sense

Brutality and Compassionate Voices   109

of grievous necessity than with one of unsettling brutality. The audience's compassion for the Jews is therefore not achieved through emulation of the Christian protagonists' emotions, but instead though a moral evaluation of their lack of restraint, which crystallizes in the suffering of the besieged. The emerging representational aesthetic is best understood, as we will see, in relation to more critical historical accounts of the harms of war and crusading. While the final stages of the siege see Titus proffering mercy to the Jews, a comparison with *The Siege*'s sources – Josephus's *De bello Iudaico* and Ranulph Higden's *Polychronicon*, for these passages – reveals that his merciful intentions are downplayed, and are promptly reneged on as he vehemently resolves "neuer pyte ne pees profre hem more / Ne gome þat he gete may to no grace taken" (1179–80).[55] In fact, not only does the *Siege*-author omit numerous instances of virtuous pity, which feature in Josephus's and Higden's narratives, but he or she also foregrounds the Christians' lack thereof, particularly when confronted with the possibility of plunder.[56] In a similar effort, the poet heightens the unbridled passions at play in the enactment of divine vengeance on the battlefield. As noted by Elisa Narin van Court, the romance proceeds to a key inversion in reworking its sources: it is no longer the Jews who are spurred by immoderate rage, but Vespasian who is depicted as "neuer ... so wroþe" (375), "wode we[ll]ande wroþ" (385), and "wroþ as a wode bore" (785), repeatedly cursing his enemies to the devil.[57] The Jews, on the other hand, are described as brave, valiant, and noble (621, 625, 867).

Anxieties about the morality of violence are most palpable in the romance's treatment of Jewish suffering and grief. After an initial battle that leaves the field drenched in blood, judgment is rendered on the Jewish high priest Caiaphas, held responsible for Christ's death, and his twelve clerks.[58] Caiaphas's fate is staged as a grotesque, distorted reproduction of the suffering and crucifixion of Christ. Flayed alive, dragged behind horses, and hung upside down on high gallows with wild animals shredding his flesh, Caiaphas is pierced and tortured to death (697–708). His torment is heightened through the accretion of details absent from the poem's source (here, Roger d'Argenteuil's *Bible en françois*), as is the reaction of the Jewish onlookers – one of empathic sorrow, leading to collective suicide:[59]

> þe Iewes walten ouer þe walles for wo at þat tyme;
> Seuen hundred slow hemself for sorow of here clerkes.
> Somme hent he[m by þe] heere and fram þe hed pulled
> And somme [doun] for deil + dasch[e]n to grounde. (713–16)

Caiaphas's execution marks the culmination of the Christian collaborative endeavor to avenge Christ's death. Yet the narrative conveys trauma and intolerable pain, rather than triumph. Acts of self-sacrifice spurred by despair had special resonance in crusade history, recalling pogroms against Europe's Jewish communities that accompanied the First, Second, and Third Crusades, but also, as discussed below, large-scale suicides of Muslims during the siege of Jerusalem in 1099. The pogroms, although subsumed into a crusading logic of revenge against God's enemies,[60] were condemned by many contemporaries as manifestations of the worst excesses of militant Christian fervor. Both Jewish and Christian authors stressed the unbridled passions, brutality, and greed of the crusaders responsible for the massacres of 1096 in the Rhineland and 1190 at York, while deploying similar discursive dynamics as *The Siege* to frame the collective suicides provoked by these attacks. In his report of the slaughters of 1096 at the inception of the First Crusade, Albert of Aachen foregrounds the anger, brutality, and mercilessness of the crusaders, which he contrasts with the anguish of the Jews, as men, women, and children opt for death at each other's hands over the ruthless treatment of the assailants: "Matres pueris lactentibus, quod dictu nefas est, guttura ferro secabant, alios transforabant, uolentes pocius sic propriis manibus perire, quam incircumcisorum armis extingui" (Mothers with children at the breast – how horrible to relate – would cut their throats with knives, would stab others, preferring that they should die thus at their own hands, rather than be killed by the weapons of the uncircumcised).[61] The Christians' bloodthirstiness is similarly set against the Jews' extreme suffering, culminating in collective suicide and infanticide, in Hebrew chronicler Eliezer bar Nathan's report of the same events.[62] This is also the case in William of Newburgh's account of the massacres of 1190 at the outset of the Third Crusade; inflamed by fury (*furor*), the mob is portrayed as raging against the Jews of Lynn, Stamford, and York, who are driven to respond to Christian violence with self-inflicted death.[63]

What is particularly striking about *The Siege*'s treatment of crusade warfare is that, like Albert of Aachen's report of the events of 1096, the narrative is punctuated by empathic authorial pronouncements such as "was deil to byholde" (645), "was pite to byholde" (1247), "þat deil was to hure" (1101), "were [tore] forto telle" (1069), or "bot alle was boteles bale" (1145). These interjections, by which the author inserts himself or herself in the narrative to elicit compassion for the Jewish victims, feature prominently around the infamous episode of infanticide and cannibalism. The scene directly follows Titus's healing from sickness through "hate" and

Brutality and Compassionate Voices

"hote yre," offering an immediate counterpoint to the poem's endorsement of restorative violence. The force of the cure-through-anger metaphor is juxtaposed with equally potent imagery invoked to convey the emotional and physical distress of the Jews. In the *Siege*-poet's version, the troubles of the town become "[tore] forto telle" (1069), as the besieged are afflicted with sorrow (1079), having neither food to eat nor water to drink, except for the tears they wept (1074). In line with the romance's general concern with the suffering of Jewish women,[64] Mary's act of cannibalistic infanticide is no longer decried as horrid, unnatural, and spurred by fury, as in Higden and Josephus's accounts,[65] but is transformed into one of piteous grief, performed in despair by a "myld" and "worþi" mother (1081 and 1093):

> Rostyþ rigge and rib with rewful wordes,
> Sayþ, "sone, vpon eche side our sorow is alofte:
> Batail about þe borwe our bodies to quelle;
> Withyn h[u]nger so hote þat ne3 our herte brestyþ." (1083–86)

The infanticidal mother responds to extreme conditions with equally extreme actions, similar in scope and tenor to those in Eliezer bar Nathan's report of the massacres of 1096: "The most gentle and tender of women slaughtered the child of her delight."[66] In both accounts, the performance of infanticide reflects negatively not on the Jewish community but on the Christian violence and horrific circumstances to which its members respond. Eliezer's sorrow – "It is for them that I weep, that tears drop from my eye"[67] – is paralleled in *The Siege* by that of the Jewish witnesses to the scene:

> [Forþ] þey went for wo wep[ande sore]
> And sayn, "alas in þis lif how longe schul we dwelle?
> 3it beter were at o brayde in batail to deye
> þan þus in langur to lyue and lengþen our fyne." (1097–1100)

In the cognate passages of the *Siege*-poet's sources, the onlookers' stupefaction and horror convey outright condemnation of an unspeakable crime, branded as heinous and abhorrent.[68] Here, their sorrow and the act itself operate in a different register, as comments on the direness of their fate at the hands of merciless Christians. The crusade has become a force of destruction and a source of unbearable misery.

Acts of infanticide and cannibalism, when they occurred (or were believed to have occurred), were often framed by medieval authors in such a way as to convey moral evaluation of the persons or conditions that provoked them. Marino Sanudo, for instance, tells of a Christian woman who, following Ṣalāḥ al-Dīn's conquest of Jerusalem in 1187, kills her own son in despair upon arriving in Tripoli and being stripped of her vital belongings by fellow coreligionists: "Supra modum animo perturbate, & spiritu tristitiae & desperationis absorpta, in marinas iecit undas filium ex se natum" (After this treatment, with mind disturbed, in a spirit of sadness, and oppressed by desperation she threw her own son into the sea). Infanticide is presented as an extreme physical manifestation of emotional agony, triggered by the "crudelitatis excessum" (excessive cruelty) of the men of Tripoli.[69] Cannibalism was also an act that demanded moral assessment, with some authors directing censure at the perpetrators and others at those who prompted the act. For example, when Guillaume le Breton relates the cannibalism of the besieged at Château Gaillard, a Norman fortress captured by Philip II of France in 1204, the perpetrators are portrayed as pitiful victims of the cruelty and inhumanity of the French besiegers.[70] If Josephus's and Higden's narratives present Mary's cannibalism as evidence of the monstrosity of the Jews, thus justifying their final destruction in the eyes of the Romans,[71] The Siege instead imbues the act with pathos and humanity, causing it to reflect critically on the unbridled rage and violence of the crusaders.

Moral Discomfort and the Jerusalem Massacres of 1099

The event that would have immediately come to mind for readers and listeners of The Siege is the Christian siege of Jerusalem during the First Crusade. As Akbari has noted, the Roman siege of 70 CE and the crusader siege of 1099 were intertwined, not only in chronicles, but also in integrated chronologies such as Lambert of Saint-Omer's Liber floridus, and through the homonymous relationship they shared, where vernacular texts with the same title could refer to either of the two events.[72] The history of the conquest of Jerusalem in 1099 was well known through such popular chronicles as those of Robert of Reims and William of Tyre, which circulated widely in vernacular translations in the fourteenth and fifteenth centuries.[73] Marcus Bull and Damien Kempf observe that "no other event in the Middle Ages stimulated such a large burst of historical writing."[74] That the massacres of Jerusalem – which most claimed were unprecedented[75] – raised moral questions for European chroniclers is evinced by just how variegated their accounts were when it came to the tone they employed and the details they included or omitted.[76] Akbari has drawn attention to important resemblances between the depiction of Jews in The Siege and that of Muslims in First Crusade chronicles: scenes where both

Moral Discomfort and the Jerusalem Massacres 113

are reduced to faceless, nameless bodies, are ascribed opulent wealth, and are characterized as misbelievers.[77] But while Akbari sees a transfer of identity occurring in *The Siege*'s scenes of compassion-arousing Jewish suffering, whereby the Jews are momentarily likened to Christians rather than Muslims,[78] I instead argue that the dominant representational economy is maintained. Indeed, a number of First Crusade narratives express ambivalence similar to *The Siege* toward Christian displays of excessive violence, also by dwelling compassionately on the suffering and human costs involved. The Jews of *The Siege* preserve their status as non-Christian enemies of the crusaders, even when portrayed sympathetically, and as such, they continue to illuminate the romance's crusade rhetoric.

The most emblematic scene of the crusader conquest of 1099 was likely that of the crusaders wading in streams of Muslim blood up to their horses' knees, disseminated in the high and later Middle Ages in such influential works as the chronicles of Siegebert of Gembloux and Otto of Freising, and Vincent of Beauvais's *Speculum historiale*.[79] In Siegebert's version, which spawned numerous continuations, the paraphrase includes a portrayal of the crusaders raging uncontrollably.[80] The *Siege* uses the same imagery when relating the initial battle in front of the city. It describes the Christians as "gre[m]ed griffouns" (556), hacking down thousands of "heþen," so that "baches [streams] woxen ablode about in þe vale" (563) and "kne-depe in þe dale dascheden stedes" (576),[81] and the survivors as retreating to Jerusalem "with mychel wo" (616). As in *The Siege*, the moral implications of slaughter on such a scale were not lost on many chroniclers of the First Crusade. Significantly, they conveyed ambivalence through the same representational means as *The Siege*: authorial interjections of shock, horror, and empathy; unrestrained, violent emotions pitted against extreme, poignant distress; the translation of impotence and emotional agony into self-inflicted death; and the suffering and killing of noncombatants, women especially.

The anonymous author of the *Gesta Francorum*, for example, relates the crusaders' frenzy upon breaching Jerusalem's defenses, inflicting a massacre such (*talis occisio*) that the blood in Solomon's Temple was up to their ankles. The tone is uncritical at first, but when the crusaders' bloodthirstiness prompts them to ignore the protection their leaders had granted the survivors, sneaking up to the temple's roof and cutting down men and women so that many are driven to throw themselves headlong to the earth, the author has Tancred rebuke them.[82] The episode is also recorded by Gilo of Paris, who contrasts Tancred's and Gaston of Béarn's feelings of mercy with the crusaders' insatiable lust for blood: "Mane dato non plenus

114   Therapeutic Crusading and Excessive Violence

adhuc tot cladibus ultor / Miles id exiguum quod adhuc superesse sciebat / Sanguinis in paucis furatur" (When morning came, the knights' vengeance was still not sated by the downfall of so many, and in slaughtering a few they stole what little amount of blood they knew still remained to be shed).[83] The author elaborates on the fate of the Muslims trapped on the temple's roof, impelled with manly courage (*animoque uirili*) to run upon each other's swords. The survivors' sorrow is foregrounded as they collect and pile up the bodies of the dead: "Gentiles nondum dampnati flendo legebant / Et congesta simul ducebant montis ad instar" (the heathens who had not yet been destroyed wept as they picked them up and collected them together, heaping them up like a mountain).[84] Nowhere else in Gilo of Paris's narrative is the Muslims' distress given such prominence as in this instance of rampant and unsanctioned vindictiveness.

If these two authors' opinions of the massacres remain somewhat conjectural in the absence of more explicit markers of ambivalence, the same cannot be said of the accounts of Albert of Aachen (who appears to have relied on the oral reports of crusaders upon their return to Europe) and William of Tyre (who wrote at the request of King Amaury of Jerusalem).[85] While vindicating the capture of Jerusalem as God's right-eous judgment, William betrays clear moral reservations about the magni-tude of the slaughter.[86] His disapproval of the crusaders – at the outset portrayed as "infidelium cruorem sitiens, et ad caedem omnino proclivis" (athirst for the blood of the enemy and wholly intent upon destruction)[87] – crystallizes in the following description, which wraps up his report of the initial carnage: "Tanta autem per urbem erat strages hostium, tantaque sanguinis effusio, ut etiam victoribus posset taedium et horrorem ingerere" (So frightful was the massacre throughout the city, so terrible the shedding of blood, that even the victors experienced sensations of horror and loathing).[88] William's picture of the crusaders' horror and disgust was replicated in important later works, such as Roger of Wendover's *Flores historiarum* and Matthew Paris's *Chronica majora*.[89] William invokes the term *strages* (massacre) throughout his account, vividly describing headless bodies, mutilated limbs, and the cold-blooded extermination of men, women, and children. His perspective merges with that of the victims: "Verum et ipsos victores a planta pedis usque ad verticem cruore madentes peridulosum erat conspicere, et horrorem quemdam inferebant occurenti-bus" (Still more dreadful was it to gaze upon the victors themselves, dripping with blood from head to foot, an ominous sight which brought terror to all who met them).[90] As in *The Siege*, this transferal of authorial sympathy, the extent of the slaughter, the mercilessness of the crusaders,

Moral Discomfort and the Jerusalem Massacres

and the anguish of the victims forbid acceptance of the depicted violence as normatively meritorious.

Albert of Aachen's account is even more explicitly critical of the crusaders. In a lengthy report colored by emotive contrasts and mostly narrated from the victims' viewpoint, Albert tells of a massacre that took place on the third day after the capture of the city. The crusaders are cast as pitiless in their anger, "puellas uero, mulieres, matronas nobiles, et foetas, cum pueris tenellis detruncantes aut lapidibus obruentes" (beheading or striking down with stones girls, women, noble ladies, even pregnant women, and very young children).[91] This depiction recalls *The Siege*'s horrific portrayal of a pregnant woman hit on the womb by a stone during an attack spurred by Christian wrath.[92] Albert notes that the massacre is officially sanctioned by the expedition's leaders, yet his tone suggests lamentable excess and a transgression of the boundaries of acceptable human conduct:

> Econtra puelle, mulieres, matrone, metu momentanee mortis angustiate, et horrore grauissime necis concusee, Christianos in iugulum utriusque sexus bachantes ac seuientes, medios pro liberanda uita amplexabantur. Quedam pedibus eorum aduoluebantur, de uita et salute sua illos nimium miserando fletu et eiulatu sollicitantes. Pueri uero quinquennii aut triennii matrum patrumque crudelem casum intuentes, una fletum et miserum clamorem multiplicabant. Sed frustra hec pietatis et misericordie signa fiebant. Nam Christiani neci sic totum animum laxauerant, ut non sugens masculus aut femina nedum infans unius anni uiuens manum percussoris euaderet.

> By contrast [to the crusaders], girls, women, ladies, tormented by fear of imminent death, and horror-struck by the violent slaughter, were embracing the Christians in their midst even as they were raving and venting their rage on the throats of both sexes, in the hope of saving their lives. Some were wound about the Christians' feet, begging them with piteous weeping and wailing for their lives and safety. When children of five or three years old saw the cruel fate of their mothers and fathers, of one accord they intensified the weeping and wretched clamor. But they were making these signals for pity and mercy in vain. For the Christians gave over their whole hearts to the slaughter, so that not a suckling little male child or female, not even an infant of one year would escape alive the hand of the murderer.[93]

What William's and Albert's accounts both vividly and troublingly capture, as does *The Siege*, is the degeneration of righteous vengeance into ferocious bloodlust. Like *The Siege*, their reports register profound anxieties about the bloodthirstiness of crusaders, the harms of unbridled violence, and war's capacity for horror.

In its evocation of the events of 1099, *The Siege* turns to a historical moment when the ideology of crusade as vengeance was being put to the test for the first time. The taking of Jerusalem in 1099 was certainly a triumph that Christendom would strive to relive for centuries. During the later Middle Ages, this aspiration was endowed with a curative dimension, representing the way to restore Christendom to "good health." Yet the siege of 1099 also went down in history as an unprecedented massacre, epitomized by the horrific image of the crusaders riding up to their horses' knees in the blood of the slain. Accordingly, chroniclers dealt with the event in different ways: some with adamant vindication and others with discomfort and disapproval. *The Siege*, I have argued, comes closer in tone to the latter group. If the Christian characters of *The Siege* are certainly at odds with Augustinian precepts of compassionate suffering with the enemy, the romance's audience, on the other hand, is invited to acknowledge the horror, cruelty, and misery of war, and to lament the Jews' fate with "animi dolore" (anguish of soul).

RICHARD COEUR DE LION AND THE BOUNDARIES OF RELIGIOUS VIOLENCE

Similar tensions agitate the semihistorical, semifantastical romance of *RCL*. In its portrayal of King Richard, his belligerent disposition, and violent actions that sometimes seem praiseworthy and are at others infused with ambivalence, *RCL* arouses mixed feelings. Critics have often interpreted the king's objectionable actions – cannibalism, above all – as troubling to modern readers but not to medieval audiences, who are assumed to have viewed them as expressions of Christian heroism, crusade ideology, and nationalist fervor.[94] Yet the legacy of Richard I in medieval England was by no means entirely positive. Although acclaimed by many as an archetype of knightly valor, a model crusader, and an expert in warfare, he was also condemned for his moral and chivalric excesses. Accusations of cruelty and excessive violence were rife, disseminated by the chronicles of Ralph of Coggeshall, Gervase of Canterbury, and Gerald of Wales.[95] Jean Flori speculates that such assessments may have originated in Richard's wholesale massacre of Muslim prisoners at Acre in 1191, compounded by other breaches to chivalric ethics, such as the violation of oaths.[96] Richard's ambivalent reputation persisted in the post-1291 era, propagated by influential works such as John Bromyard's *Summa praedicantium* and Ranulph Higden's *Polychronicon*.[97] The latter, in particular, gives a very mixed

Moral Discomfort and the Jerusalem Massacres 117

rendering of Richard's life, derived from a no longer extant account by Stephen Langton. According to Higden, the king's reign was, from the outset, blemished by the "cruel dedes" perpetrated against Jewish communities during his coronation, which he had failed to punish. He then incurred the wrath of his counselors by selling lands and castles, emptying "meny men purses and bagges" to finance his Holy Land campaign. The crusade is declared to be grounded "nou3t onliche in holy entent and for cause of [þe] fey, but for to desire of her owne helthe and hope of greet hap and fortune." While Richard is not singled out for blame, the failure of the expedition is imputed to the "evel dedes" of the crusaders.[98] The king's shortcomings are most directly broached near the end of his life in an episode, also recorded by Roger of Howden, that sees the crusade preacher Fulk of Neuilly accusing him of pride, cupidity, and lechery.[99] Glorified but also disputed, Richard I represented a choice persona for romance writers to explore both the heroic and ambivalent aspects of chivalric violence.

In this subchapter, I reassess previous scholarship on *RCL* by exposing a subtext of evaluation and critique of Richard's violent acts, introduced in key episodes in the romance's textual transmission. The king's cultural liminality, I suggest, was exploited in the course of the romance's complex manuscript history to question and elicit reflection on the boundaries of acceptable and reprehensible crusader conduct. Nowhere is the romance's preoccupation with the nature, limitations, and effects of violence more evident than in the scenes of cannibalism, which count among a number of late fourteenth-century "romance-like" interpolations, contained principally in what critics refer to as the A-version, grafted onto the earlier and more "historical" B-version of the text.[100] While scholars have mostly considered Richard's cannibalism in terms of its negotiations of nationhood, race, and theology,[101] I will instead situate it within the context of moral discourses on violence at play in other literary and historical treatments of crusader cannibalism. This tradition underpins *RCL*'s two episodes of anthropophagy: the first encodes religious warfare as politically healthy, while the second exposes the cruel, ferocious impulses it could arouse. As we will see, this second episode conforms to a tendency in earlier noncrusading scenes (also in the A-version) to interrogate Richard's actions by emphasizing the pain and protests of bereaved friends and relatives. *RCL* sets up continuities in its characterization of Christians and Muslims: both are presented as sorrowful, fearful, and righteously angry victims of Richard's unbridled violence.

Ambivalence in the Interpolations

The episodes of cannibalism emerged in *RCL*'s manuscript history in the late fourteenth century alongside the interpolation of approximately 1,200 lines to the beginning of the romance, relating the king's demonic heritage, the tournament in which he contends disguised, and his preparatory crusade and imprisonment in Germany. These additions, which first appear in London, British Library, MS Egerton 2862 (c. 1390) and Cambridge, Gonville and Caius College, MS 175 (c. 1400), exhibit concern with unsettling aspects of Richard's background and behavior.[102] The narrative's focal point of emotional response is established early on in Richard's demonic origins. In search of "þe ffeyrest wymman þat wore on liff" (51) for Richard's father, Henry, to marry, the messengers who are sent out happen upon a ship of fabulous yet distressing powers, belonging to Cassodorien's father, Corbaryng, king of Antioch. The initial reaction of these Christian knights is, significantly, intense anguish (58). The sentiment of uneasiness that the narrative pins on the demonic queen is reinforced when, on the morning following her wedding with Henry, she reveals her physical inability to witness the Eucharist and faints: "þe qwene fel in swowne adoun; / þe folk wondryd and were adrad" (190–91). Her unorthodox response to the holy sacrament – aligning her with other alleged slanderers of the Eucharist, notably witches[103] – is reiterated when, fifteen years later (but only a few lines later in the narrative), upon being prevented from withdrawing from mass, she yet again succeeds in escaping the imposed outcome, this time flying out of a window in the church's roof (227–34). These events would have evoked for contemporary audiences the legend of the Angevin dynasty's descent from the devil, disseminated, for example, by Higden's *Polychronicon*. Like others, Higden used the legend as ammunition for critique: to support charges of royal tyranny and cruelty.[104] Yet the introduction of Cassodorien in the A-version manuscripts does more than construct Richard's identity as demonic. It ascribes to him Muslim ancestry: Corbaryng, Cassodorien's father and king of Antioch, is a name the text appropriates from the Muslim leader of the *Chanson d'Antioche*, whose conversion to Christianity is recounted by the *Chrétienté Corbaran*.[105]

The connection between Richard's demonic origins and his violent temperament is established when he fights anonymously in a tournament before embarking on a preparatory crusade to the Holy Land.[106] Richard's feats of arms are presented as heroic yet harmful to the chivalric community of which he is a member. Here and elsewhere in the A-version interpolations, Richard's actions are placed under close moral scrutiny through a consistent mode of narration: they are first recounted by the narrator, and then again by members of the injured parties. Richard, dressed in black, riding "as he were wood" (463) and charging "full egerly" (290), leaves the first knight who challenges him "nye deed" (294) – which generates, according to Sir Thomas of Moulton's recounting of events, dread on the part of the onlookers (482). Richard's second contender is less fortunate. The king, described as "stout and sauage" (485), wielding his shaft "wiþ gret rage" (486), kills both man and horse: "His necke he brake there a two: / His horse and he fell to grounde, / And dyed bothe in that stounde" (298–300). In response to this, a third knight, who will thereafter rise to the challenge, decries the damage inflicted on the knightly fellowship: "þis is a deuyl, and no man, / þat oure folk felles and sleth!" (500–1).[107] Finally, when Richard unhorses this third contestant, a "hardy and good" knight (305), all others remain paralyzed, fearing for their lives: "Off hym þey were adred ful sore / þat non durste jouste wiþ hym efft: / Lest he hadde hem here lyf bereft" (514–16). Sir Thomas and Sir Fulk repeatedly describe Richard as "woode," "wroþ," "egre," "grym," and "sterne," compounding these characterizations with accusations of devilishness (500, 529–30, 574). At the close of the episode, the king attempts to mitigate Thomas's and Fulk's righteous indignation by revealing his previously concealed identity: "Takes nou3t to greef, for it was j" (586).

Ascribing excessive, objectionable knightly anger and bloodshed to Satan's influence was a common authorial practice, as Kate McGrath has shown in analyzing eleventh- and twelfth-century Anglo-Norman historical accounts. The purpose of such analogies was to signal the emotion's status not as *bona ira* (good anger) but as a deadly sin.[108] This narrative strategy was also deployed in crusade accounts to condemn wrathful dissension among Christians. The eyewitness report of the siege of Lisbon (1147), for instance, imputes outbreaks of anger that threaten to destroy the Christian army from the inside to the poison of the devil's malice (*malitie virus*).[109] Infighting that permeates chronicles of the Third Crusade was also perceived as the devil's work.[110] In his mid fourteenth-century *De itinere Terrae Sanctae liber*, Ludolph of Suchem ascribes the fall of crusader Acre to the citizens' "odiosam discordiam" (hateful quarrels), which, instigated by Satan, result in considerable Christian bloodshed.[111] Richard's displays of wrathful violence against fellow Christians precede his crusade expedition, yet imputing them to the devil produces an effect that is similar to the scenarios above. It highlights the prejudicial impact of inwardly directed violence on the Christian collective.

120   Therapeutic Crusading and Excessive Violence

Upon returning from his scouting expedition to the Holy Land, Richard ungraciously rebuffs a minstrel, finds himself accused of spying on King Modard's land, and is thrown into prison.[112] The arrest is certainly presented as unfair, but so too is Richard's treatment of Modard's son, Ardour, who challenges the English king to a contest of strength: each man is allowed to give the other a single barehanded blow. After receiving "an eere cloute" delivered in conformity with their agreement, Richard deems that Ardour "dyde hym wronge" and wrathfully swears vengeance (760–64). At this point, however, the narrative emphasizes Ardour's goodwill, courtesy, and desire for a fair fight:

> The kynges sone with good wyll
> Badde they sholde haue theyr fyll,
> Bothe of drynke, and eke of mete,
> Of the best that they wolde ete,
> That he myght not awyte
> For feblenes his dente to smyte;
> And into bedde be brought to reste,
> To quyte his that he be preste.
> The kynges sone was curtese,
> That nyghte he made hym well at ease. (765–74)

Despite this honorable treatment, Richard, concealed in the privacy of his cell, applies a layer "thycke and more" (781) of hard beeswax over his fist to inflict as much harm as possible. Ardour, described as "a trewe man" (786), faces the king and receives his blow without flinching but is struck "ded as ony ston" (798). Richard's urge to consummate his vengeance (763–64, 783–84), the lethal consequence of such spite, and the inequitable nature of the blow expose him as prone to excess and deceitful.[113] The episode makes clear that "curtese," Ardour's defining attribute, is lacking in Richard.

Informed of the death of his son, Modard exclaims, "Allas . . . now haue j non!" (802), a conventional formula used in medieval laments for the dead to elicit compassion.[114] But Modard is unable to say more and falls to the ground "as man þat was jn woo jbounde" (804). Fuller exploitation of the compassion-arousing potential of the situation occurs with the arrival of Modard's wife:

> "Allas," sche sayde, "hou may þis bene?
> Why is þis sorwe and þis ffare?
> Who has brou3t yow alle in care?"
> "Dame," he sayde, "wost þou nou3t
> þy ffayre sone to deþe is brou3t!
> Syþþen þat I was born to man,

Ambivalence in the Interpolations

Swylke sorwe hadde j neuere nan!
Alle my ioye is turnyd to woo,
Ffor sorwe j wole myseluen sloo!"
Whenne þe qwene vndyrstood,
Ffor sorwe, sertys, sche wax nygh wood.
Her kerchefs she drewe, her heer also,
"Alas," she sayd, "what shall j do!"
Sche cratched hereselff in þe bysage,
As a wymman þat was in rage.
þe face fomyd al on blood,
Sche rente þe robe þat sche in stood,
Wrong here handes þat sche was born:
"Jn what manere is my sone jlorn?" (816–34)

The passage's rhetorical effectiveness is achieved through the intensification of the verbal and somatic manifestations of grief (from swooning and threats of suicide to self-laceration), dramatic interplay between bereaved husband and wife, repetition of the conventional "Alas," parallel phrases (such as "As man þat was jn woo jbounde" and "As a wymman þat was in rage"), and sibilance, which enhances the tone of frenzy and despair. Parental sorrow gives grounds for corrective action, which the romance's audience can only construe as legitimate in view of Richard's immoral deeds – his "dedes þat aren vnwrest," as put by Modard (874). At this point, Modard is presented as giving Richard's fate a great deal of thought, acting rationally rather than impulsively. He summons his wisest advisors (936–37) – figures of utmost importance to the virtuous governance of kings[115] – and together, they spend long hours pondering the most adequate "iugement" to administer for this "gret tresoun" (950–51). After three days of juridical deliberation, one of these men, Sir Eldrys, urges Modard to "doo, be my resoun" (1001) and choose a fierce lion, abstain from feeding it – and from feeding Richard – for three days, and release it into the king's cell. But in a scene that supplies the king with his famous epithet, Richard tears the lion's heart out, carries it into the hall, seasons it with salt, and eats it in front of the stunned and horrified Modard. At yet another key moment, the king's violence is imputed to his devilish disposition: "Iwis, as j vnyrstonde can, / þis is a deuyl and no man" (1111–12). Richard's escape is triumphant. Yet the means by which it is achieved – trickery and calculated brutality in dealing with Ardour – and the consequence of his actions – the agony of parents deprived of their only son – do not rest easily with the romance's audience. The question of what means are morally permissible to achieve victory will again be raised in the cannibalism episodes, but in a context of crusade.

Cannibalism in Crusade Historiography and Literature

The most extensive scholarly treatment of the cultural legacy and literary repercussions of the acts of cannibalism perpetrated by Christian soldiers during the First Crusade is found in Geraldine Heng's *Empire of Magic*. Heng situates the crusaders' cannibalism at the siege of Ma'arra in 1098 as a point of cultural neurosis, of such traumatic tenor as to produce centuries of fiction of collective repression.[116] The chronicle reports of the episode certainly exhibit the linguistic features that modern theorists assign to the narration of trauma.[117] The quasi-inexpressibility of the event, induced by famine, is conveyed through verbal constructions such as "dicere perhorreo" (I shudder to say), "Pudet referre" (It is shameful to report), "quod etiam dictu horribile" (a horrible thing to have to describe), "Mirabile dictu et auribus horrendum" (It is extraordinary to relate and horrifying to the ears), "quod nefas est dicere nedum facere" (it is wicked to tell, let alone to do), and "Proh pudor! heu facinus!" (For shame, the dreadful deed!).[118] These interjections suggest an experience so revolting as to demand explicit moral qualification. Unlike Mary's anthropophagy in *The Siege*, hardly any attempt is made to alleviate the culpability of the crusaders. The juridical grounds for the distress elicited by the act are clearly articulated in the account of Gilo of Paris: "Tendit in illicitum, facit hoc quod ius prohibebat" (They veered toward what was not right, and did what common law forbids).[119] In preparing and consuming what some referred to as "banquets of men,"[120] the crusaders regressed to an animal-like state; as put by Ralph of Caen, "Vorando aemulati sunt feras, torrendo homines, sed caninos" (In devouring them, the Christians looked like beasts, like dogs roasting men).[121] The sight of crusaders feasting on Muslim corpses was so appalling that it was even said to have prompted Christian desertions from the campaign.[122]

Yet despite its traumatic resonance, the incident was not repressed, as Heng suggests, but was told at length in various forms throughout the high and later Middle Ages.[123] Some of the earliest chronicles to comment on the incident paved the way for subsequent understandings of cannibalism as ideologically double-edged. Raymond of Aguilers conjectures the psychological impact of the crusaders' anthropophagy on Muslim witnesses, framing it as an extreme act of cruelty and yet fiercely effective in military terms: "Et quis poterit sustinere hanc gentem que tam obstinata atque crudelis est, ut per annum non poterit revocari ab obsidione Antiochie, fame, vel gladio, vel aliquibus periculis, et nunc carnibus humanis vescitur?" (And who can stand against a people so resolute and cruel that, after a year of not backing away from the siege of Antioch, neither through hunger, sword, nor any other danger, they now eat human flesh?).[124] The notion of cannibalism as a tactic of intimidation is further attested by the account of William of Tyre, though the author is careful to specify that the act is not literal but staged. Conceived as a remedy for the "malady" of Muslim spies within the Christian camp, the roasting and make-believe consumption of Muslim flesh establishes the Franks' reputation as a nation of unrivaled, beast-like cruelty: "His qui eos miserant dicentes quoniam populus hic quarumlibet nationum, sed et feratum exuperat seviciam" (To those who had sent them they reported that this people surpassed every other nation and even beasts in cruelty).[125] Cannibalism is no longer performed out of necessity but is simulated for political ends as a theatrical maneuver, thus eluding moral condemnation.

Despite this early awareness of the act's potential to serve as a resource of holy warfare, the *literal* ingestion of Muslim flesh and its implications of inhumanity never rested easily with authors. Cannibalism came to stand as a symbol for the brutality of crusade: a form of extreme violence that certainly bore fruit, but nonetheless infringed on Christian morality. This duality of perception is evident in the tendency of certain authors to divorce cannibalism from the main body of the crusaders by ascribing it to the Tafurs, a marginalized group of soldiers viewed as barely human, often associated with the devil, and renowned for their ferocity.[126] The liminal status of this semiautonomous rabble of soldiers allowed for an acknowledgement of the atrocities and excesses of divinely approved warfare that did not incriminate the crusader army as a whole.[127] In the *Chanson d'Antioche*, the brutality of the Tafurs, shown at its most extreme in the ingestion of Muslim flesh, is identified by Peter the Hermit as a requirement of war. Yet at the same time, the Turks' responses of sorrow and protest against this "grande cruelté" (great cruelty) – "Ço ne sont pas François,ançois sont vif malfé" (These are not Frenchmen, they are living devils!) – take the form of legitimate and serious accusations, prompting Bohemond to devolve collective responsibility onto the Tafur king whose hateful impulses, he claims, could not be contained.[128] In the *Conquête de Jérusalem*, the Tafurs are likewise both encouraged and shunned. Their military contributions and useful powers of intimidation are underscored, but their "démezure," "meschanceté," and the rumors of anthropophagy that surround them set them apart from the rest of the Christian host, associating them with the remote, flesh-eating races that fight alongside the Muslims.[129]

124   Therapeutic Crusading and Excessive Violence

This tendency to call upon the Tafurs to account for the darkest impulses of crusading is borne out in William of Tudela's rendering of the infamous massacre of Béziers during the Albigensian Crusade. The author downplays the crusaders' liability for the event by imputing the most atrocious acts of violence to a band of unruly servant boys referred to as "ribauts" and "tafurs."[130] This type of wholesale massacre was certainly militarily profitable, as William states, but its human consequences were a source of such discomfort as to require moral dissociation through the assignment of a scapegoat. Here, as in the above texts, the "Tafurs," and the unbridled violence they incarnate, are both an intrinsic part and an aberration of the ideology of crusade. Their presence within these narratives suggests an acute awareness of the morally transgressive potential of the passions at play in religious warfare. This type of brutality was, however, carefully confined to the margins so as to prevent it from reflecting negatively on the dominant ethos of the movement.

The more "comfortable" option, as attested by most *chansons de geste*, was to impute these anthropophagic practices and their connotations of extreme ferocity to the Muslims of fantasy. These depictions, as noted by Jill Tattersall, take the form of counteraccusations to the events of the First Crusade, similar in nature to the romance motif of the "afflicted Muslim," which, as discussed in Chapter 1, projected Christian anxieties and insecurities.[131] Representations of Muslim cannibalism were influenced by the so-called "monstrous races" tradition.[132] Like the cannibals of ancient ethnography, these portrayals went hand in hand with an animal-like propensity for cruelty, mercilessness, and immoderate violence. The *Chanson de Guillaume*, for instance, inscribes the Muslims' taste for human flesh, "cun dragun e leppart," into a general characterization of their bloodthirstiness in battle.[133] In the *Prise d'Orange*, also part of the Guillaume cycle, the threat of being eaten "sanz pain et sanz farine" is used as a shorthand for the merciless treatment that Guillaume is warned to expect if he is taken captive by his Muslim enemies.[134] The conflation of Muslim cannibalism with other forms of censured brutality is brought to a new level in *Floovant*, which situates the act alongside threats of dismemberment, quartering, hanging, and death by burning.[135] These *chanson de geste* depictions of Muslim cannibalism clearly contribute to a discourse of ethically ambivalent violence. Conforming to wider historiographical formulations, this type of cannibalism of "pleasure," often combined with animal or devilish imagery, served as a mark of savagery, conveying unregeneracy and excess. In the trajectory mapped out here, the extreme brutality contained in this form of militant anthropophagy is thus at the

Cannibalism of Necessity and Pleasure

RCL invokes this tradition in its two episodes of anthropophagy, which, put together, encapsulate the moral tensions in late medieval perceptions of crusader violence. The first of these episodes constructs Richard's cannibalism as a matter of necessity: the king falls severely ill, collectively bringing "al Crystyndom to mekyl woo" (3028); unable to cater to his craving for roast pork, his men clean, scrape, and cook the body of a Muslim man, which Richard unwittingly consumes, resulting in his restoration to health. His renewed vigor takes the form of incensed ("wood") martial relish: "Armes me in myn armure, / Ffor loue off Cryst oure creature!" (3131–32). This yearning for home (i.e., English) food, offset only by the tastiness and restorative power of Muslim flesh, reconfigures Richard's historical illness, which, according to the chronicles, contributed to his truce with Ṣalāḥ al-Dīn and departure from the Third Crusade.[136] Richard's withdrawal was synonymous with the resumption of warfare in western Europe; as put by Marino Sanudo, it led to "implacabili odio mutuo" (implacable and mutual hatred) between the English and French kings in their territorial conflicts in Normandy.[137] This first cannibalism scene would no doubt have resonated with post-1291 perceptions of the ailments of Christendom and the crusade's healing potential. The substitution of English food with Muslim flesh as the remedy for the king's affliction and, by extension, that of "al Crystyndom," appeals to the familiar dilemma of inwardly and outwardly directed royal emotions or, as medieval affective psychology viewed them, "appetites."[138] In prescribing the violent sacrifice of a Muslim man and the absorption of his body to heal the king and palliate the lure of home, the romance rectifies the "errors" of history.

The second anthropophagy episode, set in the context of an ambassadorial dinner, is of a different nature. The romance operates a key transition: cannibalism is no longer framed as circumstantially requisite, as necessary for the good health of the king and the Christian community, but is defined as an act of premeditated brutality and pleasure, aligning Richard with the depraved Tafur and Muslim human-eaters of *chansons de geste*. What is at stake in this second scene, as in *The Siege*, is not so much the ideological foundation of crusading as the appetite for violence and baser instincts the enterprise could satisfy. As in the *Otuel* romances considered in Chapter 2, the critique of Christian conduct is effected through the medium of Muslim antagonists.[139] The narrative emphasizes the ambassadors' claim to the moral high ground by dwelling at length, and with distinct sympathy, on the emotive impact and familial implications of their loss.

Ṣalāḥ al-Dīn's emissaries, at first deceptively welcomed as "frendes" (3444),[140] are then contemptuously seated at "a syde-table" (3446) – an insult in itself[141] – containing salt but not bread, water, or wine (3447–48) and presented with the cooked decapitated heads of members of their nearest kin, whose private execution Richard had previously orchestrated. The king had requested that these heads be carefully shaven and displayed on platters, each face identified by a name tag, slanted upward, and molded into a grotesque grin (3427–33). While playing on a recognizable register of militaristic black humor,[142] the romance narrates the ambassadors' reaction – a mix of wrath, sorrow, and fear – in pitiful terms:

> þeroff they had all grame!
> What þey were whenne þey seyen,
> þe teres ran out off here eyen;
> And whenne þey þe lettre redde,
> To be slayn fful sore þey dredde.
> Kyng R. hys eyen on hem þrewe,
> Hou þey begunne to chaunge here hewe.
> For here ffrendes þey sy3yd sore,
> þat þey hadde lost for euermore.
> Off here kynde blood þey were. (3464–73)

This response, recalling that of Modard and his wife during the imprisonment scene, brings Richard's behavior into moral focus. Observed by the complacent monarch who proceeds to eat one of the heads "wiþ herte good" (3481), Ṣalāḥ al-Dīn's men can only conclude that Richard must be "wood" and that he is "þe deuelys broþir" (3483 and 3484). The king's acts conjure not only the ethically transgressive cannibalism of the French epic, but also other quasi-cannibalistic rituals of battle imputed in European literature and historiography to cultural Others.[143] Gerald of Wales, for instance, tells of the exhilarative frenzy of the Irish king Dermot MacMurrough, reveling in triumph as he identifies two hundred decapitated enemy heads laid at his feet: "Unius etiam, quem magis inter ceteros exosum habuerat, capite per aures et comas ad os erecto, crudeli morsu et valde inhumano nares et labra dente corrosit" (He lifted up to his mouth

Cannibalism of Necessity and Pleasure 127

the head of one he particularly loathed, and taking it by the ears and hair, gnawed at the nose and cheeks – a cruel and most inhuman act).[144] Richard's brutality operates in a similar register of taboo behavioral excess. Despite his status as a romance hero, the protests of his enemies are normative and relatable, demanding moral consideration of the lengths to which his violent "appetites" take him.

The king's troubling demeanor is reinforced by the incongruous emotions he exhibits and verbalizes. He assumes a wrathful stance in response to his guests' anguish and makes an astounding request for them to cheer up, be at ease, and eat their fill of their friends' and families' boiled heads:

> Abouten hym gan loke ful 3erne,
> Wiþ wraþ semblaunt, and eyen sterne.
> þe messangers þoo he bad:
> "Ffor my loue bes alle glad,
> And lokes 3e be weel at eese!
> Why kerue 3e nou3t off 3oure mese,
> And eetes ffaste as j doo?" (3487–93)

Richard's wrathful mercilessness prompts further association of his violence with cruelty, and his position of king with that of devil. The envoys are taunted, treated with derision, and contemptuously insulted – their anger is therefore justified – whereas Richard conveys his wrath with no heed to his terrified victims.[145] Combining humiliation with brutal physical abuse in the context of ambassadorial exchange, the king's actions clearly violate the boundaries of acceptable royal – or human – prerogative.[146] Eventually, after the ambassadors are again described as crippled by fear (3495–99), Richard orders that the heads be brought away and that proper food and drinks be served – a dinner that his guests, overwhelmed with dread and grief (3634–38), are unable to partake in. In a curious attempt to apologize, Richard asserts that they need not be "squoymous," that "þis is þe manner off myn hous" (3509–12). He follows this by justifying his alleged ignorance of Muslim culinary customs, resorting to his identity as "kyng, Cristen, and trewe" (3514). He then expresses worry that his good name would be stained by a pejorative reputation on account of him being "so euyl off maneres" (3519). The narrative thus has Richard admitting to a breach of ethics while asserting that among the crusaders of his "hous," the act is customary. The peripheral practices of *chansons de geste* are transferred to the center, raising the stakes considerably. In *RCL*, it is not marginalized "Tafurs" who embody the darkest impulses of crusading, its dehumanizing and morally corruptive potential, but the king and the crusader army as a whole.

128 Therapeutic Crusading and Excessive Violence

The human consequences of Richard's conduct finally receive closest scrutiny in the lengthy account of these events delivered to Ṣalāḥ al-Dīn by the envoys. This report fulfils the same narrative function as those of Sir Thomas and Sir Fulk following the precrusade tournament, and that of Modard after his son's death: to give voice to aggrieved victims. Exclamations of sorrow – "Ffor sorwe we wende ffor to deye!" and "Ffor sorwe þoo we gan to syke" (3596 and 3604) – punctuate the narrative as one of the emissaries lists the names of the relatives and friends whose heads they were served for consumption by the "sterne" King Richard (3591–604). Pronouncements of grief and dread are juxtaposed with alarming characterizations of the king:[147]

> Vs þouȝte oure herte barst ryȝt insunder,
> Lord, ȝit þou myȝt here a wundyr!
> Beffore Kyng Rycharde a knyȝt in haste
> Karff off þe hed, and he eet ffaste.
> Wiþ teeþ he grond þe flessch ful harde,
> As a wood lyoun he ffarde,
> Wiþ hys eyen stepe and grym;
> And spak, and we behelde hym,
> Ffor drede we wende ffor to sterue;
> He bad vs þat we scholde kerue
> Oure mes, and eeten as he dede. (3605–15)

Vigorously gnawing the flesh of a human head with cruel, glistening eyes, Richard is likened to a ferocious beast. The speaker's rhetoric of Christian bestial cruelty and emphatically humanized Muslim response culminates in the narration of Richard's promise to wage what can only be categorized as inhumane warfare: to "nouȝt lete on lyue / In al þy land, man, chyld, ne wyne" but to "slee alle þat he may fynde, / Seþe þe fflesch, and wiþ teeþ grynde" (3649–52). In the moral economy of the romance, this type of insatiable hunger for martial annihilation operates as a deviation from the violence of necessity and political sustainability contained in the first cannibalistic act. Echoing Richard's Christian victims, Ṣalāḥ al-Dīn expresses righteous "yre" while his advisors lament: "It is a deuyl wiþout ffayle" (3657, 3664).

That this episode was perceived by English audiences as disturbing, eliciting responses of disapproval and disgust, may well have been the reason that it was omitted from the fifteenth-century B-version manuscripts, only to reemerge in the two early prints made by Wynkyn de Worde (1509 and 1528). Indeed, of the seven extant manuscripts of the romance, only three contain Richard's anthropophagic feast,[148] which suggests that the passage may have suffered from limited popularity. Along with Caius 175, the most "contaminated," "romance-like" manuscript containing the episodes of cannibalism is the London Thornton (London, British Library, MS Additional 31042), in which *RCL* appears alongside *The Siege*, the second of three romances copied by Robert Thornton featuring acts of anthropophagy. The third is the alliterative *Morte Arthure*, preserved in Lincoln Cathedral Library, MS 91. In this poem, the trope of cannibalism also has an evaluative dimension. The Genoese monster of the *Morte*, cast as a tyrant, giant, cannibal, and rapist, embodies the form of ethically monstrous brutality that Richard's cannibalism for pleasure would have evoked.[149] In all three romances copied by Thornton, cannibalism is symptomatic of the extreme emotions involved in the performance of, or response to, morally questionable violence.

Thus, *The Siege* and *RCL* mobilize a representational aesthetic that is at odds with the triumphant crusading spirit that modern scholars have often assigned to them. Other texts invoking similar discursive dynamics could be cited: Orderic Vitalis's report of the Harrying of the North; the *Canso de la crozada* (on the Albigensian Crusade); Froissart's account of the Sack of Limoges; and the N-Town Plays' rendering of the Slaughter of the Innocents – all juxtapose unbridled anger with compassion-arousing sorrow to express ambivalence or assign blame.[150] The notion that anger was the root of morally transgressive violence was well established in Middle English literature. Chaucer's *Parson's Tale* associates the "cursed synne of Ire" with manslaughter, while his *Knight's Tale* features "crueel Ire, reed as any gleende" and "Woodnesse, laughynge in his rage" as allegorized sponsors for military atrocity.[151] Gower defines "wrathe" in terms of heat, asserting "That all a mannes pacience / Is fyred of the violence."[152] In the C-text of *Piers Plowman*, Langland has Wrath declare that he "wol gladliche smyte / Both with stone and with staf and stele vppon [his] enemye."[153] Hoccleve's *Regiment of Princes* opposes the benefits of "concord" with the detriments of "ire," and bemoans the "sorwe lamentable" caused by the Hundred Years War.[154]

Scholars have long recognized that criticism of inter-Christian warfare was an important feature of late fourteenth-century English literature.[155] What I hope to have shown is that anxieties about the morality of violence extended to crusade narratives. I close this chapter with an excerpt from the most well-informed account of the Crusade of Nicopolis to have reached us: the chronicle of Michel Pintoin, monk of Saint-Denis. There is no gloss of idealism in Pintoin's account, only biting criticism of

130   Therapeutic Crusading and Excessive Violence

Christian soldiers for their pride and presumption (as seen in Chapter 2), but also anger.[156] When, succumbing to wrath, the crusaders brutally kill the Ottoman prisoners they had taken – executions that are similar in scope to those performed by Richard to stage his cannibal feast – the author condemns the act as antithetical to the tenets of Christianity and decries the human costs:

> Dies erat dominica ultima mensis septembris, cum rumor adventus hostium innotuit. Quo territi qui Nycopolim obsidebant, redierunt, soluta obsidione, subsannantibus civibus cum ignominiosis verbis. Unde nostri ad iracundiam provocati, ut fidelium relacione notum fuit, ex concepto dolore iniquitatem inauditam pepererunt, quam scribere siccis oculis non valemus. Tunc illis excidit fidelitatis tenor, hucusque eciam infidelibus inviolabiliter obervatus; nam quotquot ex adversariis se fidelitati eorum submiserant, spretis condicionibus cum juramento firmatis, o Deus ulcionum et humanorum actuum censor equissime, occidi crudeliter preceperunt.

> It was the last Sunday of the month of September that it became known that the Turks were approaching. Our soldiers, frightened, lifted the siege on Nicopolis and broke camp amid the taunts of the citizens. According to trustworthy reports, our men were so roused by anger that out of the pain they felt they committed an act of unthinkable cruelty which I cannot tell of without shedding tears. Forgetting the responsibilities of their faith, which had until then been scrupulously observed when dealing with the infidels, and disregarding the agreements they had made – Oh God, fair judge of the vengeances and actions of men! – they cruelly executed all of the prisoners that had surrendered to them.[157]

Pintoin conveys in direct, admonitory language what *The Siege* and *RCL* convey implicitly and dramatically, deploying well-established literary strategies and complex intertextual allusions: the degeneration of crusade warfare into violence that exceeds what is morally permissible. These romances partake in the broader, familiar tension between ideals of crusading and the complications involved in their human enactment.

Conclusion

This book has argued for an understanding of post-1291 crusade culture as ambivalent and self-critical, animated by tensions and debates, and fraught with anxiety. Middle English crusade romances uphold ideals of crusading, whether by promoting "curative" violence, deploying a rhetoric of compassionate vengeance for the crucifixion of Christ, or enjoining sorrowful solidarity for injured Christians. But they also articulate anxieties about issues as fundamental and diverse as God's endorsement of the enterprise, the allure of Islam, Christendom's beleaguered state and internal divisions, the inadequacy of Christian warriors vis-à-vis their Muslim counterparts, the baser instincts and selfish ambitions crusading could satisfy, and the violence it involves. These anxieties, or "uneasy concerns," are religious as much as they are political, providential as much as moral, historical as much as literary.

Some of these anxieties – about the morality of violence and the motives of those who fought – go back to the early days of the enterprise. Others were engendered and perpetuated by the long series of Muslim victories and territorial (re)conquests that took place in the eastern Mediterranean, Anatolia, and the Balkans. Crusading defeats raised troubling questions: Had God abandoned his followers? Did he support the enemy? Was Muhammad more powerful than Christ? In the real world, such doubts were voiced by laypeople, clerics, and crusaders in Europe and the Near East. In the world of fiction, they were both assimilated to the Christian self and projected onto the Muslim Other. Beneath the ubiquitous motif of the "afflicted Muslim," commonly viewed by scholars as a mere literary construct, lies a fascinating history of blasphemy and religious doubt. Conventionally, of course, crusading defeats were interpreted as manifestations of divine anger against Christian sinfulness. The *peccatis exigentibus hominum* logic goes a long way in explaining why post-1291 crusade romances temper triumphalism with self-criticism, rarely imagine the Christian community as harmoniously unified, and often ascribe to

132   Conclusion

Muslim characters behaviors and emotions that reflect unfavorably on Christians. The reason that providential questions – such as "if Christians were defeated on account of their sins, had Muslims achieved victory on account of their moral merits?" – are so important to understanding medieval European views of Muslims and Islam is that they were asked by those (like John Bromyard) who had little experience of the peoples they described and those who had traveled extensively. As we saw in Chapter 2, the Italian missionary Riccoldo da Monte di Croce based his assessment of Islamic deeds, what he calls "opera perfectionis" (works of perfection), on both providential beliefs and sustained interaction with the Muslim communities of Baghdad.

Bringing out the heterogeneity of, and conflicts within, post-1291 crusade culture has involved placing Middle English romances in dialogue with diverse materials, many of them relatively neglected by scholars. Crusade romances take up and endorse ideas that feature in ecclesiastical propaganda. But they also dramatically enact invectives against heaven found in poetry, letters, and chronicles produced in Latin Christendom (England, France, Germany, and Italy) and the Near East. They creatively adapt "reverse Orientalism," an international, cross-generic mode in which Muslim figures look down on and offer damning critiques of Christians. They intervene in debates on conflicting "philosophies" of crusading that played out in the realm of love and were of primary concern to poets (Gower, Chaucer, and Machaut), writers of chivalric treatises (Geoffroi de Charny and Philippe de Mézières), and chroniclers of the Baltic *reysen* (Nicolaus of Jeroschin and Peter Suchenwirt). They engage with centuries-long dilemmas about the morality and human toll of religious warfare, even as they assert its politically healthy nature. These romances resist totalizing assessments, demanding instead to be integrated within, and considered key constituents of, a multivocal political culture. What makes them such remarkable cultural objects is the sheer variety of modes, traditions, and perspectives they accommodate, both individually and as a group.

Even as I have sought to cast a wide net in my coverage of primary sources, I have attempted to do justice to the translational or adaptive processes by which (most) Middle English crusade romances were created. On close examination, these romances reveal themselves to be accomplished literary works subject to what Bernard Cerquiglini calls *variance* – that is, the creative innovations of writers who thrived on the challenges and pleasures of rewriting and reinventing.[1] The author of *The Sultan of Babylon* turns the archetypal villain Laban of *La destruction de Rome* and

Fierabras into a worthy conqueror who enacts divine vengeance against sinful Christian Romans and whose spiritual crises, mirroring Charlemagne's fits of rage, perform complex cultural work. The adaptors of the *Otuel* story enhance the eponymous character's strength and moral qualities while transforming Roland and Oliver, Europe's paragons of chivalry, into disruptive troublemakers. Guy of Warwick's postconfessional life is made more exemplary to accentuate the critique of his love-spurred, worldly career. *The Siege of Jerusalem* recasts the Jews as compassion-arousing victims of merciless Roman leaders of a righteous crusade that degenerates into wanton cruelty. The interpolations to *Richard Coeur de Lion* invite moral scrutiny of the king's violent actions by exposing their adverse effects on families and chivalric communities, both Christian and Muslim. Writers of crusade romances took a serious approach to translation or adaptation, inscribing in their productions the greatest pressures and preoccupations of the world in which they lived. They knew what their audiences expected: topical, historically evocative stories that stimulated reflection, dialogue, and debate.

In the Introduction, I pointed to some key differences in the reception of Edward Said's *Orientalism* between scholars of medieval crusade literature and modern colonial fiction, citing work by Lisa Lowe, Elleke Boehmer, Jennifer Yee, Priyamvada Gopal, and others to frame my contributions. I end this book with a sense of the enduring productiveness of such debates, well over forty years since the publication of *Orientalism*, and of the possibilities for research ahead. In *Insurgent Empire* (2019), which takes as its subject indigenous anticolonial resistance and British dissent during the nineteenth to mid twentieth centuries, Gopal makes a powerful argument about the study of history: we need to attend to broad cultural developments in Europe engendered not just by European expansion but also by non-European opposition.[2] The foregoing chapters (especially the first and second) have explored the role of Muslim Levantine reconquests, and the subsequent rise of the Ottomans, in shaping and diversifying crusade culture, focusing on Middle English romances and their contexts. But there is, I believe, a need for a full-length study of the transformative pressures exerted by these geopolitical developments not only on "crusade culture" but on culture more generally – a new history of medieval European views of, and self-definition in relation to, Muslims and Islam.[3] Drawing on a pan-European archive, such a study would offer an alternative to the scholarly narrative that sees conquests and postconquest conditions (peaceful or otherwise) as the primary catalysts to cultural change in Latin Christendom.[4] It would more fully establish the

Conclusion

importance of the Ayyūbids, Mamlūks, and Ottomans in European history.[5] And it would open up areas of inquiry where scholars of this subject have yet to fully venture: analogical thinking in relation to Islam; shared moral values; anti-Orientalism; resistance to dominant racial ideologies; criticism of Europe in a global frame; the place of Muslims in debates on universal salvation; and nascent, if imperfect, ideas of equality.[6]

It is perhaps fitting to close with the qualified anticrusade argument, grounded in imperfect ideas of equality, voiced by the French lawyer Honorat Bovet in his widely disseminated *Arbre des batailles* (1387). Bovet writes that Christians have a superior claim to the Holy Land, which they gained through the Passion of Christ. But he refutes Christendom's right, and the lawfulness of papal indulgences, to wage war against Muslim peoples over any other territory on account of God's benevolence to all humans, "la creature humaine," regardless of religious belief. God graces the lands of Christians and Muslims equally with good corn and good fruit. Muslims, like Christians, have science and a sense of discretion to lead them in justice, as well as kingdoms, empires, sacred texts, and their faith. "Et doncques puisque Dieu leur a donné tant de biens pourquoy les leur osteroient les Chrestiens?" (And so, since God has given them so many blessings, why should Christians take these from them?).[7]

Notes

Introduction

1 On the later crusades, see, to start, Norman Housley, *The Later Crusades: From Lyons to Alcazar, 1274–1580* (Oxford: Oxford University Press, 1992); and Timothy Guard, *Chivalry, Kingship and Crusade: The English Experience in the Fourteenth Century* (Woodbridge, UK: Boydell Press, 2013). The most comprehensive recent general histories of the crusades are Christopher Tyerman, *God's War: A New History of the Crusades* (London: Penguin, 2007); and Paul Cobb, *The Race for Paradise: An Islamic History of the Crusades* (Oxford: Oxford University Press, 2014).

2 An influential collection of essays arguing for the multivocality and conflictual investments of medieval Latin and vernacular European cultures, but not concerned with crusade culture or the genre of romance, is Rita Copeland (ed.), *Criticism and Dissent in the Middle Ages* (Cambridge: Cambridge University Press, 1996).

3 The term may also be used in a variety of more specialized ways, including to designate clinical disorders, hardwired responses to potential threats, and existential angst. On the general sense of the term, see *anxiety* and *anxietas* in the *Oxford English Dictionary* (*OED*) and the *Dictionary of Medieval Latin from British Sources* (*DMLBS*); on its history, see further William J. Bouwsma, "Anxiety and the Formation of Early Modern Culture," in Barbara C. Malament (ed.), *After the Reformation: Essays in Honor of J. H. Hexter* (Philadelphia: University of Pennsylvania Press, 1980), pp. 215–46. While I see post-1291 crusade culture as troubled by anxieties, I do not seek to corroborate the idea, upheld by Bouwsma and others, that the European later Middle Ages were "an age of unusual anxiety" in a general sense (p. 217).

4 See, e.g., the *DMLBS*, which distinguishes between "anxius" (durable) and "angor" (temporary); and, in the *OED*, the section on "Age of Anxiety."

5 While the connection between modern colonial novels and medieval crusade romances has not (to my knowledge) previously been made, that between novels and romances more generally has been debated extensively: see, e.g., Karen Sullivan, *The Danger of Romance: Truth, Fantasy, and Arthurian Fictions* (Chicago: University of Chicago Press, 2018), pp. 26–59; Helen Swift, "Late

135

136   *Notes to page 2*

Medieval Precursors to the Novel: 'Aucune chose de nouvel,'" in Adam Watt (ed.), *The Cambridge History of the Novel in French* (Cambridge: Cambridge University Press, 2021), pp. 19–37.

6 Edward W. Said, *Orientalism* (London: Penguin, 1978; repr. 1995), p. 42; Lisa Lowe, *Critical Terrains: French and British Orientalisms* (Ithaca, NY: Cornell University Press, 1992), p. 28; Yumna Siddiqi, *Anxieties of Empire and the Fiction of Intrigue* (New York: Columbia University Press, 2008), p. 5. Some of the earliest scholars to critique *Orientalism* on these grounds are Albert Hourani, "The Road to Morocco," *New York Review of Books*, 26 (1979), 27–30 (esp. pp. 29–30); James Clifford, "On Orientalism," *History and Theory*, 19 (1980), 204–23 (for a general assessment of *Orientalism*'s tendency to relapse "into the essentializing modes it attacks," see p. 219); and Dennis Porter, "*Orientalism* and Its Problems," in Francis Barker, Peter Hulme, Margaret Iverson, and Diane Loxley (eds.), *The Politics of Theory: Proceedings of the Essex Sociology of Literature Conference, University of Essex* (Colchester, UK: University of Essex, 1983), pp. 179–93. In the Arab world, Said's book was also criticized for its "totalizing" and "essentialist mode": see Emmanuel Sivan, "Edward Said and His Arab Reviewers," in *Interpretations of Islam: Past and Present* (Princeton, NJ: Darwin Press, 1985), pp. 133–54. On the intellectual, ethical, and political questions raised by Said's homogenizing approach, see further Aijaz Ahmad, *In Theory: Classes, Nations, Literatures* (London: Verso, 1992), pp. 159–219 (esp. pp. 162–68); Robert Young, *White Mythologies: Writing History and the West* (London: Routledge, 1990), pp. 126–40; Ali Behdad, *Belated Travelers: Orientalism in the Age of Colonial Dissolution* (Durham, NC: Duke University Press, 1994), pp. 9–13; and Leela Gandhi, *Postcolonial Theory: A Critical Introduction*, 2nd ed. (New York: Columbia University Press, 2019; 1st ed. 1998), pp. 77–80, who writes that Said "defeats the logic of his own intellectual egalitarianism by producing and confirming a reversed stereotype: the racist Westerner. After *Orientalism*, it becomes our task not only to demonstrate the ambivalence of the Oriental stereotype, but also – and crucially – to refuse the pleasures of an Occidental stereotype" (p. 79). See also, more recently, the introductions to Rahul Sapra, *The Limits of Orientalism: Seventeenth-Century Representations of India* (Newark: University of Delaware Press, 2011); Srinivas Aravamudan, *Enlightenment Orientalism: Resisting the Rise of the Novel* (Chicago: University of Chicago Press, 2012); and Jennifer Yee, *The Colonial Comedy: Imperialism in the French Realist Novel* (Oxford: Oxford University Press, 2016).

7 Edward W. Said, *Culture and Imperialism* (London: Vintage Books, 1993). Srinivas Aravamudan's explanation of Said's position in *Culture and Imperialism* is useful: Said argues for the capacity of colonial literatures to "stage resistance to crude imperialist uses": "Orientalism," in David Kastan (ed.), *The Oxford Encyclopaedia of British Literature* (Oxford: Oxford University Press, 2006), pp. 143–50 (p. 148). Said appears to have conceived *Culture and Imperialism* in part as a response to the early reception of

Orientalism: see his comments on Lowe's *Critical Terrains* in *Culture and Imperialism*, pp. xxiv–xxv; see also Joseph A. Buttigieg and Paul A. Bové, "An Interview with Edward W. Said," *boundary 2*, 20 (1993), 1–25 (p. 2); and Valerie Kennedy, *Edward Said: A Critical Introduction* (Oxford: Wiley-Blackwell, 2000), pp. 82–83. On Said's trajectory from *Orientalism* to *Culture and Imperialism* in relation to the work of Erich Auerbach, see Joe Cleary, "Said, Postcolonial Studies, and World Literature," in Bashir Abu-Manneh (ed.), *After Said: Postcolonial Literary Studies in the Twenty-First Century* (Cambridge: Cambridge University Press, 2019), pp. 129–46 (p. 133).

8 Said, *Culture and Imperialism*, pp. xx, xxv, 320.

9 On modern colonial novels, as well as the work by Elleke Boehmer (*Colonial and Postcolonial Literature* [Oxford: Oxford University Press, 1995]), Priyamvada Gopal (*Insurgent Empire: Anticolonial Resistance and British Dissent* [London: Verso, 2019]), and Jennifer Yee (*Colonial Comedy*), see, e.g., Siddiqi, *Anxieties of Empire*; Patrick Brantlinger, *Victorian Literature and Postcolonial Studies* (Edinburgh: Edinburgh University Press, 2009); and Laura Chrisman, *Postcolonial Contraventions: Cultural Readings of Race, Imperialism, and Transnationalism* (Manchester, UK: Manchester University Press), pp. 51–70. For Chrisman, while more nuanced than *Orientalism*, *Culture and Imperialism* itself is overly homogenizing in its approach (see esp. pp. 53–54).

10 Scholars arguing for the transformative pressures exerted by colonial losses and indigenous resistance on colonial literatures have sometimes situated their assessments against Homi K. Bhabha's notion of ambivalence as inscribed "at the very origins of colonial authority" (*The Location of Culture*, 2nd ed. [London: Routledge, 2004; 1st ed. 1994], p. 135). See esp. Priyamvada Gopal, *Insurgent Empire*, pp. 14–15 and 19–21, who builds on Leela Gandhi's critique of the "subtle determinism" in Bhabha's theories of ambivalence (Leela Gandhi, *Affective Communities: Anticolonial Thought, Fin-de-Siècle Radicalism, and the Politics of Friendship* [Durham, NC: Duke University Press, 2006], pp. 5–6).

11 Elleke Boehmer, *Colonial and Postcolonial Literature*, pp. 98–101, 138–56 (citation at p. 98). On Western critiques related to colonialism during the eighteenth to mid twentieth centuries, a field that bridges postcolonial studies and imperial historiography, see further Robert Young, *Postcolonialism: An Historical Introduction* (Oxford: Blackwell, 2001), pp. 73–112; Gopal, *Insurgent Empire*; Gandhi, *Affective Communities* and her 2019 epilogue essay, "If This Were a Manifesto for Postcolonial Thinking," to the second edition of Gandhi, *Postcolonial Theory*, pp. 178–80; Stephen Howe, *Anticolonialism in British Politics: The Left and the End of Empire* (Oxford: Oxford University Press, 1993); Gregory Claeys, *Imperial Sceptics: British Critics of Empire, 1850–1920* (Cambridge: Cambridge University Press, 2010); Mira Matikkala, *Empire and Imperial Ambition: Liberty, Englishness and Anti-Imperialism in Late Victorian Britain* (London: I. B. Tauris, 2011); Nicholas

138   *Notes to pages 3–4*

Owen, *The British Left and India: Metropolitan Anti-Imperialism, 1885–1947* (Oxford: Oxford University Press, 2007); and the classic study by Bernard Porter, *Critics of Empire: British Radicals and the Imperial Challenge*, 2nd ed. (London: I. B. Tauris, 2008; 1st ed. 1968).

12 Boehmer, *Colonial and Postcolonial Literature*, p. 145.

13 Gopal, *Insurgent Empire*, p. 454.

14 Yee, *Colonial Comedy*, pp. 28, 143. In this respect, Yee's approach resembles that of Lisa Lowe, who examines the relation between "dominant orientalist formations" and "emergent challenges to those formations" (*Critical Terrains*, p. 9); and that of Rahul Sapra, who explores "moments of resistance that can disrupt the discourse of 'Orientalism'" (*Limits of Orientalism*, p. 12).

15 Previous scholarship invested in decentering Orientalism as an explanatory framework for understanding medieval Christian–Muslim relations has tended to focus not on histories of crusade and countercrusade, as I do here, but rather on "histories of peaceful contact": see esp. Sharon Kinoshita's important *Medieval Boundaries: Rethinking Difference in Old French Literature* (Philadelphia: University of Pennsylvania Press, 2006) (citation at p. 236). Another branch of medieval postcolonialism departing from the Orientalist model is on travel writing concerned principally with *non-Muslim* peoples: see Simon Gaunt, *Marco Polo's "Le Devisement du Monde": Voice, Language and Diversity* (Cambridge, UK: D. S. Brewer, 2013), esp. chapter 4; Kim M. Phillips, *Before Orientalism: Asian Peoples and Cultures in European Travel Writing, 1245–1510* (Philadelphia: University of Pennsylvania Press, 2014); Shirin A. Khanmohamadi, *In Light of Another's World: European Ethnography in the Middle Ages* (Philadelphia: University of Pennsylvania Press, 2013). Khanmohamadi's study does, however, have one chapter on encounters with Muslims on crusade (chapter 4, at pp. 88–112, on Jean de Joinville's *Vie de Saint Louis*). For an incisive critique of the early reception of *Orientalism* in medieval studies, see Sharon Kinoshita, "Deprovincializing the Middle Ages," in Rob Wilson and Christopher Leigh Connery (eds.), *The Worlding Project: Doing Cultural Studies in the Era of Globalization* (Santa Cruz, CA: New Pacific Press, 2007), pp. 61–75.

16 John V. Tolan, *Saracens: Islam in the Medieval European Imagination* (New York: Columbia University Press, 2002), pp. xviii, 105–34. For Tolan, the Muslim Other in epic and romance is "an essential foil for Christian virtue" (p. 129).

17 Suzanne Conklin Akbari, *Idols in the East: European Representations of Islam and the Orient, 1100–1450* (Ithaca, NY: Cornell University Press, 2009), pp. 159–99, 206–18 (citations at pp. 1 and 3). Akbari's important study allows for more ambivalence than does *Orientalism*, but locates that ambivalence not so much in crusade epics and romances as in works by Dante Alighieri and John Mandeville: see esp. pp. 53–66 and 228–35.

18 Geraldine Heng, *Empire of Magic: Medieval Romance and the Politics of Cultural Fantasy* (New York: Columbia University Press, 2003), pp. 68, 197, 242. However, rather than engage with Said, Heng engages directly with

Notes to page 4 139

Michel Foucault, whose theories on the relationship between power and knowledge underpin Said's conception of Orientalism.

19 Heng, *Empire of Magic*, pp. 3, 7, 93, 226.

20 Geraldine Heng, *The Invention of Race in the European Middle Ages* (New York: Cambridge University Press, 2018), pp. 27, 113. The role of the crusades in stimulating ideologies of religious and racial difference is most extensively discussed in chapter 3, "War/Empire," pp. 110–80. On Heng's definition of race in relation to Said's formulation of Orientalism, see further my "Unsettling Orientalism: Toward a New History of European Representations of Muslims and Islam, c. 1200–1450," *Speculum*, 100:2 (forthcoming, April 2025).

21 Jeffrey Jerome Cohen, *Of Giants: Sex, Monsters, and the Middle Ages* (Minneapolis: University of Minnesota Press, 1999) (citation at p. 133). See also his "On Saracen Enjoyment: Some Fantasies of Race in Late Medieval France and England," *Journal of Medieval and Early Modern Studies*, 31 (2001), 113–46; and "Race," in Marion Turner (ed.), *A Handbook of Middle English Studies* (Oxford: Wiley-Blackwell, 2013), pp. 109–22, which argues that romances such as *Guy of Warwick*, *Bevis of Hampton*, and *The Sultan of Babylon* reduce "the world's messiness into clean binaries," "heroic knight" versus "monstrous Other" (pp. 109–10). See further Kofi Campbell, "Nation-Building Colonialist-Style in *Bevis of Hampton*," *Exemplaria*, 18 (2006), 205–32, which reads *Bevis of Hampton* as an "Orientalist fantasy of English Christian cohesion opposed to Saracen disintegration" and contrasts the protection offered by the Christian God with the "powerlessness" of the Muslim "gods" (pp. 209, 227); Leila K. Norako, "*Sir Isumbras* and the Fantasy of Crusade," *Chaucer Review*, 48 (2013), 166–89, which argues that *Sir Isumbras* projects "an idealized and universal version of Christianity that can, by means of its cohesion, permanently defeat Islam" and "an atemporal world wherein the lines between Self and Other are starkly drawn" (p. 167); and Janice Hawes, "Saracens in Middle English Romance," in Esra Mirze Santesso and James E. McClung (eds.), *Islam and Postcolonial Discourse* (New York: Routledge, 2016), pp. 15–30. See also, in a similar vein, the genre-based inquiries of Yin Liu, "Middle English Romance as Prototype Genre," *Chaucer Review*, 40 (2006), 335–53; and Melissa Furrow, *Expectations of Romance: The Reception of a Genre in Medieval England* (Woodbridge, UK: Boydell and Brewer, 2009), pp. 57–72 (esp. pp. 70–71). Two short essays that, while not informed by work in postcolonial studies, in my view fruitfully problematize Orientalist approaches to Middle English crusade romances are Robert Allen Rouse, "Crusaders," in Neil Cartlidge (ed.), *Heroes and Anti-Heroes in Medieval Romance* (Cambridge, UK: D. S. Brewer, 2012), pp. 173–83; and, in the same volume, Siobhain Bly Calkin, "Saracens," pp. 185–200.

22 Martin Aurell, *Des Chrétiens contre les croisades, XIIe–XIIIe siècles* (Paris: Fayard, 2013). Aurell's chronological structure is what enables him to demonstrate an increase in criticism over time. Compared to the wealth of scholarship on Western critiques of modern colonialism (a portion of which

Notes to pages 5–6

is referenced in note 11 above), the scholarship on critiques of crusading is in short supply. Aurell's book is preceded by two full-length studies that also focus on the period before 1291: Palmer A. Throop, *Criticism of the Crusade: A Study of Public Opinion and Crusade Propaganda* (Amsterdam: N. V. Swets and Zeitlinger, 1940); Elizabeth Siberry, *Criticism of Crusading, 1095–1274* (Oxford: Clarendon Press, 1985). Criticism of crusading has hitherto not been considered a subject of postcolonial literary inquiry.

23 Brief assessments of critiques related to crusading after 1291 are offered by Elizabeth Siberry, "Criticism of Crusading in Fourteenth-Century England," in Peter W. Edbury (ed.), *Crusade and Settlement: Papers Read at the First Conference of the Society for the Study of the Crusades and the Latin East* (Cardiff: University College Cardiff Press, 1985), pp. 127–34; Christopher Tyerman, *England and the Crusades, 1095–1588* (Chicago: University of Chicago Press, 1988), pp. 261–62; and Housley, *Later Crusades*, pp. 377–82.

24 In the rest of this book, unless quoting from primary sources, I use the term "Muslim" rather than "Saracen." Usage of the term "Saracen" is being reassessed in medieval studies. Discussions that I have found illuminating include Shokoofeh Rajabzadeh, "The Depoliticized Saracen and Muslim Erasure," *Literature Compass*, 16 (2019), 1–8; Jerold C. Frakes, *Vernacular and Latin Literary Discourses of the Muslim Other in Medieval Germany* (New York: Palgrave, 2011), pp. 38–40; and Hélène Sirantoine, "What's in a Word? Naming 'Muslims' in Medieval Christian Iberia," in Chris Jones, Conor Kostick, and Klaus Oschema (eds.), *Making the Medieval Relevant: How Medieval Studies Contribute to Improving Our Understanding of the Present* (Berlin: De Gruyter, 2020), pp. 225–38. On the construct of the polytheistic Muslim, see my discussion in Chapter 1.

25 Here, I adapt the phrase "dream of conversion," coined by Robert I. Burns, "Christian-Islamic Confrontation in the West: The Thirteenth-Century Dream of Conversion," *American Historical Review*, 76 (1971), 1386–434.

26 This is the central assertion of my "Unsettling Orientalism."

27 See Tolan, *Saracens*, pp. 135–69 (on Muhammad as heresiarch); Heng, *Invention of Race*, pp. 113, 116–18 (on anti-Muslim polemics and caricatures Muhammad) and pp. 127–35 (on legends of the Assassins serving to promote the idea that intemperance, unbridled sexuality, sensory pleasures, irrationality, deceit, and lack of moral discipline were the characteristics of Islam); and Akbari, *Idols in the East*, pp. 159–89 (on the stereotype of the intemperate, impetuous Muslim) and pp. 221–35 (on stories of Muhammad).

28 No modern edition of Bromyard's *Summa praedicantium* has yet been published. The text is, however, available in a late sixteenth-century transcription: John Bromyard, *Summa praedicantium* (Vienna: Apud Dominicum Nicolinum, 1586). On the date of the *Summa*, see Leonard E. Boyle, "The Date of the *Summa praedicantium* of John Bromyard," *Speculum*, 48 (1973), 533–37.

29 Bromyard, *Summa praedicantium*, "Crux," 17.32–33.

Notes to pages 6–7 141

30 Bromyard, *Summa praedicantium*, "Adulterium," 17.9–10; "Anima," 23.15; "Elemosina," 3.28.

31 Most of the scholarship that does reference wider traditions of crusade writing is on two romances: *Richard Coeur de Lion* and *The Siege of Jerusalem*, which are commonly placed in dialogue with pre-1291 crusade documents; I discuss this scholarship in Chapter 4. On issues that have taken precedence over crusade traditions in otherwise richly contextualized assessments of romances of religious warfare, see further my discussion in Chapter 1, p. 18; and Chapter 3, pp. 71–72, 74 and notes 1, 5, 14, 20.

32 On the cultural turn in crusade studies, see, e.g., Megan Cassidy-Welch and Anne E. Lester, "Memory and Interpretation: New Approaches to the Study of the Crusades," *Journal of Medieval History*, 40 (2014), 225–36.

33 As put by Robert Allen Rouse, "Scholarship on the articulation of English identity during the medieval period has been somewhat of a boom industry over the past twenty-five years": review of Emily Dolmans, *Writing Regional Identities in Medieval England: From the "Gesta Herwardi" to "Richard Coer de Lyon"* (Woodbridge, UK: D. S. Brewer, 2020), *Studies in the Age of Chaucer*, 44 (2022), 395–97. As well as Dolmans's recent study, see, e.g., Thorlac Turville-Petre, *England the Nation: Language, Literature and National Identity, 1290–1340* (Oxford: Oxford University Press, 1996), pp. 108–41; Diane Speed, "The Construction of the Nation in Medieval Romance," in Carol Meale (ed.), *Readings in Medieval English Romance* (Cambridge, UK: D. S. Brewer, 1994), pp. 135–57; Siobhain Bly Calkin, *Saracens and the Making of English Identity: The Auchinleck Manuscript* (New York: Routledge, 2005); Robert Allen Rouse, *The Idea of Anglo-Saxon England in Middle English Romance* (Cambridge, UK: D. S. Brewer, 2005), pp. 70–92; Thomas H. Crofts and Robert Allen Rouse, "Middle English Popular Romance and National Identity," in Raluca L. Radulescu and Cory James Rushton (eds.), *A Companion to Medieval Popular Romance* (Cambridge, UK: D. S. Brewer, 2009), pp. 79–95; and Marisa Libbon, *Talk and Textual Production in Medieval England* (Columbus: The Ohio State University Press, 2021), pp. 107–73. The scholarship to most fully integrate the study of nationhood with the study of crusade culture is on the romance of *Richard Coeur de Lion*: see esp. Suzanne Conklin Akbari, "The Hunger for National Identity in *Richard Coeur de Lion*," in Robert M. Stein and Sandra Pierson Prior (eds.), *Reading Medieval Culture: Essays in Honor of Robert W. Hanning* (Notre Dame, IN: University of Notre Dame Press, 2005), pp. 198–227; Suzanne M. Yeager, *Jerusalem in Medieval Narrative* (Cambridge: Cambridge University Press, 2008), pp. 48–77; and Heng, *Empire of Magic*, pp. 61–113.

34 Lee Manion, *Narrating the Crusades: Loss and Recovery in Medieval and Early Modern English Literature* (Cambridge: Cambridge University Press, 2014).

35 Ardis Butterfield, *The Familiar Enemy: Chaucer, Language, and Nation in the Hundred Years War* (Oxford: Oxford University Press, 2009); David Wallace, *Premodern Places: Calais to Surinam, Chaucer to Aphra Behn* (Malden, MA: Blackwell, 2004). Recent studies include Marion Turner, *Chaucer:*

142 *Notes to pages 7–8*

A European Life (Princeton, NJ: Princeton University Press, 2019); Elizaveta Strakhov, *Continental England: Form, Translation, and Chaucer in the Hundred Years' War* (Columbus: The Ohio State University Press, 2022); and Philip Knox, *The "Romance of the Rose" and the Making of Fourteenth-Century English Literature* (Oxford: Oxford University Press, 2022).

36 I discuss two romances for which there are no extant Anglo-Norman or Latin source materials: *The Siege of Milan* and *Richard Coeur de Lion*.

37 Bernard Cerquiglini, *Éloge de la variante: Histoire critique de la philologie* (Paris: Seuil, 1989), translated into English by Betsy Wing as *In Praise of the Variant: A Critical History of Philology* (Baltimore: Johns Hopkins University Press, 1999). For Cerquiglini, "variance" is observable not just across, but also within, manuscripts: see further Arthur Bahr, "Miscellaneity and Variance in the Medieval Book," in Michael Johnston and Michael Van Dussen (eds.), *The Medieval Manuscript Book: Cultural Approaches* (Cambridge: Cambridge University Press, 2015), pp. 181–98. On the New Philology, a diverse set of attitudes toward medieval literatures and manuscripts that developed in the wake of Cerquiglini's study, see the critical overviews by Sarah Kay, "Analytical Survey 3: The New Philology," *New Medieval Literatures*, 3 (1999), 295–326; and Susan Yager, "New Philology," in Albrecht Classen (ed.), *Handbook of Medieval Studies: Terms, Methods, Trends* (Berlin: De Gruyter, 2010), pp. 999–1006. A number of other studies have informed my thinking about translation/adaptation, including Rita Copeland, *Rhetoric, Hermeneutics, and Translation in the Middle Ages: Academic Traditions and Vernacular Texts* (Cambridge: Cambridge University Press, 1991); Ivana Djordjević, "Mapping Medieval Translation," in Judith Weiss, Jennifer Fellows, and Morgan Dickson (eds.), *Medieval Insular Romance: Translation and Innovation* (Cambridge, UK: D. S. Brewer, 2000), pp. 7–23; Phillipa Hardman and Marianne Ailes, *The Legend of Charlemagne in Medieval England: The Matter of France in Middle English and Anglo-Norman Literature* (Cambridge, UK: D. S. Brewer, 2017); and Jeanette Beer (ed.), *A Companion to Medieval Translation* (Leeds, UK: Arc Humanities Press, 2019).

38 See Chapter 1, note 53; p. 44 and note 99.

39 See Chapter 1, pp. 37–40; Chapter 2, pp. 62–64; and Chapter 4, pp. 108–9.

40 See Chapter 1, pp. 40–42; and Chapter 2, pp. 56–57.

41 See Chapter 4, pp. 117, 120–21, and 126–28.

42 In treating emotions as an aspect of my methodology, I am taking up the call of scholars such as Barbara H. Rosenwein and Johannes Lang not for separate histories of feeling but for studies that, aimed at intervening in various critical debates, systematically incorporate emotions into their analyses: see Jan Plamper, "The History of Emotions: An Interview with William Reddy, Barbara Rosenwein, and Peter Stearns," *History and Theory*, 49 (2010), 237–65 (p. 260); Barbara H. Rosenwein, "Problems and Methods in the History of Emotions," *Passions in Context*, 1 (2010), 1–32 (p. 24); and

Notes to page 8 143

Johannes Lang, "New Histories of Emotion," *History and Theory*, 57 (2018), 104–20 (pp. 117–20).

43 Many introductory studies are available; a particularly concise and readable one is Barbara H. Rosenwein and Riccardo Cristiani, *What Is the History of Emotions?* (Cambridge, UK: Polity Press, 2018).

44 Anthony Bale, *Feeling Persecuted: Christians, Jews, and Images of Violence in the Middle Ages* (London: Reaktion, 2010); Rita Copeland, *Emotion and the History of Rhetoric in the Middle Ages* (Oxford: Oxford University Press, 2021); Sarah McNamer, *Affective Meditation and the Invention of Compassion* (Philadelphia: University of Pennsylvania Press, 2010); Sif Ríkharðsdóttir, *Emotion in Old Norse Literature: Translations, Voices, Contexts* (Cambridge, UK: D. S. Brewer, 2017); Megan Moore, *The Erotics of Grief: Emotions and the Construction of Privilege in the Medieval Mediterranean* (Ithaca, NY: Cornell University Press, 2021). Collections of essays include Glenn D. Burger and Holly A. Crocker (eds.), *Medieval Affect, Feeling, and Emotion* (Cambridge: Cambridge University Press, 2019); Stephanie Trigg (ed.), "Pre-Modern Emotions," special issue, *Exemplaria*, 26 (2014); Frank Brandsma, Carolyne Larrington, and Corinne Saunders (eds.), *Emotions in Medieval Arthurian Literature: Body, Mind, Voice* (Cambridge, UK: D. S. Brewer, 2015); and Mary C. Flannery (ed.), *Emotion and Medieval Textual Media* (Turnhout: Brepols, 2018).

45 In crusade studies, this area of investigation was prefigured by Jonathan Riley-Smith in his influential "Crusading as an Act of Love," *History*, 65 (1980), 177–92. See Stephen J. Spencer, *Emotions in a Crusading Context, 1095–1291* (Oxford: Oxford University Press, 2019); and the work of Susanna A. Throop: *Crusading as an Act of Vengeance 1095–1216* (Farnham, UK: Ashgate, 2011); "Zeal, Anger and Vengeance: The Emotional Rhetoric of Crusading," in Susanna A. Throop and Paul R. Hyams (eds.), *Vengeance in the Middle Ages: Emotion, Religion, and Feud* (Farnham, UK: Ashgate, 2010), pp. 177–201; and "Acts of Vengeance, Acts of Love: Crusading Violence in the Twelfth Century," in Laura Ashe and Ian Patterson (eds.), *War and Literature* (Cambridge, UK: D. S. Brewer, 2014), pp. 3–20. See also Stephen Benett, "Fear and Its Representation in the First Crusade," *Ex Historia*, 4 (2012), 29–54; Sophia Menache, "Emotions in the Service of Politics: Another Perspective on the Experience of Crusading (1095–1187)," in Susan B. Edgington and Luis García-Guijarro (eds.), *Jerusalem the Golden: The Origins and Impact of the First Crusade* (Turnhout: Brepols, 2014), pp. 235–54; and, by the same author, "Love of God or Hatred of Your Enemy? The Emotional Voices of the Crusades," *Mirabilia*, 10 (2010), 1–20.

46 Of course, the history of emotions is just one approach to studying the feelings, thoughts, ideologies, and experiences articulated in literary texts. While not framed as contributions to the history of emotions, two recent studies of crusade literature provide important insights for scholars working in that field: Marisa Galvez's *The Subject of Crusade: Lyric, Romance, and Materials, 1150 to 1500* (Chicago: University of Chicago Press, 2020), which

144 *Notes to pages 8–10*

identifies in lyric poems and other materials a "courtly crusade idiom" that illuminates the "ethical unsettledness" and "hesitations" of crusaders who left their homes, loved ones, and earthly duties to engage in holy war (pp. 2, 6, 21); and Stefan Vander Elst's *The Knight, the Cross, and the Song: Crusade Propaganda and Chivalric Literature, 1100–1400* (Philadelphia: University of Pennsylvania Press, 2017), pp. 124–88, which argues that tropes of courtly love in crusade romances and *chansons de geste* served a propagandist function.

47 Sara Ahmed, *The Cultural Politics of Emotion*, 2nd. ed. (Edinburgh: Edinburgh University Press, 2014; 1st ed. New York: Routledge, 2004); and her "Affective Economies," *Social Text*, 79 (2004), 117–39; Gandhi, *Affective Communities*; Jane Lydon, *Imperial Emotions: The Politics of Empathy across the British Empire* (Cambridge: Cambridge University Press, 2020).

48 See, notably, the sources compiled in Christoph T. Maier (ed. and trans.), *Crusade Propaganda and Ideology: Model Sermons for the Preaching of the Cross* (Cambridge: Cambridge University Press, 2000); and Jean Flori, *Prêcher la croisade (XIe–XIIIe siècle): Communication et propagande* (Paris: Perrin, 2012). Numerous sermons and encyclicals are also collected in Jonathan Riley-Smith and Louise Riley-Smith, *The Crusades: Idea and Reality, 1095–1274* (London: Edward Arnold, 1981); Norman Housley (ed. and trans.), *Documents on the Later Crusades, 1274–1580* (Basingstoke, UK: Macmillan Press, 1996); and Jessalynn Bird, Edward Peters, and James Powell (eds. and trans.), *Crusade and Christendom: Annotated Documents in Translation from Innocent III to the Fall of Acre, 1187–1291* (Philadelphia: University of Pennsylvania Press, 2013).

49 Ahmed, "Affective Economies," pp. 119–20.

50 The trajectory traced here finds support in Aurell's *Des Chrétiens contre les croisades*, discussed above, but also, in a different way, in M. Cecilia Gaposchkin's *Invisible Weapons: Liturgy and the Making of Crusade Ideology* (Ithaca, NY: Cornell University Press, 2017), which argues for a shift in the liturgy of the crusades toward the more introspective, penitential, and reformative as expedition after expedition ended in failure. See chapters 2 and 6.

51 Albert of Aachen, *Historia Ierosolimitana: History of the Journey to Jerusalem*, ed. and trans. Susan B. Edgington (Oxford: Oxford University Press, 2007), 6, 30, pp. 442–43.

52 For an overview and critique of some influential work in affect studies, see Ruth Leys, "The Turn to Affect: A Critique," *Critical Inquiry*, 37 (2011), 434–72. On the implications of such terminological choices, see further Stephanie Trigg, "Introduction: Emotional Histories – Beyond the Personalization of the Past and the Abstraction of Affect Theory," *Exemplaria*, 26 (2014), 3–15; and, by the same author, "Affect Theory," in Susan Broomhall (ed.), *Early Modern Emotions: An Introduction* (London: Routledge, 2017), pp. 10–13.

53 This definition is from Barbara H. Rosenwein, "Worrying about Emotions in History," *American Historical Review*, 107 (2002), 821–45 (p. 837). On the

Notes to page 10

emergence of social constructionism in the field of anthropology, its roots in the field of cognitive psychology, and its introduction into historical studies, see Rosenwein, "Problems and Methods in the History of Emotions," pp. 5–12; Damien Boquet and Piroska Nagy, "Pour une histoire des émotions. L'historien face aux questions contemporaines," in Damien Boquet and Piroska Nagy (eds.), *Le sujet des émotions au Moyen Âge* (Paris: Beauchesne, 2009), pp. 15–51; and Jan Plamper, *History of Emotions: An Introduction* (New York: Oxford University Press, 2015), pp. 75–146. Though the dominant approach in anthropology and historically oriented scholarship, social constructionism has not been without its critics: see esp. William M. Reddy, "Against Social Constructionism: The Historical Ethnography of Emotions," *Current Anthropology*, 38 (1997), 327–51.

54 Damien Boquet and Piroska Nagy, *Sensible Moyen Âge: Une histoire des émotions dans l'Occident medieval* (Paris: Éditions du Seuil, 2015); translated into English by Robert Shaw as *Medieval Sensibilities: A History of Emotions in the Middle Ages* (Cambridge, UK: Polity Press, 2018), p. 236. To reach these conclusions, Boquet and Nagy draw on work by Casagrande and Vecchio, some of which I cite in notes 57 and 58 below.

55 There is a vast body of scholarship on developments in the religious education of laypeople after Lateran IV. Outside the history of emotions, two recent studies are Aden Kumler, *Translating Truth: Ambitious Images and Religious Knowledge in Late Medieval France and England* (New Haven, CT: Yale University Press, 2011); and Claire M. Waters, *Translating Clergie: Status, Education, and Salvation in Thirteenth-Century Vernacular Texts* (Philadelphia: University of Pennsylvania Press, 2016).

56 See Richard Newhauser, *The Treatises on Vices and Virtues in Latin and the Vernacular* (Turnhout: Brepols, 1993), pp. 142–50.

57 Silvana Vecchio, "Passions de l'âme et péchés capitaux: Les ambiguïtés de la culture médiévale," in Christoph Flüeler and Martin Rohde (eds.), *Laster im Mittelalter/Vices in the Middle Ages* (New York: Walter de Gruyter, 2009), pp. 45–64 (p. 59).

58 Carla Casagrande and Silvana Vecchio, "Les théories des passions dans la culture médiévale," in Boquet and Nagy (eds.), *Le sujet des émotions au Moyen Âge*, pp. 107–22 (p. 122).

59 Reginald Pecock, *The Folewer to the Donet*, ed. Elsie Vaughan Hitchcock, Early English Text Society EC 4 (Oxford: Oxford University Press, 1924), p. 96.

60 Some theorists included pride and envy in taxonomies of the passions, while others did not. On Jean de la Rochelle's taxonomy, which includes them, see, e.g., Simo Knuuttila, *Emotions in Ancient and Medieval Philosophy* (Oxford: Clarendon Press, 2004), pp. 234–35; Virginia Langum, *Medicine and the Seven Deadly Sins in Late Medieval Literature and Culture* (New York: Palgrave, 2016), p. 88; and Vecchio, "Passions de l'âme et péchés capitaux," pp. 57–58.

61 Boquet and Nagy, *Medieval Sensibilities*, p. 237.

146 *Notes to pages 10–12*

62 See Tomas Zahora, "Since Feeling Is First: Teaching Royal Ethics through Managing the Emotions in the Late Middle Ages," *Parergon*, 31 (2014), 47–72.

63 A modern edition of the Latin *De regimine principum* is yet to be published. For John Trevisa's translation, see Giles of Rome, *The Governance of Kings and Princes: John Trevisa's Middle English Translation of the "De Regimine Principum" of Aegidius Romanus*, ed. David C. Fowler, Charles F. Briggs, and Paul G. Remley (New York: Garland, 1997), I, 3, pp. 113–38.

64 See Knuuttila, *Emotions in Ancient and Medieval Philosophy*, pp. 214–15.

65 On this, see Carole Rawcliffe, *Medicine and Society in Later Medieval England* (Stroud, UK: Sutton, 1995), pp. 1–25; and Langum, *Medicine and the Seven Deadly Sins*.

66 A good example of the overlap between discourses on the passions, the vices and virtues, royal governance, and the humors can be found in the French Dominican friar Laurent of Orléans's immensely popular moral treatise *La somme le roi* (composed in 1279), which also circulated widely in Middle English translations and adaptations: e.g., *The Book of Vices and Virtues*, *Adventures and Grace*, the *Ayenbite of Inwyt*, the *Book for a Simple and Devout Woman*, and William Caxton's *Royal Book*. See *La somme le roi par Frère Laurent*, ed. Edith Brayer and Anne-Françoise Leurquin-Labie (Paris: Société des Anciens Textes Français, 2008), LV, 52–71, pp. 265–66.

67 Hans Robert Jauss, *Toward an Aesthetic of Reception*, trans. Timothy Bahti (Minneapolis: University of Minnesota Press, 1982), pp. 22–25. I borrow the term "contract" from Fredric Jameson, "Magical Narratives: Romance as Genre," *New Literary History*, 7 (1975), 135–63: "Genres are essentially contracts between a writer and his readers" (p. 135). The overlap between Jameson's and Jauss's understandings of genre is noted by Helen Cooper, *The English Romance in Time: Transforming Motifs from Geoffrey of Monmouth to the Death of Shakespeare* (Oxford: Oxford University Press, 2004), p. 8n20.

68 Northrop Frye, "The Mythos of Summer: Romance" in *Anatomy of Criticism: Four Essays* (Princeton, NJ: Princeton University Press, 1957), pp. 186–206; and *The Secular Scripture: A Study of the Structure of Romance* (Cambridge, MA: Harvard University Press, 1976): "Romance avoids the ambiguities of ordinary life, where everything is a mixture of good and bad, and where it is difficult to take sides or believe that people are consistent patterns of virtue or vice. The popularity of romance, it is obvious, has much to do with its simplifying of moral facts" (pp. 35–36). For a recent assessment in this vein, see, e.g., Liu, "Middle English Romance as Prototype Genre": "It is fitting for Middle English romance to be defined in terms of prototypes, of 'best examples,' for these texts are about exemplarity" (p. 347).

69 On this, see further Roberta L. Krueger, "Introduction," in *The Cambridge Companion to Medieval Romance*, ed. Roberta L. Krueger (Cambridge: Cambridge University Press, 2000), pp. 1–9 (p. 6); Francis O'Gorman, "Realism and Romance," in Robert L. Caserio and Clement Hawes (eds.), *The Cambridge History of the English Novel* (Cambridge: Cambridge University Press, 2012), pp. 485–99 (p. 485).

Notes to pages 12–13   147

70 General genre-based discussions of Middle English romance have often featured as reference works or as introductions to edited collections: see Jane Gilbert, "A Theoretical Introduction," in Ad Putter and Jane Gilbert (eds.), *The Spirit of Medieval English Popular Romance* (Harlow, UK: Longman, 2000), pp. 15–31 (citation at p. 24); Christine Chism, "Romance," in Larry Scanlon (ed.), *The Cambridge Companion to Medieval English Literature, 1100–1500* (Cambridge: Cambridge University Press, 2009), pp. 57–70; and Neil Cartlidge, "Introduction," in Neil Cartlidge (ed.), *Heroes and Anti-Heroes in Medieval Romance*, pp. 1–8. This is not to say that Anglo-Norman romances and *chansons de geste* lack complexity of characterization; Middle English romances clearly build on the potential of their sources. On the relationship between Middle English crusade romances and *chansons de geste*, see further my "Crusade Romances and the Matter of France," in Helen Cooper and Robert R. Edwards (eds.), *The Oxford History of Poetry in English, vol. 2 (1100–1400)* (Oxford: Oxford University Press, 2023), pp. 339–55.

71 On the gentry audience of romance, see Michael Johnston, *Romance and the Gentry in Late Medieval England* (Oxford: Oxford University Press, 2014). For more general discussions, see Rosalind Field, "Romance in England, 1066–1400," in David Wallace (ed.), *The Cambridge History of Medieval English Literature* (Cambridge: Cambridge University Press, 1999), pp. 152–76 (p. 167–70); Cooper, *English Romance in Time*, pp. 11–13; Nancy Mason Bradbury, "Popular Romance," in Corinne Saunders (ed.), *A Companion to Medieval Poetry* (Chichester, UK: Wiley-Blackwell, 2010), pp. 289–307 (pp. 293–96); Derek Brewer, "The Popular English Metrical Romances," in Corinne Saunders (ed.), *A Companion to Romance: From Classical to Contemporary* (Oxford: Blackwell, 2007), pp. 45–64 (pp. 45–46); and Ad Putter, "A Historical Introduction," in Putter and Gilbert (eds.), *The Spirit of Medieval English Popular Romance*, pp. 1–15. For a discussion of the lower end of the social spectrum, see Michael Johnston, "New Evidence for the Social Reach of 'Popular Romance': The Books of Household Servants," *Viator*, 43 (2012), 303–32, who offers evidence that manuscripts of *Amis and Amiloun* and *Sir Isumbras* were owned by fifteenth-century household servants. On the oral delivery of romance, see Karl Reichl, "Orality and Performance," in Radulescu and Rushton (eds.), *A Companion to Medieval Popular Romance*, pp. 132–49; and Linda Marie Zaerr, *Performance and the Middle English Romance* (Cambridge, UK: D. S. Brewer, 2012).

72 A particularly compelling critique of the tenacious idea that Middle English romances are narratively "unsophisticated" is offered by Ralph Hanna, *London Literature, 1300–1380* (Cambridge: Cambridge University Press, 2005), pp. 104–47. Scholars of modern popular fiction have also countered earlier denigrations of that fiction as offering "uncritical gorging," emphasizing instead its ability to create enthusiasts who thrive off its pleasures and cognitive demands: see Roger Luckhurst, "The Public Sphere, Popular Culture, and the True Meaning of the Zombie Apocalypse," in David Glover (ed.), *The Cambridge Companion to Popular Fiction* (Cambridge:

148 *Notes to pages 13–18*

Cambridge University Press, 2012), pp. 68–85 (p. 68); and, in the same volume, Nicola Humble, "The Reader of Popular Fiction," pp. 86–102.

73 Cooper, *English Romance in Time*, pp. 12–13 (p. 13). On the role of debate in late medieval English culture, see further Thomas L. Reed, *Middle English Debate Poetry and the Aesthetics of Irresolution* (Columbia: University of Missouri Press, 1990). For a discussion of romance as a genre invested in asking questions, see the introduction to Katherine C. Little and Nicola McDonald (eds.), *Thinking Medieval Romance* (Oxford: Oxford University Press, 2018), pp. 1–10.

74 I discuss the historical evidence in the chapters that follow. For an overview of previous scholarly definitions of the crusade romance, see Siobhain Bly Calkin, "Crusade Romance," in Siân Echard and Robert Allen Rouse (eds.), *The Encyclopedia of British Medieval Literature* (Chichester, UK: Wiley-Blackwell, 2017), pp. 583–89.

75 This corpus of romances is largely, though not entirely, distinct from Manion's in *Narrating the Crusades*, which focuses on *Sir Isumbras, Octavian, The Sultan of Babylon,* and the B-version of *Richard Coeur de Lion* (I discuss the A-version). On these versions of *Richard Coeur de Lion*, see my discussion in Chapter 4.

Chapter 1

1 For an account of this campaign, and of other Carolingian campaigns in al-Andalus under Charlemagne's authority, see Samuel Ottewill-Soulsby, "'Those Same Cursed Saracens': Charlemagne's Campaigns in the Iberian Peninsula as Religious Warfare," *Journal of Medieval History*, 42 (2016), 405–28.

2 Robert of Reims, *Robert the Monk's History of Jerusalem: Historia Iherosolimitana*, trans. Carol Sweetenham (Aldershot, UK: Ashgate, 2006), p. 81.

3 Philippe de Mézières, *Letter to King Richard II, a Plea Made in 1395 for Peace between England and France*, ed. and trans. G. W. Coopland (Liverpool, UK: Liverpool University Press, 1975), p. 70.

4 Some examples are Robert of Reims, *Robert the Monk's History of Jerusalem*, p. 81; Ambroise, *The History of the Holy War: Ambroise's "Estoire de la Guerre Sainte,"* trans. Marianne Ailes; notes Marianne Ailes and Malcom Barber (Woodbridge, UK: Boydell Press, 2011), pp. 145–46; Helen J. Nicholson (trans.), *The Chronicle of the Third Crusade: A Translation of the "Itinerarium Peregrinorum et Gesta Regis Ricardi"* (Aldershot, UK: Ashgate, 1997), pp. 5, 21, 300; Jean Leclercq (ed.), "Un sermon prononcé pendant la guerre de Flandre sous Philippe le Bel," *Revue du moyen âge latin*, 1 (1945), 165–72; Roger Stanegrave, *Li charboclois d'armes du conquest precious de la Terre Sainte de promission*, in Jacques Paviot (ed.), *Projets de croisade (v. 1290–v. 1330)* (Paris: Académie des Inscriptions et Belles-Lettres, 2008), pp. 293–387 (p. 386); Pierre Dubois, *The Recovery of the Holy Land*, ed. and trans.

Notes to page 18

Walther I. Brandt (New York: Columbia University Press, 1956), p. 87; Marino Sanudo Torsello, *The Book of the Secrets of the Faithful Cross: Liber secretorum fidelium crucis*, trans. Peter Lock (Farnham, UK: Ashgate, 2011), p. 206; Honorat Bovet, *Medieval Muslims, Christians, and Jews in Dialogue: The "Apparicion Maistre Jehan de Meun" of Honorat Bovet*, ed. and trans. Michael Hanly (Tempe: Arizona Center for Medieval and Renaissance Studies, 2005), p. 104; and Jean Germain, "Le discours du voyage d'oultremer au très victorieux roi Charles VII, prononcé en 1452 par Jean Germain, évêque de Chalron," *Revue de l'Orient latin*, ed. C. Schefer, 5 (1895), 303–42, trans. Norman Housley (ed. and trans.), *Documents on the Later Crusades, 1274–1580* (Basingstoke, UK: Macmillan Press, 1996), pp. 142–43. See also Maurice Keen, *Chivalry* (New Haven, CT: Yale University Press, 1984), p. 107; Jace Stuckey, "Charlemagne as Crusader? Memory, Propaganda, and the Many Uses of Charlemagne's Legendary Expedition to Spain," in Matthew Gabriele and Jace Stuckey (eds.), *The Legend of Charlemagne in the Middle Ages: Power, Faith, and Crusade* (New York: Palgrave, 2008), pp. 137–52; and Anne Latowsky, "Charlemagne, Godfrey of Bouillon, and Louis IX of France," in Anthony Bale (ed.), *The Cambridge Companion to the Literature of the Crusades* (Cambridge: Cambridge University Press, 2019), pp. 200–214.

5 See, however, Lee Manion, *Narrating the Crusades: Loss and Recovery in Medieval and Early Modern English Literature* (Cambridge: Cambridge University Press, 2014), pp. 107–45, on *The Sultan of Babylon* in relation to crusading in Iberia; and Phillipa Hardman and Marianne Ailes, *The Legend of Charlemagne in Medieval England: The Matter of France in Middle English and Anglo-Norman Literature* (Cambridge, UK: D. S. Brewer, 2017), pp. 72–73, 296–97, who propose a specific crusading context (among many other non-crusading contexts) for understanding the Charlemagne romances as a group: the threat to Europe posed by the Ottomans.

6 See Robert Warm, "Identity, Narrative and Participation: Defining a Context for the Middle English Charlemagne Romances," in Rosalind Field (ed.), *Tradition and Transformation in Medieval Romance* (Cambridge, UK: D. S. Brewer, 1999), pp. 87–100; Marianne Ailes, "La réception de *Fierabras* en Angleterre," in Marc Le Person (ed.), *Le rayonnement de Fierabras dans la littérature européenne* (Lyon: Centre d'étude des Interactions Culturelles, Université Jean Moulin Lyon 3, 2003), pp. 177–89; Phillipa Hardman and Marianne Ailes, "How English Are the English Charlemagne Romances?," in Neil Cartlidge (ed.), *Boundaries in Medieval Romance* (Woodbridge, UK: D. S. Brewer, 2008), pp. 43–55; Phillipa Hardman, "Knight, King, Emperor, Saint: Portraying Charlemagne in Middle English Romance," *Reading Medieval Studies*, 38 (2012), 43–58; and Melissa Furrow, "*Chanson de geste* as Romance in England," in Laura Ashe, Ivana Djordjević, and Judith Weiss (eds.), *The Exploitations of Medieval Romance* (Cambridge, UK: D. S. Brewer, 2010), pp. 57–72.

7 Hardman and Ailes, "How English," p. 53; Ailes, "La réception de *Fierabras*," p. 189.

150   *Notes to pages 18–21*

8 Warm, "Identity, Narrative and Participation," p. 87.

9 *The Siege of Milan* is preserved uniquely in London, British Library, MS Additional 31042. I will refer to the following edition: Stephen H. A. Shepherd (ed.), *The Siege of Milan*, in *Middle English Romances* (New York: Norton, 1995), pp. 268–312.

10 *The Sultan of Babylon* also survives in a single manuscript: Princeton University Library, MS Garrett 140, c. 1450. References are given to the most recent edition: Alan Lupack (ed.), *Three Middle English Charlemagne Romances* (Kalamazoo, MI: Medieval Institute Publications, 1990), pp. 7–103. Given the echoes it contains of Langland and Chaucer, *The Sultan of Babylon* could not have been written before the end of the fourteenth century. See Lupack's introduction to *Three Middle English Charlemagne Romances*, p. 1; H. M. Smyser, "The Sowdon of Babylon and Its Author," *Harvard Studies and Notes in Philology and Literature*, 13 (1931), 185–218 (esp. pp. 203–7); and Marcel Elias, "Crusade Romances and the Matter of France," in Helen Cooper and Robert R. Edwards (eds.), *The Oxford History of Poetry in English, vol. 2 (1100–1400)* (Oxford: Oxford University Press, 2023), pp. 339–55 (pp. 348–49).

11 The other Middle English Charlemagne romance for which there is no extant source material is *Rauf Coilyear* (which is not, however, a crusade romance), composed near the end of the fifteenth century and preserved only in an edition printed in 1572.

12 Diana T. Childress, "Between Romance and Legend: 'Secular Hagiography' in Middle English Romance," *Philological Quarterly*, 57 (1978), 311–22, labels the poem a "secular hagiography" or "secular legend"; Dieter Mehl, *The Middle English Romances of the Thirteenth and Fourteenth Centuries* (London: Barnes and Noble, 1969), pp. 152–53, calls the poem a "homiletic romance"; Suzanne Conklin Akbari, "Incorporation in the *Siege of Melayne*," in Nicola McDonald (ed.), *Pulp Fictions of Medieval England: Essays in Popular Romance* (Manchester, UK: Manchester University Press, 2004), pp. 22–44, explores how hagiographic, devotional, and eucharistic themes are deployed.

13 On biblical anger, see, e.g., Laurent Smagghe, *Les émotions du prince: Émotions et discours politique dans l'espace bourguignon* (Paris: Garnier, 2012), pp. 168–72; and Yves Cattin, "Dieu d'amour, dieu de colère … justice et miséricorde dans le Proslogion (ch. VI–XI) d'Anselme de Canterbury," *Revue d'histoire et de philosophie religieuses*, 69 (1989), 423–50.

14 Lactantius, *De ira dei*, in Alexander Roberts and James Donaldson (eds.), *Ante-Nicene Fathers*, 10 vols. (Buffalo, NY: Christian Literature Publishing, 1886), VII, 18 and 21, pp. 274–75, 277.

15 Augustine, *De civitate dei*, ed. J. P. Migne, Patrologia Latina 41 (Paris: Garnier Fratres, 1864), 9, 5, col. 260; Augustine, *The City of God against the Pagans*, trans. R. W. Dyson (Cambridge: Cambridge University Press, 1998), p. 365.

16 Alcuin of York, *De virtutibus et vitiis*, ed. J. P. Migne, Patrologia Latina 101 (Paris: Garnier fratres, 1851), 31, col. 634; Rachel Stone (trans.), "Translation

Notes to pages 21–25 151

of Alcuin's *De virtutibus et vitiis liber*," *Heroic Age: A Journal of Early Medieval Northwestern Europe*, 16 (2015), XXIV, 30, http://jemne.org/issues/16/stone .php.

17 Hincmar of Reims, *De cavendis vitiis et virtutibus exercendis*, ed. Doris Nachtmann, Monumenta Germaniae Historica: Quellen zur Geistesgeschichte des Mittelalters 16 (Munich: Monumenta Germaniae Historica, 1998), pp. 153–57.

18 Thomas of Chobham, *Summa confessorum*, ed. Frederick Broomfield (Paris: Nauwelaerts, 1968), p. 414; trans. Susanna A. Throop, "Zeal, Anger and Vengeance: The Emotional Rhetoric of Crusading," in Susanna A. Throop and Paul R. Hyams (eds.), *Vengeance in the Middle Ages: Emotion, Religion, and Feud* (Farnham, UK: Ashgate, 2010), pp. 177–201 (p. 190).

19 Thomas Aquinas, *The "Summa Theologica" of Thomas Aquinas*, trans. Fathers of the English Dominican Province (London: Burns Oates and Washbourne, 1922), IIa 2ae 158, 1–8.

20 In Trevisa's translation of Giles, *The Governance of Kings and Princes: John Trevisa's Middle English Translation of the "De Regimine Principum" of Aegidius Romanus*, ed. David C. Fowler, Charles F. Briggs, and Paul G. Remley (New York: Garland, 1997), I, 3, pp. 128–29.

21 Geoffrey Chaucer, "The Parson's Tale," in Larry D. Benson (ed.), *The Riverside Chaucer*, 3rd ed. (Oxford: Oxford University Press, 2008; 1st ed. 1987), lines 535–45.

22 Stephen D. White, "The Politics of Anger," in Barbara H. Rosenwein (ed.), *Anger's Past: The Social Uses of an Emotion in the Middle Ages* (Ithaca, NY: Cornell University Press, 1998), p. 140.

23 White, "Politics of Anger," pp. 142–44; see further Richard E. Barton, "'Zealous Anger' and the Renegotiation of Aristocratic Relationships in Eleventh and Twelfth Century France," in Rosenwein (ed.), *Anger's Past*, p. 158.

24 Throop, "Zeal, Anger and Vengeance," pp. 184–201.

25 Jacques de Vitry, I, 4, Troyes, Bibliothèque Municipale, 228, in Christoph T. Maier (ed. and trans.), *Crusade Propaganda and Ideology: Model Sermons for the Preaching of the Cross* (Cambridge: Cambridge University Press, 2000), pp. 85–86.

26 Gilbert de Tournai, III, 4, Paris, Bibliothèque Nationale de France, lat. 15953, in Maier (ed. and trans.), *Crusade Propaganda and Ideology*, pp. 200–201.

27 According to Gerd Althoff, such rituals of peace and renewed friendship possessed a contractual value: see his "Friendship and Political Order," in Julian Haseldine (ed.), *Friendship in Medieval Europe* (Stroud, UK: Sutton, 1999), pp. 91–105.

28 See David Green, *The Hundred Years War: A People's History* (New Haven, CT: Yale University Press, 2014), pp. 104–24, who notes that "defense of the realm" was "central to the promotion and manifestation of royal authority in the later Middle Ages" (p. 124); and also W. R. Jones, "The English Church

and Royal Propaganda during the Hundred Years War," *Journal of British Studies*, 19 (1979), 18–30.

29 Hugo of Lüttich, *Peregrinarius*, ed. Franz Unterkircher (Leiden: Brill, 1991), pp. 32–52, lines 399–1206.

30 On the English members of Mézières's order, see Timothy Guard, *Chivalry, Kingship and Crusade: The English Experience in the Fourteenth Century* (Woodbridge, UK: Boydell Press, 2013), pp. 171–73; Adrian Bell, "English Members of the Order of the Passion: Their Political, Diplomatic and Military Significance," in Renate Blumenfeld-Kosinski and Kiril Petkov (eds.), *Philippe de Mézières and His Age* (Leiden: Brill, 2012), pp. 321–45; and Stefan Vander Elst, "'Tu es pélerin en la sainte cité': Chaucer's Knight and Philippe de Mézières," *Studies in Philology*, 106 (2009), 379–401 (pp. 381–82).

31 Philippe de Mézières, *Le songe du vieil pelerin*, ed. G. W. Coopland, 2 vols. (Cambridge: Cambridge University Press, 1969), I, 76, pp. 396–403.

32 Mézières, *Letter to King Richard II*, ed. and trans. Coopland, pp. 26–27, 99. See further Philippe Contamine, "Guerre et paix à la fin du Moyen Age: L'action et la pensée de Philippe de Mézières (1327–1405)," in Hans-Henning Kortüm (ed.), *Krieg im Mittelalter* (Berlin: Akademie Verlag, 2001), pp. 181–96.

33 Mézières, *Letter to King Richard II*, ed. and trans. Coopland, pp. 24, 97.

34 Eustache Deschamps, "Complainte de l'Eglise," in Auguste-Henry-Edouard De Queux de Saint-Hilaire and Gaston Raynaud (eds.), *Oeuvres complètes*, 11 vols. (Paris: Firmin Didot, 1878–1903), VII, pp. 293–311.

35 John Mandeville, *The Book of John Mandeville*, ed. Tamarah Kohanski and C. David Benson (Kalamazoo, MI: Medieval Institute Publications, 2007), lines 46–48.

36 John Gower, *Vox Clamantis*, in G. C. Macaulay (ed.), *The Complete Works of John Gower*, 4 vols. (Oxford: Clarendon Press, 1899), IV, 3, lines 307–10.

37 On this, in relation to Old French, see White, "Politics of Anger," p. 135; and Robert Francis Cook, *The Sense of the "Song of Roland"* (Ithaca, NY: Cornell University Press, 1987), p. 51n69.

38 See *Middle English Dictionary* (*MED*), *tene* n.(2), 3. (c) sorrow, grief; care, anxiety, distress; 4. (a) vexation, chagrin; anger, wrath; and *gref* n., 3. (a) anger, hostility, spite; 4. (a) sorrow, mental distress. See also, on the polysemy of the Old English word *teona*, which meant "the hurt" that had been "done to someone" and which raised "the emotion of shame, anger and/or grief," Michiko Ogura, *Words and Expressions of Emotion in Medieval English* (Frankfurt: Peter Lang, 2013), p. 65.

39 See further Sarah McNamer, *Affective Meditation and the Invention of Medieval Compassion* (Philadelphia: University of Pennsylvania Press, 2010), p. 11n43. As noted by McNamer, *compassioun* is a relatively late term, appearing around 1340 and deriving from both Latin and Old French (see *MED, compassioun*, n.).

40 Paulin Paris (ed.), *La chanson d'Antioche*, 2 vols. (Paris: J. Techener, 1848), I, 32, p. 53.

Notes to pages 27–29   153

41 Odo of Deuil, *De profectione Ludovici VII in Orientem: The Journey of Louis VII to the East*, ed. and trans. Virginia Gingerich Berry (New York: W. W. Norton, 1948), pp. 6–7.

42 Jacques de Vitry, "Sermones vulgares," in J. B. Pitra (ed.), *Analecta novissima spicilegii Solesmensis: Altera continuatio*, 2 vols. (Paris: Typis Tusculanis, 1888), II, p. 421; trans. Jonathan Riley-Smith and Louise Riley-Smith, *The Crusades: Idea and Reality, 1095–1274* (London: Edward Arnold, 1981), p. 134.

43 Ibid., p. 421; trans. Riley-Smith and Riley-Smith, *Crusades: Idea and Reality*, p. 134.

44 The full-length study on vengeance is Susanna Throop, *Crusading as an Act of Vengeance* (Farnham, UK: Ashgate, 2011). Numerous other sources linking sorrow or compassion to military aid or retribution are available. See, e.g., Gunther of Pairis, "Historia Constantinopolitana," in *Exuviae sacrae Constantinopolitanae*, ed. Paul Riant, 3 vols. (Geneva: Fick, 1877), I, pp. 62–64, trans. Riley-Smith and Riley-Smith, *Crusades: Idea and Reality*, pp. 70–71; and Bernard of Clairvaux, *Epistolae*, ed. J. P. Migne, Patrologia Latina 182 (Paris: Garnier fratres), no. 363, cols. 565–67, trans. Riley-Smith and Riley-Smith, *Crusades: Idea and Reality*, pp. 95–96. This rhetoric was also used to implement papal taxes and to collect alms in exchange for indulgences: see, e.g., Augustin Theiner (ed.), *Vetera monumenta historica Hungariam sacram illustrantia*, 2 vols. (Rome: Typis Vaticanis, 1864), II, 660–62, trans. Housley (ed. and trans.), *Documents on the Later Crusades*, pp. 78–80; and Jürgen Sarnowsky (ed.), "Die Johanniter und Smyrna (1344–1402)," *Römische Quartalschrift*, 87 (1992), 70–71, trans. Housley (ed. and trans.), *Documents on the Later Crusades*, pp. 101–2.

45 Norman P. Tanner (ed.), *Decrees of the Ecumenical Councils*, 2 vols. (London: Sheed and Ward, 1990), I, p. 309.

46 See Sylvia Schein, *Fideles Crucis: The Papacy, the West, and the Recovery of the Holy Land, 1274–1314* (Oxford: Clarendon Press, 1991), pp. 114–15.

47 R. B. C. Huygens (ed.), *Excidium Aconis gestorum collectio: Magister Thadeus civis Neapolitanus, Ystoria de desolatione et conculcatione civitatis Acconensis et tocius Terre Sanctae* (Turnhout: Brepols, 2004), II, lines 750–58; my translation.

48 Philippe de Mézières, *The Life and Times of Saint Peter Thomas by Philippe de Mézières*, ed. Joachim Smet (Rome: Institutum Carmelitanum, 1954), pp. 120–21; trans. Housley (ed. and trans.), *Documents on the Later Crusades*, p. 86.

49 At lines 94–96, the emphasis is likewise on Charlemagne's duty to avenge the lord of Milan: "To Charles that beris the flour-de-lyce; / Of other kynges he berys the pryce / And he sall wreke thy wrethis alle."

50 On religious weeping, see esp. Piroska Nagy, *Le Don des larmes au Moyen Âge* (Paris: Albin Michel, 2000). The practice of calling upon God's assistance through weeping is amply documented across cultures. For instance, Elina Gertsman, "Introduction: 'Going They Wept and Wept.' Tears in Medieval

154   *Notes to pages 30–32*

Discourse," in Elina Gertsman (ed.), *Crying in the Middle Ages: Tears of History* (New York: Routledge, 2012), p. xiii, refers to St. Bernard, who "invoked the power of tears to call upon Christ to restore the dead to life." See also Rachel S. Mikva, "Weeping as Discourse between Heaven and Earth: The Transformative Power of Tears in Medieval Jewish Literature," in Gertsman (ed.), *Crying in the Middle Ages* pp. 156–72, who discusses the connection between weeping and divine mercy, and refers to biblical precedents (Psalm 56:9–10 and Isaiah 30:19); Kimberley Christine Patton, "'Howl, Weep and Moan, and Bring It Back to God': Holy Tears in Eastern Christianity," in Kimberly Christine Patton and John Stratton Hawley (eds.), *Holy Tears: Weeping in the Religious Imagination* (Princeton, NJ: Princeton University Press, 2005), pp. 255–73; and Smagghe, *Les émotions du prince*, p. 380.

51 A. Chroust (ed.), *Historia de expeditione Friderici imperatoris*, in Monumenta Germaniae Historica: Scriptores rerum Germanicarum NS 5 (Berlin: Weidmannsche Buchhandlung, 1928), p. 7; trans. Riley-Smith and Riley-Smith, *Crusades: Idea and Reality*, p. 65.

52 For similar emotional rhetoric, in a different context, see Sara Ahmed, "Affective Economies," *Social Text*, 79 (2004), 117–39; Ahmed also writes on pain, injury, and collective response in *The Cultural Politics of Emotion*, 2nd ed. (Edinburgh: Edinburgh University Press, 2014; 1st ed. New York: Routledge, 2004) (see esp. pp. 20–41).

53 Turpin's is the most accusatory of three heavenly addressed complaints in Middle English crusade literature; the other two feature in *Firumbras* and *Capystranus*. See Mary Isabelle O'Sullivan (ed.), *Firumbras*, in *Firumbras and Otuel and Roland*, Early English Text Society OS 198 (London: Oxford University Press, 1935), lines 1121–22; and Shepherd (ed.), *Capystranus*, in *Middle English Romances*, lines 465–512. The episode in *Firumbras* is unparalleled in the French source texts; for a discussion, see my "Interfaith Empathy and the Formation of Romance," in Mary C. Flannery (ed.), *Emotion and Medieval Textual Media* (Turnhout: Brepols, 2018), p. 115.

54 Maldwyn Mills, "Introduction," in *Six Middle English Romances* (London: Dent, 1973), p. xiii.

55 Akbari, "Incorporation in the *Siege of Melayne*," pp. 26–27.

56 Thomas H. Crofts and Robert Allen Rouse, "Middle English Popular Romance and National Identity," in Raluca L. Radulescu and Cory James Rushton (eds.), *A Companion to Medieval Popular Romance* (Cambridge, UK: D. S. Brewer, 2009), p. 93; Stephen Shepherd, "'This Grete Journee': *The Sege of Melayne*," in Maldwyn Mills, Jennifer Fellows, and Carol M. Meale (eds.), *Romance in Medieval England* (Cambridge: D. S. Brewer, 1991), pp. 124–25; and Shepherd (ed.), *Middle English Romances*, pp. 389–90.

57 A portion of the thirteenth-century evidence is, however, concisely discussed by Martin Aurell, *Des Chrétiens contre les croisades, XIIe–XIIIe siècles* (Paris: Fayard, 2013), pp. 299–304.

58 These accusations bear affinity with medieval Christian rituals of humiliation of the saints: see Patrick Geary, "Humiliation of Saints," in Stephen Wilson

Notes to pages 32–34 155

(ed.), *Saints and Their Cults: Studies in Religious Sociology, Folklore and History* (Cambridge: Cambridge University Press, 1983), pp. 123–40.

59 Antoine de Bastard (ed.), "La colère et la douleur d'un templier en Terre Sainte," *Revue des langues romanes*, 81 (1974), 333–73 (p. 356), lines 1–8; English translation mine.

60 Alfred Jeanroy (ed.), "Le troubadour Austorc d'Aurillac et son sirventés sur la Septième Croisade," *Romanische Forschungen*, 23 (1907), 81–88 (pp. 82–83), lines 1–2, 12, 16, 22–23; English translations mine. Both Ricaut Bonomel and Austorc d'Aurillac's songs are based on an earlier *canso* of Peirol d'Auvergne. See Jaye Puckett, "'Reconmenciez novele estoire': The Troubadours and the Rhetoric of the Later Crusades," *Modern Language Notes*, 116 (2001), 844–89 (p. 878n59).

61 Linda Paterson (ed.), "Austorc de Segret: *[No s]ai qui·m so tan suy [des]-conoyssens,*" *Lecturae tropatorum*, 5 (2012), 1–16 (p. 12): "Ni re no say tan fort suy esbaÿtz: / si Dieus nos a o dïables marritz, / que Crestïas e la ley vey perida, / e Sarrazis an trobada guandida" (I know nothing, I am so bewildered: God or a devil has so afflicted us that I see Christians and the Christian religion destroyed, and Saracens have found safe haven).

62 Matthew Paris, *Chronica majora*, ed. Henry Richards Luard, 7 vols. (London: Longman, 1872–83), v, pp. 169–70; Matthew Paris, *Chronicles of Matthew Paris: Monastic Life in the Thirteenth Century*, ed. and trans. Richard Vaughan (Gloucester, UK: Alan Sutton, 1984), p. 256.

63 Ibid., p. 170; trans. Vaughan, p. 256.

64 Salimbene de Adam, *Cronica*, ed. Giuseppe Scalia, 2 vols. (Turnhout: Brepols, 1999), II, 645, pp. 672–73; *The Chronicle of Salimbene de Adam*, ed. and trans. Joseph L. Baird, Giuseppe Baglivi, and John Robert Kane (Binghamton, NY: Medieval and Renaissance Texts and Studies, 1986), p. 453.

65 He was canonized in 1297. On the cult of Saint Louis, see M. Cecilia Gaposchkin, *The Making of Saint Louis: Kingship, Sanctity, and Crusade in the Later Middle Ages* (Ithaca, NY: Cornell University Press, 2008).

66 These letters were edited by Reinhold Röhricht in Riccoldo da Monte di Croce, "Lettres de Ricoldo de Monte-Croce sur la prise d'Acre (1291)," in *Archives de l'Orient latin*, 12 vols. (Paris: Ernest Leroux, 1884), II, pp. 258–92. They were translated into French by René Kappler in Riccoldo da Monte di Croce, *Riccold de Monte Croce: Pérégrination en Terre Sainte et au Proche Orient. Lettres sur la chute de Saint Jean d'Acre* (Paris: Champion, 1997); and into English by Rita George-Tvrtković, *A Christian Pilgrim in Medieval Iraq: Riccoldo da Montecroce's Encounter with Islam* (Turnhout: Brepols, 2012), pp. 137–73. These letters are discussed, with different emphases, by Iris Shagrir, "The Fall of Acre as a Spiritual Crisis: The Letters of Riccoldo of Monte Croce," *Revue Belge de philologie et d'histoire*, 90 (2012), 1107–20. In what follows, I refer to Röhricht's edition; all English translations are mine.

67 Riccoldo da Monte di Croce, "Lettres de Ricoldo de Monte-Croce," ed. Röhricht, pp. 269–70.

156 Notes to pages 34–38

68 Ibid., p. 288.

69 Ibid., p. 271.

70 Ibid., p. 275.

71 Ibid., p. 286.

72 Ottokar von Steiermark, *Ottokars Österreichische Reimchronik*, ed. Joseph Seemüller (Hannover: Hahn, 1890), lines 52359–63.

73 *The Sultan of Babylon* is believed to have its direct source in lost Anglo-Norman versions of *La destruction de Rome* and *Fierebras*, which in turn stem from the (Anglo-Norman) texts found in London, British Library, MS Egerton 3028. The Egerton manuscript was edited by Louis Brandin in "*La destruction de Rome* et *Fierabras*, MS Egerton 3028, Musée Britannique," *Romania*, 64 (1938), 18–100. For the antecedent, longer version of *La destruction de Rome* contained in the Hanover manuscript, see Johann Heinrich Speich (ed.), *La destructioun de Rome (d'après le ms. de Hanovre IV, 578)* (Bern: Peter Lang, 1988). On the possibility that *La destruction de Rome* was an insular text altogether, see Marianne Ailes, "What's in a Name? Anglo-Norman Romances or *Chansons de geste*?," in Rhiannon Purdie and Michael Cichon (eds.), *Medieval Romance, Medieval Contexts* (Cambridge, UK: D. S. Brewer, 2011), pp. 61–76 (pp. 66–67). For the earlier continental version of *Fierabras*, see Marc Le Person (ed.), *Fierabras: Chanson de geste du XIIe siècle* (Paris: Champion, 2003). On the possible sources, influences, and historical elements at the origin of the legend and texts of *La destruction de Rome*, see Speich's introduction to *La destructioun de Rome*, pp. 7–15. The most complete study of the relationship between the English and French renderings of *Fierabras* is Marianne Ailes, "A Comparative Study of the Medieval French and Middle English Verse Texts of the Fierabras Legend," 2 vols. (unpublished doctoral thesis, University of Reading, 1989).

74 Jeffrey Jerome Cohen, "On Saracen Enjoyment: Some Fantasies of Race in Late Medieval France and England," *Journal of Medieval and Early Modern Studies*, 31 (2001), 113–46, 113–46 (p. 126).

75 See esp. lines 995–110, 2149, 2135, and 2943–44.

76 See lines 754, 962, 2169–70, and 2458; 413–18 and 784–86; 164, 237, 935, 956, 1013, and 1756; 1051–53 ("Ferumbras with grete araye / Rode forthe, Mahounde him spede, / Tille he came nyghe there Charles lay") and 1737; 1221–22 and 1254; 49, 75, 136, 207, 979, and 2163; 447–49 (the Muslim character's salvation features in the Egerton manuscript, but the quoted line is unique to *The Sultan of Babylon*).

77 See further John V. Tolan, *Sons of Ishmael: Muslims through European Eyes in the Middle Ages* (Gainesville: University Press of Florida, 2008), pp. 79–100.

78 Roger of Wendover, *Rogeri de Wendover Chronica: Sive, Flores historiarum*, ed. Henry O. Coxe, 5 vols. (London: Sumptibus Societatis, 1841–44), IV, p. 195; Jessalynn Bird, Edward Peters, and James Powell (eds. and trans.), *Crusade and Christendom: Annotated Documents in Translation from Innocent III to the Fall of Acre, 1187–1291* (Philadelphia: University of Pennsylvania Press, 2013), pp. 245–46.

Notes to pages 38–43 157

79 Michel Pintoin, *Chronique du religieux de Saint-Denys*, ed. M. L. Bellaguet, 6 vols. (Paris: Crapelet, 1839), II, pp. 487–523 (p. 498); English translation mine.

80 H. M. Smyser has traced the first few lines of this passage (963–78) to the influence of *Piers Plowman*. See Smyser, "The Sowdon of Babylon and Its Author," 205–6.

81 Other passages in which sorrow is expressed include the following: lines 339, 362, 574, 704–6, 847, 1188, 1307, 1435, 2058, 2209; anger: lines 527, 824, 1156, 2902; fear: lines 297, 302, 486, 493–94, 659–60, 878, 1337; shame: lines 558, 567, 1275–78, 1295; joy: lines 675, 691, 854, 3199; and love of God or gods: lines 413, 425, 2841.

82 In English literature, see Cindy Vitto, *The Virtuous Pagan in Middle English Literature* (Philadelphia: American Philosophical Society, 1989); Frank Grady, *Representing Righteous Heathens in Late Medieval England* (New York: Palgrave, 2005); Alastair Minnis, "Other Worlds: Chaucer's Classicism," in Rita Copeland (ed.), *The Oxford History of Classical Reception in English Literature, vol. 1 (800–1558)* (Oxford: Oxford University Press, 2016), pp. 413–34.

83 See, e.g., Margaret A. Jubb, "Enemies in the Holy War, but Brothers in Chivalry: The Crusaders' View of Their Saracen Opponents," in Hans van Dijk and Willem Noomen (ed.), *Aspects de l'épopée romane: Mentalités, idéologies, intertextualités* (Groningen: E. Forsten, 1995), pp. 251–59.

84 On the theme of king–vassal conflict, see, e.g., François Suard, *La chanson de geste* (Paris: Presses Universitaires de France, 1993), pp. 79–80 and 93–101.

85 For the parallel passage in the Egerton manuscript, see Brandin (ed.), *Fierabras*, in "*La destruction de Rome* et *Fierabras*," lines 60–85.

86 The pervasiveness of accusations of treachery in crusade documents can be traced back to the debacle of the Second Crusade, imputed by many to the treachery of the Greeks; see Giles Constable, "The Second Crusade as Seen by Contemporaries," *Traditio*, 9 (1953), 213–79. Sarah Kay, *The Chansons de Geste in the Age of Romance: Political Fictions* (Oxford: Clarendon Press, 1995), ascribes the topos of treachery in *chansons de geste* to internal problems plaguing feudal society (p. 234).

87 See Brandin (ed.), *Fierabras*, in "*La destruction de Rome* et *Fierabras*," lines 649–717.

88 Stephen J. Spencer, *Emotions in a Crusading Context, 1095–1291* (Oxford: Oxford University Press, 2019), pp. 209–39.

89 Odo of Deuil, *La croisade de Louis VII, roi de France*, ed. Henri Waquet (Paris: P. Geuthner, 1949), p. 36; for the English translation, see James Brundage, *The Crusades: A Documentary Survey* (Milwaukee, WI: Marquette University Press, 1962), p. 108.

90 Charles Wendell David (ed. and trans.), *De expugnatione Lyxbonensi: The Conquest of Lisbon* (New York: Columbia University Press, 1936), pp. 80–81.

91 Ibid., pp. 152–53.

92 Ibid., pp. 166–67. On Christian infighting during the Second Crusade, see Constable, "Second Crusade," pp. 273–74.

158 *Notes to pages 43–44*

93 Jaques de Vitry quotes from Ecclesiastes 28:11 on the perils of anger. See Jessalynn Bird, "James of Vitry's Sermons to Pilgrims," *Essays in Medieval Studies*, 24 (2008), 81–113 (p. 98).

94 Sanudo Torsello, *Book of the Secrets of the Faithful Cross*, pp. 438–39; for the Latin, see *Gesta Dei per Francos, sive orientalium expeditionem et regni Francorum Hierosolymitani historia*, ed. J. Bongars, 2 vols. (Hannover: Typis Wechelianis, 1611), II, pp. 275–76.

95 Ludolph of Suchem, *Ludolphi de itinere terrae sanctae liber*, ed. Ferdinand Deycks (Stuttgart: Gedruckt auf Kosten des Litterarischen Vereins, 1851), p. 42; Ludolph of Suchem, *Description of the Holy Land, and of the Way Thither*, ed. and trans. Aubrey Stewart (London: Committee of the Palestine Exploration Fund, 1895; repr. Cambridge: Cambridge University Press, 2013), pp. 54–55.

96 See, e.g., Michael Camille, *The Gothic Idol: Ideology and Image-Making in Medieval Art* (Cambridge: Cambridge University Press, 1989), pp. 129–51; Marianne Ailes, "The *chanson de geste*," in Bale (ed.), *Cambridge Companion to the Literature of the Crusades*, pp. 25–38 (pp. 27–28); Sharon Kinoshita and Siobhain Bly Calkin, "Saracens as Idolaters in European Vernacular Literatures," in David Thomas and Alex Mallett (eds.), *Christian–Muslim Relations: A Bibliographical History, vol. 4 (1200–1350)* (Leiden: Brill, 2013), pp. 29–44. On the eighth- and ninth-century Byzantine origins of this construct, see Suzanne Conklin Akbari, *Idols in the East: European Representations of Islam and the Orient, 1100–1450* (Ithaca, NY: Cornell University Press, 2009), pp. 203–5.

97 On the image of the polytheistic, idolatrous Frank in Arabic jihād poetry, see Osman Latiff, *The Cutting Edge of the Poet's Sword: Muslim Poetic Responses to the Crusades* (Leiden: Brill, 2017). On the origins of this image, see G. R. Hawting, *The Idea of Idolatry and the Emergence of Islam: From Polemic to History* (Cambridge: Cambridge University Press, 1999), chapter 2.

98 See Lupack (ed.), *The Sultan*, lines 276–77 (the emotion word is "woode"); 308–12 (he turns "blake, pale and wan" and becomes "nyghe woode"); 410–11 ("wod"); 2103–15 (he "was nere wode for tene" and "made grete lamentacion"); 2431–49 (his emotional state is unspecified, but his counsellors assert that if he does not repent, "Vengeaunce shalle than on you come / With sorowe, woo and wrake"); 2493–2517 ("grete sorowe and mournyng mode"; he "cryed as he were wode"); and 2755–82 ("Whan tidynnges to him were comen / Tho was he a fulle sory man"). In the Egerton, see Brandin (ed.), *Fierabras*, in "*La destruction de Rome* et *Fierabras*," lines 1310–15.

99 The author of *Otuel and Roland* incorporates an episode of divinely directed rebuke in the passage linking the two sources he or she conflates, the *chanson de geste* of *Otinel* and the *Pseudo-Turpin Chronicle*: see O'Sullivan (ed.), *Firumbras and Otuel and Roland*, lines 1526–58. The Middle English Auchinleck *Guy of Warwick* also supplements the early thirteenth-century Anglo-Norman version with one such scene: see Julius Zupitza (ed.), *The Romance of Guy of Warwick*, Early English Text Society ES 42, 49, and 59

Notes to pages 44–47 159

(Bungay, UK: Clay and Sons, 1883, 1887, 1891; repr. London: Oxford University Press, 1966), lines 3642–54. The London Thornton version of *Richard Coeur de Lion* interpolates a twenty-two-line episode in which Muslims rebuke their gods between lines 3664 and 3665. See Karl Brunner (ed.), *Der Mittelenglische Versroman über Richard Löwenherz* (Vienna: W. Braumüller, 1913), note to lines 3664–65. See also Judith Perryman (ed.), *The King of Tars* (Heidelberg: Winter, 1980), lines 646–60; Sidney J. H. Herrtage (ed.), *Sir Ferumbras*, Early English Text Society ES 34 (London: Oxford University Press, 1879; repr. 1903 and 1966), lines 3204–8 and 4927–40; and O'Sullivan (ed.), *Firumbras*, lines 769–71, 1076, and 1385–92.

100 Akbari, *Idols in the East*, pp. 200–21 (citations at pp. 206 and 216). Geraldine Heng calls these scenes "outright literary fantasies" aimed at "racing the enemy": see Heng, *The Invention of Race in the European Middle Ages* (New York: Cambridge University Press, 2018), p. 117.

101 Gerard J. Brault, "Le portrait des Sarrasins dans les chansons de geste, image projective?," in *Au carrefour des routes d'Europe: La chanson de geste* (Aix-en-Provence: CUERMA, Université de Provence, 1987), pp. 301–11.

102 Riccoldo da Monte di Croce, "Lettres de Ricoldo de Monte-Croce," ed. Röhricht, pp. 275–76.

103 Ibid., p. 266.

104 Bastard (ed.), "La colère," 356, lines 21–23; English translation mine.

105 See, e.g., Psalms 43:23: "Arise, why sleepest thou, O Lord? Arise, and cast us not off to the end." See also Psalms 7:7, 16:13, 34:23, 41:10–11, and 77:65.

106 Jeanroy (ed.), "Le troubadour Austorc d'Aurillac," 82–83, lines 1–3, 13–24; English translation mine.

107 On Austorc, see further Linda Paterson, *Singing the Crusades: French and Occitan Lyric Responses to the Crusading Movement, 1137–1336* (Cambridge, UK: D. S. Brewer, 2018), pp. 199–201.

108 Bastard (ed.), "La colère," 357, lines 27–28; English translation mine.

109 Riccoldo da Monte di Croce, "Lettres de Ricoldo de Monte-Croce," ed. Röhricht, p. 280.

110 Ibid., pp. 275, 283–84.

111 Ibid., p. 276.

112 Paris, *Chronica majora*, ed. Luard, V, pp. 169–70; Paris, *Chronicles*, ed. and trans. Vaughan, p. 256.

113 Salimbene de Adam, *Cronica*, ed. Scalia, II, 645, pp. 672–73; *The Chronicle of Salimbene de Adam*, ed. and trans. Baird, Baglivi, and Kane, 645, p. 453.

114 As noted by A. J. Forey, "Western Converts to Islam (Later Eleventh to Later Fifteenth Centuries)," *Traditio*, 68 (2013), 153–231 (pp. 157–58).

115 See Forey, "Western Converts," pp. 170–71; Benjamin Z. Kedar, "Multidirectional Conversion in the Frankish Levant," in James Muldoon (ed.), *Varieties of Religious Conversion in the Middle Ages* (Gainesville: University Press of Florida, 1997), p. 194; and T. W. Arnold, *The Preaching of Islam: A History of the Propagation of the Muslim Faith*

160   *Notes to pages 48–50*

(London: Constable, 1913), pp. 72–76. While such cases of voluntary conversion during sustained military engagements or in their aftermath are widely attested in both Christian and Muslim sources, forced conversion following military defeat or during captivity was also very common: see Forey, "Western Converts," pp. 181–214. As seen in Riccoldo's account, discussed above, European authors also frequently commented on the conversion to Islam not just of crusaders and settlers but of Christians more generally. See also the reports of William of Tripoli, Humbert of Romans, and Fidenzio of Padua, discussed by Schein, *Fideles Crucis*, p. 97; and John V. Tolan, *Saracens: Islam in the Medieval European Imagination* (New York: Columbia University Press, 2002), pp. 204–5. For an overview of key geopolitical developments contributing to the spread of Islam from the early to the late Middle Ages, and of the various reasons for which individuals converted, see the general introduction to Nimrod Hurvitz, Christian C. Sahner, Uriel Simonsohn, and Luke Yarbrough (eds.), *Conversion to Islam in the Premodern Age: A Sourcebook* (Oakland: University of California Press, 2020), pp. 1–30; and Clint Hackenburg, "Christian Conversion to Islam," in David Thomas (ed.), *Routledge Handbook on Christian–Muslim Relations* (New York: Routledge, 2018), pp. 176–84, esp. pp. 179–81.

116 See the introduction to Hurvitz, Sahner, Simonsohn, and Yarbrough (eds.), *Conversion to Islam*, p. 10; Tolan, *Saracens*, pp. xiii–xv; and Patricia Crone, *The Nativist Prophets of Early Islamic Iran: Rural Revolt and Local Zoroastrianism* (Cambridge: Cambridge University Press, 2012), pp. 14–16, who emphasizes the wide currency of this rationale across time and place.

117 An argument that was unsurprisingly also invoked by Muslim poets and polemicists during the crusades: see, e.g., Paul Cobb, *The Race for Paradise: An Islamic History of the Crusades* (Oxford: Oxford University Press, 2014), p. 192; and Latiff, *Cutting Edge*, pp. 130–5.

118 On this, see Camille, *Gothic Idol*, pp. 129–51.

119 See, e.g., O'Sullivan (ed.), *Firumbras*, lines 265–70 and 1427–30; and Herrtage (ed.), *Sir Ferumbras*, lines 2564–75.

120 Fidenzio of Padua, *Liber recuperationis Terre Sancte*, in G. Golubovich (ed.), *Biblioteca bio-bibliografica della Terra Santa e dell'Oriente Francescano*, 20 vols. (Quaracchi: Collegio di S. Bonaventura, 1913), II, pp. 9–60 (p. 21); trans. Tolan, *Saracens*, p. 211.

121 Riccoldo da Monte di Croce, "Lettres de Ricoldo de Monte-Croce," ed. Röhricht, p. 271.

Chapter 2

1 On the equally important character of the Muslim queen or princess who converts to Christianity, see Sharon Kinoshita, *Medieval Boundaries: Rethinking Difference in Old French Literature* (Philadelphia: University of

Notes to page 50

161

Pennsylvania Press, 2006), pp. 46–73, who analyzes *La prise d'Orange*; and Suzanne Conklin Akbari, *Idols in the East: European Representations of Islam and the Orient, 1100–1450* (Ithaca, NY: Cornell University Press, 2009), pp. 173–89, who discusses the figure of Floripas in the *Fierabras* tradition. On Floripas, see also Marcel Elias, "Crusade Romances and the Matter of France," in Helen Cooper and Robert R. Edwards (eds.), *The Oxford History of Poetry in English, vol. 2 (1100–1400)* (Oxford: Oxford University Press, 2023), pp. 346–47.

2 Three Middle English adaptations of *Fierabras* survive: *Sir Ferumbras*; the fragmentary *Firumbras*; and *The Sultan of Babylon*, which conflates *Fierabras* and *La destruction de Rome*.

3 The three Middle English *Otuel* romances, not translations so much as free adaptations, are ultimately based on the Anglo-Norman version of the *chanson de geste* entitled *Otinel*, found in Cologny-Geneva, Bodmer Library MS 168 and composed sometime in the later stages of the thirteenth century. The Auchinleck and Fillingham versions are presumed to share a common lost Middle English source close to the Anglo-Norman text, whereas the Thornton version is reportedly an independent adaptation, closer to the Bodmer Library manuscript than to the other extant French version (this one of continental origin, preserved in Vatican City, Vatican Library reginenses latini MS 1616, and written during the second half of the twelfth century), yet containing points in common with both. See O'Sullivan's introduction to *Firumbras and Otuel and Roland*, Early English Text Society OS 198 (London: Oxford University Press, 1935), pp. xlviii–lx; and Paul Aebischer, *Etudes sur Otinel: De la chanson de geste à la saga norroise et aux origines de la légende* (Bern: Francke, 1960), pp. 96–104. Aebischer's book is the most comprehensive study to date of the interrelationship between the different *Otinel* texts. The continental French version of the Vatican Library manuscript, with lacunae supplied from the Anglo-Norman text of the Bodmer Library manuscript, is edited in François Guessard and Henri Victor Michelant (eds.), *Les anciens poètes de la France*, 10 vols. (Paris: F. Vieweg, 1858–70), I, pp. 1–92. The Bodmer Library manuscript is the only complete version of *Otinel*; I am grateful to Diane Speed for providing access and permission to refer to her transcription. Although research for this chapter was conducted using Speed's transcription, I also consulted the recently published edition of the Bodmer *Otinel* by Elizabeth Melick, Susanna Fein, and David Raybin (eds.), *The Roland and Otuel Romances and the Anglo-Norman "Otinel"* (Kalamazoo, MI: Medieval Institute Publications, 2019). A fragment of the Anglo-Norman version is also found in Paris, Bibliothèque Nationale, nouvelles acquisitions françaises MS 5094, edited by Ernest Langlois, "Deux fragments épiques: *Otinel, Aspremont*," *Romania*, 12 (1883), 438–58; a fragment of only four lines of the continental French version is, moreover, preserved in Paris, Bibliothèque Nationale, fonds Notre-Dame MS 273. For the dates of composition of the Old French texts, see Ronald N. Walpole, "Otinel," in Geneviève Hasnohr and Michel Zink

162   *Notes to pages 51–52*

(eds.), *Dictionnaire des lettres françaises: Le Moyen Âge*, 2nd ed. (Paris: Fayard, 1994; 1st ed. 1951), p. 1089; and Françoise Veilliard, *Bibliotheca Bodmeriana Catalogues, 2: Manuscrits français du moyen âge* (Cologny-Geneva: Bodmer Library, 1975), p. 93. I will refer to the following editions of the Middle English romances: for the Aunchileck version, Sidney J. H. Herrtage (ed.), *The Tale of Rauf Coilyear with the Fragments of Roland and Vernagu and Otuel*, Early English Text Society ES 39 (London: Oxford University Press, 1882; repr. 1931 and 1969); for the Fillingham version, O'Sullivan (ed.), *Firumbras and Otuel and Roland*; for the Thornton version, Sidney J. H. Herrtage (ed.), *The Sege off Melayne and The Romance of Duke Rowland and Sir Otuell of Spayne, Together with a Fragment of The Song of Roland*, Early English Text Society ES 35 (London: Trübner, 1880; repr. 1931).

4 See, however, with different emphases, Shirin A. Khanmohamadi, *In Light of Another's World: European Ethnography in the Middle Ages* (Philadelphia: University of Pennsylvania Press, 2013). We discuss two sources in common: Jean de Joinville's *Vie de Saint Louis* and John Mandeville's *Travels*. See also Zeynep Kocabiyikoglu Cecen, "The Use of 'The Saracen Opinion' on Knighthood in Medieval French Literature: *L'Ordene de Chevalerie* and *L'apparicion Maistre Jehan de Meun*," *Medieval History Journal*, 19 (2016), 57–92.

5 Benjamin K. Kedar, *Crusade and Mission: European Approaches towards the Muslims* (Princeton, NJ: Princeton University Press, 1984), pp. 57–65.

6 On this, see John V. Tolan, *Saracens: Islam in the Medieval European Imagination* (New York: Columbia University Press, 2002), pp. 201–2; and Elizabeth Siberry, "Missionaries and Crusaders, 1095–1274: Opponents or Allies?," *Studies in Church History*, 20 (1983), 103–10 (p. 105).

7 The most comprehensive study is Peter Jackson, *The Mongols and the West, 1221–1410* (Harlow, UK: Longman, 2005). See also "The Mongol Crusades, 1241–1262," in Jessalynn Bird, Edward Peters, and James Powell (eds. and trans.), *Crusade and Christendom: Annotated Documents in Translation from Innocent III to the Fall of Acre, 1187–1291* (Philadelphia: University of Pennsylvania Press, 2013), pp. 306–10; and Tolan, *Saracens*, pp. 200–201. On papal attempts to convert the Mongols, see Jean Richard, "Le discours missionnaire: L'exposition de la foi chrétienne dans les lettres des papes aux Mongols," in Jean Richard (ed.), *Croisés, missionnaires et voyageurs: Les perspectives orientales du monde latin medieval* (London: Variorum, 1983), pp. 257–68.

8 Bird, Peters, and Powell (eds. and trans.), *Crusade and Christendom*, pp. 307–8.

9 Matthew Paris, *Chronica majora*, ed. Henry Richards Luard, 7 vols. (London: Longman, 1872–83), IV, p. 115; Josepho Alberigo (ed.), *Conciliorum oecumenicorum decretal* (Bologna: Istituto per le Scienze Religiose, 1973), p. 297. These are translated in Bird, Peters, and Powell (eds. and trans.), *Crusade and Christendom*, pp. 311, 315, and 331.

10 Robert I. Burns, "Christian-Islamic Confrontation in the West: The Thirteenth-Century Dream of Conversion," *American Historical Review*, 76 (1971), 1386–434.

Notes to pages 52–53

11 T. Hudson Turner, "Unpublished Notices of the Times of Edward I, Especially of His Relations with the Moghul Sovereigns of Persia," *Archaeological Journal*, 8 (1851), 44–51; Sylvia Schein, *Fideles Crucis: The Papacy, the West, and the Recovery of the Holy Land, 1274–1314* (Oxford: Clarendon Press, 1991), pp. 188, 214.

12 Riccoldo da Monte di Croce, *Riccold de Monte Croce: Pérégrination en Terre Sainte et au Proche Orient. Lettres sur la chute de Saint Jean d'Acre*, ed. and trans. René Kappler (Paris: Champion, 1997), pp. 112–13. In what follows, when citing Riccoldo's *Liber peregrinationis*, I refer to Kappler's edition and modern French translation; all English translations are mine.

13 On this, see Schein, *Fideles Crucis*, pp. 162–75.

14 See Antony Leopold, *How to Recover the Holy Land: The Crusade Proposals of the Late Thirteenth and Early Fourteenth Centuries* (Aldershot, UK: Ashgate, 2000), p. 110; and Vincent J. DiMarco, "The Historical Basis of Chaucer's Squire's Tale," in Kathryn L. Lynch (ed.), *Chaucer's Cultural Geography* (New York: Routledge, 2002), pp. 56–75 (p. 64).

15 William of Adam, *How to Defeat the Saracens*, ed. Gilles Constable (Washington, DC: Dumbarton Oaks, 2012), pp. 57–61; Marino Sanudo Torsello, *The Book of the Secrets of the Faithful Cross: Liber secretorum fidelium crucis*, trans. Peter Lock (Farnham, UK: Ashgate, 2011), p. 66. On the *Directorium*, see DiMarco, "Historical Basis of Chaucer's Squire's Tale," p. 65; and Aziz Suryal Atiya, *The Crusade in the Later Middle Ages* (London: Methuen, 1938), p. 107.

16 Norman P. Tanner (ed.), *Decrees of the Ecumenical Councils*, 2 vols. (London: Sheed and Ward, 1990), I, p. 309; Rutebeuf, "Lament of the Holy Land," in Bird, Peters, and Powell (eds. and trans.), *Crusade and Christendom*, p. 393.

17 Luis Gonzalez Anton, *Las uniones aragonesas y las cortes del reino, 1283–1301*, 2 vols. (Saragossa: Consejo Superior de Investigaciones Cientificas, 1975), II, pp. 450–51; English translation mine.

18 Pamela Drost Beattie, "'Pro Exaltatione Sanctae Fidei Catholicae': Mission and Crusade in the Writings of Ramon Lull," in Larry J. Simon (ed.), *Iberia and the Mediterranean World of the Middle Ages: Studies in Honor of Robert I. Burns* (Leiden: Brill, 1995), pp. 113–29 (p. 121); Leopold, *How to Recover the Holy Land*, p. 103; Kedar, *Crusade and Mission*, p. 196.

19 Pierre Dubois, *The Recovery of the Holy Land*, ed. and trans. Walther I. Brandt (New York: Columbia University Press, 1956), pp. 41 and 118–19.

20 See further Jean Delumeau, *La peur en occident (XVIe–XVIIIe siècles): Une cité assiégée* (Paris: Fayard, 1978), esp. pp. 262–72.

21 Other attacks on Turkish-held coastline include Lampsacus (1359), Adalia (1361), Alexandria (1365), Ayas (1361, 1367), Jaffa (1367), Tripoli (1367, 1403), Beirut (1403), and Bodrum (1407). See Timothy Guard, *Chivalry, Kingship and Crusade: The English Experience in the Fourteenth Century* (Woodbridge, UK: Boydell Press, 2013), p. 22, and, more generally, pp. 21–50.

22 For a brief view, see Norman Housley, *Contesting the Crusades* (Oxford: Oxford University Press, 2006), pp. 129–32; or Christopher Tyerman,

164 *Notes to pages 54–55*

God's War: A New History of the Crusades (London: Penguin, 2007), pp. 843–45.

23 Augustin Theiner (ed.), *Vetera monumenta historica Hungariam sacram illustrantia*, 2 vols. (Rome, 1859–60) I, pp. 660, 986; Jürgen Sarnowsky, "Die Johanniter und Smyrna (1344–1402)," *Römische Quartalschrift*, 87 (1992), 45, 47–98 (p. 70). Both are translated in Norman Housley (ed. and trans.), *Documents on the Later Crusades, 1274–1580* (Basingstoke, UK: MacMillan Press, 1996), pp. 78–80 and 101–2.

24 Woodburn O. Ross (ed.), *Middle English Sermons*, Early English Text Society OS 209 (London: Oxford University Press, 1940), p. 255.

25 Philippe de Mézières, *Le songe du vieil pelerin*, ed. G. W. Coopland, 2 vols. (Cambridge: Cambridge University Press, 1969), II, 282, p. 428.

26 Unfortunately for Boucicaut, however, Murad was at peace with the Mamlūks at the time. See Denis Lalande (ed.), *Le livre des fais du bon messire Jehan le Maingre, dit Bouciquaut* (Geneva: Droz, 1985), pp. 61–62; and Denis Lalande, *Jean II le Meingre, dit Boucicaut (1366–1421): Étude d'une biographie héroïque* (Geneva: Droz, 1988), pp. 27–28.

27 Helly is said to have served under Murad for three years. See Philippe Gardette, "Jacques de Helly, figure de l'entre-deux culturel au lendemain de la défaite de Nicopolis," *Erytheia: Revista de estudios bizantinos y neogriegos*, 24 (2003), 111–24 (pp. 113–14); Kiril Petkov, "The Rotten Apple and the Good Apples: Orthodox, Catholics, and Turks in Philippe de Mézières' Crusading Propaganda," *Journal of Medieval History*, 23 (1997), 255–70 (p. 266).

28 James Hankins, "Renaissance Crusaders: Humanist Crusade Literature in the Age of Mehmed II," *Dumbarton Oaks Papers*, 49 (1995), 111–207 (p. 129); Benjamin Weber, *Lutter contre les Turcs: Les formes nouvelles de la croisade pontificale au xve siècle* (Rome: École française de Rome, 2013), pp. 54–58.

29 Peter Grillo (ed.), *La Chrétienté Corbaran*, in *The Old French Crusade Cycle VII. The Jerusalem Continuations. Part 1: La Chrétienté Corbaran* (Tuscaloosa: University of Alabama Press, 1984). See John V. Tolan, *Sons of Ishmael: Muslims through European Eyes in the Middle Ages* (Gainesville: University Press of Florida, 2008), pp. 66–78.

30 Sidney J. H. Herrtage (ed.), *Sir Ferumbras*, Early English Text Society ES 34 (London: Oxford University Press, 1879; repr. 1903 and 1966), lines 759–60. On the popularity of the *Fierabras* tradition in late medieval England, in both English and French renderings, see Marianne Ailes, "La réception de *Fierabras* en Angleterre," in Marc Le Person (ed.), *Le rayonnement de Fierabras dans la littérature européenne* (Lyon: Centre d'étude des Interactions Culturelles, Université Jean Moulin Lyon 3, 2003), pp. 177–78. On the relationship between the English and French versions, see Marianne Ailes, "Comprehension Problems and Their Resolution in the Middle English Verse Translations of *Fierabras*," *Forum for Modern Language Studies*, 35 (1999), 396–407. *Sir Ferumbras* is the closest of the three Middle English versions to the original Old French *chanson*, the "Vulgate," published as Marc Le Person (ed.), *Fierabras: Chanson de geste du XIIe siècle* (Paris: Champion,

Notes to pages 55–59 165

2003); it also bears affinities with the late fifteenth-century prose version of Bagnyon, with which it shares a common, no longer extant source. See Jehan Bagnyon, *L'histoire de Charlemagne*, ed. Hans-Erich Keller (Geneva: Droz, 1992). For instances of the amplifications mentioned above, see Herrtage (ed.), *Sir Ferumbras*, lines 54–55, 59–62, 81, 94–109, 121–23, 363, 379, and 437.

31 Judith Perryman (ed.), *The King of Tars* (Heidelberg: Winter, 1980). The chronicles in question are Matthew Paris's *Flores historiarum* and Thomas of Walsingham's *Historia Anglicana*. See Lilian Herlands Hornstein, "The Historical Background of *The King of Tars*," *Speculum*, 16 (1941), 404–14; and Dorothee Metlitzki, *The Matter of Araby in Medieval England* (New Haven, CT: Yale University Press, 1977), pp. 137–38.

32 Geoffrey Chaucer, *Man of Law's Tale*, in Larry D. Benson (ed.), *The Riverside Chaucer*, 3rd ed. (Oxford: Oxford University Press, 2008; 1st ed. 1987), lines 236–37. See Metlitzki, *Matter of Araby in Medieval England*, pp. 136–60; and Jennifer R. Goodman, "Marriage and Conversion in Late Medieval Romance," in James Muldoon (ed.), *Varieties of Religious Conversion in the Middle Ages*, (Gainesville: University Press of Florida, 1997), pp. 115–28. For a discussion of the *Man of Law's Tale* in terms of "the role of marriage, proselytizing, trade, and money as tools that further crusading goals," see Siobhain Bly Calkin, "The Man of Law's Tale and Crusade," in Christopher Cannon and Maura Nolan (eds.), *Medieval Latin and Middle English Literature: Essays in Honour of Jill Mann* (Cambridge, UK: D. S. Brewer, 2011), pp. 1–24 (pp. 2–3).

33 See also lines 31–32: "Ni3t & day it was his þout, / To bring cristendom to nout"; and 47–48: "& alle flei were togidere sworn, / flat cristendom scholde be lorn."

34 See Guessard and Michelant (eds.), *Otinel*, lines 100–150; the Anglo-Norman text follows closely.

35 The Thornton version, however, assigns a different identity to the man killed by Otuel: see Diane Speed, "Chivalric Perspectives in the Middle English Otuel Romances," in Ruth Evans, Helen Fulton, and David Matthews (eds.), *Medieval Cultural Studies: Essays in Honour of Stephen Knight* (Cardiff: University of Wales Press, 2006), pp. 213–24 (p. 216).

36 See *Middle English Dictionary (MED)*, *fêrd* n.(1), 2. something inspiring fear, danger. The semantic overlap comes from the Old English term *fêar*, meaning "sudden danger/peril": see Michiko Ogura, *Words and Expressions of Emotion in Medieval English* (Frankfurt: Peter Lang, 2013), p. 68.

37 See Guessard and Michelant (eds.), *Otinel*, lines 261–64; the Anglo-Norman text is even more succinct.

38 See also lines 563–65: "As þe king stod in doute, / He spak to his folk aboute, / & seide to alle þat þere were."

39 See further Schein, *Fideles Crucis*, p. 216.

40 See Leopold, *How to Recover the Holy Land*, p. 96; and Schein, *Fideles Crucis*, p. 122.

166   *Notes to pages 59–60*

41 Roger Stanegrave, *Li charboclois d'armes du conquest precious de la Terre Sainte de promission*, in Jacques Paviot (ed.), *Projets de croisade (v. 1290–v. 1330)* (Paris: Académie des Inscriptions et Belles-Lettres, 2008), pp. 322–23, 330–31, 373–74.

42 Sanudo Torsello, *The Book of the Secrets of the Faithful Cross*, trans. Lock, p. 417.

43 Riccoldo da Monte di Croce, "Lettres de Ricoldo de Monte-Croce sur la prise d'Acre (1291)," ed. Reinhold Röhricht, in *Archives de l'Orient latin*, 12 vols. (Paris: Ernest Leroux, 1884), II, p. 269.

44 Gilbert of Tournai, *Collectio de scandalis ecclesiae*, ed. Autbert Stroick, *Archivum Franciscanum historicum*, 24 (1931), 33–62 (p. 39); English translation mine.

45 Riccoldo da Monte di Croce, "Lettres de Ricoldo de Monte-Croce," ed. Röhricht, e.g., pp. 272–74; on Llull, see Leopold, *How to Recover the Holy Land*, p. 85.

46 Stanegrave, *Li charboclois*, in Paviot (ed.), *Projets de croisade*, p. 331.

47 Philippe de Mézières, *Letter to King Richard II, a Plea Made in 1395 for Peace between England and France*, ed. and trans. G. W. Coopland (Liverpool, UK: Liverpool University Press, 1975), pp. 24–30, 97–130; Philippe de Mézières, *Une epistre lamentable et consolatoire: Adressée en 1397 à Philippe le Hardi, duc de Bourgogne, sur la défaite de Nicopolis (1396)*, ed. Philippe Contamine and Jacques Paviot (Paris: Société de l'histoire de France, 2008), e.g., pp. 142–43, 135, 168, 171, 188; Honorat Bovet, *Medieval Muslims, Christians, and Jews in Dialogue: The "Apparicion Maistre Jehan de Meun" of Honorat Bovet*, ed. and trans. Michael Hanly (Tempe: Arizona Center for Medieval and Renaissance Studies, 2005), pp. 100–101, lines 661–64.

48 Geraldine Heng, *Empire of Magic: Medieval Romance and the Politics of Cultural Fantasy* (New York: Columbia University Press, 2003), pp. 3, 45, 46, 67, 93, 104, 281.

49 Aelred of Rielvaux, *De speculo caritatis*, in Anselme Hoste and Charles H. Talbot (eds.), *Aelredi Rievallensis. Opera Omnia, I: Opera ascetica* (Turnhout: Brepols, 1971), 2, 26, p. 102, cited in Barbara H. Rosenwein, *Generations of Feeling: A History of Emotions, 600–1700* (Cambridge: Cambridge University Press, 2016), pp. 99–100.

50 See, e.g., John Gower, *Confessio Amantis*, ed. Russell A. Peck; Latin trans. Andrew Galloway, 3 vols. (Kalamazoo, MI: Medieval Institute Publications, 2013), I, 1, line 1912; Arthur Brandeis (ed.), *Jacob's Well: An English Treatise on the Cleansing of Man's Conscience*, Early English Text Society OS 115 (London: Trübner, 1900), p. 76, line 11, and p. 78, lines 16, 31; W. N. Francis (ed.), *The Book of Vices and Virtues: A Fourteenth Century English Translation of the "Somme le roi" of Lorens d'Orléans*, Early English Text Society OS 217 (London: Oxford University Press, 1942), p. 15, lines 19, 24–25; and Harriet Hudson (ed.), *Sir Isumbras*, in *Four Middle English Romances: Sir Isumbras, Octavian, Sir Eglamour of Artois, Sir Tryamour* (Kalamazoo, MI: Medieval Institute Publications, 2006), line 31.

Notes to pages 60–62

51 See, for an overview, Carla Casagrande and Silvana Vecchio, *Histoire des péchés capitaux au Moyen Âge*, trans. Pierre-Emmanuel Dauzat (Paris: Aubier, 2002), pp. 19–65.

52 Chaucer, *Parson's Tale,* in Benson (ed.), *Riverside Chaucer*, line 402; Francis (ed.), *Book of Vices and Virtues*, p. 16, lines 31–32.

53 Francis (ed.), *Book of Vices and Virtues*, p. 17, lines 11–13.

54 Richard Lavynham, *A Litil Tretys on the Seven Deadly Sins*, ed. Johannes Petrus Wilhelmus Maria van Zutphen (Rome: Institutum Carmelitanum, 1956), p. 1.

55 Brandeis (ed.), *Jacob's Well*, p. 82, lines 14–15. See also Chaucer, *Parson's Tale,* in Benson (ed.), *Riverside Chaucer*, line 487.

56 Aelred of Rielvaux, *De speculo caritatis*, ed. Hoste and Talbot, 3, 4, p. 108; see also Rosenwein, *Generations of Feeling*, p. 79, on Alcuin of York.

57 See Casagrande and Vecchio, *Histoire des péchés capitaux*, pp. 79–80.

58 Thomas Aquinas, *The Summa Theologica of Thomas Aquinas*, trans. Fathers of the English Dominican Province (London: Burns Oates and Washbourne, 1922), IIa 2ae 36, 1; Casagrande and Vecchio, *Histoire des péchés capitaux*, p. 76. On Aquinas and the sins, see Eileen C. Sweeney, "Aquinas on the Seven Deadly Sins: Tradition and Innovation," in Richard G. Newhauser and Susan J. Ridyard (eds.), *Sin in Medieval and Early Modern Culture: The Tradition of the Seven Deadly Sins* (Woodbridge, UK: York Medieval Press, 2012), pp. 85–106. Pride and envy do not feature in Aquinas's taxonomy of the passions; they are, however, included in other influential late medieval taxonomies, such as Jean de la Rochelle's. See Simo Knuuttila, *Emotions in Ancient and Medieval Philosophy* (Oxford: Clarendon Press, 2004), pp. 234–35.

59 Middle English texts drawing upon Augustine include Chaucer, *Parson's Tale,* in Benson (ed.), *Riverside Chaucer*, line 483; Brandeis (ed.), *Jacob's Well*, p. 82, lines 23–24; and Francis (ed.), *Book of Vices and Virtues*, p. 22, lines 17–19.

60 Gower, *Confessio Amantis*, ed. Peck, II, 2, lines 68–70.

61 Mireille Vincent-Cassy, "L'envie au Moyen Âge," *Annales. Economies, Sociétés, Civilisations*, 35 (1980), 253–71; Tanner (ed.), *Decrees of the Ecumenical Councils*, I, pp. 267–68.

62 John Gower, *Vox Clamantis*, in G. C. Macaulay (ed.), *The Complete Works of John Gower*, 4 vols. (Oxford: Clarendon Press, 1899), IV, 5, line 513; John Gower, *The Major Latin Works of John Gower: The Voice of One Crying, and the Tripartite Chronicle*, trans. Eric W. Stockton (Seattle: University of Washington Press, 1962), pp. 206–7.

63 See, e.g., Auchinleck (ed. Herrtage), lines 88, 103–4, 323, 384, 581, 1144, 1275, and 1458; lines 235–40, 652–54, and 1028; lines 109–10, 235–254, 325–28, 519–24, 1071, 1151–56, and 1163–70.

64 See Fillingham (ed. O'Sullivan), lines 511–17; and Thornton (ed. Herrtage), lines 518–28.

65 The citations are from the Thornton version (ed. Herrtage), lines 764 and 766. As noted by Speed, "Chivalric Perspectives," pp. 216–17, the element of

168   *Notes to pages 63–67*

secrecy is especially pronounced in the Thornton rendering. The Auchinleck also refers to the peers' endeavors as "auntres" (lines 706 and 708).

66 See Guessard and Michelant (eds.), *Otinel*, lines 1071–82.

67 See also Calkin, "Saracens," in Neil Cartlidge (ed.), *Heroes and Anti-Heroes in Medieval Romance* (Cambridge, UK: D. S. Brewer, 2012), pp. 187–89; and, by the same author, *Saracens and the Making of English Identity: The Auchinleck Manuscript* (New York: Routledge, 2005), pp. 32–33, on this episode with different emphases.

68 Guessard and Michelant (eds.), *Otinel*, lines 1108–11.

69 Paris, *Chronica majora*, ed. Luard, V, p. 131; *Chronicles of Matthew Paris: Monastic Life in the Thirteenth Century*, ed. and trans. Richard Vaughan (Gloucester, UK: Alan Sutton, 1984), p. 227.

70 Ibid., p. 133; trans. Vaughan, pp. 228–29.

71 Ibid., p. 147; trans. Vaughan, p. 239.

72 Ibid., pp. 148–49; trans. Vaughan, pp. 240–41; "modestam" changed to nominative "modestiam."

73 Ibid., p. 151; trans. Vaughan, p. 242.

74 Jean de Joinville, *Histoire de Saint Louis, credo et lettre à Louis X*, ed. Natalis de Wailly (Paris: Firmin Didot, 1874), p. 244; *Joinville and Villehardouin: Chronicles of the Crusades*, trans. Caroline Smith (London: Penguin, 2008), p. 255.

75 Gilbert of Tournai, *Collectio de scandalis ecclesiae*, ed. Stroick, pp. 33–62; Keith Walls, *John Bromyard on Church and State: The "Summa Praedicantium" and Early Fourteenth-Century England* (Market Weighton, UK: Clayton-Thorpe, 2007), pp. 203–13, 118–20.

76 Stanegrave, *Li charboclois*, in Paviot (ed.), *Projets de croisade*, pp. 330–37.

77 John Mandeville, *The Book of John Mandeville*, ed. Tamarah Kohanski and C. David Benson (Kalamazoo, MI: Medieval Institute Publications, 2007), lines 1300–18.

78 Elizabeth Siberry, *Criticism of Crusading, 1095–1274* (Oxford: Clarendon Press, 1985), pp. 72–108.

79 John Bromyard, *Summa praedicantium* (Vienna: Apud Dominicum Nicolinum, 1586), "Crux," 17.32–3.

80 Bromyard, *Summa praedicantium*, "Adulterium," 17.9–10; "Anima," 23.15; "Elemosina," 3.28; see further Walls, *John Bromyard on Church and State*, pp. 203–5. In the absence of a modern edition of the *Summa*, Walls's book, though offering little critical engagement with the text, is useful for its summaries, translations, and references. On analogical approaches to Islam, in writings by John Bromyard, Riccoldo da Monte di Croce, Johann Schiltberger, and others, see further my "Unsettling Orientalism: Toward a New History of European Representations of Muslims and Islam, c. 1200–1450," *Speculum*, 100:2 (forthcoming, April 2025).

81 See, e.g., the two episodes in Bromyard, *Summa*, "Elemosina," 3.28–9; see further Walls, *John Bromyard*, p. 24.

82 Riccoldo da Monte di Croce, "Lettres de Ricoldo de Monte-Croce," ed. Röhricht," p. 275; English translation mine.

Notes to pages 67–68 169

83 Riccoldo da Monte di Croce, *Riccold de Monte Croce: Pérégrination*, ed. and trans. Kappler, pp. 158–73. I am not the first to note this connection: see George-Tvrtković, *A Christian Pilgrim in Medieval Iraq: Riccoldo da Montecroce's Encounter with Islam* (Turnhout: Brepols, 2012), pp. 65–66. The letters are believed to have been largely redacted in the immediate aftermath of the fall of Acre but to have been completed c. 1300, around the same as the *Liber peregrinationis*, when Riccoldo was back in Florence. See Kappler's introduction, p. 12.

84 Riccoldo da Monte di Croce, *Riccold de Monte Croce: Pérégrination*, ed. and trans. Kappler, pp. 167–73 (pp. 172–73).

85 Johann Schiltberger, *Reisen des Johannes Schiltberger aus München in Europa, Asia und Afrika von 1394 bis 1427*, ed. Karl Friedrich Neumann (Munich: Selbstverl, 1859), pp. 130–32; Rodriguez (ed.), *Muslim and Christian Contact in the Middle Ages: A Reader* (Toronto: University of Toronto Press, 2015), pp. 278–79.

86 Schiltberger, *Reisen*, pp. 132–34; translation adapted from Rodriguez, *Muslim and Christian Contact*, pp. 279–81.

87 Michel Pintoin, *Chronique du religieux de Saint-Denys*, ed. M. L. Bellaguet, 6 vols. (Paris: Crapelet, 1839), II, pp. 488–91, 494–95, 498–99 (pp. 488 and 490); English translations mine.

88 Ibid., p. 499. Here, Bāyazīd rebukes the crusaders for their vanity, gluttony, and lechery.

89 Bovet, *Medieval Muslims, Christians, and Jews in Dialogue: The "Apparicion Maistre Jehan de Meun" of Honorat Bovet*, ed. and trans. Hanly, pp. 60–61, 84–85 (line 335), 98–99 (lines 633–39), 100–1 (lines 677–78), 102–3 (line 683). The work's providential framework is presented in Bovet's dedication to Jean de Montaigu, pp. 60–61: "Car sans amender nostre vie, j'ay paour que Dieux ne nous aydera, et sy doubte que les Sarrazins durement ne griefvent Crestianté, se autrement nous ne retournons a la mercy, pitié et miséricorde de Dieu; car tout appertement il est adviz qu'il soit courroucé contre son pueple, par especial quant il nous a osté la tres clere lumiere de sainte Eglise et laissié prendre tel avancement aux annemis de nostre foy" (Because without reforming our lives, I fear that God may no longer help us, and thus fear that the Saracens may grievously afflict Christianity, unless we return to the grace, the worship, and the mercy of God; because it is quite clearly apparent that he is angry with his people, especially seeing how he has taken from us the bright light of Holy Church and allowed so much progress by the enemies of our faith).

90 John of Gaunt and Philip the Bold of Burgundy were to be the crusade's leaders, but Gaunt was forced to withdraw and Philip entrusted the leadership to his son, John of Nevers. See Christopher Tyerman, *England and the Crusades, 1095–1588* (Chicago: University of Chicago Press, 1988), pp. 300–301; John France, *The Crusades and the Expansion of Catholic Christendom, 1000–1714* (London: Routledge, 2005), pp. 375–76; and Housley, *Contesting the Crusades*, pp. 131–32. J. J. N. Palmer, *England,*

170   *Notes to pages 69–71*

France, and Christendom, 1377–99 (London: Routledge, 1972), pp. 180–210, argued that an English contingent of up to one thousand soldiers, under the orders of John Beaufort (John of Gaunt's illegitimate son), was present, but his thesis has, since its publication, failed to convince. The consensus, in the absence of further evidence, seems to be that some English knights accompanied the French and Burgundian forces.

91 Jean Froissart, *Oeuvres de Froissart*, ed. Kervyn de Lettenhove, 25 vols. (Brussels: Victor Devaux et cie, 1867–77), XV, pp. 315–16.

92 Mézières, *Une epistre lamentable et consolatoire*, ed. Contamine and Paviot, p. 113; English translation mine.

Chapter 3

1 The consensus, as noted by Rosalind Field, "From *Gui* to *Guy*: The Fashioning of a Popular Romance," in Alison Wiggins and Rosalind Field (eds.), *Guy of Warwick: Icon and Ancestor* (Cambridge, UK: D. S. Brewer, 2007), pp. 44–60 (p. 50), is that the author of *Gui de Warwick* was a canon of Osney Abbey in Oxfordshire. Emma Mason has argued that *Gui* was commissioned on the occasion of the marriage between Henry Earl of Warwick and Margery D'Oilley; the romance's purpose, Mason contends in a later article, was to retrieve the reputation of the earldom. See Mason, "Legends of the Beauchamps' Ancestors: The Use of Baronial Propaganda in Medieval England," *Journal of Medieval History*, 10 (1984), 25–40; and Mason, "Fact and Fiction in Crusading Tradition: The Earls of Warwick in the Twelfth Century," *Journal of Medieval History*, 14 (1988), 81–95.

2 Fulcher of Chartres, *The Deeds of the Franks and the Other Pilgrims to Jerusalem*, ed. Rosalind Hill (London: Nelson, 1962), pp. 1–2.

3 Bernard of Clairvaux, "Liber ad Milites Templi: De laude novae militiae," in Jean LeClercq and H. M. Rochais (eds.), *Sancti Bernardi Opera*, 8 vols. (Rome: Cistercienses, 1963), III, pp. 312–31; for the English translation, see C. Greenia (trans.), *In Praise of the New Knighthood* (Kalamazoo, MI: Cistercian Publications, 1977).

4 Jonathan Riley-Smith, "Crusading as an Act of Love," *History*, 65 (1980), 177–92; see also Christoph T. Maier (ed. and trans.), *Crusade Propaganda and Ideology: Model Sermons for the Preaching of the Cross* (Cambridge: Cambridge University Press, 2000), pp. 57–59; Michael Routledge, "Songs," in Jonathan Riley-Smith (ed.), *The Oxford History of the Crusades* (Oxford: Oxford University Press, 1999), pp. 90–110 (pp. 97–101).

5 See Velma Bourgeois Richmond, *The Legend of Guy of Warwick* (New York: Garland, 1996), pp. 49–106, who documents *Gui/Guy*'s popularity during the fourteenth century. For a list and description of the sixteen manuscripts and fragments to have reached us, see Marianne Ailes, "*Gui de Warewic* in Its Manuscript Context," in Wiggins and Field (eds.), *Guy of Warwick*, pp. 12–21. There survive five manuscripts and fragments of the Middle

Notes to pages 71–73

English version, three from the fourteenth century and two from the fifteenth century. For further details, see Alison Wiggins, "The Manuscripts and Texts of the Middle English *Guy of Warwick*," in Wiggins and Field (eds.), *Guy of Warwick*, pp. 61–80 (pp. 61–65).

6 Denis Lalande (ed.), *Le livre des fais du bon messire Jehan le Maingre, dit Bouciquaut* (Geneva: Droz, 1985); Guillaume de Machaut, *La prise d'Alixandre*, ed. and trans. R. Barton Palmer (New York: Routledge, 2002).

7 See Antony Leopold, *How to Recover the Holy Land: The Crusade Proposals of the Late Thirteenth and Early Fourteenth Centuries* (Aldershot, UK: Ashgate, 2000), pp. 96–97.

8 John Gower, *Mirour de l'Omme*, in G. C. Macaulay (ed.), *The Complete Works of John Gower*, 4 vols. (Oxford: Clarendon Press, 1899), I, lines 23893–964; John Gower, *Vox Clamantis*, in G. C. Macaulay (ed.), *The Complete Works of John Gower*, 4 vols. (Oxford: Clarendon Press, 1899), IV, 5, lines 1–292; Philippe de Mézières, *Le songe du vieil pelerin*, ed. G. W. Coopland, 2 vols. (Cambridge: Cambridge University Press, 1969), I, pp. 397 and 85; Philippe de Mézières, "Philippe de Mézières and the New Order of the Passion," ed. Abdel Hamid Hamdy, *Bulletin of the Faculty of Arts, Alexandria University*, 18 (1964), 43–104 (pp. 45–46). I discuss these sources in the body of the chapter.

9 Mézières, *Songe du vieil pelerin*, ed. Coopland, I, pp. 397 and 85.

10 Kenneth Fowler, *The King's Lieutenant: Henry of Grosmont, First Duke of Lancaster* (London: Elek, 1969), pp. 104–6; Celia M. Lewis, "History, Mission, and Crusade in the *Canterbury Tales*," *Chaucer Review*, 42 (2008), 353–82 (p. 358).

11 Timothy Guard, *Chivalry, Kingship and Crusade: The English Experience in the Fourteenth Century* (Woodbridge, UK: Boydell Press, 2013), pp. 50–51, 60–63.

12 Henry of Grosmont, *Le Livre de seyntz medicines: The Unpublished Devotional Treatise of Henry of Lancaster*, ed. E. J. Arnould (Oxford: Blackwell, 1940); John Clanvowe, *The Works of Sir John Clanvowe*, ed. V. J. Scattergood (Cambridge, UK: D. S. Brewer, 1975).

13 These examples are given by Barbara H. Rosenwein, "Who Cared about Thomas Aquinas's Theory of the Passions?," *L'Atelier du Centre de recherches historiques*, 16 (2016), https://doi.org/10.4000/acrh.7420.

14 *Guy/Gui*'s amorous ethics tend to be mentioned only in passing. The couple of studies that focus on the protagonist's identity as a crusader do not engage with wider traditions of crusade writing; see Robert Allen Rouse, "An Exemplary Life: Guy of Warwick as Medieval Culture Hero," in Wiggins and Field (eds.), *Guy of Warwick*, pp. 94–109; and Rebecca Wilcox, "Romancing the East: Greeks and Saracens in *Guy of Warwick*," in Nicola McDonald (ed.), *Pulp Fictions of Medieval England: Essays in Popular Romance* (Manchester, UK: Manchester University Press, 2004), pp. 217–40.

15 The only study, to my knowledge, to have documented the connection between crusading and love-service in post-1291 political discourse is Stefan

172 *Notes to page 73*

Vander Elst's *The Knight, the Cross, and the Song: Crusade Propaganda and Chivalric Literature, 1100–1400* (Philadelphia: University of Pennsylvania Press, 2017), which analyzes Nicolaus of Jeroschin's *Krônike von Prûzinlant*, the *chansons* of the Second Crusade Cycle, and Guillaume de Machaut's *La prise d'Alixandre* as crusade propaganda.

16 Edinburgh, National Library of Scotland, Advocates MS 19.2.1 (A; the Auchinleck manuscript), edited by Julius Zupitza, *The Romance of Guy of Warwick*, 2nd ed., Early English Text Society ES 42, 49, and 59 (London: Oxford University Press, 1966; 1st ed. as three volumes in 1883, 1887, and 1891). A is the only complete fourteenth-century Middle English version. When A was adapted, there were two versions of the Anglo-Norman *Gui* in existence (see Maldwin Mills, "Techniques of Translation in the Middle English Versions of *Guy of Warwick*," in Roger Ellis [ed.], *The Medieval Translator: II* [London: Centre for Medieval Studies, 1991], pp. 209–29 [pp. 210–11]). According to Mills, the first – and earliest – is best represented in the text of Edwardes manuscript (British Library MS Additional 38662) (E) (1225–50), edited by Alfred Ewert, *Gui de Warewic: Roman du XIIIe siècle* (Paris: Champion, 1932) and translated into modern English by Judith Weiss, *Boeve de Haumtone and Gui de Warewic* (Tempe: Arizona Center for Medieval and Renaissance Studies, 2008); and the second appears in Cambridge Corpus Christi College MS 50 (C) (end thirteenth century); and, in a more reworked form, in Wolfenbüttel Herzog August Bibliothek MS Aug. 87.4 (G) (late thirteenth to early fourteenth century). While the resemblances (first noted by Mills) between the unpublished text of G and the Auchinleck version "limit the relevance of many pronouncements on the relationship between the Anglo-Norman and Middle English texts" (Ivana Djordjevic, "*Guy of Warwick* as a Translation," in Wiggins and Field [eds.], *Guy of Warwick*, pp. 27–43 [p. 42]), I rely on Mills's assertion that the second half of A (Guy's post-confessional life) bears far more resemblance to E than G (p. 215). I have also consulted Ewert's critical notes on the manuscript variations between E and C when comparing E and A.

17 See, e.g., Wilcox, "Romancing the East"; Wiggins, "Manuscripts and Texts," p. 69; and Siobhain Bly Calkin, *Saracens and the Making of English Identity: The Auchinleck Manuscript* (New York: Routledge, 2005), pp. 19–20.

18 See Paul Price, "Confessions of a Godless Killer: *Guy of Warwick* and Comprehensive Entertainment," in Judith Weiss, Jennifer Fellows, and Morgan Dickson (eds.), *Medieval Insular Romance: Translation and Innovation* (Cambridge, UK: D. S. Brewer, 2000), pp. 93–110 (p. 107); William Calin, *The French Tradition and the Literature of Medieval England* (Toronto: University of Toronto Press, 1995), p. 86; Susan Crane, "Guy of Warwick and the Question of Exemplary Romance," *Genre*, 17 (1984), 351–74 (p. 352); and Judith Weiss, "The Exploitation of Ideas of Pilgrimage and Sainthood in *Gui de Warewic*," in Laura Ashe, Ivana Djordjević, and Judith Weiss, (eds.), *The Exploitations of Medieval Romance* (Cambridge, UK: D. S. Brewer, 2010), pp. 43–56 (p. 47).

Notes to pages 73–75

19 I borrow the term "ennobling" from C. Stephen Jaeger, *Ennobling Love: In Search of a Lost Sensibility* (Philadelphia: University of Pennsylvania Press, 1999). See, in particular, chapter 11, "Virtue and Ennobling Love: Value, Worth, Reputation." While Jaeger groups religious theories and chivalric homosocial practices into a single conceptual understanding of love, I argue for the existence of fundamental tensions between the two traditions.

20 The scholarship concerned with the romance's chivalric ethics is mainly confined to close readings of the protagonist's maturation as a knight and to the historical contexts of penitential discourse. See Velma Bourgeois Richmond, *The Popularity of Middle English Romance* (Bowling Green, OH: Bowling Green University Popular Press, 1975), pp. 149–93; and Andrea Hopkins, *The Sinful Knights: A Study of Middle English Penitential Romance* (Oxford: Clarendon Press, 1990), pp. 70–118.

21 Guard, *Chivalry, Kingship and Crusade*; Christopher Tyerman, *England and the Crusades, 1095–1588* (Chicago: University of Chicago Press, 1988); Maurice Keen, "Chaucer's Knight, the English Aristocracy and the Crusade," in V. J. Scattergood and J. W. Sherbone (eds.), *English Court Culture in the Later Middle Ages* (London: Duckworth, 1983), pp. 45–61.

22 N. H. Nicolas (ed.), *The Controversy between Sir Richard Scrope and Sir Robert Grosvenor in the Court of Chivalry*, 2 vols. (London: Bentley, 1832). See Keen, "Chaucer's Knight"; and Nigel Saul, *For Honour and Fame: Chivalry in England, 1066–1500* (London: Bodley Head, 2011), pp. 115–17.

23 Nicolas (ed.), *Controversy*, II, p. 161.

24 For his full biography see Timothy Guard, "Sabraham, Nicholas (*b. c.* 1325, *d.* in or after 1399)," in *Oxford Dictionary of National Biography* (Oxford: Oxford University Press, 2004–16), www.oxforddnb.com/view/article/92452.

25 Guard, *Chivalry, Kingship and Crusade*, p. 17, divides English participation in the later crusades "into three periods of heightened activity broadly synonymous with the ebb and flow of the Anglo-French conflict: 1307–1346, 1360–1375 and 1389–1403."

26 Mason, "Legends of the Beauchamps' Ancestors"; and, by the same author, "Fact and Fiction in Crusading Tradition"; Yin Liu, "Richard Beauchamp and the Uses of Romance," *Medium Aevum*, 74 (2005), 271–87; John Frankis, "Taste and Patronage in Late Medieval England as Reflected in Versions of *Guy of Warwick*," *Medium Aevum*, 66 (1997), 80–93.

27 Guard, *Chivalry, Kingship and Crusade*, 43–45; Anthony Tuck, "Beauchamp, Thomas, Twelfth Earl of Warwick (1337x9–1401)," *Oxford Dictionary of National Biography* (Oxford: Oxford University Press, 2004–16), www.oxforddnb.com/view/article/1841.

28 On this, and other efforts by Richard Beauchamp to foster connections with Guy, see Frankis, "Taste and Patronage."

29 On this, see Mason, "Fact and Fiction," p. 90.

30 Viscount Dillon and W. St John Hope (eds.), *Pageant of the Birth, Life and Death of Richard Beauchamp, Earl of Warwick, 1389–1439* (London: Longmans, 1914), p. 44; Keen, "Chaucer's Knight," p. 54.

31 The classic study of amorous discourse and chivalry in the Arthurian tradition is Richard Barber, *The Knight and Chivalry*, 3rd ed. (Woodbridge, UK: Boydell Press, 1995; 1st ed. 1970), chapter 5 ("The Romances of Chivalry").

32 For a discussion of similar authorial treatments of the onset of love, see David Burnley, *Courtliness and Literature in Medieval England* (London: Longman, 1998), pp. 169–70. See also Tracy Adams, *Violent Passion: Managing Love in the Old French Verse Romance* (New York: Palgrave, 2005), pp. 37–73, who argues that "romance composers borrowed their symptoms of amor principally from Ovid's love writings" (p. 37).

33 For an excellent study of late medieval French romances of *amour* and *armes*, see Rosalind Brown-Grant, *French Romance of the Later Middle Ages: Gender, Morality, and Desire* (Oxford: Oxford University Press, 2008), chapter 1.

34 See, e.g., lines 755–56, 791–842, 1067–68, 1077–82, 1167–76, 1909–12, and 2847–56.

35 See, e.g., lines 1053–54, 4262, and 21:4–5.

36 See, e.g., lines 1070–72 ("And best is teld vnder sunner, / & mest frendes haþ y-wonne"); 1089–1108 (love of King Athelstan and Earl Rohaut after he wins "pris" in "euerich cuntre"); 1263–64 ("þer he dede him preyse miche, / þe Lombardes him loued inliche"); 1676–79 ("Gij hadde þe priis verrament. / Was þer non in al þat lond, / þat his dent miȝt astond / þer-fore men loued him swiþe miche"); 1685–88 ("Now he is comen to þe douk Reyner, / þat him loued and held dere; / He him vnder-feng wiþ worþschipe, / & dede him miche manschipe. / So long in þat cuntre bileued he is, / þat ouer alle þer he is praised y-wis"); 2875–88, 3067–74, 3287–93, 3345–46, 3375–82, 3724–26, 4103–6, 4184–89 (Emperor Hernis's love, praise, and worship); and 7135–36 (Athelstan welcomes Guy: "For he him herd preyse so miche: / þe king him loued, sikerliche"). This overlap between love and praise is, moreover, semantically ingrained: see *Middle English Dictionary* (*MED*), "louen" v.(4) and "loven" v.(2), esp. 6.

37 Also noted by Guard, *Chivalry, Kingship and Crusade*, p. 4.

38 On this, see Norman Housley, "The Crusading Movement, 1274–1700," in Riley-Smith (ed.), *Oxford History of the Crusades*, pp. 258–90 (p. 261); Christopher Tyerman, "'New Wine in Old Skins'? Crusade Literature and Crusading in the Eastern Mediterranean in the Later Middle Ages," in Jonathan Harris, Catherine Holmes, and Eugenia Russell (eds.), *Byzantines, Latins, and Turks in the Eastern Mediterranean World after 1150* (Oxford: Oxford University Press, 2012), pp. 265–89 (p. 279); and Maurice Keen, *Nobles, Knights and Men-at-Arms in the Middle Ages* (London: Hambledon, 1996), pp. 31–33.

39 Christopher Tyerman, *God's War: A New History of the Crusades* (London: Penguin, 2007), p. 855; Guard, *Chivalry, Kingship and Crusade*, p. 76 (see note 15 for a full list of Garter knights who served in Prussia).

40 See Albert S. Cook, "Beginning the Board in Prussia," *Journal of English and Germanic Philology*, 14 (1915), 375–88.

41 Tyerman, *God's War*, p. 885. See also Tyerman, *England and the Crusades*, p. 260.

Notes to pages 77–79

42 These examples are given by Guard, *Chivalry, Kingship and Crusade*, pp. 67–68; and Tyerman, *England and the Crusades*, p. 260.

43 Guard, *Chivalry, Kingship and Crusade*, p. 124.

44 See, e.g., Cook, "Beginning the Board in Prussia," p. 183; and William Urban, "The Teutonic Knights and Baltic Chivalry," *Historian*, 56 (1994), 519–30 (p. 523).

45 Jean Froissart, *Chroniques*, ed. Siméon Luce, 15 vols. (Paris: Mme Ve. J. Renouard, 1869–1975), VII, p. 145.

46 Norman Housley describes Boucicaut's life as an "incessant search for battle-fields on which he could earn praise for his prowess." See Housley, "One Man and His Wars: The Depiction of Warfare by Marshal Boucicaut's Biographer," *Journal of Medieval History*, 29 (2003), 27–40 (p. 30). On Boucicaut's biog-raphy, see also Denis Lalande, *Jean II le Meingre, dit Boucicaut (1366–1421): Étude d'une biographie héroïque* (Geneva: Droz, 1988).

47 Lalande (ed.), *Le livre des fais*, e.g., I, 11, pp. 40–42; I, 17, pp. 65–67; I, 19, pp. 80–82.

48 Ibid. I, 11, p. 42.

49 Ibid, I, 8, p. 28.

50 Ibid. I, 8–9, pp. 27–35 (pp. 27, 31). The chapter headings read: "Ci parle d'amours, en demonstrant par quelle maniere les bons doivent amer pour devenir vaillans"; and "Ci dit comment amours et desir d'estre ame crut en Bouciquaut courage et voulente d'estre vaillant et chevalereux." The centrality of love in upholding the knightly archetype to which Boucicaut aspired is, moreover, vividly reflected in the foundation of his very own order of chivalry, "L'Ordre de la Dame Blanche en Escu Vert," which purported to protect defenseless women against oppressive lords. See I, 38, pp. 160–71.

51 Subsequent passages are slightly more specific, referring to "sa dame" as an incentive for chivalric pursuits beginning in Prussia. See ibid., I, 11, pp. 40–41.

52 Ibid., I, 19, pp. 80–81.

53 See Lalande (ed.), *Le livre des fais*, e.g., I, 10, p. 37 (Louis II of Bourbon dubs Boucicaut knight at the age of twelve); I, 12, p. 43 (the author elaborates on Louis's love for Boucicaut); I, 13, p. 47 (Louis makes Boucicaut his lieutenant in the aftermath of a campaign in Guyenne); I, 16, p. 64 (Philippe of Artois, out of love for Boucicaut, commends him to Charles VI); I, 17, p. 65 (assertion of Charles VI's love for Boucicaut); and I, 19, p. 78 (Charles VI's "moult grant amour" for Boucicaut provides grounds for his appointment as marshal of France).

54 Ibid., I, 22, pp. 88–89; see also I, 16, p. 62, on Boucicaut's visit to Hungary.

55 Geoffroi de Charny, *The Book of Chivalry of Geoffroi de Charny*, trans. Richard W. Kaeuper and Elspeth Kennedy (Philadelphia: University of Pennsylvania Press, 1996). Charny took part in the 1345 crusade to Smyrna with Humbert of Vienna. On Charny's career and the influences on his book, see Kaeuper's introduction, pp. 3–64.

56 Charny, *Book of Chivalry*, trans. Kaeuper and Kennedy, 12, pp. 94–95, and 20, pp. 120–23.

176   *Notes to pages 79–83*

57 Ibid., 17–18, pp. 104–7.
58 Guillaume de Machaut, *Oeuvres*, ed. Ernest Hoepffner, 3 vols. (Paris: Firmin Didot, 1908–21), II, pp. 206–212, lines 1345–1504.
59 Machaut, *La prise d'Alixandre*, ed. Palmer, lines 181–88.
60 Ibid., lines 269–71.
61 See, for instance, Peter's reaction on being abandoned by his men after the taking of Alexandria, ibid., lines 3558–62: "Lors dist honneur · anours · et dames / que direz vous quant vous verrez / ces gens qui sont si esserez / certes jamais naront honnour / par droit · fors toute deshonneur" (Then he said "honor, love, and ladies! / What will you say when you see / These men drawn up here in their ranks? / Surely they will never have any claim / On honor but complete dishonor instead"). Worldly and divine love in fact find a form of conceptual unity in the figure of the Virgin Mary, cast in the double role of goddess and lover (see, e.g., lines 8765–67). Peter's status as a *miles Christi* is established from the inception through a divine message (lines 307–10) and is maintained throughout the narrative.
62 Nicolaus von Jeroschin, *The Chronicle of Prussia by Nicolaus von Jeroschin: A History of the Teutonic Knights in Prussia, 1190–1331*, trans. Mary Fischer (Farham, UK: Ashgate, 2010), p. 130. On this, and for other relevant passages, see further Vander Elst, *The Knight, the Cross, and the Song*, pp. 124–55.
63 Albert's interest in the crusade is bluntly stated: to be dubbed knight, thus acquiring higher honor (according to the poet) than that provided by his noble birth. Peter Suchenwirt's work was translated by Cook, "Beginning the Board in Prussia," pp. 378–87 (see pp. 378 and 382–83).
64 On this, see Joachim Bumke, *Courtly Culture: Literature and Society in the High Middle Ages*, trans. Thomas Dunlap (Berkeley: University of California Press, 1991; 1st ed. in German 1987), pp. 368–69.
65 Andreas Capellanus, *Andreas Capellanus on Love*, ed. and trans. P. G. Walsh (London: Duckworth, 1982), pp. 287–325, esp. pp. 287–301.
66 Albert Pauphilet (ed.), *La queste del Saint Graal* (Paris: Champion, 1923), pp. 66–67.
67 Honorat Bovet, *The Tree of Battles*, ed. and trans. G. W. Coopland (Liverpool: Liverpool University Press, 1949), pp. 143–44.
68 William Caxton (trans.), *The Book of the Knight of the Tower*, ed. M.Y. Offord, Early English Text Society SS 2 (London: Oxford University Press, 1971), p. 164.
69 Christine de Pizan, *Le livre des trois vertus*, ed. Charity Cannon Willard (Paris: Librairie Honoré Champion, 1989), pp. 116–18 (p. 116); Christine de Pizan, *The Treasure of the City of Ladies, or, The Book of the Three Virtues*, trans. Sarah Lawson (Harmondsworth, UK: Penguin, 1985), pp. 102–3 (p. 102).
70 H. S. Offler, "Thomas Bradwardine's 'Victory Sermon' in 1346," in A. I. Doyle (ed.), *Church and Crown in the Fourteenth Century* (Aldershot, UK: Ashgate, 2000), pp. 1–40 (at pp. 6 and 13 of introduction; paragraph 32 of Latin text).

Notes to pages 83–86   177

71 Ghillebert de Lannoy, *Oeuvres de Ghillebert de Lannoy: Voyageur, diplomate et moraliste*, ed. C. Potvin (Louvain: Lefever, 1878), p. 450.

72 In the early thirteenth-century *Gui*, the protagonist blames himself, not Felice, for his companions' deaths. See Ewert (ed.) and Weiss (trans.), *Gui*, line 1423. The lines blaming Felice were interpolated in the late thirteenth-century Anglo-Norman version contained in Cambridge Corpus Christi College MS 50.

73 Whereas *Gui* features the death of seven companions, ascribed to their lack of armor, the Auchinleck increases this number to thirty and omits reference to the armor. See Ewert (ed.) and Weiss (trans.), *Gui*, lines 4668 and 4699–4700. See also *Guy*, lines 7105–6, which feature the protagonist's dedication to Felice taking precedence over his friendship with Tirri: "No were it for þe loue of mi leman, / Nold ich neuer wende þe fram." Guy's departure leads to Tirri's imprisonment for felony and the seizure of his lands (147:1–152:12).

74 Herhaud's role as guarantor of the worldly value system of his protégé is established when Guy appeals to him for advice (*consilium*) and aid (*auxilium*) in the lead-up to the two first major conflicts they engage in (the battle of Segyn against the German emperor Reiner, and the defense of Emperor Hernis of Constantinople against the Saracen forces). In both cases, Herhaud's concerns are with the opportunities for "pris" and "los" afforded to Guy by these expeditions (see lines 1909–12 and 2847–56). For a useful discussion of heterosexual love as a "functional" way of gaining status in competition with other men, see Ruth Mazo Karras, *From Boys to Men: Formations of Masculinity in Late Medieval Europe* (Philadelphia: University of Pennsylvania Press, 2003), pp. 47–57.

75 The passage corresponding to Auchinleck lines 25:7–9 in *Gui* reads: "Mais pur lui unc rien ne fis, / Pur ço sui las e chaitif" (But I never did anything for Him, and so I am wretched and despicable); Ewert (ed.) and Weiss (trans.), *Gui*, lines 7625–26.

76 For instances of these elaborations, see lines 22:11, 26:5, 29:9, 37:8–9, 84:8–9 (barefoot trope, poor clothes, and begging); 89:5–9, 197:5–6, 221:5–6 (rejection of material wealth); 21:11–12, 22:1, 25:11–12 (emotional dimension of compunction); 25:2–3, 26:1–2, 27:11–12, 44:6, 47:10, 107:8 (devotion to the Passion and divine guidance); and 36:5–7, 44:1–45:2, 142:4–6, 179:8 (penitential pilgrimage and love of God).

77 The Auchinleck version, moreover, enhances this tension between "old" and "new" life by a change in meter, from rhyming couplets to tail-rhyme stanzas, just before the account of Guy's wedding with Felice and the conversion scene. On this metrical change, see, e.g., Price, "Confessions of a Godless Killer," pp. 97–100; and Field, "From *Gui* to *Guy*," pp. 56–57.

78 Gower, *Mirour de l'Omme*, in Macaulay (ed.), *Complete Works of John Gower*, I, lines 23893–23964 (quotations at lines 23895, 23898, 23901–3, and 23961); John Gower, *Mirour de l'Omme: The Mirror of Mankind*, trans. William Burton Wilson and Nancy Wilson Van Baak (East Lansing, MI: Colleagues Press, 1992), pp. 312–15.

178   *Notes to pages 86–89*

79 Ibid., lines 23941–52; trans. Wilson and Van Baak, p. 313.

80 John Gower, *Confessio Amantis*, ed. Russell A. Peck; Latin trans. Andrew Galloway, 3 vols. (Kalamazoo, MI: Medieval Institute Publications, 2013), II, 4, lines 1664–65.

81 Gower, *Vox Clamantis*, in Macaulay (ed.), *Complete Works of John Gower*, IV, 5, lines 1–292; *The Major Latin Works of John Gower: The Voice of One Crying, and the Tripartite Chronicle*, trans. Eric W. Stockton (Seattle: University of Washington Press, 1962), V, 1–6, pp. 196–204.

82 Geoffrey Chaucer, *The Book of the Duchess,* in Larry D. Benson (ed.), *The Riverside Chaucer*, 3rd ed. (Oxford: Oxford University Press, 2008; 1st ed. 1987), lines 1019–33.

83 On the Order of the Passion, see further Philippe Contamine, "'Les princes, barons et chevaliers qui a la chevalerie au service de Dieu se sont ja vouez': Recherches prosopographiques sur l'ordre de la Passion de Jésus-Christ (1385–1395)," in Martin Nejedly and Jaroslav Svátek (eds.), *La noblesse et la croisade à la fin du Moyen Age: France, Bourgogne, Bohême* (Toulouse: FRAMESPA-UMR, 2009), pp. 43–64; and Andrea Tarnowski, "Material Examples: Philippe de Mézières' Order of the Passion," *Yale French Studies*, 110 (2006), 163–75.

84 Tyerman, "'New Wine in Old Skins,'" p. 275.

85 Mézières, *Songe du vieil pelerin*, ed. Coopland, I, pp. 397 and 85; English translation mine.

86 Mézières, "Philippe de Mézières and the New Order of the Passion," ed. Hamdy, pp. 45–46; English translation mine. The *Sustance de la chevalerie de la passion de Jhesu Crist* details the order's foundational premise, values, and objectives.

87 Grosmont, *Le Livre de seyntz medicines*, ed. Arnould, p. 77, line 11, and p. 78, lines 18–19; Grosmont, *The Book of Holy Medicines*, trans. Catherine Batt (Tempe: Arizona Center for Medieval and Renaissance Studies, 2014), pp. 143–44.

88 Mézières, "Philippe de Mézières and the New Order of the Passion," ed. Hamdy, p. 64; English translation mine.

89 Tarnowski, "Material Examples," p. 166.

90 On Grosmont and the importance of humility, modeled on Christ, see *Book of Holy Medicines*, trans. Batt, pp. 106–12.

91 Ibid., pp. 64, 85–86, 90–91, 102. On Mézières and the social function of crusader dress, see Anne Romine, "Philippe de Mézières (c. 1327–1405) and the Controversy over Crusader Dress in the Fourteenth Century," *Allegorica*, 29 (2013), 36–51.

92 Albrecht Classen, "Introduction: Friendship – The Quest for a Human Ideal and Value from Antiquity to the Early Modern Time," in Albrecht Classen and Marilyn Sandidge (eds.), *Friendship in the Middle Ages and Early Modern Age* (New York: Walter de Gruyter, 2010), pp. 1–183; Klaus Oschema, "Sacred or Profane? Reflections on Love and Friendship in the Middle Ages," in Laura Gowing, Michael Hunter, and Miri Rubin (eds.), *Love,*

Friendship, and Faith in Europe, 1300–1800 (Basingstoke, UK Palgrave, 2005), pp. 43–65. See also Reginald Hyatte, *The Arts of Friendship: The Idealization of Friendship in Medieval and Early Renaissance Literature* (Leiden: Brill, 1994), pp. 43–86.

93 Aristotle, *The Nicomachean Ethics*, ed. and trans. H. Rackham (Cambridge, MA: Loeb, 1926), VIII, 3; Cicero, *Laelius de amicitia*, ed. and trans. Robert Combès (Paris: Belles Lettres, 1983).

94 See Oschema, "Sacred or Profane?," p. 47.

95 Augustine, *The Soliloquies of St. Augustine*, trans. Rose Elizabeth Cleveland (London: Williams and Norgate, 1910), 1, 12, p. 20, and 1, 13, p. 22; Augustine, *The Confessions*, ed. and trans. Philip Burton (New York: Knopf, 2001), p. 74; Aelred of Rielvaux, *Spiritual Friendship*, ed. and trans. Lawrence C. Braceland and Marsha L. Dutton (Collegeville, MN: Liturgical Press, 2010), 1, 8, and 2, 18. And, for a discussion, see Classen, "Introduction," pp. 14–18 and 30–37.

96 Thomas Aquinas, *The "Summa Theologica" of Thomas Aquinas*, trans. Fathers of the English Dominican Province (London: Burns Oates and Washbourne, 1922), IIa 2ae 23, 1 and 3.

97 Innocent III, "Quia maior," in Georgine Tangl (ed.), *Studien zum Register Innocenz III* (Weimar: H. Böhlau, 1929), p. 90; trans. Jonathan Riley-Smith and Louise Riley-Smith, *The Crusades: Idea and Reality, 1095–1274* (London: Edward Arnold, 1981), p. 120.

98 "In dilligendo proximum ex caritate non diligimus nisi Deum" (We in fact love but God when we love our neighbour out of charity). Eudes of Châteauroux, "Sermo in conversione Sancti Pauli et exhortatio ad assumendam crucem," in Maier (ed. and trans.), *Crusade Propaganda and Ideology*, pp. 130–31.

99 As further exemplified by propagandists' frequent citation of Matthew 16:24: "If any man will come after me, let him deny himself and take up his cross and follow me." See, e.g., Rosalind Hill (ed.), *Gesta Francorum et aliorum Hierosolimitanorum: The Deeds of the Franks and the Other Pilgrims to Jerusalem* (Edinburgh: Nelson, 1962), p. 1.

100 The report of Martin's sermon is given by Gunther of Pairis. See Gunther of Pairis, "Historia Constantinopolitana," in Paul Riant (ed.), *Exuviae sacrae Constantinopolitanae*, 3 vols. (Geneva: Fick, 1877), I, p. 64; trans. Riley-Smith and Riley-Smith, *Crusades: Idea and Reality*, p. 71.

101 Robert Somerville (ed.), *The Councils of Urban II* (Amsterdam: Hakkert, 1972), p. 74; Anton Chroust (ed.), *Quellen zur Geschichte des Kreuzzuges Kaiser Friedrichs I* (Berlin: Weidmannsche Buchhandlung, 1928), p. 9; cited in Christopher Tyerman, *How to Plan a Crusade: Reason and Religion in the High Middle Ages* (London: Allen Lane, 2015), p. 139.

102 Tyerman, *How to Plan a Crusade*, p. 139.

103 Christine Chism, "Friendly Fire: The Disastrous Politics of Friendship in the Alliterative *Morte Arthure*," *Arthuriana*, 20 (2010), 66–88 (p. 82); and, by the same author, "Romance," in Larry Scanlon (ed.), *The Cambridge*

180 *Notes to pages 91–94*

Companion to Medieval English Literature, 1100–500 (Cambridge: Cambridge University Press, 2009), pp. 57–70 (see pp. 61–62 for a discussion of *Amis and Amiloun*).

104 The wrathful nature of Guy's decision is conveyed to the emperor by Herhaut in a later passage: "'Sir,' quaþ he, 'it is Gij, / þat in wreþe fram þe wil parti; / Vnto þe soudan he wil fare'" (3325–27).

105 *Gui* reads: "Quant Gui ot que ço fu Terri, / Le preux, le vaillant, le hardi, / De pité comence a plorer" (When Gui heard it was Terri, the brave, the valiant, the bold, he began to weep for pity); Ewert (ed.) and Weiss (trans.), lines 4787–89.

106 In *Gui*, the protagonist's rationale for the oath, omitted in the Middle English version, reads thus: "'Sire Terri,' ço dist Gui le ber, / 'Mult grant honur fait vus ai, / Quant pur vus tant sejurné ai / En cest pais e en ceste cité; / Mult m'en devez saveir bon gré'" (And noble Gui said: "My lord Terri, I have done you much honour by staying behind so long in this land and in this city; you ought to be very grateful to me"). Ibid., lines 5040–44.

107 The stipulations of mutual devotion inherent in the troth-plight are couched in the following terms: "Ich wil þat we be treuþe-pliȝt / & sworn breþer anon riȝt / . . . / Vnder-stond now to mi resoun, / þat noiþer oþer after þis / No faile oþer while he liues is" (4907–12). The benefits that Tirri derives from the bond are enumerated at lines 7041–70.

108 Historians have argued for understandings of sworn associations of brotherhood as determined by protection, defense, and armed aggression (Brent D. Shaw, "Ritual Brotherhood in Roman and Post-Roman Society," *Traditio*, 52 [1997], 327–55 [pp. 329, 350, 354]); as legal bonds of mutual aid (Maurice Keen, "Brotherhood in Arms," *History*, 47 [2007], 1–17); as motivated by material profit (K. B. McFarlane, "A Business Partnership in War and Administration, 1421–1445," *English Historical Review*, 78 [1963], 290–309 [p. 291]); as accepted components of ecclesiastical practice (Alan Bray, *The Friend* [Chicago: University of Chicago Press, 2003], p. 25); and as a form of institutionalized gay marriage (John Boswell, *Same-Sex Unions in Premodern Europe* [New York: Villiard Books, 1994]).

109 Lines 46:1–2 and 138:7. *Gui* does not explicitly couch the protagonist's motives in terms of love: "Pur vus me sui ore combat" (For your benefit I have just fought now); Ewert (ed.) and Weiss (trans.), line 8937.

110 *Gui* likewise portrays the protagonist's relationship with God as a feudal one but omits the language of friendship. See ibid., lines 8309–26.

111 On this, see Maier (ed. and trans.), *Crusade Propaganda and Ideology*, pp. 56–57.

112 Guy's rejection of "gold" and "fe" is unparalleled in *Gui*, as is the emphasis on his love for Tirri. See Ewert (ed.) and Weiss (trans.), lines 10227–31. Leaving Tirri, Guy offers cautionary advice on how to be a good steward and eschew the mistakes of the "prout" Duke Berard (230:1–231:6).

113 See also line 243:10 ("Bid him for seynt Charite") and line 245:7 ("'Pilgrim,' quaþ þe king, 'par charite'"). The corresponding passages of *Gui* likewise

Notes to pages 94–95

posit divine love, brotherly charity, and compassion as motives for action, but less emphatically; the repeated reference to "seynt Charite" is, for instance, unparalleled. See ibid., lines 10925–11008.

114 Guy's example is held up for emulation in the final lines of the poem: "Now god leue ous to liue so, / þat we may þat ioie com to. / Amen, par charité" (299:8, 10–12). The phrase "par charité" does not feature in *Gui*.

115 Charles Swan and Wynnard Hooper (eds. and trans.), *Gesta Romanorum* (New York: Dover, 1959), tale 172, "Of Mental Constancy," pp. 325–33.

116 Georgiana Lea Morril (ed.), *Speculum Gy de Warewyke* (London: Trübner, 1898). The treatise is also contained in the Auchinleck manuscript. For a view that contemporaries saw little relationship between the two works, see, e.g., A. S. G. Edwards, "The *Speculum Guy de Warwick* and Lydgate's *Guy of Warwick*: The Non-Romance Middle English Translation," in Wiggins and Field (eds.), *Guy of Warwick*, pp. 81–93.

117 Morril (ed.), *Speculum Gy de Warewyke*, lines 5–6. See also lines 8–9: "þu loue god ouer alle þing / And þin emcristene loue also"; and lines 324–44: "For i wole speken of charite / . . . / Hit is, loue god ouer alle þing, / In þouht, in dede, and in speking. / And if þu wolt euere come þerto, / An-oþer þing þu most do: / þu most loue, hu-so hit be, / þin emcristene forþ wid þe / . . . / For men seiþ soþ, bi wit[te] myne: / 'Whoso loueþ me, he loueþ myne.' / But þu loue [þyn em] cristene þat bi þe be, / þat alday [þou] mait hem ise, / Hou maitou loue god, I ne can deuise, / Whom þu miht sen on none wyse!"

118 Ibid., particularly lines 28–36, 81–96, 113–14, 149–57, 679–83.

119 See Rutebeuf, "Lament of the Holy Land," in Jessalynn Bird, Edward Peters, and James Powell (eds. and trans.), *Crusade and Christendom: Annotated Documents in Translation from Innocent III to the Fall of Acre, 1187–1291* (Philadelphia: University of Pennsylvania Press, 2013), p. 393.

120 Fidenzio of Padua, *Liber recuperationis Terrae Sanctae*, in G. Gobulovich (ed.), *Biblioteca bio-bibliografia della Terra Sancta*, 20 vols. (Quaracchi: Collegio di S. Bonaventura, 1913), II, pp. 15, 35–38. That Fidenzio emphasizes these qualities when discussing how to preserve the Holy Land is also noted by Lee Manion, *Narrating the Crusades: Loss and Recovery in Medieval and Early Modern English Literature* (Cambridge: Cambridge University Press, 2014), p. 66.

121 Ramon Llull, *Ramon Llull: A Contemporary Life*, ed. and trans. Anthony Bonner (Barcelona: Barcino-Tamesis, 2010), 1, 2, pp. 30–31.

122 Ramon Llull, *The Book of the Ordre of Chyvalry*, trans. William Caxton and ed. A. T. P. Byles, Early English Text Society OS 168 (London: Oxford University Press, 1926), pp. 92–93. On Martorell's *Tirant lo Blanc* and *Guy*, see Richmond, *Legend of Guy of Warwick*, pp. 153–62.

123 On this, see Housley, "Crusading Movement," pp. 259–63. *Sapientia* and *potestas* denoted, in sum, wise men for advice and optimized recruitment and military strategies for maximal efficacy.

124 Mézières, "Philippe de Mézières and the New Order of the Passion," ed. Hamdy, p. 48.

182   *Notes to pages 96–99*

125 On *Guy* and Gloucestershire during the fourteenth century, see Richmond, *Legend of Guy of Warwick*, p. 104. On Chaucer and *Guy*, see Laura A. Hibbard Loomis, "Chaucer and the Auchinleck MS: Thopas and *Guy of Warwick*," in Percy Waldron Lond (ed.), *Essays and Studies in Honor of Carleton Brown* (New York: New York University Press, 1940), pp. 111–28. For an account of Clanvowe's career, see K. B. McFarlane, *Lancastrian Kings and Lollard Knights* (Oxford: Clarendon Press, 1972), pp. 151–85.

126 See Guard, *Chivalry, Kingship and Crusade*, pp. 10 and 37–38; and Timothy Guard, "Ryvere, Sir John (*b.* 1313, *d.* after 1364)," in *Oxford Dictionary of National Biography* (Oxford: Oxford University Press, 2004–16), www.oxforddnb.com/view/article/92453.

127 He drives the point home by specifying that ignoring *caritas* is the way to eternal damnation: "And alle þoo þat loue not so God and here neiȝebour þei been in þe broode wey þat leedeþ to þe deeth of helle peyne þat euere shalle lasten." Clanvowe, *Works of Sir John Clanvowe*, ed. Scattergood, pp. 79–80, lines 855–58. The passage on divine and neighborly love spans lines 795–870 (i.e., to the end of the treatise).

128 See John Scattergood, "The Date of Sir John Clanvowe's *The Two Ways* and the 'Reinvention of Lollardy,'" *Medium Aevum*, 79 (2010), 116–20.

129 L. C. Hector and Barbara F. Harvey (eds. and trans.), *The Westminster Chronicle: 1381–1394* (Oxford: Clarendon Press, 1982), pp. 480–81.

130 On this, see Siegrid Düll, Anthony Luttrell, and Maurice Keen, "Faithful unto Death: The Tomb Slab of Sir William Neville and Sir John Clanvowe, Constantinople 1391," *Antiquaries Journal*, 71 (1991), 174–90 (esp. p. 184); and Bray, *Friend*, pp. 17–19.

131 N. H. Nicolas (ed.), *Testamenta vetusta*, 2 vols. (London: Nichols and Son, 1826), I, p. 164.

132 Maurice Keen, "Chaucer and Chivalry Revisited," in Matthew Strickland (ed.), *Armies, Chivalry and Warfare in Medieval Britain and France* (Stamford, UK: P. Watkins, 1998), pp. 1–12 (p. 11).

133 Chaucer, "General Prologue," in Benson (ed.), *Riverside Chaucer*, lines 43–100. See further Marcel Elias, "Chaucer and Crusader Ethics: Youth, Love, and the Material World," *Review of English Studies*, 70 (2019), 618–39.

Chapter 4

1 John Gower, *Vox Clamantis*, in G. C. Macaulay (ed.), *The Complete Works of John Gower*, 4 vols. (Oxford: Clarendon Press, 1899), IV, 3, lines 307–10.

2 John Gower, *The Minor Latin Works*, ed. and trans. R. F. Yeager; with *In Praise of Peace*, ed. Michael Livingston (Kalamazoo, MI: Medieval Institute Publications, 2005), lines 249–51.

3 John Gower, *Confessio Amantis*, ed. Russell A. Peck; Latin trans. Andrew Galloway, 3 vols. (Kalamazoo, MI: Medieval Institute Publications, 2013), II, 3, lines 2488–90, 2492–94.

Notes to pages 99–100   183

4 Ibid., II, 4, lines 1679–81.

5 On Ralph Niger's critique of crusading on moral and providential grounds, see George B. Flahiff, "*Deus non vult:* A Critic of the Third Crusade," *Mediaeval Studies*, 9 (1947), 162–88 (p. 171); on Wolfram von Eschenbach's ambivalence, see J. A. Hunter, "Wolfram's Attitude to Warfare and Killing," *Reading Medieval Studies*, 8 (1982), 97–114; for Humbert of Romans's response to moral objections to crusading, see "Opus tripartitum," ed. E. Brown, *Fasciculus rerum expetendarum et fugiendarum*, 2 vols. (London: Impensis Richardi Chiswell, 1690), II, pp. 191–98, trans. Jonathan Riley-Smith and Louise Riley-Smith, *The Crusades: Idea and Reality, 1095–1274* (London: Edward Arnold, 1981), pp. 103–17 (pp. 104–6). See also Benjamin Kedar, *Crusade and Mission: European Approaches towards the Muslims* (Princeton, NJ: Princeton University Press, 1984), pp. 97–99, as well as my discussion of accounts of the crusader siege of Jerusalem in 1099 in this chapter.

6 John Wyclif, *Select English Works of John Wyclif*, ed. Thomas Arnold, 3 vols. (Oxford: Clarendon Press, 1869–71), III, p. 139; see also Elizabeth Siberry, "Criticism of Crusading in Fourteenth-Century England," in Peter W. Edbury (ed.), *Crusade and Settlement: Papers Read at the First Conference of the Society for the Study of the Crusades and the Latin East* (Cardiff: University College Cardiff Press, 1985), pp. 127–34 (p. 128).

7 John Trefnant, *The Register of John Trefnant, Bishop of Hereford (A.D. 1389–1404)*, ed. William W. Capes (Hereford, UK: Wilson and Phillips, 1914), pp. 360–61 (on Walter Brut), pp. 368 (on William Swinderby), and p. 377 (for a refutation of Swinderby's arguments by William of Colwyll and John Netton). See further Ben Lowe, *Imagining Peace: A History of Early English Pacifist Ideas, 1340–1560* (University Park: Pennsylvania State University Press, 1997), p. 119; Siberry, "Criticism of Crusading," p. 128.

8 H. S. Cronin (ed.), "The Twelve Conclusions of the Lollards," *English Historical Review*, 22 (1907), 292–304 (p. 302).

9 Celia M. Lewis, "History, Mission, and Crusade in the *Canterbury Tales*," *Chaucer Review*, 42 (2008), 353–82, esp. pp. 357–59; see also Christopher Tyerman, *England and the Crusades, 1095–1588* (Chicago: University of Chicago Press, 1988), pp. 264–65.

10 John Clanvowe, *The Works of Sir John Clanvowe*, ed. V. J. Scattergood (Cambridge, UK: D. S. Brewer, 1975), pp. 20 and 69.

11 Henry of Grosmont, *Le livre de seyntz medicines: The Unpublished Devotional Treatise of Henry of Lancaster*, ed. E. J. Arnould (Oxford: Blackwell, 1940), p. 17; and Lewis, "History, Mission, and Crusade," p. 358.

12 On Bromyard's critique of inter-Christian warfare, see Lowe, *Imagining Peace*, pp. 111–12.

13 Keith Walls, *John Bromyard on Church and State: The "Summa Praedicantium" and Early Fourteenth-Century England* (Market Weighton, UK: Clayton-Thorpe, 2007), pp. 206, 213.

184 *Notes to pages 100–102*

14 Philippe de Mézières, "Philippe de Mézières and the New Order of the Passion," ed. Abdel Hamid Hamdy, *Bulletin of the Faculty of Arts, Alexandria University*, 18 (1964), 43–104 (p. 67). The importance of avoiding inhumane warfare was also emphasized in the context of the Hussite Crusades: see Norman Housley, *Religious Warfare in Europe, 1400–1536* (Oxford: Oxford University Press, 2008), pp. 164–66.

15 See also my discussion of Honorat Bovet's anticrusade stance in the Conclusion.

16 See esp. Marino Sanudo Torsello, *The Book of the Secrets of the Faithful Cross: Liber secretorum fidelium crucis*, trans. Peter Lock (Farnham, UK: Ashgate, 2011), pp. 29–30; and the many passages in Philippe de Mézières, *Letter to King Richard II, a Plea Made in 1395 for Peace between England and France*, ed. and trans. G. W. Coopland (Liverpool, UK: Liverpool University Press, 1975). I discuss these sources in the body of the chapter; relevant passages are referenced in notes 36, 37, and 38.

17 Geraldine Heng, *Empire of Magic: Medieval Romance and the Politics of Cultural Fantasy* (New York: Columbia University Press, 2003), pp. 61–113; Nicola McDonald, "Eating People and the Alimentary Logic of *Richard Coeur de Lion*," in Nicola McDonald (ed.), *Pulp Fictions of Medieval England: Essays in Popular Romance* (Manchester, UK: Manchester University Press, 2004), pp. 124–50; Suzanne M. Yeager, *Jerusalem in Medieval Narrative* (Cambridge: Cambridge University Press, 2008), pp. 48–77; Heather Blurton, *Cannibalism in High Medieval English Literature* (Basingstoke, UK: Palgrave, 2007), pp. 105–31.

18 Ralph Hanna and David Lawton (eds.), *The Siege of Jerusalem,* Early English Text Society OS 320 (Oxford: Oxford University Press, 2003). See Hanna and Lawton's introduction for the dating of the text, its manuscripts, and its sources. On the poet's reliance on John of Tynemouth, unidentified by Hanna and Lawton, see Andrew Galloway, "Alliterative Poetry in Old Jerusalem: *The Siege of Jerusalem* and Its Sources," in John A. Burrow and Hoyt N. Duggan (eds.), *Medieval Alliterative Poetry: Essays in Honour of Thorlac Turville-Petre* (Dublin: Four Courts, 2010), pp. 85–106.

19 *The Siege of Jerusalem* is found alongside *Richard Coeur de Lion, Duke Roland and Sir Otuel of Spain*, and *The Siege of Milan* in London, British Library, MS Additional 31042 (London Thornton), and alongside *Octavian* and *Sir Isumbras* in London, British Library, MS Cotton Caligula A.ii.

20 William of Tyre, *A History of Deeds Done beyond the Sea*, trans. Emily A. Babcock and A. C. Krey, 2 vols. (New York: Columbia University Press, 1887–1961), I, 8, p. 341. The Old French *Eracles* survives in no less than sixty-four manuscripts and was translated into Castilian in the late thirteenth century, Italian in the mid fourteenth, and English by Caxton in 1481 (for Caxton's version, see *A Middle English Chronicle of the First Crusade: The Caxton Eracles*, ed. Dana Cushing, 2 vols. [Lewiston, NY: Edwin Miller, 2001]). Albert of Aachen, *Historia Ierosolimitana: History of the Journey to*

Notes to pages 102–104 185

Jerusalem, ed. and trans. Susan B. Edgington (Oxford: Oxford University Press, 2007), 4, 24, p. 433.

21 Sanudo Torsello, *Book of the Secrets of the Faithful Cross*, trans. Lock, pp. 191–94.

22 Pierre Dubois, *The Recovery of the Holy Land*, ed. and trans. Walther I. Brandt (New York: Columbia University Press, 1956), p. 77.

23 Interestingly, as will be discussed in this chapter, it is to promote the virtue of compassion that Titus and Vespasian are invoked. See Mézières, *Letter to King Richard II*, ed. and trans. Coopland, pp. 16–17.

24 Mary Hamel, "*The Siege of Jerusalem* as a Crusading Poem," in Barbara N. Sargent-Baur (ed.), *Journeys toward God: Pilgrimage and Crusade* (Kalamazoo, MI: Medieval Institute Publications), pp. 177–94; Roger Nicholson, "Haunted Itineraries: Reading the *Siege of Jerusalem*," *Exemplaria*, 14 (2002), 447–84.

25 Elisa Narin van Court, "*The Siege of Jerusalem* and Augustinian Historians: Writing about Jews in Fourteenth-Century England," *Chaucer Review*, 29 (1995), 227–48; Bonnie Millar, *The "Siege of Jerusalem" in Its Physical, Literary, and Historical Contexts* (Dublin: Four Courts, 2000), pp. 141–80; Michael Johnston, "Robert Thornton and *The Siege of Jerusalem*," *Yearbook of Langland Studies*, 23 (2009), 125–62; Suzanne M. Yeager, "Jewish Identity in *The Siege of Jerusalem* and Homiletic Texts: Models of Penance and Victims of Vengeance for the Urban Apocalypse," *Medium Aevum*, 80 (2011), 56–84.

26 Suzanne Conklin Akbari, "Placing the Jews in Late Medieval England," in Ivan Davidson Kalmar and Derek J. Penslar (eds.), *Orientalism and the Jews* (Waltham, MA: Brandeis University Press, 2005), pp. 32–50; Suzanne Conklin Akbari, *Idols in the East: European Representations of Islam and the Orient, 1100–1450* (Ithaca, NY: Cornell University Press, 2009), pp. 124–33; Suzanne M. Yeager, "*The Siege of Jerusalem* and Biblical Exegesis: Writing about Romans in Fourteenth-Century England," *Chaucer Review*, 39 (2004), 70–102; Marco Nievergelt, "The *Sege of Melayne* and the *Siege of Jerusalem*: National Identity, Beleaguered Christendom, and Holy War during the Great Papal Schism," *Chaucer Review*, 49 (2015), 402–26; Christine Chism, *Alliterative Revivals* (Philadelphia: University of Pennsylvania Press, 2002), pp. 155–88.

27 Akbari, *Idols in the East*, p. 129.

28 Yeager, "*The Siege of Jerusalem* and Biblical Exegesis," p. 71.

29 See Carole Rawcliffe, *Medicine and Society in Later Medieval England* (Stroud, UK: Sutton, 1995), pp. 1–25.

30 It is noted in passing by Hamel, "*The Siege of Jerusalem* as a Crusading Poem," p. 178. For noncrusading treatments of the theme, in *The Siege* and other narratives of the *Vengeance de Nostre-Seigneur* tradition, see Yeager, "Jewish Identity in *The Siege of Jerusalem*"; and Maija Birenbaum, "Affective Vengeance in Titus and Vespasian," *Chaucer Review*, 43 (2009), 330–44.

31 On this, see H. E. J. Cowdrey, "Cluny and the First Crusade," *Revue bénédictine*, 83 (1973), 283–311 (pp. 301–2). The encyclical can be found

186   *Notes to pages 104–106*

in Sergius IV, "Encyclique de Sergius IV relative à un projet de croisade," ed. Jules Lair, *Bibliothèque de l'école des chartres*, 18 (1857), pp. 246–53, and was translated into English by Thomas G. Waldman in "The 'Encyclical' of 'Sergius IV,'" in *The First Crusade: The Chronicle of Fulcher of Chartres and Other Source Materials*, ed. Edward Peters, 2nd ed. (Philadelphia: University of Pennsylvania Press, 1998; 1st ed. 1971), pp. 298–302.

32 Susan B. Edgington and Carol Sweetenham (trans.), *The "Chanson d'Antioche": An Old French Account of the First Crusade* (Farnham: Ashgate, 2011). See the introduction, pp. 38–39, on the later versions.

33 Sergius IV, "Encyclique de Sergius IV," ed. Lair, pp. 250–51; Sergius IV, *First Crusade*, trans. Waldman and ed. Peters, pp. 299–300.

34 "Amis," dist Nostre Sire, "saciés a ensient / Que dela oltremer venront novele gent, / De la mort de lor pere pranderont venjement /. . . / Et ki pris et finés iert en cel errement / L'arme del cors ira en nostre salvement" ("My friend," said Our Lord, "be assured that a new race will come from over the sea to avenge the death of their Father . . . The soul of every man who is taken and killed on this journey will receive My salvation"). Suzanne Duparc-Quioc (ed.), *La chanson d'Antioche* (Paris: P. Geuthner, 1976), laisse 11, lines 205–11; Edgington and Sweetenham (trans.), *The "Chanson d'Antioche,"* p. 107.

35 Ibid., laisse 13, line 246, and laisse 14, lines 262–63; trans. Edgington and Sweetenham, pp. 108–9.

36 Book 1 is prescribed as a syrup to liberate and cleanse; book 2 aims to induce health and perfect freedom; and book 3 instructs on conservation against relapse. Sanudo Torsello, *Book of the Secrets of the Faithful Cross*, trans. Lock, pp. 29–30.

37 Mézières, *Letter to King Richard II*, ed. and trans. Coopland, pp. 30, 46, 103.

38 Ibid., p. 31. For a brief summary of these ideas, see Philippe Contamine, "'Les princes, barons et chevaliers qui a la chevalerie au service de Dieu se sont ja vouez': Recherches prosopographiques sur l'ordre de la Passion de Jésus-Christ (1385–1395)," in Martin Nejedly and Jaroslav Svátek (eds.), *La noblesse et la croisade à la fin du Moyen Age: France, Bourgogne, Bohême* (Toulouse: FRAMESPA-UMR, 2009), pp. 43–64 (p. 44).

39 Mézières, "Philippe de Mézières and the New Order of the Passion," ed. Hamdy, p. 43.

40 Also noted by Yeager, "*The Siege of Jerusalem* and Biblical Exegesis," pp. 76–77.

41 The text does not specify that the man Josephus brings is a Jew, but the context makes clear that he is brought from within the city and is undoubtedly a Jew. This contrasts with the main source for this section of the narrative, the *Legenda aurea*, where the man is a former servant of Titus. See the notes to these lines in Hanna and Lawton's edition, pp. 144–45.

42 See Simo Knuuttila, *Emotions in Ancient and Medieval Philosophy* (Oxford: Clarendon Press, 2004), pp. 214–15; Peter King, "Emotions in Medieval Thought," in Peter Goldie (ed.), *Oxford Handbook of Philosophy of Emotion*

Notes to pages 106–107 187

(Oxford: Oxford University Press, 2009), pp. 167–87 (pp. 167–68); and Michael Livingston (ed.), *The Siege of Jerusalem*, (Kalamazoo, MI: Medieval Institute Publications, 2004), note to lines 1049–62.

43 Richard Lavynham, *A Litil Tretys on the Seven Deadly Sins*, ed. Johannes Petrus Wilhelmus Maria van Zutphen (Rome: Institutum Carmelitanum, 1956), p. 11.

44 Thomas Aquinas, *The "Summa Theologica" of Thomas Aquinas*, trans. Fathers of the English Dominican Province (London: Burns Oates and Washbourne, 1922), IIa 2ae 158, 4.

45 Siegried Wenzel (ed. and trans.), *Fasciculus morum: A Fourteenth-Century Preacher's Handbook* (University Park: Pennsylvania State University Press, 1989), pp. 118–21, cited in Daniel Lord Smail, "Hatred as a Social Institution," *Speculum*, 76 (2001), 90–126; for Giles of Rome, in John Trevisa's Middle English translation, see Giles of Rome, *The Governance of Kings and Princes: John Trevisa's Middle English Translation of the "De Regimine Principum" of Aegidius Romanus*, ed. David C. Fowler, Charles F. Briggs, and Paul G. Remley (New York: Garland, 1997), I, 3, 7, p. 128.

46 Giles of Rome, *Governance of Kings and Princes*, trans. Trevisa and ed. Fowler, Briggs, and Remley, I, 3, 7, p. 127.

47 Augustine, *De civitate dei*, ed. J. P. Migne, Patrologia Latina 41 (Paris: Garnier Fratres, 1864), 19, 7, col. 634; Augustine, *The City of God against the Pagans*, trans. R. W. Dyson (Cambridge: Cambridge University Press, 1998), p. 929.

48 "Tradidit enim Deus noster crucis adversarios in manibus nostris. Severissima namque super eos ultio divina adeo incubuit, ut dum urbem destructam castrumque eversum, agros depopulatos, terram in solitudinem redactam, nullum in agris incolam, luctus gemitusque eorum conspicimus, vicis eorum et eventus malorum misereri libeat, condolerique et compati eorum infirmitatibus, et quod nondum finem habeant flagella celestis iusticie, certe quia nec inter nos Christianos etiam correcte sunt inter flagella actionis culpe" (For our God has delivered the enemies of the cross into our hands. And divine vengeance has pressed upon them with such severity that, as we see the city in ruins and the castle overthrown, the fields depopulated, the land reduced to solitude, with no inhabitant in the fields, and as we behold their mourning and lamentations, we are inclined to feel pity for them in their vicissitudes and evil fortunes and to suffer with them on account of their infirmities and to feel sorry that the lashings of divine justice are not yet at an end; and particularly are we moved to sorrow because not even among us Christians have sins been corrected amid the scourgings of his action). Charles Wendell David (ed. and trans.), *De expugnatione Lyxbonensi: The Conquest of Lisbon* (New York: Columbia University Press, 1936), pp. 182–83.

49 Ibid., pp. 182–83. Similar directives were given by authors of guidebooks on chivalry and warfare. Honorat Bovet declares that all good Catholics must feel grief and pity in the face of tribulations and wars; and Christine de Pizan situates compassionate sorrow for the fate of enemies as a stipulation for virtuous princes. See Honorat Bovet, *The Tree of Battles*, ed. and trans.

188   *Notes to pages 107–110*

G. W. Coopland (Liverpool: Liverpool University Press, 1949), p. 91; and
Christine de Pizan, *The Book of the Body Politic*, ed. and trans. Kate Langdon
Forhan (Cambridge: Cambridge University Press, 1994), pp. 15 and 29.

50 Sanudo Torsello, *Book of the Secrets of the Faithful Cross*, trans. Lock, p. 236.

51 Ibid., pp. 191–92. See, for the original Latin, *Gesta Dei per Francos, sive
orientalium expeditionem et regni Francorum Hierosolymitani historia*, ed.
J. Bongars, 2 vols. (Hannover: Typis Wechelianis, 1611), II, p. 119.

52 Mézières, *Letter to King Richard II*, ed. and trans. Coopland, pp. 17, 89.

53 Ibid., pp. 17, 90.

54 Other examples include Guillaume de Machaut, *La prise d'Alixandre*, ed. and
trans. R. Barton Palmer (New York: Routledge, 2002), lines 6976–78, where
the author presents Peter I of Cyprus torn between joy and grief in battle; and
Bovet, *Tree of Battles*, p. 112, where Julius Caesar is portrayed as weeping over
the decapitated head of Pompey.

55 On the Romans' mercy and compassion in Josephus and Higden, see
Josephus, *The Jewish War*, ed. and trans. Gaalya Cornfeld (Grand Rapids,
MI: Zondervan, 1982), e.g., V, 4, 361, p. 381; V, 4, 372, p. 382; X, 6, 450,
p. 389; V, 7, 522, pp. 395–96; VI, 3, 215, p. 417; and Ranulph Higden,
*Polychronicon Ranulphi Higden Monachi Cestrensis; together with the English
Translation of John Trevisa and of an Unknown Writer of the Fifteenth Century*,
ed. Joseph Rawson Lumby, Rolls Series 41, 9 vols. (London: Longman,
1865–86) IV, esp. pp. 438–39, where the author claims that the Romans
were more merciful of the Jews than were the Jews with each other.

56 See lines 641–44 and 1169–72.

57 Van Court, "*The Siege of Jerusalem* and Augustinian Historians," p. 234. For
Vespasian's cursing, see lines 677 and 786.

58 On the torture of Christ by the Jews, see lines 503–4; on the execution of
Caiaphas as vengeance for the Passion, see lines 725–28.

59 Unlike Roger d'Argenteuil's *Bible en françois*, *The Siege* specifies that Caiaphas
is tortured from prime until sundown (707); has the Romans pierce his sides
(also 707), thus making the parallel with Christ's crucifixion more explicit;
and gives the number of Jews who commit suicide. For the corresponding
passages of the *Bible en françois*, which served as the *Siege*-author's sole source
for lines 205–80 and 321–728, see A. E. Ford (ed.), *La vengeance de Nostre-
Seigneur* (Turnhout: Brepols, 1993), pp. 116–17, lines 460–81. See further
Phyllis Moe, "The French Source of the Alliterative *Siege of Jerusalem*,"
Medium Aevum, 39 (1970), 147–54.

60 On this, see Jeremy Cohen, *Sanctifying the Name of God: Jewish Martyrs and
Jewish Memories of the First Crusade* (Philadelphia: University of Pennsylvania
Press, 2004), pp. 1–9 (esp. pp. 1–4).

61 Albert of Aachen, *Historia Ierosolimitana*, ed. and trans. Edgington, 1, 27,
pp. 52–53. For a discussion of the evaluative rhetoric of anger in Latin
accounts of the Rhineland massacres, see Kate McGrath, "The 'Zeal of
God': The Representation of Anger in the Latin Crusade Accounts of the
1096 Rhineland Massacres," in Kristine T. Utterback and Merrall Llewelyn

Price (eds.), *Jews in Medieval Christendom: "Slay Them Not"* (Leiden: Brill, 2013), pp. 25–44.

62 Eliezer bar Nathan, *The Persecutions of 1096*, in *The Jews and the Crusaders: The Hebrew Chronicles of the First and Second Crusades*, trans. Shlomo Eidelberg (Madison: University of Wisconsin Press, 1977), pp. 83–84.

63 William of Newburgh, *Historia de rebus anglicis*, in Richard Howlett (ed.), *Chronicles of the Reigns of Stephen, Henry II, and Richard I*, Rolls Series 82, 4 vols. (London: Longman, 1884–89), I, 4, 7–10, pp. 308–22. Though not carried out exclusively by crusaders, the anti-Jewish uprisings of 1190 are aligned at the outset with the religious zeal of Richard I's expedition to the Holy Land (see already p. 279, and pp. 310 and 313–14). On Josephus's influence on Newburgh's account, see van Court, "*The Siege of Jerusalem* and Augustinian Historians," pp. 239–41.

64 See esp. lines 1247–1252: "þe peple in þe pauyment was pite to byholde / þat were enfamy[n]ed [and] def[e]te wham hem fode wanted. / Was noȝt on ladies lafte bot þe lene bones / þat were fleschy byfore and fayre on to loke; / Burges with balies as barels or þat tyme / No gretter þan a grehounde to grype on þe medil."

65 Josephus, *Jewish War*, ed. and trans. Cornfeld, VI, 3, 199, 200, 204, pp. 416–17; Higden, *Polychronicon Ranulphi Higden*, ed. Lumby, pp. 444–47.

66 Eliezer bar Nathan, *Persecutions of 1096*, trans. Eidelberg, p. 83.

67 Ibid., p. 85.

68 See esp. Josephus, *Jewish War*, ed. and trans. Cornfeld, VI, 3, 212, p. 417; and Higden, *Polychronicon Ranulphi Higden*, ed. Lumby, pp. 446–47.

69 Sanudo Torsello, *Book of the Secrets of the Faithful Cross*, trans. Lock, pp. 306–7; *Gesta Dei per Francos*, ed. Bongars, pp. 192–93.

70 Guillaume le Breton, *La Philippide*, in F. Guizot (ed.), *Collection de mémoires relatifs à l'histoire de France* 12 (Paris: Brière, 1825), pp. 197–99.

71 Josephus, *Jewish War*, ed. and trans. Cornfeld, VI, 3, 214–216, pp. 417–18; and Higden, *Polychronicon Ranulphi Higden*, ed. Lumby, pp. 446–47. In John Trevisa's translation of Higden in the same volume: "We come to a bataille of men, but now I see þat we fiȝteþ aȝenst bestes … but þese men devoureþ here owne children: þanne destroye we hem, for alle hir dedes stinkeþ."

72 Suzanne Conklin Akbari, "Erasing the Body: History and Memory in Medieval Siege Poetry," in Nicholas Paul and Suzanne M. Yeager (eds.), *Remembering the Crusades: Myth, Image, and Identity* (Baltimore: Johns Hopkins University Press, 2012), pp. 146–73 (pp. 157–58).

73 On the popularity, translation, and dissemination of Robert's and William's chronicles, see Carol Sweetenham's introduction to Robert of Reims, *Robert the Monk's History of the First Crusade* (Aldershot, UK: Ashgate, 2005), trans. Carol Sweetenham, pp. 8–11; and Benjamin Z. Kedar, "The Jerusalem Massacre of July 1099 in the Western Historiography of the Crusades," *Crusades*, 3 (2004), 15–75 (pp. 31–35).

190   *Notes to pages 112–114*

74 Marcus Bull and Damien Kempf, "Introduction," in *Writing the Early Crusades: Text, Transmission, and Memory* (Woodbridge, UK: Boydell Press, 2014), pp. 1–8 (p. 2).

75 This claim finds its origin in the anonymous *Gesta Francorum*: "Tales occisiones de paganorum gente nullus unquam audiuit nec uidit ... et nemo scit numerum eorum nisi solus Deus" (No-one has ever seen or heard of such a slaughter of pagans ... and no-one save God alone knows how many there were). Rosalind Hill (ed.), *Gesta Francorum et aliorum Hierosolimitanorum: The Deeds of the Franks and the Other Pilgrims to Jerusalem* (Edinburgh: Nelson, 1962), p. 92. See also, e.g., Guibert of Nogent, *Geste de Dieu par les Frances: Histoire de la première croisade*, trans. Monique-Cécile Garand (Turnhout: Brepols, 1998), pp. 7, 245; and Peter Tudebode, *Historia de Hierosolymitano Itinere*, trans. John Hugh Hill and Laurita L. Hill (Philadelphia: American Philosophical Society, 1974), pp. 11, 120.

76 In my discussion of these accounts, I build on Kedar's important article "The Jerusalem Massacre of July 1099."

77 Akbari, "Placing the Jews," pp. 37–39; Akbari, *Idols in the East*, pp. 127–28. The indebtedness of *The Siege*'s depictions of Jewish affluence to First Crusade chronicles was first noted by Chism, *Alliterative Revivals*, pp. 320–25.

78 Akbari, "Placing the Jews," pp. 39–43; Akbari, *Idols in the East*, pp. 129–33.

79 See Kedar, "The Jerusalem Massacre of July 1099," p. 31. As noted by Kedar, the scene, which finds its origin in a letter by the crusade's leaders to Pope Urban II, "came to epitomize the conquest of Jerusalem for generations of Westerners." The scene was also taken up at the end of the fifteenth century by Felix Fabri; see *The Wanderings of Felix Fabri*, trans. Aubrey Stewart (London: Palestine Pilgrims' Text Society, 1892), 3, p. 308.

80 Siegebert of Gembloux, *Chronica*, ed. L. C. Bethmann, Monumenta Germaniae Historica: Scriptores 6 (Hanover: Hahn, 1844), p. 368.

81 Also, lines 603–5: "So was þe bent ouerbrad, blody byrunne, / With ded bodies about – alle þe brod vale – / Myȝt no stede doun stap bot on stele wede." See also Akbari, "Placing the Jews," p. 39.

82 Hill (ed.), *Gesta Francorum*, pp. 91–92.

83 Gilo of Paris, *The "Historia vie Hierosolimitane" of Gilo of Paris and a Second Anonymous Author*, ed. and trans. C. W. Grocock and J. E. Siberry (Oxford: Clarendon Press, 1997), pp. 248–49, lines 344–46. Tancred's and Gaston's feelings of mercy are highlighted at lines 332–33: "Et eis sua signa dederunt / Tancretius Gastonque, piis affectibus acti" (And Tancred and Gaston gave them their banners, prompted by feelings of mercy).

84 Ibid., pp. 250–51, lines 359–61. A similar image of the crusaders wrathfully cutting down their enemies, driven to commit suicide out of terror and grief, is found in Robert of Reims's ambivalent rendering of the taking of Antioch in 1098. See Robert of Reims, *The "Historia Iherosolimitana" of Robert the Monk*, ed. Damien Kempf and Marcus Bull (Woodbridge, UK: Boydell Press, 2013), 8, p. 87; and *Robert the Monk's History of the First Crusade*, trans. Sweetenham, p. 185.

Notes to pages 114–117 191

85 It is relevant that William knew of the accounts of Albert of Aachen, Fulcher of Chartres, and Baudri of Bourgueil: see the introduction to William of Tyre, *History of Deeds*, trans. Babcock and Krey, p. 29.

86 My assessment aligns with Kedar, "Jerusalem Massacre of July 1099," pp. 26–27.

87 William of Tyre, *History of Deeds*, trans. Babcock and Krey, I, 8, 19, p. 370.

88 Ibid., I, 8, 19, p. 371.

89 See Roger of Wendover, *Roger of Wendover's Flowers of History*, trans. J. A. Giles, 4 vols. (Felinfach: Llanerch, 1993–96), I, 2, p. 433; Matthew Paris, *Chronica Majora*, ed. Henry Richards Luard, 7 vols. (London: Longman, 1872–83), II, pp. 101–2.

90 William of Tyre, *History of Deeds*, trans. Babcock and Krey, I, 8, 19, p. 372.

91 Albert of Aachen, *Historia Ierosolimitana*, ed. and trans. Edgington, 6, 30, pp. 440–43.

92 The offensive is launched with Vespasian described thus: "þan wroþ as a wode bore he wendeþ his bridul: / 3if 3e as dogges wold dey, þe deuel haue þat recche!'" (785–86, 829–32).

93 Albert of Aachen, *Historia Ierosolimitana*, ed. and trans. Edgington, 6, 30, pp. 442–43.

94 Yeager, *Jerusalem in Medieval Narrative*, pp. 48–77; Suzanne Conklin Akbari, "The Hunger for National Identity in *Richard Coeur de Lion*," in Robert M. Stein and Sandra Pierson Prior (eds.), *Reading Medieval Culture: Essays in Honor of Robert W. Hanning* (Notre Dame, IN: University of Notre Dame Press, 2005), pp. 198–227; Alan S. Ambrisco, "Cannibalism and Cultural Encounters in *Richard Coeur de Lion*," *Journal of Medieval and Early Modern Studies*, 29 (1999), 499–528; Heng, *Empire of Magic*, pp. 63–113; McDonald, "Eating People," pp. 124–50.

95 On this, see Jean Flori, *Richard Coeur de Lion: Le roi chevalier* (Paris: Payot, 1999), pp. 416–17.

96 Ibid., pp. 418–22. This type of massacre was, according to Flori, most commonly ascribed to populations deemed "savage" and "barbarian."

97 Bromyard denounced Richard for his lapse into vanity and pride; see Timothy Guard, *Chivalry, Kingship and Crusade: The English Experience in the Fourteenth Century* (Woodbridge, UK: Boydell Press, 2013), p. 178.

98 The quotations are from John Trevisa's translation. See Higden, *Polychronicon Ranulphi Higden*, ed. Lumby, VIII, pp. 85, 89, 91, 119, and 121.

99 Ibid., VIII, p. 159.

100 The distinction between B-version and A-version manuscripts was originally made by Karl Brunner in his introduction to *Der Mittelenglische Versroman über Richard Löwenherz*, (Vienna: W. Braumüller, 1913), pp. 1–24, which remains the most comprehensive scholarly edition of the romance. Version B manuscripts: Edinburgh, National Library of Scotland, MS Advocates 19.2.1 (the Auchinleck MS) (c. 1330); London, College of Arms, MS Arundel 58 (c. 1400–1450); London, British Library, MS Egerton 2862

(*olim* Trentham-Sutherland) (c. 1390); London, British Library, MS Harley 4690 (fifteenth century); Oxford, Bodleian Library, MS Douce 228 (late fifteenth century). Version A manuscripts: Cambridge, Gonville and Caius College, MS 175/96 (c. 1400); London, British Library, MS Additional 31042 (the London Thornton MS) (c. 1440). Brunner's edition is based on the Gonville and Caius College, MS 175/96 (c. 1400) supplemented by one of the two early prints of the text by Wynkyn de Worde (1509 and 1528). Brunner's B-A distinction, and the classification of the former as "historical" and the latter as "romance-like," is, however, problematic because all extant manuscripts, apart from the earliest, the fragmentary Auchinleck, contain a certain amount of interpolated "romance" material. The designation of Egerton 2862 as a B-version manuscript is particularly problematic given that it is unique within B to contain the episodes of cannibalism. For a detailed table of the passages contained in each of the different manuscripts, see Brunner's introduction, pp. 15–17.

101 See Yeager, *Jerusalem in Medieval Narrative*, pp. 48–77; Akbari, "Hunger for National Identity"; Ambrisco, "Cannibalism and Cultural Encounters"; Heng, *Empire of Magic*, pp. 63–113; and McDonald, "Eating People."

102 London, British Library, MS Egerton 2862 (c. 1390) contains the episodes of cannibalism, but its opening lines are illegible (the manuscript begins at line 1857). The 1,200-line interpolation to the start of the narrative occurs after line 35 of the Auchinleck manuscript and is found in its most complete form in the A-version manuscripts, starting with Cambridge, Gonville and Caius College, MS 175 (c. 1400), which also contains the cannibalism episodes. Despite the fragmentary state of the Auchinleck, which breaks off at an earlier point in the narrative (at the start of the siege of Acre), the cannibalism episodes are consensually assumed to be later additions. They have no historical foundation in Richard's life, and, as noted by Philida Schellekens, their style, subject matter, and a number of linguistic features set them apart from the base narrative of the B version, which deals with historically attested events (see Philida M. T. A. Schellekens [ed.], "An Edition of the Middle English Romance: *Richard Coeur de Lion*," 2 vols. [unpublished doctoral thesis, Durham University, 1989], II, pp. 33 and 62). For a more extensive treatment of the romance's manuscript history, see Marcel Elias, "Violence, Excess, and the Composite Emotional Rhetoric of *Richard Coeur de Lion*," *Studies in Philology*, 114 (2017), 1–38.

103 Jeffrey Burton Russel, *Witchcraft in the Middle Ages* (Ithaca, NY: Cornell University Press, 1984), p. 167.

104 I quote here from John Trevisa's translation: "Also of þis Henry [Henry II, Richard's father] while he was a child y-norsched in þe kynges court of Fraunce, seynt Bernard þe abbot propheciede and saide in presence of þe kynges, 'Of þe devel he come, and to þe devel he schal'; and menede þerby boþe þe tyraundise of his fader Geffray þat geldede the bisshop of Sagye, and his owne cruelnesse þat slou3 seynt Thomas of Caunterbury." Higden, *Polychronicon Ranulphi Higden*, ed. Lumby, VIII, p. 35. The legend was

Notes to pages 118–120 193

invoked by Scottish chroniclers to support charges of treachery. See Walter Bower, *Scotichronicon*, ed. D. E. R. Watt, 9 vols. (Aberdeen: Aberdeen University Press, 1987–98), V, pp. 16–19; Dan Embree, Edward Donald Kennedy, and Kathleen Daly (eds.), *Short Scottish Prose Chronicles* (Woodbridge, UK: Boydell Press, 2012), pp. 40–1, 56, 131, 270, and 285; and Katherine H. Terrell, "'Lynealy discendit of þe devill': Genealogy, Textuality, and Anglophobia in Medieval Scottish Chronicles," *Studies in Philology*, 108 (2011), 320–44.

105 As noted by Akbari, "Hunger for National Identity," p. 201.

106 Tournaments were often organized to accompany crusade preparations. See, e.g., Simon D. Lloyd, *English Society and the Crusade, 1216–1307* (Oxford: Clarendon Press, 1988), pp. 19–20.

107 Compare this, for instance, with the sentiments aroused by Guy of Warwick: "þai seyden hem among / þe pilgrim was non erþely man; / It was an angel, from heuen cam" (188:3–5). Guy in turn characterizes the Muslim giant Amoraunt thus: "It is . . . no mannes sone: / It is a deuel fram helle come" (95:10–11).

108 Kate McGrath, "The Politics of Chivalry: The Function of Anger and Shame in Eleventh- and Twelfth-Century Anglo-Norman Historical Narratives," in Belle S. Tuten and Tracey L. Billado (eds.), *Feud, Violence and Practice: Essays in Medieval Studies in Honor of Stephen D. White* (Farnham, UK: Ashgate, 2010), pp. 55–69 (pp. 65–66).

109 David (ed. and trans.), *De expugnatione Lyxbonensi*, pp. 166–67.

110 On this, see John V. Tolan, *Sons of Ishmael: Muslims through European Eyes in the Middle Ages* (Gainesville: University Press of Florida, 2008), pp. 82 and 85.

111 Ludolph of Suchem, *Ludolphi de itinere terrae sanctae liber*, ed. Ferdinand Deycks (Stuttgart: Gedruckt auf Kosten des Litterarischen Vereins, 1851), p. 42.

112 Richard's ungracious treatment of the minstrel is an interesting choice on the part of the adaptor in view of the popular legend of Blondel, which appears in earliest form in a thirteenth-century French prose chronicle. The legend tells of a minstrel who shows his dedication to Richard I by finding the location of the German prison in which the king is incarcerated, traveling and singing songs from castle to castle until finally hearing the captive monarch's voice in reply. See John Gillingham, "Some Legends of Richard the Lionheart: Their Development and Their Influence," in Janet Nelson (ed.), *Richard Coeur de Lion in History and Myth* (London: King's College Centre for Late Antique and Medieval Studies, 1992), pp. 51–69 (p. 55).

113 While fighting fairly is, to a degree, a modern misconception of chivalry, the violation of agreed-upon terms of combat was widely condemned. See, e.g., Flori, *Richard Coeur de Lion*, pp. 424–32; and, on Froissart's conception of chivalry, according to which "good knights fought fairly," Warren C. Brown, *Violence in Medieval Europe* (Harlow, UK: Longman, 2010), p. 280.

194   *Notes to pages 120–123*

114 The full-length study is Velma Bourgeois Richmond, *Laments for the Dead in Medieval Narrative* (Pittsburgh, PA: Duquesne University Press, 1966).

115 See Gerd Althoff, *Family, Friends and Followers*, trans. Christopher Caroll (Cambridge: Cambridge University Press, 2004; 1st ed. in German 1990); and his "Friendship and Political Order," in Julian Haseldine (ed.), *Friendship in Medieval Europe* (Stroud, UK: Sutton, 1999), pp. 91–105.

116 Heng, *Empire of Magic*, pp. 21–61.

117 On a trauma theory and crusade literature, see Siobhain Bly Calkin, "Narrating Trauma? Captured Cross Relics in Chronicles and *Chansons de Geste*," *Exemplaria*, 33 (2021), 19–43. In relation to noncrusading materials, see also Catherine A. M. Clarke, "Signs and Wonders: Writing Trauma in Twelfth-Century England," *Reading Medieval Studies*, 35 (2009), 55–77.

118 Fulcher of Chartres, *A History of the Expedition to Jerusalem, 1095–1127*, trans. Rita Ryan (Knoxville: University of Tennessee Press, 1969), 1, 15, p. 112; Ralph of Caen, *The Gesta Tancredi of Ralph of Caen: A History of the Normans on the First Crusade*, trans. Bernard S. Bachrach and David S. Bachrach (Aldershot, UK: Ashgate, 2005), p. 116; Robert of Reims, *Historia Iherosolimitana*, ed. Kempf and Bull, 8, p. 88; Albert of Aachen, *Historia Ierosolimitana*, ed. and trans. Edgington, 5, 29, pp. 374–75; Gilo of Paris, *Historia vie Hierosolimitane*, ed. and trans. Grocock and Siberry, 8, pp. 214–15.

119 Gilo of Paris, *Historia vie Hierosolimitane*, ed. and trans. Grocock and Siberry, 8, pp. 214–15.

120 See Jay Rubenstein, "Cannibals and Crusaders," *French Historical Studies*, 31 (2008), 525–52 (p. 538).

121 Ralph of Caen, *Gesta Tancredi in expeditione Hierosolymitana*, in *Recueil des historiens des croisades. Historiens occidentaux* (Paris: Académie des Inscriptions et Belles-Lettres, 1844–95), III, 97, p. 675; Ralph of Caen, *Gesta Tancredi of Ralph of Caen*, trans. Bachrach and Bachrach, p. 116.

122 Raymond of Aguilers, *Le "Liber" de Raymond d'Aguilers*, ed. John Hugh and Laurita L. Hill; introduction and notes trans. Philippe Wolff (Paris: P. Geuthner, 1969), p. 101.

123 The evidence is discussed by Rubenstein, "Cannibals and Crusaders"; see, in relation to Heng's argument, pp. 528–29.

124 Raymond of Aguilers, *Liber*, ed. Hugh and Hill, p. 101; English translation mine.

125 William of Tyre, *History of Deeds*, trans. Babcock and Krey, I, 4, 23, p. 222.

126 The most important scholarship on the Tafurs is Lewis A. Sumberg, "The Tafurs and the First Crusade," *Mediaeval Studies*, 21 (1959), 224–46; Jill Tattersall, "Anthropophagi and Eaters of Raw Flesh in French Literature of the Crusade Period: Myth, Tradition and Reality," *Medium Aevum*, 57 (1998), 240–53; and Magali Janet, "Les scènes de cannibalisme aux abords d'Antioche dans les récits de la première croisade: Des chroniques à la chanson de croisade," *Bien dire et bien aprandre*, 22 (2004), 179–91.

127 See Edgington and Sweetenham's introduction to *The "Chanson d'Antioche,"* pp. 59 and 73–74.

Notes to pages 123–126

128 Duparc-Quioc (ed.), *La chanson d'Antioche*, pp. 218–21.

129 See esp. Tattersall, "Anthropophagi and Eaters of Raw Flesh," pp. 247–49.

130 William of Tudela (and anonymous successor), *The Song of the Cathar Wars: A History of the Albigensian Crusade*, trans. Janet Shirley (Aldershot, UK: Ashgate, 1996) omits reference to the Tafurs; see the Old Occitan original: *Histoire de la croisade contre les hérétiques albigeois*, ed. C. Fauriel (Paris: Imprimerie Royale, 1837), 18, p. 33.

131 Tattersall, "Anthropophagi and Eaters of Raw Flesh," p. 248.

132 Blurton, *Cannibalism in High Medieval English Literature*, p. 107.

133 Duncan McMillan (ed.), *La chanson de Guillaume*, 2 vols. (Paris: Picard, 1949), I, lines 1717–20.

134 C. Régnier (ed.), *La prise d'Orange* (Paris: Klincksieck, 1972), lines 341–47.

135 François Guessard and Henri Victor Michelant (eds.), *Floovant*, in *Les anciens poètes de la France*, 10 vols. (Paris: F. Vieweg, 1860), I, lines 1836–43.

136 See, e.g., Helen J. Nicholson (trans.), *The Chronicle of the Third Crusade: A Translation of the "Itinerarium Peregrinorum et Gesta Regis Ricardi"* (Aldershot, UK: Ashgate, 1997), 6, 27–28, pp. 370–72.

137 Sanudo Torsello, *Gesta Dei*, ed. Bongars, pp. 200, 202; Sanudo Torsello, *Book of the Secrets of the Faithful Cross*, trans. Lock, pp. 317, 321.

138 Following Aristotle, medieval philosophers distinguished the intellective and sensitive parts of the soul, which each had cognitive and appetitive faculties. Some thinkers (like Thomas Aquinas) confined emotions to the sensitive appetite while others (like John Duns Scotus and William of Ockham) identified emotions as features of appetite in general, sometimes as sensitive reactions, and sometimes as intellective attitudes. For an overview, see King, "Emotions in Medieval Thought," pp. 167–88.

139 Siobhain Bly Calkin, "Saracens," in Neil Cartlidge (ed.), *Heroes and Anti-Heroes in Medieval Romance* (Cambridge, UK: D. S. Brewer, 2012), pp. 198–99, also comments on how the episode of cannibalism signals troubling aspects of Richard's behavior, focusing on the issue of dynastic succession.

140 Manipulating the language of friendship to deceive was often frowned upon; see, e.g., C. Stephen Jaeger, *Ennobling Love: In Search of a Lost Sensibility* (Philadelphia: University of Pennsylvania Press, 1999), p. 19. See also Chapter 3 of the present study, on Morgadour's use of the language of friendship to lure Guy into a trap in *Guy of Warwick*.

141 An interesting parallel is found in the Austrian poet Walther von der Vogelweide's *Novellino*, where Ṣalāḥ al-Dīn is portrayed as denouncing Christian kings for eating at tables more elevated than those of their subjects. See Walther von der Vogelweide, *The Single-Stanza Lyrics*, ed. and trans. Frederick Goldin (New York: Routledge, 2003), p. xxv.

142 Lesley A. Coote, "Laughing at Monsters in *Richard Cœur de Lyon*," in Adrian P. Tudor and Alan Hindley (eds.), *Grant Risée? The Medieval Comic Presence: Essays in Memory of Brian J. Levy* (Turnhout: Brepols, 2006), pp. 193–211; Heng, *Empire of Magic*, pp. 73–78.

196 *Notes to pages 126–129*

143 For a discussion of accusations of "savage" and "uncivilized" warfare imputed by English authors to the Irish, Irish-speaking Scots, and Welsh, see John Gillingham, "Conquering the Barbarians: War and Chivalry in Twelfth-Century Britain," *Haskins Society Journal*, 4 (1992), 67–84. According to Larissa Tracy, many authors attempted to define English identity in opposition to brutality and torture: see *Torture and Brutality in Medieval Literature: Negotiations of National Identity* (Cambridge, UK: D. S. Brewer, 2012).

144 Gerald of Wales, *Expugnatio Hibernica: The Conquest of Ireland*, ed. and trans. A. B. Scott and F. X. Martin (Dublin: Royal Irish Academy, 1978), 4, 15–23, pp. 36–37.

145 According to Giles of Rome's *Super rhetoricum*, what differentiates a good king's anger from a tyrant's wrath is that the latter does not subside in response to fear and trembling. See Bénédicte Sère, "Déshonneur, outrages et infamie aux sources de la violence d'après le *Super rhetoricorum* de Gilles de Rome," in François Foronda, Christine Barralis, and Bénédicte Sère (eds.), *Violences souveraines au Moyen Âge: Travaux d'une école historique* (Paris: Presses Universitaires de France, 2010), pp. 103–12 (p. 109).

146 Paul R. Hyams notes that many medieval English writers disapproved of kings and lords who inflicted harm and humiliation to defenseless victims; see *Rancor and Reconciliation in Medieval England* (Ithaca, NY: Cornell University Press, 2003), p. 52.

147 See also lines 3613 ("Ffor drede we wende ffor to sterue"), 3619 ("Ffor drede hou we begunne to quake"), 3634 ("Ffor drede and dool we wende to deye"), and 3638 ("So sory were we þenne for drede").

148 London, British Library, MS Egerton 2862 (c. 1390); Cambridge, Gonville and Caius College, MS 175/96 (c. 1400); London, British Library, MS Additional 31042 (c. 1440).

149 Larry D. Benson (ed.), *Alliterative Morte Arthure*, rev. Edward E. Foster (Kalamazoo, MI: Medieval Institute Publications, 1994), lines 842–55.

150 See Orderic Vitalis, *The Ecclesiastical History of Orderic Vitalis*, ed. and trans. Marjorie Chibnall, 6 vols. (Oxford: Clarendon Press, 1969–80), II, 4, pp. 231–32; Jean Froissart, *Chroniques*, ed. Siméon Luce, 15 vols. (Paris: Mme Ve. J. Renouard, 1869–1975), VII, p. 250; and Douglas Sugano (ed.), "Slaughter of the Innocents; Death of Herod," in *The N-Town Plays* (Kalamazoo, MI: Medieval Institute Publications, 2007), esp. lines 89–104. The composite *Canso de la crozada* is particularly illuminating because it allows for a comparison between different authorial usages of emotional language within the same narrative. William of Tudela, the author of the first 131 laisses, shows support for the northern French of Simon de Montfort by stressing their composure and restraint, while largely omitting reference to the physical and emotional consequences of their actions; by contrast, William's anonymous continuer, who sides with the Cathars, repeatedly presents Simon as merciless and wrathful beyond reason, while emphasizing the grief, anguish, and fear of his victims. See William of

Tudela (and anonymous successor), *Song of the Cathar Wars*, trans. Janet Shirley, on Simon's unbridled wrath, e.g., laisses 171–73, pp. 105–10; 179–80, pp. 117–18; and on the anguish, grief, and terror of the Cathars, e.g., laisses 176, p. 112; 178, p. 115; 198, p. 156.

151 Chaucer, *The Parson's Tale*, in Larry D. Benson (ed.), *The Riverside Chaucer*, 3rd ed. (Oxford: Oxford University Press, 2008; 1st ed. 1987), lines 532–78; from the same volume, *The Knight's Tale*, lines 1997, 2011.

152 Gower, *Confessio Amantis*, ed. Peck, II, 3, lines 23–24. On Chaucer, Gower, and war, see Nigel Saul, "A Farewell to Arms? Criticism of Warfare in Late Fourteenth-Century England," in Chris Given-Wilson (ed.), *Fourteenth Century England* (Woodbridge, UK: Boydell Press, 2002), pp. 131–46; and R. F. Yeager, "Pax Poetica: On the Pacifism of Chaucer and Gower," *Studies in the Age of Chaucer*, 9 (1987), 97–121.

153 William Langland, *Piers Plowman: A Parallel Text Edition of the A, B, C and Z Versions*, ed. A. V. C. Schmidt, 2 vols. (London: Longman, 1995–2008), I, C.6, lines 105–6. On anger in Langland, see Paul Megna, "Langland's Wrath: Righteous Anger Management in *The Vision of Piers Plowman*," *Exemplaria*, 25 (2013), 130–51.

154 Thomas Hoccleve, *The Regiment of Princes*, ed. Charles R. Blyth (Kalamazoo, MI: Medieval Institute Publications, 1999), lines 5195–5201, 5229–30.

155 Saul, "A Farewell to Arms?"; Yeager, "Pax Poetica"; Lowe, *Imagining Peace*, pp. 68–147; John Barnie, *War in Medieval Society: Social Values and the Hundred Years War, 1377–99* (London: Weidenfeld and Nicolson, 1974), pp. 117–38.

156 Michel Pintoin, *Chronique du religieux de Saint-Denys*, ed. M. L. Bellaguet, 6 vols. (Paris: Crapelet, 1839), II, pp. 487–96, 508–11.

157 Ibid., p. 500; English translation mine.

Conclusion

1 Bernard Cerquiglini, *Éloge de la variante: Histoire critique de la philologie* (Paris: Seuil, 1989); translated into English by Betsy Wing as *In Praise of the Variant: A Critical History of Philology* (Baltimore: Johns Hopkins University Press, 1999).

2 Priyamvada Gopal, *Insurgent Empire: Anticolonial Resistance and British Dissent* (London: Verso, 2019), pp. 1–32. Gopal, at pp. 9–13, buttresses her argument with Michel-Rolph Trouillot, *Silencing the Past: Power and the Production of History* (Boston: Beacon Press, 1995).

3 I introduce this book in my "Unsettling Orientalism: Toward a New History of European Representations of Muslims and Islam, c. 1200–1450," *Speculum*, 100:2 (forthcoming, April 2025).

4 The classic study of European expansion and cultural change during the high Middle Ages is Robert Bartlett, *The Making of Europe: Conquest, Colonization,*

198   *Notes to pages 133–134*

and Cultural Change, 950–1350 (Princeton, NJ: Princeton University Press, 1993).

5 The place of the Ottomans in European cultural history is better established than that of the Ayyūbids and Mamlūks, but scholarship on the subject has focused principally on the early modern period, not the later Middle Ages. On early modern Anglo-Ottoman relations, see, e.g., Nabil Matar, *Islam in Britain, 1558–1685* (Cambridge: Cambridge University Press, 1998); Nabil Matar and Gerald MacLean, *Britain and the Islamic World, 1558–1713* (Oxford: Oxford University Press, 2011); Gerald MacLean, *Looking East: English Writing and the Ottoman Empire before 1800* (Basingstoke, UK: Palgrave, 2007); and Daniel J. Vitkus, *Turning Turk: English Theater and the Multicultural Mediterranean, 1570–1630* (New York: Palgrave, 2003).

6 On anti-Orientalism in British and Irish modernist poetry, see Jahan Ramazani, *A Transnational Poetics* (Chicago: University of Chicago Press, 2009), pp. 109–14; and, by the same author, *Poetry in a Global Age* (Chicago: University of Chicago Press, 2020), pp. 133–54.

7 Honorat Bovet, *"L'Arbre des Batailles" d'Honoré Bonet*, ed. Ernest Nys (Brussels: Muquardt, 1883), pp. 86–87; Honorat Bovet, *The Tree of Battles*, ed. and trans. G. W. Coopland (Liverpool: Liverpool University Press, 1949), pp. 126–27. On Bovet's little-studied anticrusade stance, see further Aziz Suryal Atiya, *The Crusade of Nicopolis* (London: Methuen, 1934), p. 123.

Bibliography

Primary Sources

Aelred of Rielvaux. *De speculo caritatis*, in Anselme Hoste and Charles H. Talbot (eds.), *Aelredi Rievallensis. Opera Omnia, I: Opera ascetica*. Turnhout: Brepols, 1971.
    Spiritual Friendship, ed. and trans. Lawrence C. Braceland and Marsha L. Dutton. Collegeville, MN: Liturgical Press, 2010.
Alberigo, Josepho (ed.). *Conciliorum oecumenicorum decretal*. Bologna: Istituto per le Scienze Religiose, 1973.
Albert of Aachen. *Historia Ierosolimitana: History of the Journey to Jerusalem*, ed. and trans. Susan B. Edgington. Oxford: Oxford University Press, 2007.
Alcuin of York. *De virtutibus et vitiis*, ed. J. P. Migne, Patrologia Latina 101. Paris: Garnier fratres, 1851.
Ambroise. *The History of the Holy War: Ambroise's "Estoire de la Guerre Sainte,"* trans. Marianne Ailes; notes Marianne Ailes and Malcom Barber. Woodbridge, UK: Boydell Press, 2011.
Aquinas, Thomas. *The "Summa Theologica" of Thomas Aquinas*, trans. Fathers of the English Dominican Province. London: Burns Oates and Washbourne, 1922.
Aristotle. *The Nicomachean Ethics*, ed. and trans. H. Rackham. Cambridge, MA: Loeb, 1926.
Augustine. *The City of God against the Pagans*, trans. R. W. Dyson. Cambridge: Cambridge University Press, 1998.
    Confessions, ed. and trans. Philip Burton. New York: Knopf, 2001.
    De civitate dei, ed. J. P. Migne, Patrologia Latina 41. Paris: Garnier fratres, 1864.
    The Soliloquies of St. Augustine, trans. Rose Elizabeth Cleveland. London: Williams and Norgate, 1910.
Bagnyon, Jehan. *L'histoire de Charlemagne*, ed. Hans-Erich Keller. Geneva: Droz, 1992.
Bastard, Antoine de (ed.). "La colère et la douleur d'un templier en Terre Sainte." *Revue des langues romanes*, 81 (1974), 333–73.
Benson, Larry D. (ed.). *Alliterative Morte Arthure*; rev. Edward E. Foster. Kalamazoo, MI: Medieval Institute Publications, 1994.

200 *Bibliography*

Bernard of Clairvaux. *In Praise of the New Knighthood*, trans. D. O'Donovan and C. Greenia. Kalamazoo, MI: Cistercian Publications, 1977.

"Liber ad Milites Templi: De laude novae militiae," in Jean LeClercq and H. M. Rochais (eds.), *Sancti Bernardi Opera*, 8 vols. Rome: Editiones Cistercienses, 1963, III, pp. 312–31.

Bird, Jessalynn, Edward Peters, and James Powell (eds. and trans.). *Crusade and Christendom: Annotated Documents in Translation from Innocent III to the Fall of Acre, 1187–129.* Philadelphia: University of Pennsylvania Press, 2013.

Bovet, Honorat. *"L'Arbre des Batailles" d'Honore Bonet*, ed. Ernest Nys. Brussels: Muquardt, 1883.

Medieval Muslims, Christians, and Jews in Dialogue: The "Apparicion Maistre Jehan de Meun" of Honorat Bovet, ed. and trans. Michael Hanly. Tempe: Arizona Center for Medieval and Renaissance Studies, 2005.

The Tree of Battles, ed. and trans. G. W. Coopland. Liverpool: Liverpool University Press, 1949.

Bower, Walter. *Scotichronicon*, ed. D. E. R. Watt, 9 vols. Aberdeen: Aberdeen University Press, 1987–98.

Brandeis, Arthur (ed.). *Jacob's Well: An English Treatise on the Cleansing of Man's Conscience*, Early English Text Society OS 115. London: Trübner, 1900.

Brandin, Louis (ed.). *"La destruction de Rome* et *Fierabras*, MS Egerton 3028, Musée Britannique." *Romania*, 64 (1938), 18–100.

Bromyard, John. *Summa praedicantium*. Vienna: Apud Dominicum Nicolinum, 1586.

Brundage, James (ed.). *The Crusades: A Documentary Survey*. Milwaukee, WI: Marquette University Press, 1962.

Brunner, Karl (ed.). *Der Mittelenglische Versroman über Richard Löwenherz*. Vienna: W. Braumüller, 1913.

Capellanus, Andreas. *Andreas Capellanus on Love*, ed. and trans. P. G. Walsh. London: Duckworth, 1982.

Caxton, William (trans.). *The Book of the Knight of the Tower*, ed. M. Y. Offord, Early English Text Society SS 2. London: Oxford University Press, 1971.

A Middle English Chronicle of the First Crusade: The Caxton Eracles, ed. Dana Cushing, 2 vols. Lewiston, NY: Edwin Miller, 2001.

Chaucer, Geoffrey. *The Riverside Chaucer*, 3rd ed., ed. Larry D. Benson. Oxford: Oxford University Press, 2008; 1st ed. 1987.

Christine de Pizan. *The Book of the Body Politic*, ed. and trans. Kate Langdon Forhan. Cambridge: Cambridge University Press, 1994.

Le livre des trois vertus, ed. Charity Cannon Willard. Paris: Librairie Honoré Champion, 1989.

The Treasure of the City of Ladies, or, The Book of the Three Virtues, trans. Sarah Lawson. Harmondsworth, UK: Penguin, 1985.

Chroust, Anton (ed.). *Historia de expeditione Friderici imperatoris*, in Monumenta Germaniae historica: Scriptores rerum Germanicarum NS 5. Berlin: Weidmannsche Buchhandlung, 1928, pp. 1–115.

Quellen zur Geschichte des Kreuzzuges Kaiser Friedrichs I. Berlin: Weidmannsche Buchhandlung, 1928.

Cicero. *Laelius de amicitia,* ed. and trans. Robert Combès. Paris: Belles Lettres, 1983.

Clanvowe, John. *The Works of Sir John Clanvowe,* ed. V. J. Scattergood. Cambridge, UK: D. S. Brewer, 1975.

Cronin, H. S. (ed.). "The Twelve Conclusions of the Lollards." *English Historical Review,* 22 (1907), 292–304.

David, Charles Wendell (ed. and trans.). *De expugnatione Lyxbonensi: The Conquest of Lisbon.* New York: Columbia University Press, 1936.

Deschamps, Eustache. "Complainte de l'Eglise," in Auguste-Henry-Edouard De Queux de Saint-Hilaire and Gaston Raynaud (eds.), *Oeuvres complètes,* 11 vols. Paris: Firmin Didot, 1878–1903, VII, pp. 293–311.

Dillon, Viscount, and W. St John Hope (eds.). *Pageant of the Birth, Life and Death of Richard Beauchamp, Earl of Warwick, 1389–1439.* London: Longmans, 1914.

Dubois, Pierre. *The Recovery of the Holy Land,* ed. and trans. Walther I. Brandt. New York: Columbia University Press, 1956.

Duparc-Quioc, Suzanne (ed.). *La chanson d'Antioche.* Paris: P. Geuthner, 1976.

Edgington, Susan B., and Carol Sweetenham (trans.). *The "Chanson d'Antioche": An Old French Account of the First Crusade.* Farnham, UK: Ashgate, 2011.

Embree, Dan, Edward Donald Kennedy, and Kathleen Daly (eds.). *Short Scottish Prose Chronicles.* Woodbridge, UK: Boydell Press, 2012.

Ewert, Alfred (ed.). *Gui de Warewic: Roman du XIIIe siècle.* Paris: Champion, 1932.

Fabri, Felix. *The Wanderings of Felix Fabri,* trans. Aubrey Stewart. London: Palestine Pilgrims' Text Society, 1892.

Fidenzio of Padua. *Liber recuperations Terre Sancte,* in G. Gobulovich (ed.), *Biblioteca bio-bibliografica della Terra Santa e dell'Oriente Francescano,* 20 vols. Quaracchi: Collegio di S. Bonaventura, 1913, II, pp. 9–60.

Ford, A. E. (ed.). *La vengeance de Nostre-Seigneur: The Old and Middle French Versions.* Turnhout: Brepols, 1993.

Francis, W. N. (ed.). *The Book of Vices and Virtues: A Fourteenth Century English Translation of the "Somme le Roi" of Lorens d'Orléans,* Early English Text Society OS 217. London: Oxford University Press, 1942.

Froissart, Jean. *Chroniques,* ed. Siméon Luce, 15 vols. Paris: Mme Ve. J. Renouard, 1869–1975.

Oeuvres de Froissart, ed. Kervyn de Lettenhove, 25 vols. Brussels: Victor Devaux et cie, 1867–1877.

Fulcher of Chartres. *The Deeds of the Franks and the Other Pilgrims to Jerusalem,* ed. Rosalind Hill. London: Nelson, 1962.

The First Crusade: The Chronicle of Fulcher of Chartres and Other Source Materials, ed. Edward Peters, 2nd ed. Philadelphia: University of Pennsylvania Press, 1998; 1st ed. 1971.

A History of the Expedition to Jerusalem, 1095–1127, trans. Rita Ryan. Knoxville: University of Tennessee Press, 1969.

Bibliography

Geoffroi de Charny. *The Book of Chivalry of Geoffroi de Charny*, trans. Richard W. Kaeuper and Elspeth Kennedy. Philadelphia: University of Pennsylvania Press, 1996.

Gerald of Wales. *Expugnatio Hibernica: The Conquest of Ireland*, ed. and trans. A. B. Scott and F. X. Martin. Dublin: Royal Irish Academy, 1978.

Germain, Jean. "Le discours du voyage d'oultremer au très victorieux roi Charles VII, prononcé en 1452 par Jean Germain, évêque de Chalron," ed. C. Schefer. *Revue de l'Orient latin*, 5 (1895), 303–42.

Ghillebert de Lannoy. *Oeuvres de Ghillebert de Lannoy: Voyageur, diplomate et moraliste*, ed. C. Potvin. Louvain: Lefever, 1878.

Gilbert of Tournai. *Collectio de scandalis ecclesiae*, ed. Autbert Stroick. *Archivum Franciscanum historicum*, 24 (1931), 33–62.

Giles of Rome. *The Governance of Kings and Princes: John Trevisa's Middle English Translation of the "De Regimine Principum" of Aegidius Romanus*, ed. David C. Fowler, Charles F. Briggs, Paul G. Remley. New York: Garland, 1997.

Gilo of Paris. *The "Historia vie Hierosolimitane" of Gilo of Paris and a Second Anonymous Author*, ed. and trans. C. W. Grocock and J. E. Siberry. Oxford: Clarendon Press, 1997.

Gower, John. *Confessio Amantis*, ed. Russell A. Peck, trans. Andrew Galloway, 3 vols. Kalamazoo, MI: Medieval Institute Publications, 2013.

The Major Latin Works of John Gower: The Voice of One Crying, and the Tripartite Chronicle, trans. Eric W. Stockton. Seattle: University of Washington Press, 1962.

The Minor Latin Works, ed. and trans. R. F. Yeager; with *In Praise of Peace*, ed. Michael Livingston. Kalamazoo, MI: Medieval Institute Publications, 2005.

Mirour de l'Omme, in G. C. Macaulay (ed.), *The Complete Works of John Gower*, 4 vols. Oxford: Clarendon Press, 1899, I, pp. 1–334.

Mirour de l'Omme: The Mirror of Mankind, trans. William Burton Wilson and Nancy Wilson Van Baak. East Lansing, MI: Colleagues Press, 1992.

Vox Clamantis, in G. C. Macaulay (ed.), *The Complete Works of John Gower*, 4 vols. Oxford: Clarendon Press, 1899, IV, pp. 3–313.

Grillo, Peter (ed.). *La Chrétienté Corbaran*, in *The Old French Crusade Cycle VII. The Jerusalem Continuations. Part 1: La Chrétienté Corbaran*. Tuscaloosa: University of Alabama Press, 1984.

Guessard, François, and Henri Victor Michelant (eds.). *Floovant*, in *Les anciens poètes de la France*, 10 vols. Paris: Vieweg, 1858–70, I.

Otinel, in *Les anciens poètes de la France*, 10 vols. Paris: Vieweg, 1858–70, I.

Guibert of Nogent. *Geste de Dieu par les Frances: Histoire de la première croisade*, trans. Monique-Cécile Garand. Turnhout: Brepols, 1998.

Guillaume de Machaut. *Oeuvres*, ed. Ernest Hoepffner, 3 vols. Paris: Firmin Didot, 1908–21, II.

La prise d'Alixandre, ed. and trans. R. Barton Palmer. New York: Routledge, 2002.

Bibliography

Guillaume le Breton. *La Philippide*, in F. Guizot (ed.), *Collection de mémoires relatifs à l'histoire de France* 12. Paris: Brière, 1825.

Gunther of Pairis. "Historia Constantinopolitana," in Paul Riant (ed.), *Exuviae sacrae Constantinopolitanae*, 3 vols. Geneva: Fick, 1877, I, pp. 57–126.

Hanna, Ralph, and David Lawton (eds.). *The Siege of Jerusalem*, Early English Text Society OS 320. Oxford: Oxford University Press, 2003.

Hector, L. C., and Barbara F. Harvey (eds. and trans.), *The Westminster Chronicle: 1381–1394*. Oxford: Clarendon Press, 1982.

Henry of Grosmont. *The Book of Holy Medicines*, trans. Catherine Batt. Tempe: Arizona Center for Medieval and Renaissance Studies, 2014.

Le livre de seyntz medicines: The Unpublished Devotional Treatise of Henry of Lancaster, ed. E. J. Arnould. Oxford: Blackwell, 1940.

Herrtage, Sidney J. H. (ed.). *The Sege off Melayne and The Romance of Duke Rowland and Sir Otuell of Spayne, Together with a Fragment of The Song of Roland*, Early English Text Society ES 35. London: Trübner, 1880; repr. 1931.

Sir Ferumbras, Early English Text Society ES 34. London: Oxford University Press, 1879; repr. 1903 and 1966.

The Tale of Rauf Coilyear with the Fragments of Roland and Vernagu and Otuel, Early English Text Society ES 39. London: Trübner, 1882; repr. 1931 and 1969.

Higden, Ranulph. *Polychronicon Ranulphi Higden Monachi Cestrensis; Together with the English Translation of John Trevisa and of an Unknown Writer of the Fifteenth Century*, ed. Joseph Rawson Lumby, Rolls Series 41, 9 vols. London: Longman, 1865–86.

Hill, Rosalind (ed.). *Gesta Francorum et aliorum Hierosolimitanorum: The Deeds of the Franks and the Other Pilgrims to Jerusalem*. Edinburgh: Nelson, 1962.

Hincmar of Reims. *De cavendis vitiis et virtutibus exercendis*, ed. Doris Nachtmann, Monumenta Germaniae Historica: Quellen zur Geistesgeschichte des Mittelalters 16. Munich: Monumenta Germaniae Historica, 1998.

Hoccleve, Thomas. *The Regiment of Princes*, ed. Charles R. Blyth. Kalamazoo, MI: Medieval Institute Publications, 1999.

Housley, Norman (ed. and trans.). *Documents on the Later Crusades, 1274–1580*. Basingstoke, UK: Macmillan Press, 1996.

The Later Crusades: From Lyons to Alcazar, 1274–1580. Oxford: Oxford University Press, 1992.

Hudson, Harriet (ed.). *Sir Isumbras*, in *Four Middle English Romances: Sir Isumbras, Octavian, Sir Eglamour of Artois, Sir Tryamour*. Kalamazoo, MI: Medieval Institute Publications, 1996.

Hugo of Lüttich. *Peregrinarius*, ed. Franz Unterkircher. Leiden: Brill, 1991.

Humbert of Romans. "Opus tripartitum," ed. E. Brown, *Fasciculus rerum expetendarum et fugiendarum*, 2 vols. London: Impensis Richardi Chiswell, 1690, II, pp. 191–98.

Hurvitz, Nimrod, Christian C. Sahner, Uriel Simonsohn, and Luke Yarbrough (eds.). *Conversion to Islam in the Premodern Age: A Sourcebook.* Oakland: University of California Press, 2020.

Huygens, R. B. C. (ed.). *Excidium Aconis gestorum collectio: Magister Thadeus civis Neapolitanus, Ystoria de desolatione et conculcatione civitatis Acconensis et tocius Terre Sanctae.* Turnhout: Brepols, 2004.

Innocent III. "Quia maior," in Georgine Tangl (ed.), *Studien zum Register Innocenz III.* Weimar: H. Böhlau, 1929.

Jacques de Vitry. "Sermones vulgares," in J. B. Pitra (ed.), *Analecta novissima spicilegii Solesmensis: Altera continuatio,* 2 vols. Paris: Typis Tusculanis, 1888, II.

Jean de Joinville. *Histoire de Saint Louis, credo et lettre à Louis X,* ed. Natalis de Wailly. Paris: Firmin Didot, 1874.

Joinville and Villehardouin: Chronicles of the Crusades, trans. Caroline Smith. London: Penguin, 2008.

Jeanroy, Alfred (ed.). "Le troubadour Austorc d'Aurillac et son sirventés sur la Septième Croisade." *Romanische Forschungen,* 23 (1907), 81–88.

Josephus. *The Jewish War,* ed. and trans. Gaalya Cornfeld. Grand Rapids, MI: Zondervan, 1982.

Lactantius. *De ira dei,* in Alexander Roberts and James Donaldson (eds.), *Ante-Nicene Fathers,* 10 vols. Buffalo, NY: Christian Literature Publishing, 1886, VII.

Lalande, Denis (ed.). *Le livre des fais du bon messire Jehan le Maingre, dit Bouciquaut.* Geneva: Droz, 1985.

Langland, William. *Piers Plowman: A Parallel Text Edition of the A, B, C and Z Versions,* ed. A. V. C. Schmidt, 2 vols. London: Longman, 1995–2008.

Laurent of Orléans. *La somme le roi par Frère Laurent,* ed. Edith Brayer and Anne-Françoise Leurquin-Labie. Paris: Société des Anciens Textes Français, 2008.

Lavynham, Richard. *A Litil Tretys on the Seven Deadly Sins,* ed. Johannes Petrus Wilhelmus Maria van Zutphen. Rome: Institutum Carmelitanum, 1956.

Leclercq, Jean (ed.). "Un sermon prononcé pendant la guerre de Flandre sous Philippe le Bel." *Revue du moyen âge latin,* 1 (1945), 165–72.

Livingston, Michael (ed.). *The Siege of Jerusalem.* Kalamazoo, MI: Medieval Institute Publications, 2004.

Llull, Ramon. *The Book of the Ordre of Chyvalry,* trans. William Caxton and ed. Alfred T. P. Byles, Early English Text Society OS 168. London: Oxford University Press, 1926.

Ramon Llull: A Contemporary Life, ed. and trans. Anthony Bonner. Barcelona: Barcino-Tamesis, 2010.

Ludolph of Suchem. *Description of the Holy Land, and of the Way Thither,* ed. and trans. Aubrey Stewart. London: Committee of the Palestine Exploration Fund, 1895); repr. Cambridge: Cambridge University Press, 2013.

Ludolphi de itinere terrae sanctae liber, ed. Ferdinand Deycks. Stuttgart: Gedruckt auf Kosten des Litterarischen Vereins, 1851.

Bibliography

205

Lupack, Alan (ed.). *The Sultan of Babylon*, in *Three Middle English Charlemagne Romances*. Kalamazoo, MI: Medieval Institute Publications, 1990, pp. 7–103.

Maier, Christoph T. (ed. and trans.). *Crusade Propaganda and Ideology: Model Sermons for the Preaching of the Cross*. Cambridge: Cambridge University Press, 2000.

Mandeville, John. *The Book of John Mandeville*, ed. Tamarah Kohanski and C. David Benson. Kalamazoo, MI: Medieval Institute Publications, 2007.

McMillan, Duncan (ed.). *La chanson de Guillaume*, 2 vols. Paris: Picard, 1949.

Melick, Elizabeth, Susanna Fein, and David Raybin (eds.). *The Roland and Otuel Romances and the Anglo-Norman "Otinel."* Kalamazoo, MI: Medieval Institute Publications, 2019.

Morrill, Georgiana Lea (ed.). *Speculum Gy de Warewyke*. London: Trübner, 1898.

Nathan, Eliezer bar. *The Persecutions of 1096*, in *The Jews and the Crusaders: The Hebrew Chronicles of the First and Second Crusades*, trans. Shlomo Eidelberg. Madison: University of Wisconsin Press, 1977.

Nicholson, Helen J. (trans.). *The Chronicle of the Third Crusade: A Translation of the "Itinerarium Peregrinorum et Gesta Regis Ricardi."* Aldershot, UK: Ashgate, 1997.

Nicolas, N. H. (ed.). *The Controversy between Sir Richard Scrope and Sir Robert Grosvenor in the Court of Chivalry*, 2 vols. London: Bentley, 1832.

Testamenta vetusta, 2 vols. London: Nichols and Son, 1826.

Nicolaus von Jeroschin. *The Chronicle of Prussia by Nicolaus von Jeroschin: A History of the Teutonic Knights in Prussia, 1190–1331*, trans. Mary Fischer. Farham, UK: Ashgate, 2010.

Odo of Deuil. *De profectione Ludovici VII in Orientem: The Journey of Louis VII to the East*, ed. and trans. Virginia Gingerich Berry. New York: W. W. Norton, 1948.

La croisade de Louis VII, roi de France, ed. Henri Waquet. Paris: P. Geuthner, 1949.

O'Sullivan, Mary Isabelle (ed.). *Firumbras and Otuel and Roland*, Early English Text Society OS 198. London: Oxford University Press, 1935.

Ottokar von Steiermark. *Ottokars Österreichische Reimchronik*, ed. Joseph Seemüller. Hannover: Hahn, 1890.

Paris, Matthew. *Chronica majora*, ed. Henry Richards Luard, 7 vols. London : Longman, 1872–83.

Chronicles of Matthew Paris: Monastic Life in the Thirteenth Century, ed. and trans. Richard Vaughan. Gloucester: Alan Sutton, 1984.

Paris, Paulin (ed.). *La chanson d'Antioche*, 2 vols. Paris: J. Techener, 1848, I.

Paterson, Linda (ed.). "Austorc de Segret: *[No s]ai qui·m so tan suy [des]conoyssens.*" *Lecturae tropatorum*, 5 (2012), 1–16.

Pauphilet, Albert (ed.). *La queste del Saint Graal*. Paris: Champion, 1923.

Pecock, Reginald. *The Folewer to the Donet*, ed. Elsie Vaughan Hitchcock, Early English Text Society EC 4. London: Oxford University Press, 1924.

Perryman, Judith (ed.). *The King of Tars*. Heidelberg: Winter, 1980.

206   *Bibliography*

Person, Marc Le (ed.). *Fierabras: Chanson de geste du XIIe siècle.* Paris: Champion, 2003.

Philippe de Mézières. *Une epistre lamentable et consolatoire: Adressée en 1397 à Philippe le Hardi, duc de Bourgogne, sur la défaite de Nicopolis (1396),* ed. Philippe Contamine and Jacques Paviot. Paris: Société de l'Histoire de France, 2008.

Letter to King Richard II, a Plea Made in 1395 for Peace between England and France, ed. and trans. G. W. Coopland. Liverpool,UK: Liverpool University Press, 1975.

The Life and Times of Saint Peter Thomas by Philippe de Mézières, ed. Joachim Smet. Rome: Institutum Carmelitanum, 1954.

"Philippe de Mézières and the New Order of the Passion," ed. Abdel Hamid Hamdy. *Bulletin of the Faculty of Arts, Alexandria University,* 18 (1964), 43–104.

Le songe du vieil pelerin, ed. G. W. Coopland, 2 vols. Cambridge: Cambridge University Press, 1969.

Pintoin, Michel. *Chronique du religieux de Saint-Denys,* ed. M. L. Bellaguet, 6 vols. Paris: Crapelet, 1839.

Ralph of Caen. *The Gesta Tancredi of Ralph of Caen: A History of the Normans on the First Crusade,* trans. Bernard S. Bachrach and David S. Bachrach. Aldershot, UK: Ashgate, 2005.

Gesta Tancredi in expeditione Hierosolymitana, in *Recueil des historiens des croisades. Historiens occidentaux.* Paris: Académie des Inscriptions et Belles-Lettres, 1844–95.

Raymond of Aguilers. *Le "Liber" de Raymond d'Aguilers,* ed. John Hugh and Laurita L. Hill; introduction and notes trans. Philippe Wolff. Paris: P. Geuthner, 1969.

Régnier, C. (ed.). *La prise d'Orange.* Paris: Klincksieck, 1972.

Riccoldo da Monte di Croce. "Lettres de Ricoldo de Monte-Croce sur la prise d'Acre (1291)," ed. Reinhold Röhricht, in *Archives de l'Orient latin,* 12 vols. Paris: Ernest Leroux, 1884, II, 258–92.

Riccold de Monte Croce: Pérégrination en Terre Sainte et au Proche Orient. Lettres sur la chute de Saint Jean d'Acre, ed. and trans. René Kappler. Paris: Champion, 1997.

Riley-Smith, Jonathan, and Louise Riley-Smith. *The Crusades: Idea and Reality, 1095–1274.* London: Edward Arnold, 1981.

Robert of Reims. *The "Historia Iherosolimitana" of Robert the Monk,* ed. Damien Kempf and Marcus Bull. Woodbridge, UK: Boydell Press, 2013.

Robert the Monk's History of the First Crusade, trans. Carol Sweetenham. Aldershot, UK: Ashgate, 2005.

Robert the Monk's History of Jerusalem: Historia Iherosolimitana, trans. Carol Sweetenham. Aldershot, UK: Ashgate, 2006.

Rodriguez, Jarbel (ed.). *Muslim and Christian Contact in the Middle Ages: A Reader.* Toronto: University of Toronto Press, 2015.

Roger of Wendover. *Roger of Wendover's Flowers of History,* trans. J. A. Giles, 4 vols. Felinfach: Llanerch, 1993–96.

Bibliography

Rogeri de Wendover Chronica: Sive, Flores historiarum, ed. Henry O. Coxe, 5 vols. London: Sumptibus Societatis, 1841–44, IV.

Ross, Woodburn O. (ed.). *Middle English Sermons*, Early English Text Society OS 209. London: Oxford University Press, 1940.

Rutebeuf. "Lament of the Holy Land," in *Crusade and Christendom: Annotated Documents in Translation from Innocent III to the Fall of Acre, 1187–1291*, ed. and trans. Jessalynn Bird, Edward Peters, and James Powell. Philadelphia: University of Pennsylvania Press, 2013, pp. 389–93.

Salimbene de Adam. *The Chronicle of Salimbene de Adam*, ed. and trans. Joseph L. Baird, Giuseppe Baglivi, and John Robert Kane. Binghamton, NY: Medieval and Renaissance Texts and Studies, 1986.

Cronica, ed. Giuseppe Scalia, 2 vols. Turnhout: Brepols, 1999.

Sanudo Torsello, Marino. *The Book of the Secrets of the Faithful Cross: Liber secretorum fidelium crucis*, trans. Peter Lock. Farnham, UK: Ashgate, 2011.

Gesta Dei per Francos, sive orientalium expeditionem et regni Francorum Hierosolymitani historia, ed. J. Bongars, 2 vols. Hannover: Typis Wechelianis, 1611, II.

Schellekens, Philida M. T. A. (ed.). "An Edition of the Middle English Romance: *Richard Coeur de Lion*," 2 vols. Unpublished doctoral thesis, Durham University (1989).

Schiltberger, Johann. *Reisen des Johannes Schiltberger aus München in Europa, Asia und Afrika von 1394 bis 1427*, ed. Karl Friedrich Neumann. Munich: Selbstverl, 1859.

Sergius IV. "The 'Encyclical' of 'Sergius IV,'" trans. Thomas G. Waldman, in *The First Crusade: The Chronicle of Fulcher of Chartres and Other Source Materials*, ed. Edward Peters, 2nd ed. Philadelphia: University of Pennsylvania Press, 1998; 1st ed. 1971, pp. 298–302.

"Encyclique de Sergius IV relative à un projet de croisade," ed. Jules Lair. *Bibliothèque de l'école des chartres*, 18 (1857), 246–53.

Shepherd, Stephen H. A. (ed.). *The Siege of Milan*, in *Middle English Romances*. New York: Norton, 1995, pp. 268–312.

Siegebert of Gembloux. *Chronica*, ed. L. C. Bethmann, Monumenta Germaniae Historica: Scriptores 6. Hanover: Hahn, 1844.

Speich, Johann Heinrich (ed.). *La destructioun de Rome (d'après le ms. de Hanovre IV, 578)*. Bern: Peter Lang, 1988.

Stanegrave, Roger. *Li charboclois d'armes du conquest precious de la Terre Sainte de promission*, in Jacques Paviot (ed.), *Projets de croisade (v. 1290–v. 1330)*. Paris: Académie des Inscriptions et Belles-Lettres, 2008, pp. 293–387.

Stone, Rachel (trans.). "Translation of Alcuin's *De virtutibus et vitiis liber*." *Heroic Age: A Journal of Early Medieval Northwestern Europe*, 16 (2015), http://jemne.org/issues/16/stone.php.

Sugano, Douglas (ed.). "Slaughter of the Innocents; Death of Herod," in *The N-Town Plays*. Kalamazoo, MI: Medieval Institute Publications, 2007.

Swan, Charles, and Wynnard Hooper (eds. and trans.). *Gesta Romanorum*. New York: Dover, 1959.

208 *Bibliography*

Tanner, Norman P. (ed.). *Decrees of the Ecumenical Councils*, 2 vols. London: Sheed and Ward, 1990.

Theiner, Augustin (ed.). *Vetera monumenta historica Hungariam sacram illustrantia*, 2 vols. Rome: Typis Vaticanis, 1859–60.

Thomas of Chobham. *Summa confessorum*, ed. Frederick Broomfield. Paris: Nauwelaerts, 1968.

Trefnant, John. *The Register of John Trefnant, Bishop of Hereford (A.D. 1389–1404)*, ed. William W. Capes. Hereford, UK: Wilson and Phillips, 1914.

Tudebode, Peter. *Historia de Hierosolymitano Itinere*, trans. John Hugh Hill and Laurita L. Hill. Philadelphia: American Philosophical Society, 1974.

Vitalis, Orderic. *The Ecclesiastical History of Orderic Vitalis*, ed. and trans. Marjorie Chibnall, 6 vols. Oxford: Clarendon Press, 1969–80.

Walther von der Vogelweide. *The Single-Stanza Lyrics*, ed. and trans. Frederick Goldin. New York: Routledge, 2003.

Weiss, Judith (trans.). *Boeve de Haumtone and Gui de Warewic*. Tempe: Arizona Center for Medieval and Renaissance Studies, 2008.

William of Adam. *How to Defeat the Saracens*, ed. Gilles Constable. Washington, DC: Dumbarton Oaks, 2012.

William of Newburgh. *Historia de rebus anglicis*, in Richard Howlett (ed.), *Chronicles of the Reigns of Stephen, Henry II, and Richard I*, Rolls Series 82, 4 vols. London: Longman, 1884–89.

William of Tudela (and anonymous successor). *Histoire de la croisade contre les hérétiques albigeois*, ed. C. Fauriel. Paris: Imprimerie Royale, 1837.

The Song of the Cathar Wars: A History of the Albigensian Crusade, trans. Janet Shirley. Aldershot, UK: Ashgate, 1996.

William of Tyre. *A History of Deeds Done beyond the Sea*, trans. Emily A. Babcock and A. C. Krey, 2 vols. New York: Columbia University Press, 1887–1961.

Wyclif, John. *Select English Works of John Wyclif*, ed. Thomas Arnold, 3 vols. Oxford: Clarendon Press, 1869–71.

Zupitza, Julius (ed.). *The Romance of Guy of Warwick*, 2nd ed., Early English Text Society ES 42, 49, and 59. London: Oxford University Press, 1966; 1st ed. as three volumes in 1883, 1887, and 1891.

Secondary Sources

Adams, Tracy. *Violent Passion: Managing Love in the Old French Verse Romance*. New York: Palgrave, 2005.

Aebischer, Paul. *Études sur Otinel: De la chanson de geste à la saga norroise et aux origines de la légende*. Bern: Francke, 1960.

Ahmad, Aijaz. *In Theory: Classes, Nations, Literatures*. London: Verso, 1992.

Ahmed, Sara. "Affective Economies." *Social Text*, 79 (2004), 117–39.

The Cultural Politics of Emotion, 2nd ed. Edinburgh: Edinburgh University Press, 2014; 1st ed. New York: Routledge, 2004.

Bibliography

Ailes, Marianne. "A Comparative Study of the Medieval French and Middle English Verse Texts of the Fierabras Legend," 2 vols. Unpublished doctoral thesis, University of Reading, 1989.

"The *chanson de geste*," in Anthony Bale (ed.), *The Cambridge Companion to the Literature of the Crusades*. Cambridge: Cambridge University Press, 2019, pp. 25–38.

"Comprehension Problems and Their Resolution in the Middle English Verse Translations of *Fierabras*." *Forum for Modern Language Studies*, 35 (1999), 396–407.

"*Gui de Warewic* in Its Manuscript Context," in Alison Wiggins and Rosalind Field (eds.), *Guy of Warwick: Icon and Ancestor*. Cambridge, UK: D. S. Brewer, 2007, pp. 12–21.

"La réception de *Fierabras* en Angleterre," in Marc Le Person (ed.), *Le rayonnement de Fierabras dans la littérature européenne*. Lyon: Centre d'étude des Interactions Culturelles, Université Jean Moulin Lyon 3, 2003, pp. 177–89.

"What's in a Name? Anglo-Norman Romances or Chansons de geste?," in Rhiannon Purdie and Michael Cichon (eds.), *Medieval Romance, Medieval Contexts*. Cambridge, UK: D. S. Brewer, 2011, pp. 61–76.

Akbari, Suzanne Conklin. "Erasing the Body: History and Memory in Medieval Siege Poetry," in Nicholas Paul and Suzanne M. Yeager (eds.), *Remembering the Crusades: Myth, Image, and Identity*. Baltimore: Johns Hopkins University Press, 2012, pp. 146–73.

"The Hunger for National Identity in *Richard Coeur de Lion*," in Robert M. Stein and Sandra Pierson Prior (eds.), *Reading Medieval Culture: Essays in Honor of Robert W. Hanning*. Notre Dame, IN: University of Notre Dame Press, 2005, pp. 198–227.

Idols in the East: European Representations of Islam and the Orient, 1100–1450. Ithaca, NY: Cornell University Press, 2009.

"Incorporation in the *Siege of Melayne*," in Nicola McDonald (ed.), *Pulp Fictions of Medieval England: Essays in Popular Romance*. Manchester, UK: Manchester University Press, 2004, pp. 22–44.

"Placing the Jews in Late Medieval England," in Ivan Davidson Kalmar and Derek J. Penslar (eds.), *Orientalism and the Jews*. Hanover, NH: University Press of New England, 2005, pp. 34–45.

Althoff, Gerd. *Family, Friends and Followers*, trans. Christopher Caroll. Cambridge: Cambridge University Press, 2004; 1st ed. in German 1990.

"Friendship and Political Order," in Julian Haseldine (ed.), *Friendship in Medieval Europe*. Stroud, UK: Sutton, 1999, pp. 91–105.

"*Ira regis*: Prolegomena to a History of Royal Anger," in Barbara H. Rosenwein (ed.), *Anger's Past: The Social Uses of an Emotion in the Middle Ages*. Ithaca, NY: Cornell University Press, 1998, pp. 59–74.

Ambrisco, Alan S. "Cannibalism and Cultural Encounters in *Richard Coeur de Lion*." *Journal of Medieval and Early Modern Studies*, 29 (1999), 499–528.

Aravamudan, Srinivas. *Enlightenment Orientalism: Resisting the Rise of the Novel*. Chicago: University of Chicago Press, 2012.

Bibliography

"Orientalism," in David Kastan (ed.), *The Oxford Encyclopaedia of British Literature*. Oxford: Oxford University Press, 2006, pp. 143–50.

Arnold, T. W. *The Preaching of Islam: A History of the Propagation of the Muslim Faith*. London: Constable, 1913.

Atiya, Aziz Suryal. *The Crusade in the Later Middle Ages*. London: Methuen, 1938. *The Crusade of Nicopolis*. London: Methuen, 1934.

Aurell, Martin. *Des Chrétiens contre les croisades, XIIe–XIIIe siècles*. Paris: Fayard, 2013.

Bahr, Arthur. "Miscellaneity and Variance in the Medieval Book," in Michael Johnston and Michael Van Dussen (eds.), *The Medieval Manuscript Book: Cultural Approaches*. Cambridge: Cambridge University Press, 2015, pp. 181–98.

Bale, Anthony. *Feeling Persecuted: Christians, Jews, and Images of Violence in the Middle Ages*. London: Reaktion, 2010.

Bancourt, Paul. *Les musulmans dans les chansons de geste du Cycle du roi*. Aix-en-Provence: Université de Provence, 1982.

Barber, Richard. *The Knight and Chivalry*, 3rd ed. Woodbridge, UK: Boydell Press, 1995; 1st ed. 1970.

Barnie, John. *War in Medieval Society: Social Values and the Hundred Years War, 1377–99*. London: Weidenfeld and Nicolson, 1974.

Bartlett, Robert. *The Making of Europe: Conquest, Colonization, and Cultural Change, 950–1350*. Princeton, NJ: Princeton University Press, 1993.

Barton, Richard E. "'Zealous Anger' and the Renegotiation of Aristocratic Relationships in Eleventh and Twelfth Century France," in Barbara H. Rosenwein (ed.), *Anger's Past: The Social Uses of an Emotion in the Middle Ages*. Ithaca, NY: Cornell University Press, 1998, pp. 153–70.

Beattie, Pamela Drost. "'*Pro Exaltatione Sanctae Fidei Catholicae*': Mission and Crusade in the Writings of Ramon Lull," in Larry J. Simon (ed.), *Iberia and the Mediterranean World of the Middle Ages: Studies in Honor of Robert I. Burns*. Leiden: Brill, 1995, pp. 113–29.

Beer, Jeanette (ed.). *A Companion to Medieval Translation*. Leeds, UK: Arc Humanities Press, 2019.

Behdad, Ali. *Belated Travelers: Orientalism in the Age of Colonial Dissolution*. Durham, NC: Duke University Press, 1994.

Bell, Adrian. "English Members of the Order of the Passion: Their Political, Diplomatic and Military Significance," in Renate Blumenfeld-Kosinski and Kiril Petkov (eds.), *Philippe de Mézières and His Age*. Leiden: Brill, 2012, pp. 321–45.

Bellis, Joanna, and Laura Slatter (eds.). *Representing War and Violence, 1250–1600*. Woodbridge, UK: Boydell Press, 2016.

Benett, Stephen. "Fear and Its Representation in the First Crusade." *Ex Historia*, 4 (2012), 29–54.

Bhabha, Homi K. *The Location of Culture*, 2nd ed. London: Routledge, 2004; 1st ed. 1994.

Bird, Jessalynn. "James of Vitry's Sermons to Pilgrims." *Essays in Medieval Studies*, 24 (2008), 81–113.

Bibliography

Birenbaum, Maija. "Affective Vengeance in Titus and Vespasian." *Chaucer Review*, 43 (2009), 330–44.

Blurton, Heather. *Cannibalism in High Medieval English Literature*. Basingstoke, UK: Palgrave, 2007.

Boehmer, Elleke. *Colonial and Postcolonial Literature*. Oxford: Oxford University Press, 1995.

Boquet, Damien, and Piroska Nagy. *Medieval Sensibilities: A History of Emotions in the Middle Age*, trans. Robert Shaw. Cambridge, UK: Polity Press, 2018.
"Pour une histoire des émotions: L'historien face aux questions contemporaines," in Damien Boquet and Piroska Nagy (eds.), *Le sujet des émotions au Moyen Âge*. Paris: Beauchesne, 2009, pp. 15–51.
Sensible Moyen Âge: Une histoire des émotions dans l'Occident medieval. Paris: Éditions du Seuil, 2015.

Boswell, John B. *Same-Sex Unions in Premodern Europe*. New York: Villiard Books, 1994.

Bouwsma, William J. "Anxiety and the Formation of Early Modern Culture," in Barbara C. Malament (ed.), *After the Reformation: Essays in Honor of J. H. Hexter*. Philadelphia: University of Pennsylvania Press, 1980, pp. 215–46.

Boyle, Leonard E. "The Date of the *Summa praedicantium* of John Bromyard." *Speculum*, 48 (1973), 533–37.

Bradbury, Nancy Mason. "Popular Romance," in Corinne Saunders (ed.), *A Companion to Medieval Poetry*. Chichester, UK: Wiley-Blackwell, 2010, pp. 289–307.

Brandsma, Frank, Carolyne Larrington, and Corinne Saunders (eds.). *Emotions in Medieval Arthurian Literature: Body, Mind, Voice*. Cambridge, UK: D. S. Brewer, 2015.

Brantlinger, Patrick. *Victorian Literature and Postcolonial Studies*. Edinburgh: Edinburgh University Press, 2009.

Brault, Gerard J. "Le portrait des Sarrasins dans les chansons de geste, image projective?," in *Au carrefour des routes d'Europe: La chanson de geste*. Aix-en-Provence: CUERMA, Université de Provence, 1987, pp. 301–11.

Bray, Alan. *The Friend*. Chicago: University of Chicago Press, 2003.

Brewer, Derek. "The Popular English Metrical Romances," in Corinne Saunders (ed.), *A Companion to Romance: From Classical to Contemporary*. Oxford: Blackwell, 2004, pp. 45–64.

Brown, Warren C. *Violence in Medieval Europe*. Harlow, UK: Longman, 2010.

Brown-Grant, Rosalind. *French Romance of the Later Middle Ages: Gender, Morality, and Desire*. Oxford: Oxford University Press, 2008.

Bull, Marcus, and Damien Kempf (eds.). *Writing the Early Crusades: Text, Transmission, and Memory*. Woodbridge, UK: Boydell Press, 2014.

Bumke, Joachim. *Courtly Culture: Literature and Society in the High Middle Ages*, trans. Thomas Dunlap. Berkeley: University of California Press, 1991; 1st ed. in German 1987.

Burger, Glenn D., and Holly A. Crocker (eds.). *Medieval Affect, Feeling, and Emotion*. Cambridge: Cambridge University Press, 2019.

Bibliography

Burnley, David. *Courtliness and Literature in Medieval England*. London: Longman, 1998.

Burns, Robert I. "Christian-Islamic Confrontation in the West: The Thirteenth-Century Dream of Conversion." *American Historical Review*, 76 (1971), 1386–434.

Butterfield, Ardis. *The Familiar Enemy: Chaucer, Language, and Nation in the Hundred Years War*. Oxford: Oxford University Press, 2009.

Calin, William. *The French Tradition and the Literature of Medieval England*. Toronto: University of Toronto Press, 1995.

Calkin, Siobhain Bly. "Crusade Romance," in Siân Echard and Robert Allen Rouse (eds.), *The Encyclopedia of British Medieval Literature*. Chichester, UK: Wiley-Blackwell, 2017, pp. 583–89.

"The Man of Law's Tale and Crusade," in Christopher Cannon and Maura Nolan (eds.), *Medieval Latin and Middle English Literature: Essays in Honour of Jill Mann*. Cambridge, UK: D. S. Brewer, 2011, pp. 1–24.

"Narrating Trauma? Captured Cross Relics in Chronicles and *Chansons de Geste*." *Exemplaria*, 33 (2021), 19–43.

"Saracens," in Neil Cartlidge (ed.), *Heroes and Anti-Heroes in Medieval Romance*. Cambridge, UK: D. S. Brewer, 2012, pp. 185–200.

Saracens and the Making of English Identity: The Auchinleck Manuscript. New York: Routledge, 2005.

Camille, Michael. *The Gothic Idol: Ideology and Image-Making in Medieval Art*. Cambridge: Cambridge University Press, 1989.

Campbell, Kofi. "Nation-Building Colonialist-Style in *Bevis of Hampton*." *Exemplaria*, 18 (2006), 205–32.

Cartlidge, Neil. "Introduction," in Neil Cartlidge (ed.), *Heroes and Anti-Heroes in Medieval Romance*. Cambridge, UK: D. S. Brewer, 2012, pp. 1–8.

Casagrande, Carla, and Silvana Vecchio. *Histoire des péchés capitaux au Moyen Âge*, trans. Pierre-Emmanuel Dauzat. Paris: Aubier, 2002.

"Les théories des passions dans la culture médiévale," in Damien Boquet and Piroska Nagy, *Le sujet des émotions au Moyen Âge*. Paris: Beauchesne, 2009, pp. 107–22.

Cassidy-Welch, Megan, and Anne E. Lester. "Memory and Interpretation: New Approaches to the Study of the Crusades." *Journal of Medieval History*, 40 (2014), 225–36.

Cattin, Yves. "Dieu d'amour, dieu de colère ... justice et miséricorde dans le Proslogion (ch. VI–XI) d'Anselme de Canterbury." *Revue d'histoire et de philosophie religieuses*, 69 (1989), 423–50.

Cecen, Zeynep Kocabiyikoglu. "The Use of 'The Saracen Opinion' on Knighthood in Medieval French Literature: *L'Ordene de Chevalerie* and *L'apparicion Maistre Jehan de Meun*.'" *Medieval History Journal*, 19 (2016), 57–92.

Cerquiglini, Bernard. *Éloge de la variante: Histoire critique de la philologie*. Paris: Seuil, 1989.

In Praise of the Variant: A Critical History of Philology, trans. Betsy Wing. Baltimore: Johns Hopkins University Press, 1999.

Bibliography

Childress, Diana T. "Between Romance and Legend: 'Secular Hagiography' in Middle English Romance." *Philological Quarterly*, 57 (1978), 311–22.

Chism, Christine. *Alliterative Revivals*. Philadelphia: University of Pennsylvania Press, 2002.

"Friendly Fire: The Disastrous Politics of Friendship in the Alliterative *Morte Arthure*." *Arthuriana*, 20 (2010), 66–88.

"Romance," in Larry Scanlon (ed.), *The Cambridge Companion to Medieval English Literature, 1100–1500*. Cambridge: Cambridge University Press, pp. 57–70.

Chrisman, Laura. *Postcolonial Contraventions: Cultural Readings of Race, Imperialism, and Transnationalism*. Manchester, UK: Manchester University Press, 2003.

Claeys, Gregory. *Imperial Sceptics: British Critics of Empire, 1850–1920*. Cambridge: Cambridge University Press, 2010.

Clarke, Catherine A. M. "Signs and Wonders: Writing Trauma in Twelfth-Century England." *Reading Medieval Studies*, 35 (2009), 55–77.

Classen, Albrecht. "Introduction: Friendship – The Quest for a Human Ideal and Value from Antiquity to the Early Modern Time," in Albrecht Classen and Marilyn Sandidge (eds.), *Friendship in the Middle Ages and Early Modern Age*. New York: Walter de Gruyter, 2010, pp. 1–183.

Cleary, Joe. "Said, Postcolonial Studies, and World Literature," in Bashir Abu-Manneh (ed.), *After Said: Postcolonial Literary Studies in the Twenty-First Century*. Cambridge: Cambridge University Press, 2019, pp. 129–46.

Clifford, James. "On Orientalism." *History and Theory*, 19 (1980), 204–23.

Cobb, Paul. *The Race for Paradise: An Islamic History of the Crusades*. Oxford: Oxford University Press, 2014.

Cohen, Jeffrey Jerome. *Of Giants: Sex, Monsters, and the Middle Ages*. Minneapolis: University of Minnesota Press, 1999.

"On Saracen Enjoyment: Some Fantasies of Race in Late Medieval France and England." *Journal of Medieval and Early Modern Studies*, 31 (2001), 113–46.

"Race," in Marion Turner (ed.), *A Handbook of Middle English Studies*. Oxford: Wiley-Blackwell, 2013, pp. 109–22.

Cohen, Jeremy. *Sanctifying the Name of God: Jewish Martyrs and Jewish Memories of the First Crusade*. Philadelphia: University of Pennsylvania Press, 2004.

Constable, Giles. "The Second Crusade as Seen by Contemporaries." *Traditio*, 9 (1953), 213–79.

Contamine, Philippe. "Guerre et paix à la fin du Moyen Age: L'action et la pensée de Philippe de Mézières (1327–1405)," in Hans-Henning Kortüm (ed.), *Krieg im Mittelalter*. Berlin: Akademie Verlag, 2001, pp. 181–96.

"'Les princes, barons et chevaliers qui a la chevalerie au service de Dieu se sont ja vouez': Recherches prosopographiques sur l'ordre de la Passion de Jésus-Christ (1385–1395)," in Martin Nejedly and Jaroslav Svátek (eds.), *La noblesse et la croisade à la fin du Moyen Age: France, Bourgogne, Bohême*. Toulouse: FRAMESPA-UMR, 2009, pp. 43–64.

Cook, Albert S. "Beginning the Board in Prussia." *Journal of English and Germanic Philology*, 14 (1915), 375–88.

Cook, Robert Francis. *The Sense of the "Song of Roland."* Ithaca, NY: Cornell University Press, 1987.

Cooper, Helen. *The English Romance in Time: Transforming Motifs from Geoffrey of Monmouth to the Death of Shakespeare.* Oxford: Oxford University Press, 2004.

Coote, Lesley A. "Laughing at Monsters in *Richard Cœur de Lyon*," in Adrian P. Tudor and Alan Hindley (eds.), *Grant Risée? The Medieval Comic Presence: Essays in Memory of Brian J. Levy.* Turnhout: Brepols, 2006, pp. 193–211.

Copeland, Rita (ed.). *Criticism and Dissent in the Middle Ages.* Cambridge: Cambridge University Press, 1996.

 Emotion and the History of Rhetoric in the Middle Ages. Oxford: Oxford University Press, 2021.

 Rhetoric, Hermeneutics and Translation in the Middle Ages: Academic Traditions and Vernacular Texts. Cambridge: Cambridge University Press, 1991.

Cowdrey, H. E. J. "Cluny and the First Crusade." *Revue bénédictine*, 83 (1973), 283–311.

Crane, Susan. "Guy of Warwick and the Question of Exemplary Romance." *Genre*, 17 (1984), 351–74.

Crofts, Thomas H., and Robert Allen Rouse. "Middle English Popular Romance and National Identity," in Raluca L. Radulescu and Cory James Rushton (eds.), *A Companion to Medieval Popular Romance.* Cambridge, UK: D. S. Brewer, 2009, pp. 79–95.

Crone, Patricia. *The Nativist Prophets of Early Islamic Iran: Rural Revolt and Local Zoroastrianism.* Cambridge: Cambridge University Press, 2012.

Daniel, Norman. *Heroes and Saracens: An Interpretation of the Chansons de Geste.* Edinburgh: Edinburgh University Press, 1984.

Delumeau, Jean. *La peur en occident (XVIe–XVIIIe siècles): Une cité assiégée.* Paris: Fayard, 1978.

DiMarco, Vincent J. "The Historical Basis of Chaucer's Squire's Tale," in Kathryn L. Lynch (ed.), *Chaucer's Cultural Geography.* New York: Routledge, 2002, pp. 56–75.

Djordjević, Ivana. "*Guy of Warwick* as a Translation," in Alison Wiggins and Rosalind Field (eds.), *Guy of Warwick: Icon and Ancestor.* Cambridge, UK: D. S. Brewer, 2007, pp. 27–43.

 "Mapping Medieval Translation," in Judith Weiss, Jennifer Fellows, and Morgan Dickson (eds.), *Medieval Insular Romance: Translation and Innovation.* Cambridge, UK: D. S. Brewer, 2000, pp. 7–23.

Dolmans, Emily. *Writing Regional Identities in Medieval England: From the "Gesta Herwardi" to "Richard Coer de Lyon."* Woodbridge, UK: D. S. Brewer, 2020.

Downes, Stephanie, Andrew Lynch, and Katrina O'Loughlin (eds.). *Emotions and War: Medieval to Romantic Literature.* Basingstoke, UK: Palgrave, 2015.

Düll, Siegrid, Anthony Luttrell, and Maurice Keen. "Faithful unto Death: The Tomb Slab of Sir William Neville and Sir John Clanvowe, Constantinople 1391." *Antiquaries Journal*, 71 (1991), 174–90.

Bibliography

Edwards, A. S. G. "The *Speculum Guy de Warwick* and Lydgate's *Guy of Warwick*: The Non-Romance Middle English Translation," in Alison Wiggins and Rosalind Field (eds.), *Guy of Warwick: Icon and Ancestor*. Cambridge, UK: D. S. Brewer, 2007, pp. 81–93.

Elias, Marcel. "Chaucer and Crusader Ethics: Youth, Love, and the Material World." *Review of English Studies*, 70 (2019), 618–39.

"Crusade Romances and the Matter of France," in Helen Cooper and Robert R. Edwards (eds.), *The Oxford History of Poetry in English, vol. 2 (1100–1400)*. Oxford: Oxford University Press, 2023, pp. 339–55.

"Interfaith Empathy and the Formation of Romance," in Mary C. Flannery (ed.), *Emotion and Medieval Textual Media*. Turnhout: Brepols, 2018, pp. 99–124.

"Unsettling Orientalism: Toward a New History of European Representations of Muslims and Islam, c. 1200–1450." *Speculum*, 100:2 (forthcoming, April 2025).

"Violence, Excess, and the Composite Emotional Rhetoric of *Richard Coeur de Lion*." *Studies in Philology*, 114 (2017), 1–38.

Fellows, Jennifer. "From *Gui* to *Guy*: The Fashioning of a Popular Romance," in Alison Wiggins and Rosalind Field (eds.), *Guy of Warwick: Icon and Ancestor*. Cambridge, UK: D. S. Brewer, 2007, pp. 44–60.

Field, Rosalind. "Romance in England, 1066–1400," in David Wallace (ed.), *The Cambridge History of Medieval English Literature*. Cambridge: Cambridge University Press, 1999, pp. 152–76.

Flahiff, George B. "*Deus Non Vult*: A Critic of the Third Crusade." *Mediaeval Studies*, 9 (1947), 162–88.

Flannery, Mary C. (ed.). *Emotion and Medieval Textual Media*. Turnhout: Brepols, 2018.

Flori, Jean. *Prêcher la croisade (XIe–XIIIe siècle): Communication et propaganda*. Paris: Perrin, 2012.

Richard Coeur de Lion: Le roi chevalier. Paris: Payot, 1999.

Forey, A. J. "Western Converts to Islam (Later Eleventh to Later Fifteenth Centuries)." *Traditio*, 68 (2013), 153–231.

Fowler, Kenneth. *The King's Lieutenant: Henry of Grosmont, First Duke of Lancaster*. London: Elek, 1969.

Frakes, Jerold C. *Vernacular and Latin Literary Discourses of the Muslim Other in Medieval Germany*. New York: Palgrave, 2011.

France, John. *The Crusades and the Expansion of Catholic Christendom, 1000–1714*. London: Routledge, 2005.

Frankis, John. "Taste and Patronage in Late Medieval England as Reflected in Versions of *Guy of Warwick*." *Medium Aevum*, 66 (1997), 80–93.

Frye, Northrop. *Anatomy of Criticism: Four Essays*. Princeton, NJ: Princeton University Press, 1957.

The Secular Scripture: A Study of the Structure of Romance. Cambridge, MA: Harvard University Press, 1976.

Furrow, Melissa. "*Chanson de Geste* as Romance in England," in Laura Ashe, Ivana Djordjević, and Judith Weiss (eds.), *The Exploitations of Medieval Romance*. Cambridge, UK: D. S. Brewer, 2010, pp. 57–72.

Expectations of Romance: The Reception of a Genre in Medieval England. Woodbridge, UK: Boydell and Brewer, 2009.

Galloway, Andrew. "Alliterative Poetry in Old Jerusalem: *The Siege of Jerusalem* and Its Sources," in John A. Burrow and Hoyt N. Duggan (eds.), *Medieval Alliterative Poetry: Essays in Honour of Thorlac Turville-Petre*. Dublin: Four Courts, 2010, pp. 85–106.

Galvez, Marisa. *The Subject of Crusade: Lyric, Romance, and Materials, 1150 to 1500*. Chicago: University of Chicago Press, 2020.

Gandhi, Leela. *Affective Communities: Anticolonial Thought, Fin-de-Siècle Radicalism, and the Politics of Friendship*. Durham, NC: Duke University Press, 2006.

Postcolonial Theory: A Critical Introduction, 2nd ed. New York: Columbia University Press, 2019; 1st ed. 1998.

Gaposchkin, M. Cecilia. *Invisible Weapons: Liturgy and the Making of Crusade Ideology*. Ithaca, NY: Cornell University Press, 2017.

The Making of Saint Louis: Kingship, Sanctity, and Crusade in the Later Middle Ages. Ithaca, NY: Cornell University Press, 2008.

Gardette, Philippe. "Jacques de Helly, figure de l'entre-deux culturel au lendemain de la défaite de Nicopolis." *Erytheia: Revista de estudios bizantinos y neogriegos*, 24 (2003), 111–24.

Gaunt, Simon. "Can the Middle Ages Be Postcolonial?" *Comparative Literature*, 61 (2009), 160–76.

Marco Polo's "Le Devisement du Monde": Voice, Language and Diversity. Cambridge, UK: D. S. Brewer, 2013.

Geary, Patrick. "Humiliation of Saints," in Stephen Wilson (ed.), *Saints and Their Cults: Studies in Religious Sociology, Folklore and History*. Cambridge: Cambridge University Press, 1983, pp. 123–40.

George-Tvrtković, Rita. *A Christian Pilgrim in Medieval Iraq: Riccoldo da Montecroce's Encounter with Islam* Turnhout: Brepols, 2012.

Gertsman, Elina (ed.). "Introduction: 'Going They Wept and Wept.' Tears in Medieval Discourse," in Elina Gertsman (ed.), *Crying in the Middle Ages: Tears of History*. New York: Routledge, 2012.

Gilbert, Jane. "A Theoretical Introduction," in Ad Putter and Jane Gilbert (eds.), *The Spirit of Medieval English Popular Romance*. Harlow, UK: Longman, 2000, pp. 15–31.

Gillingham, John. "Conquering the Barbarians: War and Chivalry in Twelfth-Century Britain." *Haskins Society Journal*, 4 (1992), 67–84.

"Some Legends of Richard the Lionheart: Their Development and Their Influence," in Janet Nelson (ed.), *Richard Coeur de Lion in History and Myth*. London: King's College Centre for Late Antique and Medieval Studies, 1992, pp. 51–69.

Glover, David (ed.). *The Cambridge Companion to Popular Fiction*. Cambridge: Cambridge University Press, 2012.

Gonzalez Anton, Luis. *Las uniones aragonesas y las cortes del reino, 1283–1301*, 2 vols. Saragossa: Consejo Superior de Investigaciones Cientificas, 1975, II.

Bibliography

Goodman, Jennifer R. "Marriage and Conversion in Late Medieval Romance," in James Muldoon (ed.), *Varieties of Religious Conversion in the Middle Ages.* Gainesville: University Press of Florida, 1997, pp. 115–28.

Gopal, Priyamvada. *Insurgent Empire: Anticolonial Resistance and British Dissent.* London: Verso, 2019.

Grady, Frank. *Representing Righteous Heathens in Late Medieval England.* New York: Palgrave, 2005.

Green, David. *The Hundred Years War: A People's History.* New Haven, CT: Yale University Press, 2014.

Guard, Timothy. *Chivalry, Kingship and Crusade: The English Experience in the Fourteenth Century.* Woodbridge, UK: Boydell Press, 2013.

"Ryvere, Sir John (*b.* 1313, *d.* after 1364)," *Oxford Dictionary of National Biography.* Oxford: Oxford University Press, 2004–16, www.oxforddnb .com/view/article/92453.

"Sabraham, Nicholas (*b. c.* 1325, *d.* in or after 1399)," in *Oxford Dictionary of National Biography.* Oxford: Oxford University Press, 2004–16, www .oxforddnb.com/view/article/92452.

Hackenburg, Clint. "Christian Conversion to Islam," in David Thomas (ed.), *Routledge Handbook on Christian-Muslim Relations.* New York: Routledge, 2018, pp. 176–84.

Hamel, Mary. "The Siege of Jerusalem as a Crusading Poem," in Barbara N. Sargent-Baur (ed.), *Journeys toward God: Pilgrimage and Crusade.* Kalamazoo, MI: Medieval Institute Publications, pp. 177–94.

Hankins, James. "Renaissance Crusaders: Humanist Crusade Literature in the Age of Mehmed II." *Dumbarton Oaks Papers,* 49 (1995), 111–207.

Hanna, Ralph. *London Literature, 1300–1380.* Cambridge: Cambridge University Press, 2005.

Hardman, Phillipa. "Knight, King, Emperor, Saint: Portraying Charlemagne in Middle English Romance." *Reading Medieval Studies,* 38 (2012), 43–58.

Hardman, Phillipa, and Ailes, Marianne. "How English Are the English Charlemagne Romances?," in Neil Cartlidge (ed.), *Boundaries in Medieval Romance.* Woodbridge, UK: D. S. Brewer, 2008, pp. 43–55.

The Legend of Charlemagne in Medieval England: The Matter of France in Middle English and Anglo-Norman Literature. Cambridge, UK: D.S. Brewer, 2017.

Hawes, Janice. "Saracens in Middle English Romance," in Esra Mirze Santesso and James E. McClung (eds.), *Islam and Postcolonial Discourse.* New York: Routledge, 2016, pp. 15–30.

Hawting, G. R. *The Idea of Idolatry and the Emergence of Islam: From Polemic to History.* Cambridge: Cambridge University Press, 1999.

Heng, Geraldine. *Empire of Magic: Medieval Romance and the Politics of Cultural Fantasy.* New York: Columbia University Press, 2003.

The Invention of Race in the European Middle Ages. New York: Cambridge University Press, 2018).

Bibliography

Hibbard Loomis, Laura A. "Chaucer and the Auchinleck MS: Thopas and *Guy of Warwick*," in Percy Waldron Lond (ed.), *Essays and Studies in Honor of Carleton Brown*. New York: New York University Press, 1940, pp. 111–28.

Hopkins, Andrea. *The Sinful Knights: A Study of Middle English Penitential Romance*. Oxford: Clarendon Press, 1990.

Hornstein, Lilian Herlands. "The Historical Background of *The King of Tars*." *Speculum*, 16 (1941), 404–14.

Hourani, Albert. "The Road to Morocco." *New York Review of Books*, 26 (1979), 27–30.

Housley, Norman. *Contesting the Crusades*. Oxford: Oxford University Press, 2006.

Crusading and Warfare in Medieval and Renaissance Europe. Aldershot, UK: Ashgate, 2001.

"The Crusading Movement, 1274–1700," in Jonathan Riley-Smith (ed.), *The Oxford History of the Crusades*. Oxford: Oxford University Press, 1999, pp. 258–90.

The Later Crusades: From Lyons to Alcazar, 1274–1580. Oxford: Oxford University Press, 1992.

"One Man and His Wars: The Depiction of Warfare by Marshal Boucicaut's Biographer." *Journal of Medieval History*, 29 (2003), 27–40.

Religious Warfare in Europe, 1400–1536. Oxford: Oxford University Press, 2008.

Howe, Stephen. *Anticolonialism in British Politics: The Left and the End of Empire*. Oxford: Oxford University Press, 1993.

Humble, Nicola. "The Reader of Popular Fiction," in David Glover (ed.), *The Cambridge Companion to Popular Fiction*. Cambridge: Cambridge University Press, 2012, pp. 86–102.

Hunter, J. A. "Wolfram's Attitude to Warfare and Killing." *Reading Medieval Studies*, 8 (1982), 97–114.

Hyams, Paul R. *Rancor and Reconciliation in Medieval England*. Ithaca, NY: Cornell University Press, 2003.

Hyatte, Reginald. *The Arts of Friendship: The Idealization of Friendship in Medieval and Early Renaissance Literature*. Leiden: Brill, 1994.

Jackson, Peter. *The Mongols and the West, 1221–1410*. Harlow, UK: Longman, 2005.

Jaeger, C. Stephen. *Ennobling Love: In Search of a Lost Sensibility*. Philadelphia: University of Pennsylvania Press, 1999.

Jameson, Fredric. "Magical Narratives: Romance as Genre." *New Literary History*, 7 (1975), 135–63.

Janet, Magali. "Les scènes de cannibalisme aux abords d'Antioche dans les récits de la première croisade: Des chroniques à la chanson de croisade." *Bien dire et bien aprandre*, 22 (2004), 179–91.

Jauss, Hans Robert. *Toward an Aesthetic of Reception*, trans. Timothy Bahti. Minneapolis: University of Minnesota Press, 1982.

Johnston, Michael. "New Evidence for the Social Reach of 'Popular Romance': The Books of Household Servants." *Viator*, 43 (2012), 303–32.

Bibliography

"Robert Thornton and *The Siege of Jerusalem.*" *Yearbook of Langland Studies*, 23 (2009), 125–62.

Romance and the Gentry in Late Medieval England. Oxford: Oxford University Press, 2014.

Jones, Terry. *Chaucer's Knight: The Portrait of a Medieval Mercenary.* London: Weidenfeld and Nicolson, 1980.

Jones, W. R. "The English Church and Royal Propaganda during the Hundred Years War." *Journal of British Studies*, 19 (1979), 18–30.

Jubb, Margaret. "The Crusaders' Perceptions of Their Opponents," in Helen J. Nicholson (ed.), *Palgrave Advances in the Crusades.* Basingstoke, UK: Palgrave, 2005, pp. 225–44.

"Enemies in the Holy War, but Brothers in Chivalry: The Crusaders' View of Their Saracen Opponents," in Hans van Dijk and Willem Noomen (eds.), *Aspects de l'épopée romane: Mentalités, idéologies, intertextualités.* Groningen: E. Forsten, 1995, pp. 251–59.

Kaeuper, Richard. *Chivalry and Violence in Medieval Europe.* New York: Oxford University Press, 1999.

Karras, Ruth Mazo. *From Boys to Men: Formations of Masculinity in Late Medieval Europe.* Philadelphia: University of Pennsylvania Press, 2003.

Kay, Sarah. "Analytical Survey 3: The New Philology." *New Medieval Literatures*, 3 (1999), 295–326.

The Chansons de Geste in the Age of Romance: Political Fictions. Oxford: Clarendon Press, 1995.

Kedar, Benjamin K. *Crusade and Mission: European Approaches towards the Muslims.* Princeton, NJ: Princeton University Press, 1984.

"The Jerusalem Massacre of July 1099 in the Western Historiography of the Crusades." *Crusades*, 3 (2004), 15–75.

"Multidirectional Conversion in the Frankish Levant," in James Muldoon (ed.), *Varieties of Religious Conversion in the Middle Ages.* Gainesville: University Press of Florida, 1997, pp. 190–99.

Keen, Maurice. "Brotherhood in Arms." *History*, 47 (2007), 1–17.

"Chaucer and Chivalry Revisited," in Matthew Strickland (ed.), *Armies, Chivalry and Warfare in Medieval Britain and France.* Stamford, UK: P. Watkins, 1998, pp. 1–12.

"Chaucer's Knight, the English Aristocracy and the Crusade," in V. J. Scattergood and J. W. Sherbone (eds.), *English Court Culture in the Later Middle Ages.* London: Duckworth, 1983, pp. 45–61.

Chivalry. New Haven, CT: Yale University Press, 1984.

Nobles, Knights and Men-at-Arms in the Middle Ages. London: Hambledon, 1996.

Kennedy, Valerie. *Edward Said: A Critical Introduction.* Oxford: Wiley-Blackwell, 2000.

Khanmohamadi, Shirin A. *In Light of Another's World: European Ethnography in the Middle Ages.* Philadelphia: University of Pennsylvania Press, 2013.

King, Peter. "Emotions in Medieval Thought," in Peter Goldie (ed.), *Oxford Handbook of Philosophy of Emotion.* Oxford: Oxford University Press, 2009, pp. 167–87.

Bibliography

Kinoshita, Sharon. "Deprovincializing the Middle Ages," in Rob Wilson and Christopher Leigh Connery (eds.), *The Worlding Project: Doing Cultural Studies in the Era of Globalization*. Santa Cruz, CA: New Pacific Press, 2007, pp. 61–75.

Medieval Boundaries: Rethinking Difference in Old French Literature. Philadelphia: University of Pennsylvania Press, 2006.

"'Pagans Are Wrong and Christians Are Right': Alterity, Gender, and Nation in the *Chanson de Roland*." *Journal of Medieval and Early Modern Studies*, 31 (2001), 79–111.

Kinoshita, Sharon, and Siobhain Bly Calkin. "Saracens as Idolaters in European Vernacular Literatures," in David Thomas and Alex Mallett (eds.), *Christian–Muslim Relations: A Bibliographical History, vol. 4 (1200–1350)*. Leiden: Brill, 2013, pp. 29–44.

Knox, Philip. *The "Romance of the Rose" and the Making of Fourteenth-Century English Literature*. Oxford: Oxford University Press, 2022.

Knuuttila, Simo. *Emotions in Ancient and Medieval Philosophy*. Oxford: Clarendon Press, 2004.

Krueger, Roberta L. "Introduction," in Roberta L. Krueger (ed.), *The Cambridge Companion to Medieval Romance*. Cambridge: Cambridge University Press, 2000, pp. 1–9.

Kumler, Aden. *Translating Truth: Ambitious Images and Religious Knowledge in Late Medieval France and England*. New Haven, CT: Yale University Press, 2011.

Lalande, Denis. *Jean II le Meingre, dit Boucicaut (1366–1421): Étude d'une biographie héroïque*. Geneva: Droz, 1988.

Lampert-Weissig, Lisa. *Medieval Literature and Postcolonial Studies*. Edinburgh: Edinburgh University Press, 2010.

Lang, Johannes. "New Histories of Emotion." *History and Theory*, 57 (2018), 104–20.

Langlois, Ernest. "Deux fragments épiques: *Otinel, Aspremont*." *Romania*, 12 (1883), 438–58.

Langum, Virginia. *Medicine and the Seven Deadly Sins in Late Medieval Literature and Culture*. New York: Palgrave, 2016.

Larrington, Carolyne. "The Psychology of Emotion and Study of the Medieval Period." *Early Medieval Europe*, 10 (2001), 251–56.

Latiff, Osman. *The Cutting Edge of the Poet's Sword: Muslim Poetic Responses to the Crusades*. Leiden: Brill, 2017.

Latowsky, Anne. "Charlemagne, Godfrey of Bouillon, and Louis IX of France," in Anthony Bale (ed.), *The Cambridge Companion to the Literature of the Crusades*. Cambridge: Cambridge University Press, 2019, pp. 200–214.

Leopold, Antony. *How to Recover the Holy Land: The Crusade Proposals of the Late Thirteenth and Early Fourteenth Centuries*. Aldershot, UK: Ashgate, 2000.

Lewis, Celia M. "History, Mission, and Crusade in the *Canterbury Tales*." *Chaucer Review*, 42 (2008), 353–82.

Leys, Ruth. "The Turn to Affect: A Critique." *Critical Inquiry*, 37 (2011), 434–72.

Bibliography

Libbon, Marisa. *Talk and Textual Production in Medieval England*. Columbus: The Ohio State University Press, 2021.

Little, Katherine C., and Nicola McDonald (eds.). *Thinking Medieval Romance*. Oxford: Oxford University Press, 2018.

Liu, Yin. "Middle English Romance as Prototype Genre." *Chaucer Review*, 40 (2006), 335–53.

"Richard Beauchamp and the Uses of Romance." *Medium Aevum*, 74 (2005), 271–87.

Lloyd, Simon D. *English Society and the Crusade, 1216–1307*. Oxford: Clarendon Press, 1988.

Lowe, Ben. *Imagining Peace: A History of Early English Pacifist Ideas, 1340–1560*. University Park: Pennsylvania State University Press, 1997.

Lowe, Lisa. *Critical Terrains: French and British Orientalisms*. Ithaca, NY: Cornell University Press, 1992.

Lower, Michael. *The Tunis Crusade of 1270: A Mediterranean History*. Oxford: Oxford University Press, 2018.

Luckhurst, Roger. "The Public Sphere, Popular Culture, and the True Meaning of the Zombie Apocalypse," in David Glover (ed.), *The Cambridge Companion to Popular Fiction*. Cambridge: Cambridge University Press, 2012, pp. 68–85.

Lydon, Jane. *Imperial Emotions: The Politics of Empathy across the British Empire*. Cambridge: Cambridge University Press, 2020.

MacLean, Gerald. *Looking East: English Writing and the Ottoman Empire before 1800*. Basingstoke, UK: Palgrave, 2007.

Manion, Lee. *Narrating the Crusades: Loss and Recovery in Medieval and Early Modern English Literature*. Cambridge: Cambridge University Press, 2014.

Mason, Emma. "Fact and Fiction in Crusading Tradition: The Earls of Warwick in the Twelfth Century." *Journal of Medieval History*, 14 (1988), 81–95.

"Legends of the Beauchamps' Ancestors: The Use of Baronial Propaganda in Medieval England." *Journal of Medieval History*, 10 (1984), 25–40.

Mastnak, Tomaz. *Crusading Peace: Christendom, the Muslim World, and Western Political Order*. Berkeley: University of California Press, 2002.

Matar, Nabil. *Islam in Britain, 1558–1685*. Cambridge: Cambridge University Press, 1998.

Matar, Nabil, and Gerald MacLean. *Britain and the Islamic World, 1558–1713*. Oxford: Oxford University Press, 2011.

Matikkala, Mira. *Empire and Imperial Ambition: Liberty, Englishness and Anti-Imperialism in Late Victorian Britain*. London: I. B. Tauris, 2011.

McDonald, Nicola. "Eating People and the Alimentary Logic of *Richard Coeur de Lion*," in Nicola McDonald (ed.), *Pulp Fictions of Medieval England: Essays in Popular Romance*. Manchester, UK: Manchester University Press, 2004, pp. 124–50.

McFarlane, K. B. "A Business Partnership in War and Administration, 1421–1445." *English Historical Review*, 78 (1963), 290–309.

Lancastrian Kings and Lollard Knights. Oxford: Clarendon Press, 1972.

McGrath, Kate. "The Politics of Chivalry: The Function of Anger and Shame in Eleventh- and Twelfth-Century Anglo-Norman Historical Narratives," in Belle S. Tuten and Tracey L. Billado (eds.), *Feud, Violence and Practice: Essays in Medieval Studies in Honor of Stephen D. White*. Farnham, UK: Ashgate, 2010, pp. 55–69.

"The 'Zeal of God': The Representation of Anger in the Latin Crusade Accounts of the 1096 Rhineland Massacres," in Kristine T. Utterback and Merrall Llewelyn Price (eds.), *Jews in Medieval Christendom: "Slay Them Not."* Leiden: Brill, 2013, pp. 25–44.

McNamer, Sarah. *Affective Meditation and the Invention of Medieval Compassion*. Philadelphia: University of Pennsylvania Press, 2010.

Megna, Paul. "Langland's Wrath: Righteous Anger Management in *The Vision of Piers Plowman.*" *Exemplaria*, 25 (2013), 130–51.

Mehl, Dieter. *The Middle English Romances of the Thirteenth and Fourteenth Centuries*. London: Barnes and Noble, 1969.

Menache, Sophia. "Emotions in the Service of Politics: Another Perspective on the Experience of Crusading (1095–1187)," in Susan B. Edgington and Luis García-Guijarro (eds.), *Jerusalem the Golden: The Origins and Impact of the First Crusade*. Turnhout: Brepols, 2014, pp. 235–54.

"Love of God or Hatred of Your Enemy? The Emotional Voices of the Crusades." *Mirabilia*, 10 (2010), 1–20.

Metlitzki, Dorothee. *The Matter of Araby in Medieval England*. New Haven, CT: Yale University Press, 1977.

Mikva, Rachel S. "Weeping as Discourse between Heaven and Earth: The Transformative Power of Tears in Medieval Jewish Literature," in Elina Gertsman (ed.), *Crying in the Middle Ages: Tears of History*. New York: Routledge, 2012, pp. 156–72.

Millar, Bonnie. *The "Siege of Jerusalem" in Its Physical, Literary, and Historical Contexts*. Dublin: Four Courts, 2000.

Mills, Maldwin. "Introduction," in *Six Middle English Romances*. London: Dent, 1973, pp. vii–xxxi.

"Techniques of Translation in the Middle English Versions of *Guy of Warwick*," in Roger Ellis (ed.), *The Medieval Translator: II*. London: Centre for Medieval Studies, 1991, pp. 209–29.

Minnis, Alastair. "Other Worlds: Chaucer's Classicism," in Rita Copeland (ed.), *The Oxford History of Classical Reception in English Literature, vol. 1 (800–1558)*. Oxford: Oxford University Press, 2016, pp. 413–34.

Moe, Phyllis. "The French Source of the Alliterative *Siege of Jerusalem.*" *Medium Aevum*, 39 (1970), 147–54.

Moore, Megan. *The Erotics of Grief: Emotions and the Construction of Privilege in the Medieval Mediterranean*. Ithaca, NY: Cornell University Press, 2021.

Nagy, Pirsoka. *Le Don des larmes au Moyen Âge*. Paris: Albin Michel, 2000.

Newhauser, Richard. *The Treatises on Vices and Virtues in Latin and the Vernacular*. Turnhout: Brepols, 1993.

Bibliography

Nicholson, Roger. "Haunted Itineraries: Reading the *Siege of Jerusalem*." *Exemplaria*, 14 (2002), 447–84.

Nievergelt, Marco. "*The Sege of Melayne* and *The Siege of Jerusalem*: National Identity, Beleaguered Christendom, and Holy War during the Great Papal Schism." *Chaucer Review*, 49 (2015), 402–26.

Norako, Leila K. "*Sir Isumbras* and the Fantasy of Crusade." *Chaucer Review*, 48 (2013), 166–89.

Offler, H. S. "Thomas Bradwardine's 'Victory Sermon' in 1346," in A. I. Doyle (ed.), *Church and Crown in the Fourteenth Century*. Aldershot, UK: Ashgate, 2000, pp. 1–40.

O'Gorman, Francis. "Realism and Romance," in Robert L. Caserio and Clement Hawes (eds.), *The Cambridge History of the English Novel*. Cambridge: Cambridge University Press, 2012, pp. 485–99.

Ogura, Michiko. *Words and Expressions of Emotion in Medieval English*. Frankfurt: Peter Lang, 2013.

Oschema, Klaus. "Sacred or Profane? Reflections on Love and Friendship in the Middle Ages," in Laura Gowing, Michael Hunter, and Miri Rubin (eds.), *Love, Friendship, and Faith in Europe, 1300–1800*. Basingstoke, UK: Palgrave, 2005, pp. 43–65.

Ottewill-Soulsby, Samuel. "'Those Same Cursed Saracens': Charlemagne's Campaigns in the Iberian Peninsula as Religious Warfare." *Journal of Medieval History*, 42 (2016), 405–28.

Owen, Nicholas. *The British Left and India: Metropolitan Anti-Imperialism, 1885–1947*. Oxford: Oxford University Press, 2007.

Palmer, J. J. N. *England, France, and Christendom, 1377–99*. London: Routledge, 1972.

Paterson, Linda. *Singing the Crusades: French and Occitan Lyric Responses to the Crusading Movement, 1137–1336*. Cambridge, UK: D. S. Brewer, 2018.

Patton, Kimberley Christine. "'Howl, Weep and Moan, and Bring It Back to God': Holy Tears in Eastern Christianity," in Kimberly Christine Patton and John Stratton Hawley (eds.), *Holy Tears: Weeping in the Religious Imagination*. Princeton, NJ: Princeton University Press, 2005, pp. 255–73.

Paul, Nicholas, and Suzanne Yeager (eds.). *Remembering the Crusades: Myth, Image and Identity*. Baltimore: John Hopkins University Press, 2012.

Pearsall, Derek. "The Pleasure of Popular Romance: A Prefatory Essay," in Rhiannon Purdie and Michael Cichon (eds.), *Medieval Romance, Medieval Contexts*. Cambridge, UK: D. S. Brewer, 2011, pp. 9–18.

Petkov, Kiril. "The Rotten Apple and the Good Apples: Orthodox, Catholics, and Turks in Philippe de Mézières' Crusading Propaganda." *Journal of Medieval History*, 23 (1997), 255–70.

Phillips, Kim M. *Before Orientalism: Asian Peoples and Cultures in European Travel Writing, 1245–1510*. Philadelphia: University of Pennsylvania Press, 2014.

Plamper, Jan. "The History of Emotions: An Interview with William Reddy, Barbara Rosenwein, and Peter Stearns." *History and Theory*, 49 (2010), 237–65.

Bibliography

History of Emotions: An Introduction. New York: Oxford University Press, 2015.

Porter, Bernard. *Critics of Empire: British Radicals and the Imperial Challenge*, 2nd ed. London: I. B. Tauris, 2008; 1st ed. 1968.

Porter, Dennis. "*Orientalism* and Its Problems," in Francis Barker, Peter Hulme, Margaret Iverson, and Diane Loxley (eds.), *The Politics of Theory: Proceedings of the Essex Sociology of Literature Conference, University of Essex*. Colchester, UK: University of Essex, 1983, pp. 179–93.

Price, Paul. "Confessions of a Godless Killer: *Guy of Warwick* and Comprehensive Entertainment," in Judith Weiss, Jennifer Fellows, and Morgan Dickson (eds.), *Medieval Insular Romance: Translation and Innovation*. Cambridge, UK: D. S. Brewer, 2000, pp. 93–110.

Puckett, Jaye. "'Reconmenciez novele estoire': The Troubadours and the Rhetoric of the Later Crusades." *Modern Language Notes*, 116 (2001), 844–89.

Putter, Ad. "A Historical Introduction," in Ad Putter and Jane Gilbert (eds.), *The Spirit of Medieval English Popular Romance*. Harlow, UK: Pearson, 2000, pp. 1–15.

Rajabzadeh, Shokoofeh. "The Depoliticized Saracen and Muslim Erasure." *Literature Compass*, 16 (2019), 1–8.

Ramazani, Jahan. *Poetry in a Global Age*. Chicago: University of Chicago Press, 2020.

A Transnational Poetics. Chicago: University of Chicago Press, 2009.

Rawcliffe, Carole. *Medicine and Society in Later Medieval England*. Stroud, UK: Sutton, 1995.

Reddy, William M. "Against Social Constructionism: The Historical Ethnography of Emotions." *Current Anthropology*, 38 (1997), 327–51.

Reed, Thomas L. *Middle English Debate Poetry and the Aesthetics of Irresolution*. Columbia: University of Missouri Press, 1990.

Reichl, Karl. "Orality and Performance," in Raluca L. Radulescu and Cory James Rushton (eds.), *A Companion to Medieval Popular Romance*. Cambridge, UK: D. S. Brewer, 2009, pp. 132–49.

Richard, Jean. "Le discours missionnaire: L'exposition de la foi chrétienne dans les lettres des papes aux Mongols," in Jean Richard (ed.), *Croisés, missionnaires et voyageurs: Les perspectives orientales du monde latin medieval*. London: Variorum, 1983, pp. 257–68.

Richmond, Velma Bourgeois. *Laments for the Dead in Medieval Narrative*. Pittsburgh, PA: Duquesne University Press, 1966.

The Legend of Guy of Warwick. New York: Garland, 1996.

The Popularity of Middle English Romance. Bowling Green, OH: Bowling Green University Popular Press, 1975.

Ríkharðsdóttir, Sif. *Emotion in Old Norse Literature: Translations, Voices, Contexts*. Cambridge, UK: D. S. Brewer, 2017.

Riley-Smith, Jonathan. *The Crusades: A Short History*. London: Athlone, 1992.

"Crusading as an Act of Love." *History*, 65 (1980), 177–92.

"Peace Never Established: The Case of the Kingdom of Jerusalem." *Transactions of the Royal Historical Society*, 28 (1978), 82–102.

Bibliography

Romine, Anne. "Philippe de Mézières (c. 1327–1405) and the Controversy over Crusader Dress in the Fourteenth Century." *Allegorica*, 29 (2013), 36–51.

Rosenwein, Barbara H. *Emotional Communities in the Early Middle Ages*. Ithaca, NY: Cornell University Press, 2006.

Generations of Feeling: A History of Emotions, 600–1700. Cambridge: Cambridge University Press, 2016.

"Problems and Methods in the History of Emotions." *Passions in Context*, 1 (2010), 1–32.

"Who Cared about Thomas Aquinas's Theory of the Passions?" *L'Atelier du Centre de recherches historiques*, 16 (2016), https://doi.org/10.4000/acrh.7420.

"Worrying about Emotions in History." *American Historical Review*, 107 (2002), 821–45.

Rosenwein, Barbara H., and Riccardo Cristiani. *What Is the History of Emotions?* Cambridge, UK: Polity Press, 2018.

Rouse, Robert Allen. "Crusaders," in Neil Cartlidge (ed.), *Heroes and Anti-Heroes in Medieval Romance*. Cambridge, UK: D. S. Brewer, 2012, pp. 173–83.

"An Exemplary Life: Guy of Warwick as Medieval Culture Hero," in Alison Wiggins and Rosalind Field (eds.), *Guy of Warwick: Icon and Ancestor*. Cambridge, UK: D. S. Brewer, 2007, pp. 94–109.

The Idea of Anglo-Saxon England in Middle English Romance. Cambridge, UK: D. S. Brewer, 2005.

Review of Emily Dolmans, *Writing Regional Identities in Medieval England: From the "Gesta Herwardi" to "Richard Coer de Lyon"* (Cambridge, UK: D. S. Brewer, 2020). *Studies in the Age of Chaucer*, 44 (2022), 395–97.

Routledge, Michael. "Songs," in Jonathan Riley-Smith (ed.), *The Oxford History of the Crusades*. Oxford: Oxford University Press, 1999, pp. 90–110.

Rubenstein, Jay. "Cannibals and Crusaders." *French Historical Studies*, 31 (2008), 525–52.

Russel, Jeffrey Burton. *Lucifer: The Devil in the Middle Ages*. Ithaca, NY: Cornell University Press, 1986.

Witchcraft in the Middle Ages. Ithaca, NY: Cornell University Press, 1984.

Said, Edward W. *Culture and Imperialism*. London: Vintage Books, 1993.

"An Interview with Edward W. Said." *boundary* 2, 20 (1993), 1–25.

Orientalism. London: Penguin, 1978; repr., 1995.

Sapra, Rahul. *The Limits of Orientalism: Seventeenth-Century Representations of India*. Newark: University of Delaware Press, 2011.

Sarnowsky, Jürgen. "Die Johanniter und Smyrna (1344–1402)." *Römische Quartalschrift*, 87 (1992), 47–98.

Saul, Nigel. "A Farewell to Arms? Criticism of Warfare in Late Fourteenth-Century England," in Chris Given-Wilson (ed.), *Fourteenth Century England*. Woodbridge, UK: Boydell Press, 2002, pp. 131–46.

For Honour and Fame: Chivalry in England, 1066–1500. London: Bodley Head, 2011.

Scattergood, John. "The Date of Sir John Clanvowe's *The Two Ways* and the 'Reinvention of Lollardy.'" *Medium Aevum*, 79 (2010), 116–20.

226   *Bibliography*

Schein, Sylvia. *Fideles Crucis: The Papacy, the West, and the Recovery of the Holy Land*. Oxford: Clarendon Press, 1991.

Sère, Bénédicte. "Déshonneur, outrages et infamie aux sources de la violence d'après le *Super rhetoricorum* de Gilles de Rome," in François Foronda, Christine Barralis, and Bénédicte Sère (eds.), *Violences souveraines au Moyen Âge: Travaux d'une école historique*. Paris: Presses Universitaires de France, 2010, pp. 103–12.

Shagrir, Iris. "The Fall of Acre as a Spiritual Crisis: The Letters of Riccoldo of Monte Croce." *Revue Belge de philologie et d'histoire*, 90 (2012), 1107–20.

Shaw, Brent D. "Ritual Brotherhood in Roman and Post-Roman Society." *Traditio*, 52 (1997), 327–55.

Shepherd, Stephen. "'This Grete Journee': *The Sege of Melayne*," in Maldwyn Mills, Jennifer Fellows, and Carol M. Meale (eds.), *Romance in Medieval England*. Cambridge, UK: D. S. Brewer, 1991, pp. 113–31.

Siberry, Elizabeth. *Criticism of Crusading, 1095–1274*. Oxford: Clarendon Press, 1985.

    "Criticism of Crusading in Fourteenth-Century England," in Peter W. Edbury (ed.), *Crusade and Settlement: Papers Read at the First Conference of the Society for the Study of the Crusades and the Latin East*. Cardiff: University College Cardiff Press, 1985, pp. 127–34.

    "Missionaries and Crusaders, 1095–1274: Opponents or Allies?" *Studies in Church History*, 20 (1983), 103–10.

Siddiqi, Yumna. *Anxieties of Empire and the Fiction of Intrigue*. New York: Columbia University Press, 2008.

Sirantoine, Hélène. "What's in a Word? Naming 'Muslims' in Medieval Christian Iberia," in Chris Jones, Conor Kostick, and Klaus Oschema (eds.), *Making the Medieval Relevant: How Medieval Studies Contribute to Improving Our Understanding of the Present*. Berlin: De Gruyter, 2020, pp. 225–38.

Sivan, Emmanuel. "Edward Said and His Arab Reviewers," in *Interpretations of Islam: Past and Present*. Princeton, NJ: Darwin Press, 1985, pp. 133–54.

Smagghe, Laurent. *Les émotions du prince: Émotions et discours politique dans l'espace bourguignon*. Paris: Garnier, 2012.

    "Sur paine d'encourir nostre indignation. Rhétorique du courroux princier dans les Pays-Bas bourguignons à la fin du Moyen Âge," in Damien Boquet and Piroska Nagy (eds.), *Politiques des émotions au Moyen Âge*. Florence: SISMEL Edizioni del Galluzzo, 2010, pp. 75–91.

Smail, Daniel Lord. "Hatred as a Social Institution." *Speculum*, 76 (2001), 90–126.

Smyser, H. M. "Charlemagne Legends," in J. B. Severs (ed.), *A Manual of the Writings in Middle English*. 11 vols. New Haven, CT: Connecticut Academy of Arts and Sciences, 1967, I, pp. 80–100.

    "The Sowdon of Babylon and Its Author." *Harvard Studies and Notes in Philology and Literature*, 13 (1931), 185–218.

Speed, Diane. "Chivalric Perspectives in the Middle English Otuel Romances," in Ruth Evans, Helen Fulton, and David Matthews (eds.), *Medieval Cultural*

Studies: Essays in Honour of Stephen Knight. Cardiff: University of Wales Press, 2006, pp. 213–24.

"The Construction of the Nation in Medieval Romance," in Carol Meale (ed.), *Readings in Medieval English Romance.* Cambridge, UK: D. S. Brewer, 1994, pp. 135–57.

Spencer, Stephen J. "Constructing the Crusader: Emotional Language in the Narratives of the First Crusade," in Susan B. Edgington and Luis Garcia-Guijarro (eds.), *Jerusalem the Golden: The Origins and Impact of the First Crusade.* Turnhout: Brepols, 2014, pp. 173–89.

Emotions in a Crusading Context, 1095–1291. Oxford: Oxford University Press, 2019.

Strakhov, Elizaveta. *Continental England: Form, Translation, and Chaucer in the Hundred Years' War.* Columbus: The Ohio State University Press, 2022.

Stuckey, Jace. "Charlemagne as Crusader? Memory, Propaganda, and the Many Uses of Charlemagne's Legendary Expedition to Spain," in Matthew Gabriele and Jace Stuckey (eds.), *The Legend of Charlemagne in the Middle Ages: Power, Faith, and Crusade.* New York: Palgrave, 2008, pp. 137–52.

Suard, François. *La chanson de geste.* Paris: Presses Universitaires de France, 1993.

Sullivan, Karen. *The Danger of Romance: Truth, Fantasy, and Arthurian Fictions.* Chicago: University of Chicago Press, 2018, pp. 26–59.

Sumberg, Lewis A. "The Tafurs and the First Crusade." *Mediaeval Studies,* 21 (1959), 224–46.

Sweeney, Eileen C. "Aquinas on the Seven Deadly Sins: Tradition and Innovation," in Richard G. Newhauser and Susan J. Ridyard (eds.), *Sin in Medieval and Early Modern Culture: The Tradition of the Seven Deadly Sins.* Woodbridge, UK: York Medieval Press, 2012, pp. 85–106.

Swift, Helen. "Late Medieval Precursors to the Novel: 'Aucune chose de nouvel,'" in Adam Watt (ed.), *The Cambridge History of the Novel in French.* Cambridge: Cambridge University Press, 2021, pp. 19–37.

Tarnowski, Andrea. "Material Examples: Philippe de Mézières' Order of the Passion." *Yale French Studies,* 110 (2006), 163–75.

Tattersall, Jill. "Anthropophagi and Eaters of Raw Flesh in French Literature of the Crusade Period: Myth, Tradition and Reality." *Medium Aevum,* 57 (1998), 240–53.

Terrell, Katherine H. "'Lynealy discendit of þe devill': Genealogy, Textuality, and Anglophobia in Medieval Scottish Chronicles." *Studies in Philology,* 108 (2011), 320–44.

Throop, Palmer A. *Criticism of the Crusade: A Study of Public Opinion and Crusade Propaganda.* Amsterdam: N. V. Swets and Zeitlinger, 1940.

Throop, Susanna A. "Acts of Vengeance, Acts of Love: Crusading Violence in the Twelfth Century," in Laura Ashe and Ian Patterson (eds.), *War and Literature.* Cambridge, UK: D. S. Brewer, 2014, pp. 3–20.

Crusading as an Act of Vengeance, 1095–1216. Farnham, UK: Ashgate, 2011.

"Zeal, Anger and Vengeance: The Emotional Rhetoric of Crusading," in Susanna A. Throop and Paul R. Hyams (eds.), *Vengeance in the Middle*

Ages: Emotion, Religion, and Feud. Farnham, UK: Ashgate, 2010, pp. 177–201.

Tolan, John V. *Saracens: Islam in the Medieval European Imagination.* New York: Columbia University Press, 2002.

Sons of Ishmael: Muslims through European Eyes in the Middle Ages. Gainesville: University Press of Florida, 2008.

Tracy, Larissa. *Torture and Brutality in Medieval Literature: Negotiations of National Identity.* Cambridge, UK: D. S. Brewer, 2012.

Trigg, Stephanie. "Affect Theory," in Susan Broomhall (ed.), *Early Modern Emotions: An Introduction.* London: Routledge, 2017, pp. 10–13.

"Introduction: Emotional Histories – Beyond the Personalization of the Past and the Abstraction of Affect Theory." *Exemplaria,* 26 (2014), 3–15.

(ed.). "Pre-Modern Emotions." Special issue, *Exemplaria,* 26 (2014).

Tuck, Anthony. "Beauchamp, Thomas, Twelfth Earl of Warwick (1337–1401)," in *Oxford Dictionary of National Biography.* Oxford: Oxford University Press, 2004–16, www.oxforddnb.com/view/article/1841.

Turner, Marion. *Chaucer: A European Life.* Princeton, NJ: Princeton University Press, 2019.

Turner, T. Hudson. "Unpublished Notices of the Times of Edward I, Especially of His Relations with the Moghul Sovereigns of Persia." *Archaeological Journal,* 8 (1851), 44–51.

Turville-Petre, Thorlac. *England the Nation: Language, Literature and National Identity, 1290–1340.* Oxford: Oxford University Press, 1996.

Tyerman, Christopher. *England and the Crusades, 1095–1588.* Chicago: University of Chicago Press, 1988.

Fighting for Christendom: Holy War and the Crusades. Oxford: Oxford University Press, 2004.

God's War: A New History of the Crusades. London: Penguin, 2007.

"The Holy Land and the Crusades of the Thirteenth and Fourteenth Centuries," in Peter W. Edbury (ed.), *Crusade and Settlement: Papers Read at the First Conference of the Society for the Study of the Crusades and the Latin East and Presented to R. C. Smail.* Cardiff: University College Cardiff Press, 1985, pp. 105–12.

How to Plan a Crusade: Reason and Religion in the High Middle Ages. London: Allen Lane, 2015.

"'New Wine in Old Skins'? Crusade Literature and Crusading in the Eastern Mediterranean in the Later Middle Ages," in Jonathan Harris, Catherine Holmes, and Eugenia Russell (eds.), *Byzantines, Latins, and Turks in the Eastern Mediterranean World after 1150.* Oxford: Oxford University Press, 2012, pp. 265–89.

Urban, William. "The Teutonic Knights and Baltic Chivalry." *Historian,* 56 (1994), 519–30.

Van Court, Elisa Narin. "*The Siege of Jerusalem* and Augustinian Historians: Writing about Jews in Fourteenth-Century England." *Chaucer Review,* 29 (1995), 227–48.

Bibliography

Vander Elst, Stefan. *The Knight, the Cross, and the Song: Crusade Propaganda and Chivalric Literature, 1100–1400*. Philadelphia: University of Pennsylvania Press, 2017.

"'Tu es pélérin en la sainte cité': Chaucer's Knight and Philippe de Mézières." *Studies in Philology*, 106 (2009), 379–401.

Vecchio, Silvana. "Passions de l'âme et péchés capitaux: Les ambiguïtés de la culture médiévale," in Christoph Flüeler and Martin Rohde (eds.), *Laster im Mittelalter/Vices in the Middle Ages*. New York: Walter de Gruyter, 2009, pp. 45–64.

Veilliard, Françoise. *Bibliotheca Bodmeriana Catalogues, 2: Manuscrits français du moyen âge*. Cologny-Geneva: Bodmer Library, 1975.

Vincent-Cassy, Mireille. "L'envie au Moyen Âge." *Annales. Economies, Sociétés, Civilisations*, 35 (1980), 253–71.

Vitkus, Daniel J. *Turning Turk: English Theater and the Multicultural Mediterranean, 1570–1630*. New York: Palgrave, 2003.

Vitto, Cindy. *The Virtuous Pagan in Middle English Literature*. Philadelphia: American Philosophical Society, 1989.

Wacks, David A. *Medieval Iberian Crusade Fiction and the Mediterranean World*. Toronto: University of Toronto Press, 2019.

Wallace, David. *Premodern Places: Calais to Surinam, Chaucer to Aphra Behn*. Malden, MA: Blackwell, 2004.

Walls, Keith. *John Bromyard on Church and State: The "Summa Praedicantium" and Early Fourteenth-Century England*. Market Weighton, UK: Clayton-Thorpe, 2007.

Walpole, Ronald N. "Otinel," in Geneviève Hasnohr, and Michel Zink (eds.), *Dictionnaire des lettres françaises: Le Moyen Âge*, 2nd ed. Paris: Fayard, 1994; 1st ed. 1951, pp. 1089–90.

Warm, Robert. "Identity, Narrative and Participation: Defining a Context for the Middle English Charlemagne Romances," in Rosalind Field (ed.), *Tradition and Transformation in Medieval Romance*. Cambridge, UK: D. S. Brewer, 1999, pp. 87–100.

Waters, Claire M. *Translating Clergie: Status, Education, and Salvation in Thirteenth-Century Vernacular Texts*. Philadelphia: University of Pennsylvania Press, 2016.

Weber, Benjamin. *Lutter contre les Turcs: Les formes nouvelles de la croisade pontificale au Xve siècle*. Rome: École française de Rome, 2013.

Weiss, Judith. "The Exploitation of Ideas of Pilgrimage and Sainthood in *Gui de Warewic*," in Laura Ashe, Ivana Djordjević, and Judith Weiss (eds.), *The Exploitations of Medieval Romance*. Cambridge, UK: D. S. Brewer, 2010, pp. 43–56.

White, Stephen D. "The Politics of Anger," in Barbara H. Rosenwein (ed.), *Anger's Past: The Social Uses of an Emotion in the Middle Ages*. Ithaca, NY: Cornell University Press, 1998, pp. 127–52.

Wiggins, Alison. "The Manuscripts and Texts of the Middle English *Guy of Warwick*," in Alison Wiggins and Rosalind Field (eds.), *Guy of Warwick: Icon and Ancestor*. Cambridge, UK: D. S. Brewer, 2007, pp. 61–80.

230   *Bibliography*

Wilcox, Rebecca. "Romancing the East: Greeks and Saracens in Guy of Warwick," in Nicola McDonald (ed.), *Pulp Fictions of Medieval England: Essays in Popular Romance*. Manchester, UK: Manchester University Press, 2004, pp. 217–40.

Yager, Susan. "New Philology," in Albrecht Classen (ed.), *Handbook of Medieval Studies: Terms, Methods, Trends*. Berlin: De Gruyter, 2010, pp. 999–1006.

Yeager, R. F. "Pax Poetica: On the Pacifism of Chaucer and Gower." *Studies in the Age of Chaucer*, 9 (1987), 97–121.

Yeager, Suzanne M. *Jerusalem in Medieval Narrative*. Cambridge: Cambridge University Press, 2008.

"Jewish Identity in *The Siege of Jerusalem* and Homiletic Texts: Models of Penance and Victims of Vengeance for the Urban Apocalypse." *Medium Aevum*, 80 (2011), 56–84.

"*The Siege of Jerusalem* and Biblical Exegesis: Writing about Romans in Fourteenth-Century England." *Chaucer Review*, 39 (2004), 70–102.

Yee, Jennifer. *The Colonial Comedy: Imperialism in the French Realist Novel*. Oxford: Oxford University Press, 2016.

Young, Robert. *Postcolonialism: An Historical Introduction*. Oxford: Blackwell, 2001.

White Mythologies: Writing History and the West. London: Routledge, 1990.

Zaerr, Linda Marie. *Performance and the Middle English Romance*. Cambridge, UK: D. S. Brewer, 2012.

Zahora, Tomas. "Since Feeling Is First: Teaching Royal Ethics through Managing the Emotions in the Late Middle Ages." *Parergon*, 31 (2014), 47–72.

Index

Acre
  and fall of (1291), 3–5, 28, 42, 50, 52, 61, 66–68, 76, 95, 119
  and letters of Riccoldo da Monte di Croce, 34, 59
  and Mamlūks, 1, 9, 43, 51, 53
  and siege of (1189–1191), 116
Adrianople, 54
Aelred of Rielvaux, 60, 89
"afflicted Muslim" motif, 14, 16, 19, 44–45, 48, 124, 131
Ahmed, Sara, 8
Ailes, Marianne, 18
Akbari, Suzanne Conklin, 3, 5, 31, 44, 102–3, 112
al-Ashraf Khalīl, 43
Albert of Aachen, 9, 102, 110, 114–15
Albigensian Crusade, 124, 129
Alcuin of York, 21, 94. *See also Liber de virtutibus et vitiis*
Alexandria, 29, 33, 74–75, 79, 93
Alliterative *Morte Arthure*, 90, 129. *See also* Robert Thornton
Amis and Amiloun, 90
Amoraunt (Guy of Warwick), 74, 84, 93
Anatolia, 1, 50, 96, 131
anger, 8, 10–11, 19–23, 33–34, 43, 47, 119, 127, 129–30
  and Albert of Aachen, 110, 115
  and Alcuin of York, 21
  and Augustine, 21
  and God, 20, 23, 26, 38, 49, 66, 131
  and grief, 27, 32
  and Henry of Grosmont, 100
  and Lactantius, 21
  and Otuel, 56
  and sorrow, 27, 101
  and *The Siege of Jerusalem*, 16, 111
  and *The Siege of Milan*, 13, 20, 22, 24, 49
  and *The Sultan of Babylon*, 13, 19, 40–42, 44, 49

and Thomas Aquinas, 21, 106
and Thomas of Chobham, 21
Anglo-Norman, 14, 119
  chansons de geste, 36
  Fierabras, 14, 36, 41
  Gui de Warewic, 15, 70–71, 73, 83, 85, 92
  Otinel, 56
  romances, 7
anthropophagy, *See* cannibalism
Apparicion maistre Jehan de Meun, 60, 68
Aquinas, Thomas, 11, 21, 61, 72, 89, 106
Arbre des batailles, 82, 134
Aristotle, 89
Arsūf, 32
Arthurian romance, 71, 75, 79
Athelston, 90
Auchinleck (manuscript), 15, 50, 56–58, 63, 73, 83, 85, 88, 92–94
Augustine (of Hippo), 21, 61, 89, 107. *See also De civitate dei*
Aurell, Martin, 4
Austorc d'Aurillac, 32, 46
Austorc de Segret, 33
Austria, 35, 52, 80
Ayyūbid(s), 9, 51, 65, 134

Baghdad, 14, 34, 132
Bale, Anthony, 8
Balkans, 1, 53, 77, 131
Baltic, 1, 5, 9, 72, 76–77, 80, 87, 132, 228
Barbary Crusade, 15, 72, 77, 96–97
Battle of Kosovo, 53
Bāyazīd I, 38, 68–69
Beauchamp, Richard, 75
Beauchamp, Thomas, 74, 77
Beauchamps, earls of Warwick, 13, 74
Beaufort, John, 77
Belisent (*Otuel* romances), 58
Béziers, 124
Bible, 20, 24, 46, 102, 109
blasphemy, 18, 31, 34, 131

231

232   Index

Boehmer, Elleke, 3, 133
Bonomel, Ricaut, 32, 46–47
The Book of the Knight of the Tower, 82
Book of the Order of Chivalry, 95. See also Ramon
  Llull
Boquet, Damien, 10
Bovet, Honorat, 60, 68, 82, 134
Bradwardine, Thomas, 82
Brault, Gerald J., 44
Bromyard, John, 5–6, 66–67, 100, 116, 132. See
  also *Summa praedicantium*
Brut, Walter, 99
Bulgaria, 53, 74
Bull, Marcus, 112
Burns, Robert I., 52
Butterfield, Ardis, 7
Byzantine (Empire), 50, 76, 81, 90, 92

Caiaphas (*The Siege of Jerusalem*), 109
cannibalism, 16, 101, 110–12, 117, 122–25, 129
  and alliterative *Morte Arthure*, 129
  and First Crusade, 101, 122
  and Guillaume le Breton, 112
  and Josephus, 111–12
  and Ranulph Higden, 111
  and Raymond of Aguilers, 122
  and *Richard Coeur de Lion* (*RCL*), 16, 101,
    116–18, 121, 125–26, 129
  and Tafurs, 123
  and William of Tyre, 123
Capellanus, Andreas, 82
caritas, 61, 73, 81, 88–89, 93–97
Cartlidge, Neil, 12
Casagrande, Carla, 10
Cassodorien (*RCL*), 118
Cerquiglini, Bernard, 7, 132
Chanson d'Antioche, 27, 104, 118
  and cannibalism, 123
Chanson de Guillaume, 124
Chanson de Roland, 18, 30
chansons de geste, 3, 7, 18, 27, 39, 44–46, 127
  and cannibalism, 124–25
  and conversion, 54
  and *Fierabras*, 36, 50
  and "noble Muslim" motif, 40
  and *Otinel*, 50
Charlemagne, 15, 18, 69, 102, 133
  and literary tradition, 18, 26, 41, 55, 70
  and *Otuel* romances, 13, 15, 51, 59–64
  and *The Siege of Milan*, 19–20, 27, 29–30, 35
  and *The Sultan of Babylon*, 14, 20, 36–43, 51
Charles VI, 18, 54
Chaucer, Geoffrey, 55, 87, 96–97, 132
  and *Book of the Duchess*, 87
  and *General Prologue*, 15, 97

and *Man of Law's Tale*, 55
and *Parson's Tale*, 21, 60, 129
Chinggis (Genghis) Khān, 51
Chism, Christine, 12, 90
chivalric
  crusading, 9, 15, 70, 94
  ethics, 60, 72, 116
  fame, 55, 76, 78
  manuals, 10, 73, 97
  piety, 94, 97
Chrétien de Troyes, 84
Chrétienté Corbaran, 55, 118. See also conversion
Christine de Pizan, 82. See also *Livre des trois vertus*
Chronica majora, 64–65, 114
Cicero, 89
Clanvowe, John, 16, 72, 97, 100. See also *The
  Two Ways*
Clarel (*Otuel* romances), 62
class, 12, 74
Classen, Albrecht, 89
Clermont, 18, 71, 90
Clifford, Lewis, 97
Cohen, Jeffrey Jerome, 36
Colebrond (*Guy of Warwick*), 74
colonial literature, 3–4, 16
compassion, 27–29, 40, 88, 100–1, 103, 108,
  120, 129
  and *The Siege of Jerusalem*, 102–3, 106,
    109–10, 133
  and *The Siege of Milan*, 27, 31
complaint literature, 20, 32
Confessio Amantis, 61, 86, 99. See also John
  Gower
Conrad, Joseph, 2
Constantinople, 1, 5, 54, 74, 76–77, 97
conversion, 5, 14, 48, 50–51, 53–55, 69, 99, 103
  and *Chrétienté Corbaran*, 118
  and dream of, 51–52, 54–56
  and *Guy of Warwick*, 70, 73, 83–85
  and *Otuel*, 14–15, 58–62, 68
  and Ramon Llull, 53, 95
  and *The Sultan of Babylon*, 19, 36, 46
Cooper, Helen, 13
Copeland, Rita, 8
Crofts, Thomas, 32
crusade chronicles, 27, 40, 102, 112
crusade propaganda, 8–9, 20, 24, 40, 76, 93, 102
crusade sermons, 8, 22, 27, 40, 90
crusading
  as chivalric, 9, 15, 70, 94
  defeats, 5, 7, 19, 32, 38, 45, 47–48, 66, 68, 131
  as healthy, 16, 101
  and pogroms, 16, 110
  as salvific, 16, 101, 106
curative violence, 102–3, 131

Index

233

Damascus, 52, 65
De civitate dei, 21, 107. *See also* Augustine (of Hippo)
De expugnatione Lyxbonensi, 42–43
De itinere terrae sanctae liber, 43, 119. *See also* Ludolph of Suchem
De regimine principum, 10, 21, 106. *See also* Giles of Rome
Deschamps, Eustache, 26
dishonor, 40, 59
Dominican(s), 5, 14, 34, 96
Dubois, Pierre, 53, 102
Duke Roland and Sir Otuel of Spain, 13, 50, 102

Edessa, 4, 9, 27
Edward I, 52–53
Edward III, 75, 96
Egerton (manuscript), 36–37, 42, 44, 118
Egypt, 9, 33, 49, 51, 66, 96
Eliezer bar Nathan, 110–11
envy, 9–11, 15, 51, 60–66, 69
Epistre au roi Richart, 18, 25, 60, 105
Eucharist, 20, 118
Eudes of Châteauroux, 89
execution(s), 1, 105, 110, 126, 129

fame, 76–77, 96–97
  chivalric, 55, 76, 78
  pursuit of, 8, 15, 72, 76, 85–86
Fasciculus morum, 106
fear, 14, 16, 22, 40, 50, 52, 55, 58–60, 126–27
  and dream of conversion, 51
  and *Otuel* romances, 50, 59, 69
Felice (*Guy of Warwick*), 15, 70, 75–76, 81, 83–85, 92
Ferumbras (*The Sultan of Babylon*), 41
Fidenzio of Padua, 48, 59, 95
Fierabras, 14, 36, 41–42, 50, 55, 133
Fifth Crusade, 28, 51, 89
Fillingham (manuscript), 50, 57–58, 63
First Crusade, 3–4, 16, 51, 55, 102, 104, 110, 113, 124
  and cannibalism, 101, 122
  and *Chanson d'Antioche*, 27, 104
  chronicles, 9, 42, 113
  and pogroms, 16
  and Pope Urban II, 18, 71
  and *The Siege of Jerusalem*, 13, 103, 112–13
Floovant, 124
Flori, Jean, 116
Fourth Crusade, 90
Fourth Lateran Council, 10, 61
Francis of Assisi, 51
fraternal love/friendship, 15, 73, 76, 78, 80, 89–96

Frederick II, 52
Froissart, Jean, 15, 69, 77, 129
Frye, Northrop, 12
Fulcher of Chartres, 71, 114
Fulk of Neuilly, 117, 128

Galilee, 48
Gandhi, Leela, 8
Ganelon (*The Siege of Milan*), 23, 25–26, 30
Garcia d'Ayerve, 53
gentry, 11–12, 25, 74
Geoffroi de Charny, 15, 79, 132. *See also Livre de chevalerie*
Gerald of Wales, 116, 126
Germany, 52, 67, 74, 76, 93, 118, 132
Gervase of Canterbury, 116
Gesta Francorum, 113
Gesta Romanorum, 94, 207
Ghāzān Khān, 52
Ghillebert de Lannoy, 83
Gilbert de Tournai, 22, 59, 66
Gilbert, Jane, 12
Giles of Rome, 10, 21, 106. *See also De regimine principum*
Gilo of Paris, 113, 122
Gloucestershire, 96
God, 14, 23, 32, 34, 37–38, 43–46, 57, 66–67, 70, 81–82, 97, 134
  and anger against, 9, 24, 27, 32, 34–35, 49
  and anger of, 20, 22–23, 26, 38, 49
  and crusading, 1, 5, 7, 13–14, 19, 32–36, 38, 48–49, 73, 83, 131
  and friendship, 89, 93
  and *Guy of Warwick*, 70, 83
  and Holy Land, 6, 66
  and Islam, 48
  and Lactantius, 21
  and love, 8, 10, 15, 61, 63, 71–72
  and *Otuel* romances, 58–59, 62
  and pride, 61
  and service to, 5–6, 15, 72–73, 80, 85
  and sleep, 45
  and will of, 1, 48, 60
Godfrey of Bouillon, 55
Gopal, Priyamvada, 3, 133
Gower, John, 15–16, 26, 55, 61, 72, 86–87, 99, 129
  and crusading for love, 86, 132
grief, 30, 33–34, 68, 101, 127–28
  and anger, 32–33
  and *Chanson d'Antioche*, 27
  compassionate, 27–29, 108
  and *Guy of Warwick*, 93
  and *The Siege of Jerusalem*, 109, 111, 121

234 Index

grief (cont.)
 and *The Siege of Milan*, 28, 31
 and *The Sultan of Babylon*, 40
Guard, Timothy, 74, 77, 96
Gui de Warewic, 15, 70
Guillaume de Machaut, 15, 71, 79, 132. *See also*
 La prise d'Alixandre

Hardman, Phillipa, 18
hate, 66, 105–6, 110
Hayton of Korykos, 52
Heng, Geraldine, 3–5, 60, 122
Henry IV, 99
Henry of Grosmont, 15, 72, 87, 100. *See also*
 Livre de seyntz medicines
Henry Scrope of Masham, 77
Hernis (*Guy of Warwick*), 76, 81, 83–84, 90–93
heroism, 4, 39, 50, 73, 77, 80, 116–18
heterosexual love, 73, 78, 81–83
Higden, Ranulph, 102, 109, 111–12, 116, 118
Hincmar of Reims, 21
history of emotions, 8
Hoccleve, Thomas, 129
Holy Land, 1, 6, 14, 25, 27–28, 35–36, 51–52,
 54, 66, 90, 118–20
 and Christian loss of, 9, 15
 and *Guy of Warwick*, 74, 85
 and Honorat Bovet, 134
 and John Bromyard, 66
 and John Gower, 99–100
 and John Ryvere, 96
 and Marino Sanudo, 43, 105
 and Philippe de Mézières, 29, 72, 102
 and pilgrimage, 93
 and Ramon Llull, 53
 and recovery treatises, 72, 95
 and Ricaut Bonomel, 32
 and Richard Beauchamp, 75
 and Second Council of Lyons, 53
Holy Sepulchre, 18, 104
Honor, 71, 77–80, 82–83
 pursuit of, 76, 90
 of Virgin Mary, 80
 of women, 79
Hospitaller, 59
humility, 68, 85, 88
humoral theory, 11, 106
Hundred Years War, 18, 25, 74, 77, 129
Hungary, 52, 68, 74, 79

idolatry, 44, 48
īlkhāns, 52, 55
Imād al-Dīn Zangī, 4, 9
imperialism, 2–3
invectives against heaven, 2, 27, 132

Islam, 3, 5, 35, 44, 54, 67, 131–34
 and conversion to, 19, 36, 46–48
 and īlkhāns, 52
 and John Bromyard, 6, 66
 and Orientalism, 3

Jacobus de Voragine, 102
Jacques de Helly, 54
Jacques de Vitry, 22, 28, 43, 51
James II, 52
Jauss, Hans Robert, 12
Jean le Maingre, 54, 71, 77–79. *See also Livre des
 fais*
Jerusalem, 28, 48, 65, 100, 103–4, 112–13,
 116
 and Ayyūbids, 9
 and *Guy of Warwick*, 93
 and Holy Sepulchre, 18
 and Jewish population, 102, 108
 and John Clanvowe, 96
 and John Ryvere, 96
 and massacres, 9, 16, 107, 112–13
 and Ṣalāḥ al-Dīn, 4, 38, 112
 and siege of, 13, 102, 105, 107, 110, 112
 and William of Tyre, 114
Jews, 16, 102–3, 105, 108–13, 116–17, 133
John of Gaunt, 77, 87
John of Tynemouth, 102
Josephus, 102, 105, 107, 109, 111–12
Judea, 48

Kedar, Benjamin, 51
Keen, Maurice, 74, 97
Kempf, Damien, 112
The King of Tars, 44, 55
knight-errantry, 15, 70–71, 74
Krônike von Prûzinlant, 15, 80. *See also* Nicolaus
 of Jeroschin

La destruction de Rome, 14, 36–37, 132
La prise d'Alixandre, 15, 71, 79. *See also*
 Guillaume de Machaut
Laban (sultan) (*The Sultan of Babylon*), 14,
 19–20, 36–46, 49, 132
Lancelot, 75, 78, 82, 87
Langton, Stephen, 117
Laurent of Orléans (Frère Laurent), 60
Lavynham, Richard, 61, 106
leprosy, 66, 103, 105
Lewis, Celia, 100
Liber de fine, 53, 59
Liber de virtutibus et vitiis, 94. *See also* Alcuin of
 York
Liber peregrinationis, 67. *See also* Riccoldo da
 Monte di Croce

Index

Livre de chevalerie, 15, 79–80. *See also* Geoffroi de Charny
Livre de seyntz medicines, 87, 100. *See also* Henry of Grosmont
Livre des fais, 15, 54, 71, 77, 80. *See also* Jean le Maingre
Livre des trois vertus, 82. *See also* Christine de Pizan
Llull, Ramon, 53, 59, 95. *See also* Book of the Order of Chivalry
Lollards, 96–97, 99–100
Lombardy, 23, 29–30, 76, 83
London, 96, 99, 118, 129
Louis VII, 42
Louis IX, 4, 9, 32, 34, 46, 49, 64
love, 9–11, 15, 17, 38, 67, 71–76, 78–83, 93–97, 132
   of God, 8, 15, 21, 40, 71, 73, 81, 85, 87, 94, 97
   and *Guy of Warwick*, 70, 72–76, 78, 80–81, 83–84, 90–92, 94, 133
   homosocial, 76, 81, 97
   and *Otuel* romances, 62
   of women, 71, 78, 82
   worldly, 15, 72, 81
Lowe, Lisa, 2, 133
Ludolph of Suchem, 43, 119. *See also De itinere terrae sanctae liber*
Lydon, Jane, 8

Macedonia, 53
MacMurrough, Dermot, 126
Mamlūk(s), 4, 9, 43, 50–54, 59–60, 94–96, 134
   and conversion, 53
   and Ghāzān Khān, 52
   reconquest of Acre, 1, 4–5, 28, 66–67
   Sultan al-Zāhir Baybars, 32
Mandeville, John, 26, 66
Manion, Lee, 6
marriage, 53, 55, 76
Marshal Boucicaut, *See* Jean le Maingre
Martin of Pairis, 90
Martorell, Joanot, 95
Mary (*The Siege of Jerusalem*), 111–12, 122
Maurice de Bruyn, 74
McGrath, Kate, 119
McNamar, Sarah, 8
Mehmed II, 54
Metlitzki, Dorothee, 55
Mills, Maldwyn, 31
Mirour de l'Omme, 86
Mongol Empire/Mongols, 5, 14, 50–55
Moore, Megan, 8
Muhammad, 5, 34, 44, 46–48, 131
Murad I, 54

Nagy, Piroska, 10
Narin van Court, Elisa, 109
neocolonial cultures, 8
Neville, William, 96
New Philology, 7
New Testament, 89
Nicolaus of Jeroschin, 15, 80, 132. *See also Krônike von Prûzinlant*
Nicopolis (Battle of), 5, 9, 15, 38, 51, 53, 60, 68–69, 77, 79, 129–30
nobility, 11, 25, 74, 77
Normandy, 74, 77, 125
North Africa, 1, 5, 7, 9, 72, 77, 87
novel, 2–3, 12
   British, 3
   modern colonial, 2
N-Town Plays, 129

Occitan, 6, 14, 32–33
Octavian, 102
Odo of Deuil, 27–28, 42
Ogier (*Otuel* romances), 15, 42, 51, 62–63, 68
Old Testament, 9, 20, 47, 89
Oliferne, 55
Oliver (*Otuel* romances), 15, 51, 55, 62–64, 68, 133
Oliver (*The Sultan of Babylon*), 41
Oliver of Paderborn, 51
Order of the Garter, 76–77
Order of the Holy Sepulchre, 96
Order of the Passion of Jesus Christ, 25, 72, 95, 97, 100, 105
Oschema, Klaus, 89
Otinel, 50–51, 55–56
Ottokar von Steiermark, 35
Ottoman Empire, 14, 53–54, 67, 77, 79, 129, 134
   and conquests of, 5, 9, 15, 50–51, 53–54, 60, 68
   and forces of, 53
   and piracy, 53
   and rise of, 4, 48, 59, 133
   and siege of Constantinople (1453), 1
   and sultans, 38, 54, 68
Otuel (*Otuel* romances), 14, 51, 56–64

Palestine, 95
Paris, 25–26, 29
Paris, Matthew, 33–34, 47, 52, 64–65, 114
Peckham, John, 10
Pecock, Reginald, 10
Peraldus, William, 21, 72. *See also Summa de vitiis*
Peter I of Cyprus, 29, 75, 79
Peter the Hermit, 27, 123

236

Index

Philippe de Mézières, 15, 29, 72, 87, 102–5, 107–8
  and *Epistre au roi Richart*, 18, 25
  and *Epistre lamentable et consolatoire*, 69
  and Order of the Passion, 25, 72, 87, 100
  and *Songe du vieil pelerin*, 54, 87
  and *Sustance de la chevalerie de la passion de Jhesu Crist*, 87, 105
Piers Plowman, 129
Pintoin, Michel, 16, 38, 68, 129–30
Polychronicon, 102, 109, 116, 118. *See also* Ranulph Higden
polytheism, 3, 44
Pope Clement V, 52
Pope Clement VI, 54
Pope Gregory VIII, 29, 90
Pope Innocent III, 89
Pope Pius II, 54
Pope Sergius IV, 104
Pope Urban II, 18, 71
postcolonial studies, 2, 4, 16
Prester John, 51
pride, 45, 60–61, 64–66, 68–69, 94, 117, 130
  and crusading defeats, 9, 64
  and envy, 9, 15, 51, 60–66, 69
  and Oliver, 15, 51
  and Roland, 15, 51, 63, 65, 69
Prise d'Orange, 124
Prose Guy, 75
Prussia, 74–75, 77, 79

Ralph of Caen, 122
Ralph of Coggeshall, 116
Raymond of Aguilers, 122
reverse Orientalism, 2, 6, 51, 68–69, 132
Riccoldo da Monte di Croce, 34, 45–48, 52, 59, 67, 132. *See also Liber peregrinationis*
Ríkharðsdóttir, Sif, 8
Robert of Artois, 65
Robert of Reims, 112
Roger of Argenteuil, 102, 109
Roger of Howden, 117
Roger of Wendover, 38, 114
Roland (*Otuel* romances), 14–15, 51, 56–58, 60–65, 68–69, 133
Roland (*The Siege of Milan*), 23, 30–31, 35
Roland (*The Sultan of Babylon*), 33, 41
Rosenwein, Barbara H., 10
Rutebeuf, 53, 94
Ryvere, John, 95–96

Sabraham, Nicholas, 74
Said, Edward, 2–4, 16, 36, 133
saints, 12, 32–34, 44, 46–47, 64

Ṣalāḥ al-Dīn, 4, 38, 112, 125–28
Salimbene de Adam, 33–34, 47
Sanudo, Marino, 43, 52, 59, 102–3, 105, 107–8, 111, 125
Schiltberger, Johann, 67
Scrope v. Grosvenor, 74
Second Boer War, 3
Second Council of Lyons, 53, 59
Second Crusade, 9, 27, 42, 66, 107
sermons, 15, 22, 54, 82
Seventh Crusade, 33, 47, 64
shame, 29, 40, 59–60, 67–68
  and fear, 11, 14, 56, 58, 60
Shepherd, Stephen, 32
Siddiqi, Yumna, 2
siege of Jerusalem
  accounts of, 9, 107
  in 1099, 112
  in 70 CE, 13, 102
siege of Lisbon, 43, 107, 119. *See also* Second Crusade
siege of Ma'arra, 16, 101, 122
Sir Ferumbras, 55
Sir Isumbras, 102
Smyrna, 53–54
sorrow, 8–9, 11, 28, 30, 32–34, 40, 85, 97, 114, 121, 123, 126, 128
  and anger, 27, 101
  and Augustine, 61, 107
  and compassion, 27–28, 129
  and *The Siege of Jerusalem*, 13, 16, 103, 109–11
  and *The Siege of Milan*, 13, 20, 27, 30, 49
  and *The Sultan of Babylon*, 20, 44, 47, 49
  and vengeance, 19, 49
Spain, 1, 5, 18, 52, 72, 74, 76–77, 87
Speculum Gy de Warewyke, 94
Spencer, Stephen, 8, 42
Stanegrave, Roger, 59, 66
Suchenwirt, Peter, 80, 132
Summa confessorum, 21
Summa de vitiis, 21, 72. *See also* William Peraldus
Summa praedicantium, 5–6, 67, 116. *See also* John Bromyard
Swinderby, William, 99
Syria, 52, 55, 95–96

Tafurs, 123–25, 127
Tarnowski, Andrea, 88
Tattersall, Jill, 124
Tervagant, 44, 46, 48
Teutonic Order, 75–76
Thadeo of Naples, 59
Third Crusade, 13, 29, 38, 90, 110, 119, 125
Thomas of Chobham, 21

Index

Thomas of Moulton (*RCL*), 119, 128
Thornton, Robert, 50, 56–58, 61, 64, 68, 129.
  See also alliterative *Morte Arthure*
Thrace, 53
Throop, Susanna A., 8, 22
Tirri (*Guy of Warwick*), 74, 83–86, 92–94
Titus (*The Siege of Jerusalem*), 13, 102–10
Tolan, John V., 3, 5
travel literature, 15, 26, 66–67
Tripoli, 48, 112
Tristan, 75, 78
Tunis, 15, 33, 49
Tunisia, 9, 96
Turpin (*The Siege of Milan*), 20, 23–26, 29–33,
  35, 45, 49
Two Ways, The, 96, 100. *See also* John Clanvowe
Tyerman, Christopher, 74, 77, 87

Vecchio, Silvana, 10
vengeance, 8, 11, 19, 28, 40, 105–7, 114,
  130–31, 133
  and anger, 22
  and Aquinas, 21
  and *Guy of Warwick*, 94
  and *RCL*, 120

and *The Siege of Jerusalem*, 101, 103–7, 109,
  115–16
and *The Siege of Milan*, 13, 23, 27–29, 49,
  101
and *The Sultan of Babylon*, 14, 20, 37–40, 49
Vespasian, 13, 102–5, 107–9
Virgin Mary, 1, 9, 14, 19, 31–36, 45, 80
Vox Clamantis, 26, 86–87, 99. *See also* John
  Gower

Wallace, David, 7
Warm, Robert, 18
White, Stephen D., 22
William of Adam, 52
William of Newburgh, 110
William of Tudela, 124
William of Tyre, 102, 112, 114–15, 123
Wyclif, John, 16, 99–100
Wynkyn de Worde, 128

Yeager, Suzanne M., 102–3
Yee, Jennifer, 3, 133
York, 10, 110

zeal, 21, 28, 30–31, 43

CAMBRIDGE STUDIES IN MEDIEVAL LITERATURE

1   ROBIN KIRKPATRICK *Dante's "Inferno": Difficulty and Dead Poetry*
2   JEREMY TAMBLING *Dante and Difference: Writing in the "Commedia"*
3   SIMON GAUNT *Troubadours and Irony*
4   WENDY SCASE *"Piers Plowman" and the New Anticlericalism*
5   JOSEPH J. DUGGAN *The "Cantar de mio Cid": Poetic Creation in Its Economic and Social Contexts*
6   RODERICK BEATON *The Medieval Greek Romance*
7   KATHRYN KERBY-FULTON *Reformist Apocalypticism and "Piers Plowman"*
8   ALISON MORGAN *Dante and the Medieval Other World*
9   ECKEHARD SIMON (ed.) *The Theatre of Medieval Europe: New Research in Early Drama*
10 MARY CARRUTHERS *The Book of Memory: A Study of Memory in Medieval Culture*
11 RITA COPELAND *Rhetoric, Hermeneutics, and Translation in the Middle Ages: Academic Traditions and Vernacular Texts*
12 DONALD MADDOX *The Arthurian Romances of Chrétien de Troyes: Once and Future Fictions*
13 NICHOLAS WATSON *Richard Rolle and the Invention of Authority*
14 STEVEN F. KRUGER *Dreaming in the Middle Ages*
15 BARBARA NOLAN *Chaucer and the Tradition of the "Roman Antique"*
16 SYLVIA HUOT *The "Romance of the Rose" and Its Medieval Readers: Interpretation, Reception, Manuscript Transmission*
17 CAROL M. MEALE (ed.) *Women and Literature in Britain, 1150–1500*
18 HENRY ANSGAR KELLY *Ideas and Forms of Tragedy from Aristotle to the Middle Ages*
19 MARTIN IRVINE *The Making of Textual Culture: "Grammatica" and Literary Theory, 350–1100*
20 LARRY SCANLON *Narrative, Authority, and Power: The Medieval Exemplum and the Chaucerian Tradition*
21 ERIK KOOPER (ed.) *Medieval Dutch Literature in Its European Context*
22 STEVEN BOTTERILL *Dante and the Mystical Tradition: Bernard of Clairvaux in the "Commedia"*
23 PETER BILLER AND ANNE HUDSON (eds.) *Heresy and Literacy, 1000–1530*
24 CHRISTOPHER BASWELL *Virgil in Medieval England: Figuring the "Aeneid" from the Twelfth Century to Chaucer*
25 JAMES SIMPSON *Sciences and the Self in Medieval Poetry: Alan of Lille's "Anticlaudianus" and John Gower's "Confessio Amantis"*

26 JOYCE COLEMAN *Public Reading and the Reading Public in Late Medieval England and France*

27 SUZANNE REYNOLDS *Medieval Reading: Grammar, Rhetoric and the Classical Text*

28 CHARLOTTE BREWER *Editing "Piers Plowman": The Evolution of the Text*

29 WALTER HAUG *Vernacular Literary Theory in the Middle Ages: The German Tradition, 800–1300, in Its European Context*

30 SARAH SPENCE *Texts and the Self in the Twelfth Century*

31 EDWIN D. CRAUN *Lies, Slander and Obscenity in Medieval English Literature: Pastoral Rhetoric and the Deviant Speaker*

32 PATRICIA E. GRIEVE *"Floire and Blancheflor" and the European Romance*

33 HUW PRYCE (ed.) *Literacy in Medieval Celtic Societies*

34 MARY CARRUTHERS *The Craft of Thought: Meditation, Rhetoric, and the Making of Images, 400–1200*

35 BEATE SCHMOLKE-HASSELMANN *The Evolution of Arthurian Romance: The Verse Tradition from Chrétien to Froissart*

36 SIÂN ECHARD *Arthurian Narrative in the Latin Tradition*

37 FIONA SOMERSET *Clerical Discourse and Lay Audience in Late Medieval England*

38 FLORENCE PERCIVAL *Chaucer's Legendary Good Women*

39 CHRISTOPHER CANNON *The Making of Chaucer's English: A Study of Words*

40 ROSALIND BROWN-GRANT *Christine de Pizan and the Moral Defence of Women: Reading beyond Gender*

41 RICHARD NEWHAUSER *The Early History of Greed: The Sin of Avarice in Early Medieval Thought and Literature*

42 MARGARET CLUNIES ROSS (ed.) *Old Icelandic Literature and Society*

43 DONALD MADDOX *Fictions of Identity in Medieval France*

44 RITA COPELAND *Pedagogy, Intellectuals, and Dissent in the Later Middle Ages: Lollardy and Ideas of Learning*

45 KANTIK GHOSH *The Wycliffite Heresy: Authority and the Interpretation of Texts*

46 MARY C. ERLER *Women, Reading, and Piety in Late Medieval England*

47 D. H. GREEN *The Beginnings of Medieval Romance: Fact and Fiction, 1150–1220*

48 J. A. BURROW *Gestures and Looks in Medieval Narrative*

49 ARDIS BUTTERFIELD *Poetry and Music in Medieval France: From Jean Renart to Guillaume de Machaut*

50 EMILY STEINER *Documentary Culture and the Making of Medieval English Literature*

51 WILLIAM E. BURGWINKLE *Sodomy, Masculinity, and Law in Medieval Literature: France and England, 1050–1230*

52 NICK HAVELY *Dante and the Franciscans: Poverty and the Papacy in the 'Commedia'*

53 SIEGFRIED WENZEL *Latin Sermon Collections from Later Medieval England: Orthodox Preaching in the Age of Wyclif*

54 ANANYA JAHANARA KABIR AND DEANNE WILLIAMS (eds.) *Postcolonial Approaches to the European Middle Ages: Translating Cultures*

55 MARK MILLER *Philosophical Chaucer: Love, Sex, and Agency in the "Canterbury Tales"*

56 SIMON A. GILSON *Dante and Renaissance Florence*

57 RALPH HANNA *London Literature, 1300–1380*

58 MAURA NOLAN *John Lydgate and the Making of Public Culture*

59 NICOLETTE ZEEMAN *"Piers Plowman" and the Medieval Discourse of Desire*

60 ANTHONY BALE *The Jew in the Medieval Book: English Antisemitisms, 1350–1500*

61 ROBERT J. MEYER-LEE *Poets and Power from Chaucer to Wyatt*

62 ISABEL DAVIS *Writing Masculinity in the Later Middle Ages*

63 JOHN M. FYLER *Language and the Declining World in Chaucer, Dante, and Jean de Meun*

64 MATTHEW GIANCARLO *Parliament and Literature in Late Medieval England*

65 D. H. GREEN *Women Readers in the Middle Ages*

66 MARY DOVE *The First English Bible: The Text and Context of the Wycliffite Versions*

67 JENNI NUTTALL *The Creation of Lancastrian Kingship: Literature, Language and Politics in Late Medieval England*

68 LAURA ASHE *Fiction and History in England, 1066–1200*

69 J. A. BURROW *The Poetry of Praise*

70 MARY CARRUTHERS *The Book of Memory: A Study of Memory in Medieval Culture (Second Edition)*

71 ANDREW COLE *Literature and Heresy in the Age of Chaucer*

72 SUZANNE M. YEAGER *Jerusalem in Medieval Narrative*

73 NICOLE R. RICE *Lay Piety and Religious Discipline in Middle English Literature*

74 D. H. GREEN *Women and Marriage in German Medieval Romance*

75 PETER GODMAN *Paradoxes of Conscience in the High Middle Ages: Abelard, Heloise, and the Archpoet*

76 EDWIN D. CRAUN *Ethics and Power in Medieval English Reformist Writing*

77 DAVID MATTHEWS *Writing to the King: Nation, Kingship, and Literature in England, 1250–1350*

78 MARY CARRUTHERS (ed.) *Rhetoric beyond Words: Delight and Persuasion in the Arts of the Middle Ages*

79 KATHARINE BREEN *Imagining an English Reading Public, 1150–1400*

80 ANTONY J. HASLER *Court Poetry in Late Medieval England and Scotland: Allegories of Authority*

81 SHANNON GAYK *Image, Text, and Religious Reform in Fifteenth-Century England*
82 LISA H. COOPER *Artisans and Narrative Craft in Late Medieval England*
83 ALISON CORNISH *Vernacular Translation in Dante's Italy: Illiterate Literature*
84 JANE GILBERT *Living Death in Medieval French and English Literature*
85 JESSICA ROSENFELD *Ethics and Enjoyment in Late Medieval Poetry: Love after Aristotle*
86 MICHAEL VAN DUSSEN *From England to Bohemia: Heresy and Communication in the Later Middle Ages*
87 MARTIN EISNER *Boccaccio and the Invention of Italian Literature: Dante, Petrarch, Cavalcanti, and the Authority of the Vernacular*
88 EMILY V. THORNBURY *Becoming a Poet in Anglo-Saxon England*
89 LAWRENCE WARNER *The Myth of "Piers Plowman": Constructing a Medieval Literary Archive*
90 LEE MANION *Narrating the Crusades: Loss and Recovery in Medieval and Early Modern English Literature*
91 DANIEL WAKELIN *Scribal Correction and Literary Craft: English Manuscripts 1375–1510*
92 JON WHITMAN (ed.) *Romance and History: Imagining Time from the Medieval to the Early Modern Period*
93 VIRGINIE GREENE *Logical Fictions in Medieval Literature and Philosophy*
94 MICHAEL JOHNSTON AND MICHAEL VAN DUSSEN (eds.) *The Medieval Manuscript Book: Cultural Approaches*
95 TIM WILLIAM MACHAN (ed.) *Imagining Medieval English: Language Structures and Theories, 500–1500*
96 ERIC WEISKOTT *English Alliterative Verse: Poetic Tradition and Literary History*
97 SARAH ELLIOTT NOVACICH *Shaping the Archive in Late Medieval England: History, Poetry, and Performance*
98 GEOFFREY RUSSOM *The Evolution of Verse Structure in Old and Middle English Poetry: From the Earliest Alliterative Poems to Iambic Pentameter*
99 IAN CORNELIUS *Reconstructing Alliterative Verse: The Pursuit of a Medieval Meter*
100 SARA HARRIS *The Linguistic Past in Twelfth-Century Britain*
101 ERIC KWAKKEL AND RODNEY THOMSON (eds.) *The European Book in the Twelfth Century*
102 IRINA DUMITRESCU *The Experience of Education in Anglo-Saxon Literature*
103 JONAS WELLENDORF *Gods and Humans in Medieval Scandinavia: Retying the Bonds*
104 THOMAS A. PRENDERGAST AND JESSICA ROSENFELD (eds.) *Chaucer and the Subversion of Form*
105 KATIE L. WALTER *Middle English Mouths: Late Medieval Medical, Religious and Literary Traditions*

106 LAWRENCE WARNER *Chaucer's Scribes: London Textual Production, 1384–1432*
107 GLENN D. BURGER AND HOLLY A. CROCKER (eds.) *Medieval Affect, Feeling, and Emotion*
108 ROBERT J. MEYER-LEE *Literary Value and Social Identity in the "Canterbury Tales"*
109 ANDREW KRAEBEL *Biblical Commentary and Translation in Later Medieval England: Experiments in Interpretation*
110 GEORGE CORBETT *Dante's Christian Ethics: Purgatory and Its Moral Contexts*
111 JONATHAN MORTON AND MARCO NIEVERGELT (eds.) *The "Roman de la Rose" and Thirteenth-Century Thought*
112 ORIETTA DA ROLD *Paper in Medieval England: From Pulp to Fictions*
113 CHRISTIANIA WHITEHEAD *The Afterlife of St Cuthbert: Place, Texts and Ascetic Tradition, 690–1500*
114 RICHARD MATTHEW POLLARD *Imagining the Medieval Afterlife*
115 DAVID G. LUMMUS *The City of Poetry: Imagining the Civic Role of the Poet in Fourteenth-Century Italy*
116 ANDREW. M. RICHMOND, *Landscapes in Middle English Romance: The Medieval Imagination and the Natural World*
117 MARK CHINCA AND CHRISTOPHER YOUNG *Literary Beginnings in the European Middle Ages*
118 MARK FAULKNER *A New Literary History of the Long Twelfth Century: Language and Literature between Old and Middle English*
119 JOSEPH TAYLOR *Writing the North of England in the Middle Ages: Regionalism and Nationalism in Medieval English Literature*
120 OLIVIA HOLMES *Boccaccio and Exemplary Literature: Ethics and Mischief in the "Decameron"*
121 TAYLOR COWDERY *Matter and Making in Early English Poetry: Literary Production from Chaucer to Sidney*
122 HARRIET SOPER *The Life Course in Old English Poetry*
123 JENNIFER A. LORDEN *Forms of Devotion in Early English Poetry: The Poetics of Feeling*
124 ANNE SCHUURMAN *The Theology of Debt in Late Medieval English Literature*
125 EMMA O. BÉRAT *Women's Genealogies in the Medieval Literary Imagination: Matrilineal Legacies in the High Middle Ages*

www.ingramcontent.com/pod-product-compliance
Ingram Content Group UK Ltd.
Pitfield, Milton Keynes, MK11 3LW, UK
UKHW041639141224
452228UK00008B/105